Christian Omnibus Vol. 1
Eight Books on Prayer

TABLE OF CONTENTS

Lord, Teach Us to Pray

~ ※ ~

By *Andrew Murray*

The 1896 Edition

~ ※ ~

LORD, TEACH US TO PRAY

OR
THE ONLY TEACHER.

The disciples had been with Christ, and seen Him pray. They had learnt to understand something of the connection between His wondrous life in public, and His secret life of prayer. They had learnt to believe in Him as a Master in the art of prayer—none could pray like Him. And so they came to Him with the request, 'Lord, teach us to pray.' And in after years they would have told us that there were few things more wonderful or blessed that He taught them than His lessons on prayer.

And now still it comes to pass, as He is praying in a certain place, that disciples who see Him thus engaged feel the need of repeating the same request, 'Lord, teach us to pray.' As we grow in the Christian life, the thought and the faith of the Beloved Master in His never-failing intercession becomes evermore precious, and the hope of being *Like Christ* in His intercession gains an attractiveness before unknown. And as we see Him pray, and remember that there is none who can pray like Him, and none who can teach like Him, we feel the petition of the disciples, 'Lord, teach us to pray,' is just what we need. And as we think how all He is and has, how He Himself is our very own, how He is Himself our life, we feel assured that we have but to ask, and He will be delighted to take us up into closer fellowship with Himself, and teach us to pray even as He prays.

Come, my brothers! Shall we not go to the Blessed Master and ask Him to enroll our names too anew in that school which He always keeps open for those who long to continue their studies in the Divine art of prayer and intercession? Yes, let us this very day say to the Master, as they did of old, 'Lord, teach us to pray.' As we meditate we shall find each word of the petition we bring to be full of meaning.

'Lord, teach us *to pray*.' Yes, *to pray*. This is what we need to be taught. Though in its beginnings prayer is so simple that the feeble child can pray, yet it is at the same time the highest and holiest work to which man can rise. It is fellowship with the Unseen and Most Holy One. The powers of the eternal world have been placed at its disposal. It is the very essence of true religion, the channel of all blessings, the secret of power and life. Not only for ourselves, but for others, for the Church, for the world, it is to prayer that God has given the right to take hold of Him and His strength. It is on prayer that the promises wait for their fulfilment, the kingdom for its coming, the glory of God for its full revelation. And for this blessed work, how slothful and unfit we are. It is only the Spirit of God can enable us to do it aright. How speedily we are deceived into a resting in the form, while the power is wanting. Our early training, the teaching of the Church, the influence of habit, the stirring of the emotions—how easily these lead to prayer which has no spiritual power, and avails but little. True prayer, that takes hold of God's strength, that availeth much, to which the gates of heaven are really opened wide—who would not cry, Oh for some one to teach me thus to pray?

Jesus has opened a school, in which He trains His redeemed ones, who specially desire it, to have power in prayer. Shall we not enter it with the petition, Lord! it is just this we need to be taught! O teach us to *pray*.

'Lord, teach *us* to pray.' Yes, *us*, Lord. We have read in Thy Word with what power Thy believing people of old used to pray, and what mighty wonders were done in answer to their prayers. And if this took place under the Old Covenant, in the time of preparation, how much more wilt Thou not now, in these days of fulfilment, give Thy people this sure sign of Thy presence in their midst. We have heard the promises given to Thine apostles of the power of prayer in Thy name, and have seen how gloriously they experienced their truth: we know for certain, they can become true to us too. We hear continually even in these days what glorious tokens of Thy power Thou dost still give to those who trust Thee fully. Lord! these all are men of like passions with ourselves; teach *us* to pray so too. The promises are for us, the powers and gifts of the heavenly world are for us. O teach *us* to pray so that we may receive abundantly. To us too Thou hast entrusted Thy work, on our prayer too the coming of Thy kingdom depends, in our prayer too Thou canst glorify Thy name; 'Lord, teach us to pray.' Yes, us, Lord; we offer ourselves as learners; we would indeed be taught of Thee. 'Lord, teach *us* to pray.'

'Lord, *teach* us to pray.' Yes, we feel the need now of being *taught* to pray. At first there is no work appears so simple; later on, none that is more difficult; and the confession is forced from us: We know not how to pray as we ought. It is true we have God's Word, with its clear and sure promises; but sin has so darkened our mind, that we know not always how to apply the Word. In spiritual things we do not always seek the most needful things, or fail in praying according to the law of the sanctuary. In temporal things we are still less able to avail ourselves of the wonderful liberty our Father has given us to ask what we need. And even when we know what to ask, how much there is still needed to make prayer acceptable. It must be to the glory of God, in full surrender to His will, in full assurance of faith, in the name of Jesus, and with a perseverance that, if need be, refuses to be denied. All this must be learned. It can only be learned in the school of much prayer, for practice makes perfect. Amid the painful consciousness of ignorance and unworthiness, in the struggle between believing and doubting, the heavenly art of effectual prayer is learnt. Because, even when we do not remember it, there is One, the Beginner and Finisher of faith and prayer, who watches over our praying, and sees to it that *in all who trust Him for it* their education in the school of prayer shall be carried on to perfection. Let but the deep undertone of all our prayer be the teachableness that comes from a sense of ignorance, and from faith in Him as a perfect teacher, and we may be sure we shall be taught, we shall learn to pray in power. Yes, we may depend upon it, He *teaches* to pray.

'*Lord*, teach us to pray.' None can teach like Jesus, none but Jesus; therefore we call on Him, 'Lord, teach us to pray.' A pupil needs a teacher, who knows his work, who has the gift of teaching, who in patience and love will descend to the pupil's needs. Blessed be God! Jesus is all this and much more. He knows what prayer is. It is Jesus, praying Himself, who teaches to pray. He knows what prayer is. He learned it amid the trials and tears of His earthly life. In heaven it is still His beloved work: His life there is prayer. Nothing delights Him more than to find those whom He can take with Him into the Father's presence, whom He can clothe with power to pray down God's blessing on those around them, whom He can train to be His fellow-workers in the intercession by which the kingdom is to be revealed on earth. He knows how to teach. Now by the urgency of felt need, then by the confidence with which joy inspires. Here by the teaching of the Word, there by the testimony of another believer who knows what it is to have prayer heard. By His Holy Spirit, He has access to our heart, and teaches us to pray by showing us the sin that hinders the prayer, or giving us the assurance that we please God. He teaches, by giving not only thoughts of what to ask or how to ask, but by breathing within us the very spirit of prayer, by living within us as the Great Intercessor. We may indeed and most joyfully say, 'Who teacheth like Him?' Jesus never taught His disciples how to preach, only how to pray. He did not speak much of what was needed to preach well, but much of praying well. To know how to speak to God is more than knowing how to speak to man. Not power with men, but power with God is the first thing. Jesus loves to teach us how to pray.

What think you, my beloved fellow-disciples! would it not be just what we need, to ask the Master for a month to give us a course of special lessons on the art of prayer? As we meditate on the words He spake on earth, let us yield ourselves to His teaching in the fullest confidence that, with such a teacher, we shall make progress. Let us take time not only to meditate, but to pray, to tarry at the foot of the throne, and be trained to the work of intercession. Let us do so in the assurance that amidst our stammerings and fears He is carrying on His work most beautifully. He will breathe His own life, which is all prayer, into us. As He makes us partakers of His righteousness and His life, He will of His intercession too. As the members of His body, as a holy priesthood, we shall take part in His priestly work of pleading and prevailing with God for men. Yes, let us most joyfully say, ignorant and feeble though we be, 'Lord, teach us to pray.'

'Lord, Teach Us To Pray.'

~ ※ ~

Blessed Lord! who ever livest to pray, Thou canst teach me too to pray, me to live ever to pray. In this Thou lovest to make me share Thy glory in heaven, that I should pray without ceasing, and ever stand as a priest in the presence of my God.

Lord Jesus! I ask Thee this day to enroll my name among those who confess that they know not how to pray as they ought, and especially ask Thee for a course of teaching in prayer. Lord! teach me to tarry with Thee in the school, and give Thee time to train me. May a deep sense of my ignorance, of the wonderful privilege and power of prayer, of the need of the Holy Spirit as the Spirit of prayer, lead me to cast away my thoughts of what I think I know, and make me kneel before Thee in true teachableness and poverty of spirit.

And fill me, Lord, with the confidence that with such a teacher as Thou art I shall learn to pray. In the assurance that I have as my teacher, Jesus, who is ever praying to the Father, and by His prayer rules the destinies of His Church and the world, I will not be afraid. As much as I need to know of the mysteries of the prayer-world, Thou wilt unfold for me. And when I may not know, Thou wilt teach me to be strong in faith, giving glory to God.

Blessed Lord! Thou wilt not put to shame Thy scholar who trusts Thee, nor, by Thy grace, would he Thee either. Amen.

'IN SPIRIT AND TRUTH'

OR

THE TRUE WORSHIPPERS.

'The hour cometh, and now is, when the true worshippers shall worship the Father in spirit and truth: for such doth the Father seek to be His worshippers. God is a Spirit: and they that worship Him must worship Him in spirit and truth.'—John iv. 23, 24.

These words of Jesus to the woman of Samaria are His first recorded teaching on the subject of prayer. They give us some wonderful first glimpses into the world of prayer. The Father *seeks* worshippers: our worship satisfies His loving heart and is a joy to Him. He seeks *true worshippers*, but finds many not such as He would have them. True worship is that which is *in spirit and truth. The Son has come* to open the way for this worship in spirit and in truth, and teach it us. And so one of our first lessons in the school of prayer must be to understand what it is to pray in spirit and in truth, and to know how we can attain to it.

To the woman of Samaria our Lord spoke of a threefold worship. There is, first, the ignorant worship of the Samaritans: 'Ye worship that which ye know not.' The second, the intelligent worship of the Jew, having the true knowledge of God: 'We worship that which we know; for salvation is of the Jews.' And then the new, the spiritual worship which He Himself has come to introduce: 'The hour is coming, and is now, when the true worshippers shall worship the Father in spirit and truth.' From the connection it is evident that the words 'in spirit and truth' do not mean, as is often thought, earnestly, from the heart, in sincerity. The Samaritans had the five books of Moses and some knowledge of God; there was doubtless more than one among them who honestly and earnestly sought God in prayer. The Jews had the true full revelation of God in His word, as thus far given; there were among them godly men, who called upon God with their whole heart. And yet not 'in spirit and truth,' in the full meaning of the words. Jesus says, '*The hour is coming, and now is:*' it is only in and through Him that the worship of God will be in spirit and truth.

Among Christians one still finds the three classes of worshippers. Some who in their ignorance hardly know what they ask: they pray earnestly, and yet receive but little. Others there are, who have more correct knowledge, who try to pray with all their mind and heart, and often pray most earnestly, and yet do not attain to the full blessedness of worship in spirit and truth. It is into this third class we must ask our Lord Jesus to take us; we must be taught of Him how to worship in spirit and truth. This alone is spiritual worship; this makes us worshippers such as the Father seeks. In prayer everything will depend on our understanding well and practicing the worship in spirit and truth.

'God is *a Spirit* and they that worship Him must worship Him *in spirit* and truth.' The first thought suggested here by the Master is that there must be harmony between God and His worshippers; such as God is, must His worship be. This is according to a principle which prevails throughout the universe: we look for correspondence between an object and the organ to which it reveals or yields itself. The eye has an inner fitness for the light, the ear for sound. The man who would truly worship God, would find and know and possess and enjoy God, must be in harmony with Him, must have a capacity for receiving Him. Because God *is Spirit*, we must worship *in spirit*. As God is, so His worshipper.

And what does this mean? The woman had asked our Lord whether Samaria or Jerusalem was the true place of worship. He answers that henceforth worship is no longer to be limited to a certain place: 'Woman, believe Me, *the hour cometh* when neither in this mountain, nor in Jerusalem, shall ye worship the Father.' As God is Spirit, not bound by space or time, but in His infinite perfection always and everywhere the same, so His worship would henceforth no longer be confined by place or form, but spiritual as God Himself is spiritual. A lesson of deep importance. How much our Christianity suffers from this, that it is confined to certain times and places. A man who seeks to pray earnestly in the church or in the closet, spends the greater part of the week or the day in a spirit entirely at variance with that in which he prayed. His worship was the work of a fixed place or hour, not of his whole being. God is a spirit: He is the Everlasting and Unchangeable One; what He is, He is always and in truth. Our worship must even so be in spirit and truth: His worship must be the spirit of our life; our life must be worship in spirit as God is Spirit.

'God is a Spirit: and they that worship Him must worship Him in spirit and truth.' The second thought that comes to us is that this worship in the spirit must come from God Himself. God is Spirit: He alone has Spirit to give. It was for this He sent His Son, to fit us for such spiritual worship, by giving us the Holy Spirit. It is of His own work that Jesus speaks when He says twice, 'The hour cometh,' and then adds, 'and is now.' He came to baptize with the Holy Spirit; the Spirit could not stream forth till He was glorified (*John i. 33, vii. 37, 38, xvi. 7*). It was when He had made an end of sin, and entering into the Holiest of all with His blood, had there on our behalf *received* the Holy Spirit (*Acts ii. 33*), that He could send Him down to us as the Spirit of the Father. It was when Christ had redeemed us, and we in Him had received the position of children, that the Father sent forth the Spirit of His Son into our hearts to cry, 'Abba, Father.' The worship in spirit is the worship of the Father in the Spirit of Christ, the Spirit of Sonship.

This is the reason why Jesus here uses the name of Father. We never find one of the Old Testament saints personally appropriate the name of child or call God his Father. The worship *of the Father* is only possible to those to whom the Spirit of the Son has been given. The worship *in spirit* is only possible to those to whom the Son has revealed the Father, and who have received the spirit of Sonship. It is only Christ who opens the way and teaches the worship in spirit.

And *in truth*. That does not only mean, *in sincerity*. Nor does it only signify, in accordance with the truth of God's Word. The expression is one of deep and Divine meaning. Jesus is 'the only-begotten of the Father, *full of* grace and *truth*.' 'The law was given by Moses; grace and *truth came* by Jesus Christ.' Jesus says, '*I am the truth* and the life.' In the Old Testament all was shadow and promise; Jesus brought and gives the reality, *the substance*, of things hoped for. In Him the blessings and powers of the eternal life are our actual possession and experience. Jesus is full of grace and truth; the Holy Spirit is the Spirit of truth; through Him the grace that is in Jesus is ours indeed, and truth a positive communication out of the Divine life. And so worship in spirit is worship *in truth*; actual living fellowship with God, a real correspondence and harmony between the Father, who is a Spirit, and the child praying in the spirit.

What Jesus said to the woman of Samaria, she could not at once understand. Pentecost was needed to reveal its full meaning. We are hardly prepared at our first entrance into the school of prayer to grasp such teaching. We shall understand it better later on. Let us only begin and take the lesson as He gives it. We are carnal and cannot bring God the worship He seeks. But Jesus came to give the Spirit: He has given Him to us. Let the disposition in which we set ourselves to pray be what Christ's words have taught us. Let there be the deep confession of our inability to bring God the worship that is pleasing to Him; the childlike teachableness that waits on Him to instruct us; the simple faith that yields itself to the breathing of the Spirit. Above all, let us hold fast the blessed truth—we shall find that the Lord has more to say to us about it—that the knowledge of the Fatherhood of God, the revelation of His infinite Fatherliness in our hearts, the faith in the infinite love that gives us His Son and His Spirit to make us children, is indeed the secret of prayer in spirit and truth. This is the new and living way Christ opened up for us. To have Christ the Son, and *The Spirit of the Son*, dwelling within us, and revealing the Father, this makes us true, spiritual worshippers.

'Lord, Teach Us To Pray.'

~ ※ ~

Blessed Lord! I adore the love with which Thou didst teach a woman, who had refused Thee a cup of water, what the worship of God must be. I rejoice in the assurance that Thou wilt no less now instruct Thy disciple, who comes to Thee with a heart that longs to pray in spirit and in truth. O my Holy Master! do teach me this blessed secret.

Teach me that the worship in spirit and truth is not of man, but only comes from Thee; that it is not only a thing of times and seasons, but the outflowing of a life in Thee. Teach me to draw near to God in prayer under the deep impression of my ignorance and my having nothing in myself to offer Him, and at the same time of the provision Thou, my Savior, makest for the Spirit's breathing in my childlike stammerings. I do bless Thee that in Thee I am a child, and have a child's liberty of access; that in Thee I have the spirit of Sonship and of worship of truth. Teach me, above all, Blessed Son of the Father, how it is the revelation of the Father that gives confidence in prayer; and let the infinite Fatherliness of God's Heart be my joy and strength for a life of prayer and of worship. Amen.

PRAY TO THY FATHER WHICH IS IN SECRET

OR
ALONE WITH GOD.

'But thou, when thou prayest, enter into thine inner chamber, and having shut thy door, pray to thy Father which is in secret, and thy Father which seeth in secret shall recompense thee.'—Matt. vi. 6.

After Jesus had called His first disciples He gave them their first public teaching in the Sermon on the Mount. He there expounded to them the kingdom of God, its laws and its life. In that kingdom God is not only King, but Father; He not only gives all, but is Himself all. In the knowledge and fellowship of Him alone is its blessedness. Hence it came as a matter of course that the revelation of prayer and the prayer-life was a part of His teaching concerning the New Kingdom He came to set up. Moses gave neither command nor regulation with regard to prayer: even the prophets say little directly of the duty of prayer; it is Christ who teaches to pray.

And the first thing the Lord teaches His disciples is that they must have a secret place for prayer; every one must have some solitary spot where he can be alone with his God. Every teacher must have a schoolroom. We have learnt to know and accept Jesus as our only teacher in the school of prayer. He has already taught us at Samaria that worship is no longer confined to times and places; that worship, spiritual true worship, is a thing of the spirit and the life; the whole man must in his whole life be worship in spirit and truth. And yet He wants each one to choose for himself the fixed spot where He can daily meet him. That inner chamber, that solitary place, is Jesus' schoolroom. That spot may be anywhere; that spot may change from day to day if we have to change our abode; but that secret place there must be, with the quiet time in which the pupil places himself in the Master's presence, to be by Him prepared to worship the Father. There alone, but there most surely, Jesus comes to us to teach us to pray.

A teacher is always anxious that his schoolroom should be bright and attractive, filled with the light and air of heaven, a place where pupils long to come, and love to stay. In His first words on prayer in the Sermon on the Mount, Jesus seeks to set the inner chamber before us in its most attractive light. If we listen carefully, we soon notice what the chief thing is He has to tell us of our tarrying there. Three times He uses the name of Father: 'Pray to *thy Father*;' '*Thy Father* shall recompense thee;' *Your Father* knoweth what things ye have need of.' The first thing in closet-prayer is: I must meet my Father. The light that shines in the closet must be: the light of the Father's countenance. The fresh air from heaven with which Jesus would have filled the atmosphere in which I am to breathe and pray, is: God's Father-love, God's infinite Fatherliness. Thus each thought or petition we breathe out will be simple, hearty, childlike trust in the Father. This is how the Master teaches us to pray: He brings us into the Father's living presence. What we pray there must avail. Let us listen carefully to hear what the Lord has to say to us.

First, '*Pray to thy Father which is in secret.*' God is a God who hides Himself to the carnal eye. As long as in our worship of God we are chiefly occupied with our own thoughts and exercises, we shall not meet Him who is a Spirit, the unseen One. But to the man who withdraws himself from all that is of the world and man, and prepares to wait upon God alone, the Father will reveal Himself. As he forsakes and gives up and shuts out the world, and the life of the world, and surrenders himself to be led of Christ into the secret of God's presence, the light of the Father's love will rise upon him. The secrecy of the inner chamber and the closed door, the entire separation from all around us, is an image of, and so a help to, that inner spiritual sanctuary, the secret of God's tabernacle, within the veil, where our spirit truly comes into contact with the Invisible One. And so we are taught, at the very outset of our search after the secret of effectual prayer, to remember that it is in the inner chamber, where we are alone with the Father, that we shall learn to pray aright. The Father is in secret: in these words Jesus teaches us where He is waiting us, where He is always to be found. Christians often complain that private prayer is not what it should be. They feel weak and sinful, the heart is cold and dark; it is as if they have so little to pray, and in that little no faith or joy. They are discouraged and kept from prayer by the thought that they cannot come to the Father as they ought or as they wish. Child of God! listen to your Teacher. He tells you that when you go to private prayer your first thought must be: The Father is in secret, the Father waits me there. Just because your heart is cold and prayerless, get you into the presence of the loving Father. As a father pitieth his children, so the Lord pitieth you. Do not be thinking of how little you have to bring God, but of how much He wants to give you. Just place yourself before, and look up into, His face; think of His love, His wonderful, tender, pitying love. Just tell Him how sinful and cold and dark all is: it is the Father's loving heart will give light and warmth to yours. O do what Jesus says: Just shut the door, and pray to thy Father, which is in secret. Is it not wonderful? to be able to go alone with God, the infinite God. And then to look up and say: My Father!

'And thy Father, which seeth in secret, will recompense thee.' Here Jesus assures us that secret prayer cannot be fruitless: its blessing will show itself in our life. We have but in secret, alone with God, to entrust our life before men to Him; He will reward us openly; He will see to it that the answer to prayer be made manifest in His blessing upon us. Our Lord would thus teach us that as infinite Fatherliness and Faithfulness is that with which God meets us in secret, so on our part there should be the childlike simplicity of faith, the confidence that our prayer does bring down a blessing. 'He that cometh to God must believe that *He is a rewarder* of them that seek Him.' Not on the strong or the fervent feeling with which I pray does the blessing of the closet depend, but upon the love and the power of the Father to whom I there entrust my needs. And therefore the Master has but one desire: Remember your Father is, and sees and hears in secret; go there and stay there, and go again from there in the confidence: He will recompense. Trust Him for it; depend upon Him: prayer to the Father cannot be vain; He will reward you openly.

Still further to confirm this faith in the Father-love of God, Christ speaks a third word: *'Your Father knoweth what things ye have need of before ye ask Him.'* At first sight it might appear as if this thought made prayer less needful: God knows far better than we what we need. But as we get a deeper insight into what prayer really is, this truth will help much to strengthen our faith. It will teach us that we do not need, as the heathen, with the multitude and urgency of our words, to compel an unwilling God to listen to us. It will lead to a holy thoughtfulness and silence in prayer as it suggests the question: Does my Father really know that I need this? It will, when once we have been led by the Spirit to the certainty that our request is indeed something that, according to the Word, we do need for God's glory, give us wonderful confidence to say, My Father knows I need it and must have it. And if there be any delay in the answer, it will teach us in quiet perseverance to hold on: Father! Thou knowest I need it. O the blessed liberty and simplicity of a child that Christ our Teacher would fain cultivate in us, as we draw near to God: let us look up to the Father until His Spirit works it in us. Let us sometimes in our prayers, when we are in danger of being so occupied with our fervent, urgent petitions, as to forget that the Father knows and hears, let us hold still and just quietly say: My Father sees, my Father hears, my Father knows; it will help our faith to take the answer, and to say: We know that we have the petitions we have asked of Him.

And now, all ye who have anew entered the school of Christ to be taught to pray, take these lessons, practice them, and trust Him to perfect you in them. Dwell much in the inner chamber, with the door shut—shut in from men, shut up with God; it is there the Father waits you, it is there Jesus will teach you to pray. To be alone in secret with the Father: this be your highest joy. To be assured that the Father will openly reward the secret prayer, so that it cannot remain unblessed: this be your strength day by day. And to know that the Father knows that you need what you ask, this be your liberty to bring every need, in the assurance that your God will supply it according to His riches in glory in Christ Jesus.

'Lord, Teach Us To Pray.'

~ ※ ~

Blessed Savior! with my whole heart I do bless Thee for the appointment of the inner chamber, as the school where Thou meetest each of Thy pupils alone, and revealest to him the Father. O my Lord! strengthen my faith so in the Father's tender love and kindness, that as often as I feel sinful or troubled, the first instinctive thought may be to go where I know the Father waits me, and where prayer never can go unblessed. Let the thought that He knows my need before I ask, bring me, in great restfulness of faith, to trust that He will give what His child requires. O let the place of secret prayer become to me the most beloved spot on earth.

And, Lord! hear me as I pray that Thou wouldest everywhere bless the closets of Thy believing people. Let Thy wonderful revelation of a Father's tenderness free all young Christians from every thought of secret prayer as a duty or a burden, and lead them to regard it as the highest privilege of their life, a joy and a blessing. Bring back all who are discouraged, because they cannot find ought to bring Thee in prayer. O give them to understand that they have only to come with their emptiness to Him who has all to give, and delights to do it. Not, what they have to bring the Father, but what the Father waits to give them, be their one thought.

And bless especially the inner chamber of all Thy servants who are working for Thee, as the place where God's truth and God's grace is revealed to them, where they are daily anointed with fresh oil, where their strength is renewed, and the blessings are received in faith, with which they are to bless their fellow-men. Lord, draw us all in the closet nearer to Thyself and the Father. Amen.

'AFTER THIS MANNER PRAY'

OR
THE MODEL PRAYER.

'After this manner therefore pray ye: Our Father which art in heaven.'
—Matt. vi. 9.

Every teacher knows the power of example. He not only tells the child what to do and how to do it, but shows him how it really can be done. In condescension to our weakness, our Heavenly Teacher has given us the very words we are to take with us as we draw near to our Father. We have in them a form of prayer in which there breathe the freshness and fulness of the Eternal Life. So simple that the child can lisp it, so divinely rich that it comprehends all that God can give. A form of prayer that becomes the model and inspiration for all other prayer, and yet always draws us back to itself as the deepest utterance of our souls before our God.

'*Our Father which art in heaven!*' To appreciate this word of adoration aright, I must remember that none of the saints had in Scripture ever ventured to address God as their Father. The invocation places us at once in the center of the wonderful revelation the Son came to make of His Father as our Father too. It comprehends the mystery of redemption—Christ delivering us from the curse that we might become the children of God. The mystery of regeneration—the Spirit in the new birth giving us the new life. And the mystery of faith—ere yet the redemption is accomplished or understood, the word is given on the lips of the disciples to prepare them for the blessed experience still to come. The words are the key to the whole prayer, to all prayer. It takes time, it takes life to study them; it will take eternity to understand them fully. The knowledge of God's Father-love is the first and simplest, but also the last and highest lesson in the school of prayer. It is in the personal relation to the living God, and the personal conscious fellowship of love with Himself, that prayer begins. It is in the knowledge of God's Fatherliness, revealed by the Holy Spirit, that the power of prayer will be found to root and grow. In the infinite tenderness and pity and patience of the infinite Father, in His loving readiness to hear and to help, the life of prayer has its joy. O let us take time, until the Spirit has made these words to us spirit and truth, filling heart and life: 'Our Father which art in heaven.' Then we are indeed within the veil, in the secret place of power where prayer always prevails.

'*Hallowed be Thy name.*' There is something here that strikes us at once. While we ordinarily first bring our own needs to God in prayer, and then think of what belongs to God and His interests, the Master reverses the order. First, *Thy* name, *Thy* kingdom, *Thy* will; then, give *us*, forgive *us*, lead *us*, deliver *us*. The lesson is of more importance than we think. In true worship the Father must be first, must be all. The sooner I learn to forget myself in the desire that He may be glorified, the richer will the blessing be that prayer will bring to myself. No one ever loses by what he sacrifices for the Father.

This must influence all our prayer. There are two sorts of prayer: personal and intercessory. The latter ordinarily occupies the lesser part of our time and energy. This may not be. Christ has opened the school of prayer specially to train intercessors for the great work of bringing down, by their faith and prayer, the blessings of His work and love on the world around. There can be no deep growth in prayer unless this be made our aim. The little child may ask of the father only what it needs for itself; and yet it soon learns to say, Give some for sister too. But the grown-up son, who only lives for the father's interest and takes charge of the father's business, asks more largely, and gets all that is asked. And Jesus would train us to the blessed life of consecration and service, in which our interests are all subordinate to the Name, and the Kingdom, and the Will of the Father. O let us live for this, and let, on each act of adoration, Our Father! there follow in the same breath, *Thy* Name, *Thy* Kingdom, *Thy* Will;—for this we look up and long.

'*Hallowed be Thy name.*' What name? This new name of Father. The word *Holy* is the central word of the Old Testament; the *name* Father of the New. In this name of Love all the holiness and glory of God are now to be revealed. And how is the name to be hallowed? By God Himself: '*I will hallow* My great name which ye have profaned.' Our prayer must be that in ourselves, in all God's children, in presence of the world, God Himself would reveal the holiness, the Divine power, the hidden glory of the name of Father. The Spirit of the Father is the *Holy* Spirit: it is only when we yield ourselves to be led *of Him*, that the name will be *hallowed* in our prayer and our lives. Let us learn the prayer: 'Our Father, hallowed be Thy name.'

'*Thy kingdom come.*' The Father is a King and has a kingdom. The son and heir of a king has no higher ambition than the glory of his father's kingdom. In time of war or danger this becomes his passion; he can think of nothing else. The children of the Father are here in the enemy's territory, where the kingdom, which is in heaven, is not yet fully manifested. What more natural than that, when they learn to hallow the Father-name, they should long and cry with deep enthusiasm: 'Thy kingdom come.' The coming of the kingdom is the one great event on which the revelation of the Father's glory, the blessedness of His children, the salvation of the world depends. On our prayers too the coming of the kingdom waits. Shall we not join in the deep longing cry of the redeemed: 'Thy kingdom come'? Let us learn it in the school of Jesus.

'*Thy will be done, as in heaven, so on earth.*' This petition is too frequently applied alone to the *suffering* of the will of God. In heaven God's will is *done*, and the Master teaches the child to ask that the will may be done on earth just as in heaven: in the spirit of adoring submission and ready obedience. Because the will of God is the glory of heaven, the doing of it is the blessedness of heaven. As the will is done, the kingdom of heaven comes into the heart. And wherever faith has accepted the Father's love, obedience accepts the Father's will. The surrender to, and the prayer for a life of heaven-like obedience, is the spirit of childlike prayer.

'*Give us this day our daily bread.*' When first the child has yielded himself to the Father in the care for His Name, His Kingdom, and His Will, he has full liberty to ask for his daily bread. A master cares for the food of his servant, a general of his soldiers, a father of his child. And will not the Father in heaven care for the child who has in prayer given himself up to His interests? We may indeed in full confidence say: Father, I live for Thy honor and Thy work; I know Thou carest for me. Consecration to God and His will gives wonderful liberty in prayer for temporal things: the whole earthly life is given to the Father's loving care.

'*And forgive us our debts as we also have forgiven our debtors.*' As bread is the first need of the body, so forgiveness for the soul. And the provision for the one is as sure as for the other. We are children, but sinners too; our right of access to the Father's presence we owe to the precious blood and the forgiveness it has won for us. Let us beware of the prayer for forgiveness becoming a formality: only what is really confessed is really forgiven. Let us in faith accept the forgiveness as promised: as a spiritual reality, an actual transaction between God and us, it is the entrance into all the Father's love and all the privileges of children. Such forgiveness, as a living experience, is impossible without a forgiving spirit to others: as *forgiven* expresses the heavenward, so *forgiving* the earthward, relation of God's child. In each prayer to the Father I must be able to say that I know of no one whom I do not heartily love.

'*And lead us not into temptation, but deliver us from the evil one.*' Our daily bread, the pardon of our sins, and then our being kept from all sin and the power of the evil one, in these three petitions all our personal need is comprehended. The prayer for bread and pardon must be accompanied by the surrender to live in all things in holy obedience to the Father's will, and the believing prayer in everything to be kept by the power of the indwelling Spirit from the power of the evil one.

Children of God! it is thus Jesus would have us to pray to the Father in heaven. O let His Name, and Kingdom, and Will, have the first place in our love; His providing, and pardoning, and keeping love will be our sure portion. So the prayer will lead us up to the true child-life: the Father all to the child, the Father all for the child. We shall understand how Father and child, the *Thine* and the *Our*, are all one, and how the heart that begins its prayer with the God-devoted Thine, will have the power in faith to speak out the Our too. Such prayer will, indeed, be the fellowship and interchange of love, always bringing us back in trust and worship to Him who is not only the Beginning but the End: 'For thine is the kingdom, and the power, and the glory, for ever, Amen.' Son of the Father, teach us to pray, 'Our Father.'

'Lord, Teach Us To Pray.'

~※~

O Thou who art the only-begotten Son, teach us, we beseech Thee, to pray, 'Our Father.' We thank Thee, Lord, for these Living Blessed Words which Thou hast given us. We thank Thee for the millions who in them have learnt to know and worship the Father, and for what they have been to us. Lord! it is as if we needed days and weeks in Thy school with each separate petition; so deep and full are they. But we look to Thee to lead us deeper into their meaning: do it, we pray Thee, for Thy Name's sake; Thy name is Son of the Father.

Lord! Thou didst once say: 'No man knoweth the Father save the Son, and he to whom the Son willeth to reveal Him.' And again: 'I made known unto them Thy name, and will make it known, that the love wherewith Thou hast loved Me may be in them.' Lord Jesus! reveal to us the Father. Let His name, His infinite Father-love, the love with which He loved Thee, according to Thy prayer, BE IN US. Then shall we say aright, 'Our Father!' Then shall we apprehend Thy teaching, and the first spontaneous breathing of our heart will be: 'Our Father, Thy Name, Thy Kingdom, Thy Will.' And we shall bring our needs and our sins and our temptations to Him in the confidence that the love of such a Father cares for all.

Blessed Lord! we are Thy scholars, we trust Thee; do teach us to pray, 'Our Father.' Amen.

How To Pray

~ ※ ~

By *R. A. Torrey*

~ ※ ~

Chapter I: The Importance of Prayer

In the 6th chapter of Ephesians in the 18th verse we read words which put the tremendous importance of prayer with startling and overwhelming force:

"Praying always with all prayer and supplication in the Spirit, and watching thereunto with all perseverance and supplication for all saints."

When we stop to weigh the meaning of these words, then note the connection in which they are found, the intelligent child of God is driven to say,

"I must pray, pray, pray. I must put all my energy and all my heart into prayer. Whatever else I do, I must pray."

The Revised Version is, if possible, stronger than the Authorized:

"With all prayer and supplication praying at all seasons in the spirit, and watching thereunto in all perseverance and supplication for all the saints."

Note the *alls*: "with *all* prayer," "at *all* seasons," "in *all* perseverance," "for *all* the saints." Note the piling up of strong words, "prayer," "supplication," "perseverance." Note once more the strong expression, "watching thereunto," more literally, "being sleepless thereunto." Paul realized the natural slothfulness of man, and especially his natural slothfulness in prayer. How seldom we pray things through! How often the church and the individual get right up to the verge of a great blessing in prayer and just then let go, get drowsy, quit. I wish that these words "being sleepless unto prayer" might burn into our hearts. I wish the whole verse might burn into our hearts.

But why is this constant, persistent, sleepless, overcoming prayer so needful?

1. First of all, *because there is a devil.*

He is cunning, he is mighty, he never rests, he is ever plotting the downfall of the child of God; and if the child of God relaxes in prayer, the devil will succeed in ensnaring him.

This is the thought of the context. The 12th verse reads:

"For our wrestling is not against flesh and blood, but against the principalities, against the powers, against the world rulers of this darkness, against the spiritual hosts of wickedness in the heavenly places." Then comes the 13th verse: "Wherefore take up the whole armor of God, that ye may be able to withstand in the evil day, and, having done all, to stand." Next follows a description of the different parts of the Christian's armor, which we are to put on if we are to stand against the devil and his mighty wiles. Then Paul brings all to a climax in the 18th verse, telling us that to all else we must add prayer—constant, persistent, untiring, sleepless prayer in the Holy Spirit, or all else will go for nothing.

2. A second reason for this constant, persistent, sleepless, overcoming prayer is that *prayer is God's appointed way for obtaining things, and the great secret of all lack in our experience, in our life and in our work is neglect of prayer.*

James brings this out very forcibly in the 4th chapter and 2nd verse of his epistle: "Ye have not because ye ask not." These words contain the secret of the poverty and powerlessness of the average Christian—neglect of prayer.

"Why is it," many a Christian is asking, "I make so little progress in my Christian life?"

"Neglect of prayer," God answers. "You have not because you ask not."

"Why is it," many a minister is asking, "I see so little fruit from my labors?"

Again God answers, "Neglect of prayer. You have not because you ask not."

"Why is it," many a Sunday-School teacher is asking, "that I see so few converted in my Sunday-School class?"

Still God answers, "Neglect of prayer. You have not because you ask not."

"Why is it," both ministers and churches are asking, "that the church of Christ makes so little headway against unbelief and error and sin and worldliness?"

Once more we hear God answering, "Neglect of prayer. You have not because you ask not."

3. The third reason for this constant, persistent, sleepless, overcoming prayer is that *those men whom God set forth as a pattern of what He expected Christians to be—the apostles—regarded prayer as the most important business of their lives.*

When the multiplying responsibilities of the early church crowded in upon them, they "called the multitude of the disciples unto them, and said, It is not reason that we should leave the Word of God, and serve tables. Wherefore, brethren, look ye out among you seven men of honest report, full of the Holy Ghost and wisdom, whom we may appoint over this business. *But we will give ourselves continually to prayer* and to the ministry of the Word." It is evident from what Paul wrote to the churches and to individuals about praying for them, that very much of his time and strength and thought was given to prayer. (Rom. 1:9; Eph. 1:15, 16; Col. 1:9; 1 Thess. 3:10; 2 Tim. 1:3).

All the mighty men of God outside the Bible have been men of prayer. They have differed from one another in many things, but in this they have been alike.

4. But there is a still weightier reason for this constant, persistent, sleepless, overcoming prayer. It is, *prayer occupied a very prominent place and played a very important part in the earthly life of our Lord.*

Turn, for example, to Mark 1:35. We read, "And in the morning, rising up a great while before day, He went out, and departed into a solitary place, and there prayed." The preceding day had been a very busy and exciting one, but Jesus shortened the hours of needed sleep that He might arise early and give Himself to more sorely needed prayer.

Turn again to Luke 6:12, where we read, "And it came to pass in those days that He went out into a mountain to pray, and continued all night in prayer to God." Our Savior found it necessary on occasion to take a whole night for prayer.

The words "pray" and "prayer" are used at least twenty-five times in connection with our Lord in the brief record of His life in the four Gospels, and His praying is mentioned in places where the words are not used. Evidently prayer took much of the time and strength of Jesus, and a man or woman who does not spend much time in prayer, cannot properly be called a follower of Jesus Christ.

5. There is another reason for constant, persistent, sleepless, overcoming prayer that seems if possible even more forcible than this, namely, *praying is the most important part of the present ministry of our risen Lord.*

Christ's ministry did not close with His death. His atoning work was finished then, but when He rose and ascended to the right hand of the Father, He entered upon other work for us just as important in its place as His atoning work. It cannot be divorced from

His atoning work; it rests upon that as its basis, but it is necessary to our complete salvation.

What that great present work is, by which He carries our salvation on to completeness, we read in Heb. 7:25, "Wherefore He is able also to save them to the uttermost that come unto God by Him, seeing *He ever liveth to make intercession for them.*" This verse tells us that Jesus is able to save us unto the uttermost, not merely *from* the uttermost, but *unto* the uttermost, unto entire completeness, absolute perfection, because He not merely died, but because He also "ever liveth." The verse also tells us for what purpose He now lives, *"to make intercession for us,"* to pray. Praying is the principal thing He is doing in these days. It is by His prayers that He is saving us.

The same thought is found in Paul's remarkable, triumphant challenge in Rom. 8:34—"Who is he that shall condemn? It is Christ Jesus that died, yea rather, that was raised from the dead, who is at the right hand of God, *who also maketh intercession for us.*"

If we then are to have fellowship with Jesus Christ in His present work, we must spend much time in prayer; we must give ourselves to earnest, constant, persistent, sleepless, overcoming prayer. I know of nothing that has so impressed me with a sense of the importance of praying at all seasons, being much and constantly in prayer, as the thought that that is the principal occupation at present of my risen Lord. I want to have fellowship with Him, and to that end I have asked the Father that whatever else He may make me, to make me at all events an intercessor, to make me a man who knows how to pray, and who spends much time in prayer.

This ministry of intercession is a glorious and a mighty ministry, and we can all have part in it. The man or the woman who is shut away from the public meeting by sickness can have part in it; the busy mother; the woman who has to take in washing for a living can have part—she can mingle prayers for the saints, and for her pastor, and for the unsaved, and for foreign missionaries, with the soap and water as she bends over the washtub, and not do the washing any more poorly on that account; the hard driven man of business can have part in it, praying as he hurries from duty to duty. But of course we must, if we would maintain this spirit of constant prayer, take time—and take plenty of it—when we shall shut ourselves up in the secret place alone with God for nothing but prayer.

6. The sixth reason for constant, persistent, sleepless, overcoming prayer is that *prayer is the means that God has appointed for our receiving mercy, and obtaining grace to help in time of need.*

Heb. 4:16 is one of the simplest and sweetest verses in the Bible,—"Let us therefore come boldly unto the throne of grace, that we may obtain mercy, and find grace to help in time of need." These words make it very plain that God has appointed a way by which we shall seek and obtain mercy and grace. That way is prayer; bold, confident, outspoken approach to the throne of grace, the most holy place of God's presence, where our sympathizing High Priest, Jesus Christ, has entered in our behalf. (Verses 14, 15.)

Mercy is what we need, grace is what we must have, or all our life and effort will end in complete failure. Prayer is the way to get them. There is infinite grace at our disposal, and we make it ours experimentally by prayer. Oh, if we only realized the fullness of God's grace, that is ours for the asking, its height and depth and length and breadth, I am sure that we would spend more time in prayer. The measure of our appropriation of grace is determined by the measure of our prayers.

Who is there that does not feel that he needs more grace? Then ask for it. Be constant and persistent in your asking. Be importunate and untiring in your asking. God delights to have us "shameless" beggars in this direction; for it shows our faith in Him, and He is mightily pleased with faith. Because of our "shamelessness" He will rise and give us as much as we need (Luke 11:8). What little streams of mercy and grace most of us know, when we might know rivers overflowing their banks!

7. The next reason for constant, persistent, sleepless, overcoming prayer is that *prayer in the name of Jesus Christ is the way Jesus Christ Himself has appointed for His disciples to obtain fullness of joy.*

He states this simply and beautifully in John 16:24, "Hitherto have ye asked nothing in My name; ask, and ye shall receive, that your joy may be fulfilled." "Made full" is the way the Revised Version reads. Who is there that does not wish his joy filled full? Well, the way to have it filled full is by praying in the name of Jesus. We all know people whose joy is filled full, indeed, it is just running over, is shining from their eyes, bubbling out of their very lips, and running off their finger tips when they shake hands with you. Coming in contact with them is like coming in contact with an electrical machine charged with gladness. Now people of that sort are always people that spend much time in prayer.

Why is it that prayer in the name of Christ brings such fullness of joy? In part, because we get what we ask. But that is not the only reason, nor the greatest. It makes God real. When we ask something definite of God, and He gives it, how real God becomes! He is right there! It is blessed to have a God who is real, and not merely an idea. I remember how once I was taken suddenly and seriously sick all alone in my study. I dropped upon my knees and cried to God for help. Instantly all pain left me—I was perfectly well. It seemed as if God stood right there, and had put out His hand and touched me. The joy of the healing was not so great as the joy of meeting God.

There is no greater joy on earth or in heaven, than communion with God, and prayer in the name of Jesus brings us into communion with Him. The Psalmist was surely not speaking only of future blessedness, but also of present blessedness when he said,

"In Thy presence is fullness of joy." (Ps. 16.11.) O the unutterable joy of those moments when in our prayers we really press into the presence of God!

Does some one say. "I have never known any such joy as that in prayer"?

Do you take enough leisure for prayer to actually get into God's presence? Do you really give yourself up to prayer in the time which you do take?

8. The eighth reason for constant, persistent, sleepless, overcoming prayer is that *prayer,* in *every care and anxiety and need of life, with thanksgiving, is the means that God has appointed for obtaining freedom from all anxiety, and the peace of God which passeth all understanding.*

"Be careful for nothing," says Paul, "but in everything by prayer and supplication with thanksgiving let your requests be made known unto God, and the peace of God which passeth all understanding, shall keep your hearts and minds through Christ Jesus." (Phil. 4:6, 7.) To many this seems at the first glance, the picture of a life that is beautiful, but beyond the reach of ordinary mortals; not so at all. The verse tells us how the life is attainable by every child of God: "Be careful for nothing," or as the Revised Version reads, "In nothing be anxious." The remainder of the verse tells us how, and it is very simple: "But in everything by prayer and supplication with thanksgiving let your requests be made known unto God." What could be plainer or more simple than that? Just keep in constant touch with God, and when any trouble or vexation, great or small, comes up, speak to Him about it, never forgetting to return thanks for what He has already done. What will the result be? "The peace of God which passeth all understanding shall guard your hearts and your thoughts in Christ Jesus."

That is glorious, and as simple as it is glorious! Thank God, many are trying it. Don't you know any one who is always serene? Perhaps he is a very stormy man by his natural make-up, but troubles and conflicts and reverses and bereavements may sweep around him, and the peace of God which passeth all understanding guards his heart and his thoughts in Christ Jesus.

We all know such persons. How do they manage it?

Just by prayer, that is all. Those persons who know the deep peace of God, the unfathomable peace that passeth all understanding, are always men and women of much prayer.

Some of us let the hurry of our lives crowd prayer out, and what a waste of time and energy and nerve force there is by the constant worry! One night of prayer will save us from many nights of insomnia. Time spent in prayer is not wasted, but time invested at big interest.

9. The ninth reason for constant, persistent, sleepless, overcoming prayer is that *prayer is the method that God Himself has appointed for our obtaining the Holy Spirit.*

Upon this point the Bible is very plain. Jesus says, "If ye then, being evil, know how to give good gifts unto your children, how much more shall your heavenly Father give the Holy Spirit to them that ask Him?" (Luke 11:13.) Men are telling us in these days, very good men too, "You must not pray for the Holy Spirit," but what are they going to do with the plain statement of Jesus Christ, "How much more will your heavenly Father give the Holy Spirit *to them that ask Him?*"

Some years ago when an address on the baptism with the Holy Spirit was announced, a brother came to me before the address and said with much feeling,

"Be sure and tell them not to pray for the Holy Spirit."

"I will surely not tell them that, for Jesus says, 'How much more shall your heavenly Father give the Holy Spirit to them that ask Him'."

"Oh, yes," he replied, "but that was before Pentecost."

"How about Acts 4:31? Was that before Pentecost, or after?"

"After, of course."

"Read it."

"'And when *they had prayed*, the place was shaken where they were assembled together; and they were all *filled with the Holy Ghost*, and they spake the Word of God with boldness.'"

"How about Acts 8:15? Was that before Pentecost or after?"

"After."

"Please read."

"'Who, when they were come down *prayed* for them, that they might receive the Holy Ghost.'"

He made no answer. What could he answer? It is plain as day in the Word of God that before Pentecost and after, the first baptism and the subsequent fillings with the Holy Spirit were received in answer to definite prayer. Experience also teaches this.

Doubtless many have received the Holy Spirit the moment of their surrender to God before there was time to pray, but how many there are who know that their first definite baptism with the Holy Spirit came while they were on their knees or faces before God, alone or in company with others, and who again and again since that have been filled with the Holy Spirit in the place of prayer!

I know this as definitely as I know that my thirst has been quenched while I was drinking water. Early one morning in the Chicago Avenue Church prayer room, where several hundred people had been assembled a number of hours in prayer, the Holy Spirit fell so manifestly, and the whole place was so filled with His presence, that no one could speak or pray, but sobs of joy filled the place. Men went out of that room to different parts of the country, taking trains that very morning, and reports soon came back of the out-pouring of God's Holy Spirit in answer to prayer. Others went out into the city with the blessing of God upon them. This is only one instance among many that might be cited from personal experience.

If we would only spend more time in prayer, there would be more fullness of the Spirit's power in our work. Many and many a man who once worked unmistakably in the power of the Holy Spirit is now filling the air with empty shoutings, and beating it with his meaningless gesticulations, because he has let prayer be crowded out. We must spend much time on our knees before God, if we are to continue in the power of the Holy Spirit.

10. The tenth reason for constant, persistent, sleepless, overcoming prayer is that *prayer is the means that Christ has appointed whereby our hearts shall not become overcharged with surfeiting and drunkenness and cares of this life, and so the day of Christ's return come upon us suddenly as a snare.*

One of the most interesting and solemn passages upon prayer in the Bible is along this line. (Luke 21:34-36) "Take heed to yourselves, lest at any time your hearts be overcharged with surfeiting and drunkenness and cares of this life, and so that day come upon you unawares. For as a snare shall it come on all them that dwell in the face of the whole earth. Watch ye therefore, and *pray always*, that ye may be accounted worthy to escape all these things that shall come to pass, and to stand before the Son of man." According to this passage there is only one way in which we can be prepared for the coming of the Lord when He appears, that is, through much prayer.

The coming again of Jesus Christ is a subject that is awakening much interest and much discussion in our day; but it is one thing to be interested in the Lord's return, and to talk about it, and quite another thing to be prepared for it. We live in an atmosphere that has a constant tendency to unfit us for Christ's coming. The world tends to draw us down by its gratifications and by its cares. There is only one way by which we can rise triumphant above these things—by constant watching unto prayer, that is, by sleeplessness unto prayer. "Watch" in this passage is the same strong word used in Eph. 6:18, and "always" the same strong phrase "in every season." The man who spends little time in prayer, who is not steadfast and constant in prayer, will not be ready for the Lord when He comes. But we may be ready. How? Pray! Pray! Pray!

11. There is one more reason for constant, persistent, sleepless, overcoming prayer, and it is a mighty one: *because of what prayer accomplishes*. Much has really been said upon that already, but there is much also that should be added.

(1) Prayer promotes our spiritual growth as almost nothing else, indeed as nothing else but Bible study; and true prayer and true Bible study go hand in hand.

It is through prayer that my sin is brought to light, my most hidden sin. As I kneel before God and pray, "Search me, O God, and know my heart; try me, and know my thoughts; and see if there be any wicked way in me," (Ps.139:23, 24), God shoots the penetrating rays of His light into the innermost recesses of my heart, and the sins I never suspected are brought to view. In answer to prayer, God washes me from mine iniquity and cleanses me from my sin (Ps. 51:2). In answer to prayer my eyes are opened to behold wondrous things out of God's Word (Ps. 119:18). In answer to prayer I get wisdom to know God's way (Jas. 1:5) and strength to walk in it. As I meet God in prayer and gaze into His face, I am changed into His own image from glory to glory (2 Cor. 3:18). Each day of true prayer life finds me liker to my glorious Lord.

John Welch, son-in-law to John Knox, was one of the most faithful men of prayer this world ever saw. He counted that day ill-spent in which seven or eight hours were not used alone with God in prayer and the study of His Word. An old man speaking of him after his death said, "He was a type of Christ."

How came he to be so like his Master?

His prayer life explains the mystery.

(2) Prayer brings power into our work.

If we wish power for any work to which God calls us, be it preaching, teaching, personal work, or the rearing of our children, we can get it by earnest prayer.

A woman with a little boy who was perfectly incorrigible, once came to me in desperation and said:

"What shall I do with him?"

I asked, "Have you ever tried prayer?"

She said that she had prayed for him, she thought. I asked if she had made his conversion and his character a matter of definite, expectant prayer. She replied that she had not been definite in the matter. She began that day, and at once there was a marked change in the child, and he grew up into Christian manhood.

How many a Sunday-school teacher has taught for months and years, and seen no real fruit from his labors, and then has learned the secret of intercession, and by earnest pleading with God, has seen his scholars brought one by one to Christ! How many a poor preacher has become a mighty man of God by casting away his confidence in his own ability and gifts, and giving himself up to God to wait upon Him for the power that comes from on high! John Livingstone spent a night, with some others likeminded, in prayer to God and religious conversation, and when he preached next day in the Kirk of Shotts five hundred people were converted, or dated some definite uplift in their life to that occasion. Prayer and power are inseparable.

(3) Prayer avails for the conversion of others.

There are few converted in this world unless in connection with some one's prayers. I formerly thought that no human being had anything to do with my own conversion, for I was not converted in church or Sunday-school, or in personal conversation with any one. I was awakened in the middle of the night and converted. As far as I can remember I had not the slightest thought of being converted, or of anything of that character, when I went to bed and fell asleep; but I was awakened in the middle of the night and converted probably inside of five minutes. A few minutes before I was about as near eternal perdition as one gets. I had one foot over the brink and was trying to get the other one over. I say I thought no human being had anything to do with it, but I had forgotten my mother's prayers, and I afterward learned that one of my college classmates had chosen me as one to pray for until I was saved.

Prayer often avails where everything else fails. How utterly all of Monica's efforts and entreaties failed with her son, but her prayers prevailed with God, and the dissolute youth became St. Augustine, the mighty man of God. By prayer the bitterest enemies of the Gospel have become its most valiant defenders, the greatest scoundrels the truest sons of God, and the vilest women the purest saints. Oh, the power of prayer to reach down, down, down, where hope itself seems vain, and lift men and women up, up, up into fellowship with and likeness to God. It is simply wonderful! How little we appreciate this marvelous weapon!

(4) Prayer brings blessings to the church.

The history of the church has always been a history of grave difficulties to overcome. The devil hates the church and seeks in every way to block its progress; now by false doctrine, again by division, again by inward corruption of life. But by prayer, a clear way can be made through everything. Prayer will root out heresy, allay misunderstanding, sweep away jealousies and animosities, obliterate immoralities, and bring in the full tide of God's reviving grace. History abundantly proves this. In the hour of darkest portent, when the case of the church, local or universal, has seemed beyond hope, believing men and believing women have met together and cried to God and the answer has come.

It was so in the days of Knox, it was so in the days of Wesley and Whitfield, it was so in the days of Edwards and Brainerd, it was so in the days of Finney, it was so in the days of the great revival of 1857 in this country and of 1859 in Ireland, and it will be so again in your day and mine. Satan has marshalled his forces. Christian science with its false Christ—a woman—lifts high its head. Others making great pretensions of apostolic methods, but covering the rankest dishonesty and hypocrisy with these pretensions, speak with loud assurance. Christians equally loyal to the great fundamental truths of the Gospel are glowering at one another with a devil-sent suspicion. The world, the flesh and the devil are holding high carnival. It is now a dark day, *but*—now "it is time for Thee, Lord, to work; for they have made void Thy law." (Ps. 119:126). And He is getting ready to work, and now He is listening for the voice of prayer. Will He hear it? Will He hear it from you? Will He hear it from the church as a body? I believe He will.

Chapter II: Praying unto God

We have seen something of the tremendous importance and the resistless power of prayer, and now we come directly to the question—how to pray with power.

1. In the 12th chapter of the Acts of the Apostles we have the record of a prayer that prevailed with God, and brought to pass great results. In the 5th verse of this chapter, the manner and method of this prayer is described in few words:

"Prayer was made without ceasing of the church *unto God* for him."

The first thing to notice in this verse is the brief expression "unto God." The prayer that has power is the prayer that is offered unto God.

But some will say, "Is not all prayer unto God?"

No. Very much of so-called prayer, both public and private, is not unto God. In order that a prayer should be really unto God, there must be a definite and conscious approach to God when we pray; we must have a definite and vivid realization that God is bending over us and listening as we pray. In very much of our prayer there is really but little thought of God. Our mind is taken up with the thought of what we need, and is not occupied with the thought of the mighty and loving Father of whom we are seeking it. Oftentimes it is the case that we are occupied neither with the need nor with the One to whom we are praying, but our mind is wandering here and there throughout the world. There is no power in that sort of prayer. But when we really come into God's presence, really meet Him face to face in the place of prayer, really seek the things that we desire *from Him*, then there is power.

If, then, we would pray aright, the first thing that we should do is to see to it that we really get an audience with God, that we really get into His very presence. Before a word of petition is offered, we should have the definite and vivid consciousness that we are talking to God, and should believe that He is listening to our petition and is going to grant the thing that we ask of Him. This is only possible by the Holy Spirit's power, so we should look to the Holy Spirit to really lead us into the presence of God, and should not be hasty in words until He has actually brought us there.

One night a very active Christian man dropped into a little prayer-meeting that I was leading. Before we knelt to pray, I said something like the above, telling all the friends to be sure before they prayed, and while they were praying, that they really were in God's presence, that they had the thought of Him definitely in mind, and to be more taken up with Him than with their petition. A few days after I met this same gentleman, and he said that this simple thought was entirely new to him, that it had made prayer an entirely new experience to him.

If then we would pray aright, these two little words must sink deep into our hearts, "*unto God.*"

2. The second secret of effective praying is found in the same verse, in the words "*without ceasing.*"

In the Revised Version, "without ceasing" is rendered "earnestly." Neither rendering gives the full force of the Greek. The word means literally "stretched-out-ed-ly." It is a pictorial word, and wonderfully expressive. It represents the soul on a stretch of earnest and intense desire. "Intensely" would perhaps come as near translating it as any English word. It is the word used of our Lord in Luke 22:44 where it is said, "He prayed more earnestly: and His sweat was as it were great drops of blood falling down to the ground."

We read in Heb. 5:7 that "in the days of His flesh" Christ "offered up prayers and supplications with strong crying and tears." In Rom. 15:30, Paul beseeches the saints in Rome to *strive* together with him in their prayers. The word translated "strive" means primarily to contend as in athletic games or in a fight. In other words, the prayer that prevails with God is the prayer into which we put our whole soul, stretching out toward God in intense and agonizing desire. Much of our modern prayer has no power in it because there is no heart in it. We rush into God's presence, run through a string of petitions, jump up and go out. If someone should ask us an hour afterward for what we prayed, oftentimes we could not tell. If we put so little heart into our prayers, we cannot expect God to put much heart into answering them.

We hear much in our day of the rest of faith, but there is such a thing as the fight of faith in prayer as well as in effort. Those who would have us think that they have attained to some sublime height of faith and trust because they never know any agony of conflict or of prayer, have surely gotten beyond their Lord, and beyond the mightiest victors for God, both in effort and prayer, that the ages of Christian history have known. When we learn to come to God with an intensity of desire that wrings the soul, then shall we know a power in prayer that most of us do not know now.

But how shall we attain to this earnestness in prayer?

Not by trying to work ourselves up into it. The true method is explained in Rom. 8:26, "And in like manner the Spirit also helpeth our infirmity: for we know not how to pray as we ought; but the Spirit Himself maketh intercession for us with groanings which cannot be uttered." The earnestness that we work up in the energy of the flesh is a repulsive thing. The earnestness wrought in us by the power of the Holy Spirit is pleasing to God. Here again, if we would pray aright, we must look to the Spirit of God to teach us to pray.

It is in this connection that fasting comes. In Dan. 9:3 we read that Daniel set his face "unto the Lord God, to seek by prayer and supplications, with fasting, and sackcloth, and ashes." There are those who think that fasting belongs to the old dispensation; but when we look at Acts 14:23, and Acts 13:2, 3, we find that it was practised by the earnest men of the apostolic day.

If we would pray with power, we should pray with fasting. This of course does not mean that we should fast every time we pray; but there are times of emergency or special crisis in work or in our individual lives, when men of downright earnestness will withdraw themselves even from the gratification of natural appetites that would be perfectly proper under other circumstances, that they may give themselves up wholly to prayer. There is a peculiar power in such prayer. Every great crisis in life and work should be met in that way. There is nothing pleasing to God in our giving up in a purely Pharisaic and legal way things which are pleasant, but there is power in that downright earnestness and determination to obtain in prayer the things of which we sorely feel our need, that leads us to put away everything, even the things in themselves most right and necessary, that we may set our faces to find God, and obtain blessings from Him.

3. A third secret of right praying is also found in this same verse, Acts 12:5. It appears in the three words "*of the church.*"

There is power in *united prayer*. Of course there is power in the prayer of an individual, but there is vastly increased power in united prayer. God delights in the unity of His people, and seeks to emphasize it in every way, and so He pronounces a special blessing upon united prayer. We read in Matt. 18:19, "If two of you shall agree on earth as touching anything that they shall ask, it shall be done for them of My Father which is in heaven." This unity, however, must be real. The passage just quoted does not say that if two shall agree in asking, but if two shall agree *as touching* anything they shall ask. Two persons might agree to ask for the same thing, and yet there be no real agreement as touching the thing they asked. One might ask it because he really desired it, the other might ask it simply to please his friend. But where there is real agreement, where the Spirit of God brings two believers into perfect harmony as concerning that which they may ask of God, where the Spirit lays the same burden on two hearts; in all such prayer there is absolutely irresistible power.

Chapter III: Obeying and Praying

1. One of the most significant verses in the Bible on prayer is 1 John 3:22. John says, "And whatsoever we ask, we receive of Him, because we keep His commandments, and do those things that are pleasing in His sight."

What an astounding statement! John says in so many words, that everything he asked for he got. How many of us can say this: "Whatsoever I ask I receive"? But John explains why this was so, "Because we keep His commandments, and do those things that are pleasing in His sight." In other words, the one who expects God to do as he asks Him, must on his part *do whatever God bids him*. If we give a listening ear to all God's commands to us, He will give a listening ear to all our petitions to Him. If, on the other hand, we turn a deaf ear to His precepts, He will be likely to turn a deaf ear to our prayers. Here we find the secret of much unanswered prayer. We are not listening to God's Word, and therefore He is not listening to our petitions.

I was once speaking to a woman who had been a professed Christian, but had given it all up. I asked her why she was not a Christian still. She replied, because she did not believe the Bible. I asked her why she did not believe the Bible.

"Because I have tried its promises and found them untrue."

"Which promises?"

"The promises about prayer."

"Which promises about prayer?"

"Does it not say in the Bible, 'Whatsoever ye ask believing ye shall receive'?"

"It says something nearly like that."

"Well, I asked fully expecting to get and did not receive, so the promise failed."

"Was the promise made to you?"

"Why, certainly, it is made to all Christians, is it not?"

"No, God carefully defines who the 'ye's' are, whose believing prayers He agrees to answer."

I then turned her to 1 John 3:22, and read the description of those whose prayers had power with God.

"Now," I said, "were you keeping His commandments and doing those things which are pleasing in His sight?"

She frankly confessed that she was not, and soon came to see that the real difficulty was not with God's promises, but with herself. That is the difficulty with many an unanswered prayer to-day: the one who offers it is not obedient.

If we would have power in prayer, we must be earnest students of His Word to find out what His will regarding us is, and then having found it, do it. One unconfessed act of disobedience on our part will shut the ear of God against many petitions.

2. But this verse goes beyond the mere keeping of God's commandments. John tells us that we must *do those things that are pleasing in His sight.*

There are many things which it would be pleasing to God for us to do which He has not specifically commanded us. A true child is not content with merely doing those things which his father specifically commands him to do. He studies to know his father's will, and if he thinks that there is any thing that he can do that would please his father, he does it gladly, though his father has never given him any specific order to do it. So it is with the true child of God. He does not ask merely whether certain things are commanded or certain things forbidden. He studies to know his Father's will in all things.

There are many Christians to-day who are doing things that are not pleasing to God, and leaving undone things which would be pleasing to God. When you speak to them about these things they will confront you at once with the question, "Is there any command in the Bible not to do this thing?" And if you cannot show them some verse in which the matter in question is plainly forbidden, they think they are under no obligation whatever to give it up; but a true child of God does not demand a specific command. If we make it our study to find out and to do the things which are pleasing to God, He will make His study to do the things which are pleasing to us. Here again we find the explanation of much unanswered prayer: We are not making it the study of our lives to know what would please our Father, and so our prayers are not answered.

Take as an illustration of questions that are constantly coming up, the matter of theater going, dancing and the use of tobacco. Many who are indulging in these things will ask you triumphantly if you speak against them, "Does the Bible say, 'Thou shalt not go to the theater'?" "Does the Bible say, 'Thou shalt not dance'?" "Does the Bible say, 'Thou shalt not smoke'?" That is not the question. The question is, Is our heavenly Father well pleased when He sees one of His children in the theater, at the dance, or smoking? That is a question for each to decide for himself, prayerfully, seeking light from the Holy Spirit. "Where is the harm in these things?" many ask. It is aside from our purpose to go into the general question, but beyond a doubt there is this great harm in many a case; they rob our prayers of power.

3. Psalm 145:18 throws a great deal of light on the question of how to pray: "The Lord is nigh unto all them that call upon Him, to all that call upon Him in truth."

That little expression "in truth" is worthy of study. If you will take your concordance and go through the Bible, you will find that this expression means "in reality," "in sincerity." The prayer that God answers is the prayer that is real, the prayer that asks for something that is sincerely desired.

Much prayer is insincere. People ask for things which they do not wish. Many a woman is praying for the conversion of her husband, who does not really wish her husband to be converted. She thinks that she does, but if she knew what would be involved in the conversion of her husband, how it would necessitate an entire revolution in his manner of doing business, and how consequently it would reduce their income and make necessary an entire change in their method of living, the real prayer of her heart would be, if she were to be sincere with God:

"O God, do not convert my husband."

She does not wish his conversion at so great cost.

Many a church is praying for a revival that does not really desire a revival. They think they do, for to their minds a revival means an increase of membership, an increase of income, an increase of reputation among the churches, but if they knew what a real revival meant, what a searching of hearts on the part of professed Christians would be involved, what a radical transformation of individual, domestic and social life would be brought about, and many other things that would come to pass if the Spirit of God was poured out in reality and power; if all this were known, the real cry of the church would be:

"O God, keep us from having a revival."

Many a minister is praying for the baptism with the Holy Spirit who does not really desire it. He thinks he does, for the baptism with the Spirit means to him new joy, new power in preaching the Word, a wider reputation among men, a larger prominence in the church of Christ. But if he understood what a baptism with the Holy Spirit really involved, how for example it would necessarily bring him into antagonism with the world, and with unspiritual Christians, how it would cause his name to be "cast out as evil," how it might necessitate his leaving a good comfortable living and going down to work in the slums, or even in some foreign land; if he understood all this, his prayer quite likely would be—if he were to express the real wish of his heart,—

"O God, save me from being baptized with the Holy Ghost."

But when we do come to the place where we really desire the conversion of friends at any cost, really desire the outpouring of the Holy Spirit whatever it may involve, really desire the baptism with the Holy Ghost come what may, where we desire anything "in truth" and then call upon God for it "in truth," God is going to hear.

Chapter IV: Praying in the Name of Christ and According to the Will of God

1. It was a wonderful word about prayer that Jesus spoke to His disciples on the night before His crucifixion, "Whatsoever ye shall ask *in My name*, that will I do, that the Father may be glorified in the Son. If ye shall ask anything in My name, I will do it."

Prayer in the name of Christ has power with God. God is well pleased with His Son Jesus Christ. He hears Him always, and He also hears always the prayer that is really in His name. There is a fragrance in the name of Christ that makes acceptable to God every prayer that bears it.

But what is it to pray in the name of Christ?

Many explanations have been attempted that to ordinary minds do not explain. But there is nothing mystical or mysterious about this expression. If one will go through the Bible and examine all the passages in which the expression "in My name" or "in His name" or synonymous expressions are used, he will find that it means just about what it does in modern usage. If I go to a bank and hand in a check with my name signed to it, I ask of that bank *in my own name*. If I have money deposited in that bank, the check will be cashed; if not, it will not be. If, however, I go to a bank with somebody else's name signed to the check, I am asking *in his name*, and it does not matter whether I have money in that bank or any other, if the person whose name is signed to the check has money there, the check will be cashed.

If, for example, I should go to the First National Bank of Chicago, and present a check which I had signed for $50.00, the paying teller would say to me:

"Why, Mr. Torrey, we cannot cash that. You have no money in this bank."

But if I should go to the First National Bank with a check for $5,000.00 made payable to me, and signed by one of the large depositors in that bank, they would not ask whether I had money in that bank or in any bank, but would honor the check at once.

So it is when I go to the bank of heaven, when I go to God in prayer. I have nothing deposited there, I have absolutely no credit there, and if I go in my own name I will get absolutely nothing; but Jesus Christ has unlimited credit in heaven, and He has granted to me the privilege of going to the bank with His name on my checks, and when I thus go, my prayers will be honored to any extent.

To pray then in the name of Christ is to pray on the ground, not of my credit, but His; to renounce the thought that I have any claims on God whatever, and approach Him on the ground of God's claims. Praying in the name of Christ is not merely adding the phrase "I ask these things in Jesus' name" to my prayer. I may put that phrase in my prayer and really be resting in my own merit all the time. On the other hand, I may omit that phrase but really be resting in the merit of Christ all the time. But when I really do approach God, not on the ground of my merit, but on the ground of Christ's merit, not on the ground of my goodness, but on the ground of the atoning blood (Heb. 10:19), God will hear me. Very much of our modern prayer is vain because men approach God imagining that they have some claim upon God whereby He is under obligations to answer their prayers.

Years ago when Mr. Moody was young in Christian work, he visited a town in Illinois. A judge in the town was an infidel. This judge's wife besought Mr. Moody to call upon her husband, but Mr. Moody replied:

"I cannot talk with your husband. I am only an uneducated young Christian, and your husband is a book infidel."

But the wife would not take no for an answer, so Mr. Moody made the call. The clerks in the outer office tittered as the young salesman from Chicago went in to talk with the scholarly judge.

The conversation was short. Mr. Moody said:

"Judge, I can't talk with you. You are a book infidel, and I have no learning, but I simply want to say if you are ever converted, I want you to let me know."

The judge replied: "Yes, young man, if I am ever converted I will let you know. Yes, I will let you know."

The conversation ended. The clerks tittered still louder when the zealous young Christian left the office, but the judge was converted within a year. Mr. Moody visiting the town again asked the judge to explain how it came about. The judge said:

"One night, when my wife was at prayer meeting, I began to grow very uneasy and miserable. I did not know what was the matter with me, but finally retired before my wife came home. I could not sleep all that night. I got up early, told my wife that I would eat no breakfast, and went down to the office. I told the clerks they could take a holiday, and shut myself up in the inner office. I kept growing more and more miserable, and finally I got down and asked God to forgive my sins, but I would not say 'for Jesus' sake,' for I was a Unitarian and I did not believe in the atonement. I kept praying 'God forgive my sins'; but no answer came. At last in desperation I cried, 'O God, for Christ's sake forgive my sins,' and found peace at once."

The judge had no access to God until he came in the name of Christ, but when he thus came, he was heard and answered at once.

2. Great light is thrown upon the subject "How to Pray" by 1 John 5:14, 15: "And this is the boldness which we have toward Him, that if we ask anything *according to His will*, He heareth us; and if we know that He heareth us whatsoever we ask, we know that we have the petitions which we have asked of Him."

This passage teaches us plainly that if we are to pray aright, we must pray according to God's will, then will we beyond a peradventure get the thing we ask of Him.

But can we know the will of God? Can we know that any specific prayer is according to His will?

We most surely can.

How?

(1) First by the Word. God has revealed His will in His Word.

When anything is definitely promised in the Word of God, we know that it is His will to give that thing. If then when I pray, I can find some definite promise of God's Word and lay that promise before God, I know that He hears me, and if I know that He hears me, I know that I have the petition that I have asked of Him. For example, when I pray for wisdom I know that it is the will of God to give me wisdom, for He says so in James 1:5: "If any of you lack wisdom, let him ask of God, that giveth to all men liberally, and upbraideth not; and it shall be given him." So when I ask for wisdom I know that the prayer is heard, and that wisdom will be given me. In like manner when I pray for the Holy Spirit I know from Luke 11:13 that it is God's will, that my prayer is heard, and that I have the petition that I have asked of Him: "If ye then, being evil, know how to give good gifts unto your children, how much more shall your heavenly Father give the Holy Spirit to them that ask Him?"

Some years ago a minister came to me at the close of an address on prayer at a Y.M.C.A. Bible school, and said,

"You have produced upon those young men the impression that they can ask for definite things and get the very things that they ask."

I replied that I did not know whether that was the impression that I produced or not, but that was certainly the impression that I desired to produce.

"But," he replied, "that is not right. We cannot be sure, for we don't know God's will."

I turned him at once to James 1:5, read it and said to him, "Is it not God's will to give us wisdom, and if you ask for wisdom do you not know that you are going to get it?"

"Ah!" he said, "we don't know what wisdom is."

I said, "No, if we did, we would not need to ask; but whatever wisdom may be, don't you know that you will get it?"

Certainly it is our privilege to know. When we have a specific promise in the Word of God, if we doubt that it is God's will, or if we doubt that God will do the thing that we ask, we make God a liar.

Here is one of the greatest secrets of prevailing prayer: To study the Word to find what God's will is as revealed there in the promises, and then simply take these promises and spread them out before God in prayer with the absolutely unwavering expectation that He will do what He has promised in His Word.

(2) But there is still another way in which we may know the will of God, that is, by the teaching of His Holy Spirit. There are many things that we need from God which are not covered by any specific promise, but we are not left in ignorance of the will of God even then. In Rom. 8:26, 27 we are told, "And in like manner the Spirit also helpeth our infirmity: for we know not how to pray as we ought; but the Spirit Himself maketh intercession for us with groanings which cannot be uttered; and He that searcheth the hearts knoweth what is the mind of the spirit, because He maketh intercession for the saints *according to the will of God*." Here we are distinctly told that the Spirit of God prays in us, draws out our prayer, in the line of God's will. When we are thus led out by the Holy Spirit in any direction, to pray for any given object, we may do it in all confidence that it is God's will, and that we are to get the very thing we ask of Him, even though there is no specific promise to cover the case. Often God by His Spirit lays upon us a heavy burden of prayer for some given individual. We cannot rest, we pray for him with groanings which cannot be uttered. Perhaps the man is entirely beyond our reach, but God hears the prayer, and in many a case it is not long before we hear of his definite conversion.

The passage 1 John 5:14, 15 is one of the most abused passages in the Bible: "This is *the confidence* that we have in Him, that, if we ask anything according to His will, He heareth us; and if we know that He hear us, whatsoever we ask, we know that we have the petitions that we desired of Him." The Holy Spirit beyond a doubt put it into the Bible to encourage our faith. It begins with "This is *the confidence* that we have in Him," and closes with "*We know* that we have the petitions that we desired of Him;" but one of the most frequent usages of this passage, which was so manifestly given to beget confidence, is to introduce an element of uncertainty into our prayers. Oftentimes when one waxes confident in prayer, some cautious brother will come and say:

"Now, don't be too confident. If it is God's will He will do it. You should put in, 'If it be Thy will.'"

Doubtless there are many times when we do not know the will of God, and in all prayer submission to the excellent will of God should underlie it; but when we know God's will, there need be no "ifs"; and this passage was not put into the Bible in order that we might introduce "ifs" into all our prayers, but in order that we might throw our "ifs" to the wind, and have "*confidence*" and "*know* that we have the petitions which we have asked of Him."

Chapter V: Praying in the Spirit

1. Over and over again in what has already been said, we have seen our dependence upon the Holy Spirit in prayer. This comes out very definitely in Eph. 6:18, "Praying always with all prayer and supplication *in the Spirit*," and in Jude 20, "Praying *in the Holy Ghost*." Indeed the whole secret of prayer is found in these three words, "in the Spirit." It is the prayer that God the Holy Spirit inspires that God the Father answers.

The disciples did not know how to pray as they ought, so they came to Jesus and said, "Lord teach us to pray." We know not how to pray as we ought, but we have another Teacher and Guide right at hand to help us (John 14:16, 17), "The Spirit helpeth our infirmity" (Rom. 8:26). He teaches us how to pray. True prayer is prayer in the Spirit; that is, the prayer the Spirit inspires and directs. When we come into God's presence we should recognize "our infirmity," our ignorance of what we should pray for or how we should pray for it, and in the consciousness of our utter inability to pray aright we should look up to the Holy Spirit, casting ourselves utterly upon Him to direct our prayers, to lead out our desires and to guide our utterance of them.

Nothing can be more foolish in prayer than to rush heedlessly into God's presence, and ask the first thing that comes into our mind, or that some thoughtless friend has asked us to pray for. When we first come into God's presence we should be silent before Him. We should look up to Him to send His Holy Spirit to teach us how to pray. We must wait for the Holy Spirit, and surrender ourselves to the Spirit, then we shall pray aright.

Oftentimes when we come to God in prayer, we do not feel like praying. What shall one do in such a case? Cease praying until he does feel like it? Not at all. When we feel least like praying is the time when we most need to pray. We should wait quietly before God and tell Him how cold and prayerless our hearts are, and look up to Him and trust Him and expect Him to send the Holy Spirit to warm our hearts and draw them out in prayer. It will not be long before the glow of the Spirit's presence will fill our hearts, and we will begin to pray with freedom, directness, earnestness and power. Many of the most blessed seasons of prayer I have ever known have begun with a feeling of utter deadness and prayerlessness, but in my helplessness and coldness I have cast myself upon God, and looked to Him to send His Holy Spirit to teach me to pray, and He has done it.

When we pray in the Spirit, we will pray for the right things and in the right way. There will be joy and power in our prayer.

2. If we are to pray with power we must pray *with faith*. In Mark 11:24 Jesus says, "Therefore I say unto you, What things soever ye desire, when ye pray, believe that ye receive them, and ye shall have them." No matter how positive any promise of God's Word may be, we will not enjoy it in actual experience unless we confidently expect its fulfillment in answer to our prayer. "If any of you lack wisdom," says James, "let him ask of God that giveth to all men liberally, and upbraideth not; and it shall be given him." Now that promise is as positive as a promise can be, but the next verse adds,

"But let him ask in faith, nothing doubting: for he that doubteth is like the surge of the sea driven by the wind and tossed. For let not that man think that he shall receive anything of the Lord." There must then be confident unwavering expectation. But there is a faith that goes beyond expectation, that believes that the prayer is heard and the promise granted. This comes out in the Revised Version of Mark 11:24, "Therefore I say unto you, All things whatsoever ye pray and ask for, believe that ye *have* received them, and ye shall have them."

But how can one get this faith?

Let us say with all emphasis, it cannot be pumped up. Many a one reads this promise about the prayer of faith, and then asks for things that he desires and tries to make himself believe that God has heard the prayer. This ends only in disappointment, for it is not real faith and the thing is not granted. It is at this point that many people make a collapse of faith altogether by trying to work up faith by an effort of their will, and as the thing they made themselves believe they expected to get is not given, the very foundation of faith is oftentimes undermined.

But how does real faith come?

Rom 10:17 answers the question: "So then faith cometh by hearing, and hearing *by the Word of God*." If we are to have real faith, we must study the Word of God and find out what is promised, then simply believe the promises of God. Faith must have a warrant. Trying to believe something that you want to believe is not faith. Believing what God says in His Word is faith. If I am to have faith when I pray, I must find some promise in the Word of God on which to rest my faith. Faith furthermore comes through the Spirit. The Spirit knows the will of God, and if I pray in the Spirit, and look to the Spirit to teach me God's will, He will lead me out in prayer along the line of that will, and give me faith that the prayer is to be answered; but in no case does real faith come by simply determining that you are going to get the thing that you want to get.

If there is no promise in the Word of God, and no clear leading of the Spirit, there can be no real faith, and there should be no upbraiding of self for lack of faith in such a case. But if the thing desired is promised in the Word of God, we may well upbraid ourselves for lack of faith if we doubt; for we are making God a liar by doubting His Word.

Chapter VI: Always Praying and Not Fainting

In two parables in the Gospel of Luke, Jesus teaches with great emphasis the lesson that men ought always to pray and not to faint. The first parable is found in Luke 11:5-8, and the other in Luke 18:1-8.

"And He said unto them, Which of you shall have a friend, and shall go unto him at midnight, and say unto him: 'Friend, lend me three loaves; for a friend of mine in his journey is come to me, and I have nothing to set before him?' And he from within shall answer and say: 'Trouble me not: the door is now shut, and my children are with me in bed. I cannot rise and give thee.' I say unto you, Though he will not rise and give him because he is his friend, yet because of his importunity he will rise and give him as many as he needeth." (Luke 11:5-8)

"And He spake a parable unto them to this end, that men always ought to pray and not to faint, saying: There was in a city a judge which feared not God, neither regarded man; and there was a widow in that city; and she came to him, saying:

"'Avenge me of mine adversary.'

"And he would not for a while; but afterward he said within himself: 'Though I fear not God, nor regard man, yet because this widow troubleth me I will avenge her, lest by her continual coming she weary me.'

"And the Lord said, Hear what the unjust judge saith. And shall not God avenge his own elect, which cry day and night unto Him, though He bear long with them? I tell you that He will avenge them speedily. Nevertheless when the Son of man cometh, shall He find faith on the earth?" (Luke 18:1-8)

In the former of these two parables Jesus sets forth the necessity of importunity in prayer in a startling way. The word rendered "importunity" means literally "shamelessness," as if Jesus would have us understand that God would have us draw nigh to Him with a determination to obtain the things we seek that will not be put to shame by any seeming refusal or delay on God's part. God delights in the holy boldness that will not take "no" for an answer. It is an expression of great faith, and nothing pleases God more than faith.

Jesus seemed to put the Syro-Phoenician woman away almost with rudeness, but she would not be put away, and Jesus looked upon her shameless importunity with pleasure, and said, "O woman, great is thy faith; be it unto thee even as thou wilt." (Matt. 15:28) God does not always let us get things at our first effort. He would train us and make us strong men by compelling us to work hard for the best things. So also He does not always give us what we ask in answer to the first prayer; He would train us and make us strong men of prayer by compelling us to pray hard for the best things. He makes us *pray through.*

I am glad that this is so. There is no more blessed training in prayer than that that comes through being compelled to ask again and again and again even through a long period of years before one obtains that which he seeks from God. Many people call it submission to the will of God when God does not grant them their requests at the first or second asking, and they say:

"Well, perhaps it is not God's will."

As a rule this is not submission, but spiritual laziness. We do not call it submission to the will of God when we give up after one or two efforts to obtain things by action; we call it lack of strength of character. When the strong man of action starts out to accomplish a thing, if he does not accomplish it the first, or second or one hundredth time, he keeps hammering away until he does accomplish it; and the strong man of prayer when he starts to pray for a thing keeps on praying until he prays it through, and obtains what he seeks. We should be careful about what we ask from God, but when we do begin to pray for a thing we should never give up praying for it until we get it, or until God makes it very clear and very definite to us that it is not His will to give it.

Some would have us believe that it shows unbelief to pray twice for the same thing, that we ought to "take it" the first time that we ask. Doubtless there are times when we are able through faith in the Word or the leading of the Holy Spirit to *claim* the first time that which we have asked of God; but beyond question there are other times when we must pray again and again and again for the same thing before we get our answer. Those who have gotten beyond praying twice for the same thing have gotten beyond their Master, (Matt. 26:44). George Muller prayed for two men daily for upwards of sixty years. One of these men was converted shortly before his death, I think at the last service that George Muller held, the other was converted within a year after his death. One of the great needs of the present day is men and women who will not only start out to pray for things, but pray on and on and on until they obtain that which they seek from the Lord.

Chapter VII: Abiding in Christ

"If ye abide in Me, and My words abide in you, ye shall ask what ye will, and it shall be done unto you." (John 15:7) The whole secret of prayer is found in these words of our Lord. Here is prayer that has unbounded power: "Ask *what ye will*, and it shall be done unto you."

There is a way then of asking and getting precisely what we ask and getting all we ask. Christ gives two conditions of this all-prevailing prayer:

1. The first condition is, "If ye abide in Me."

What is it to abide in Christ?

Some explanations that have been given of this are so mystical or so profound that to many simple-minded children of God they mean practically nothing at all; but what Jesus meant was really very simple.

He had been comparing Himself to a vine, His disciples to the branches in the vine. Some branches continued in the vine, that is, remained in living union with the vine, so that the sap or life of the vine constantly flowed into these branches. They had no independent life of their own. Everything in them was simply the outcome of the life of the vine flowing into them. Their buds, their leaves, their blossoms, their fruit, were really not theirs, but the buds, leaves, blossoms and fruit of the vine. Other branches were completely severed from the vine, or else the flow of the sap or life of the vine into them was in some way hindered. Now for us to abide in Christ is for us to bear the same relation to Him that the first sort of branches bear to the vine; that is to say, to abide in Christ is to renounce any independent life of our own, to give up trying to think our thoughts, or form our resolutions, or cultivate our feelings, and simply and constantly look to Christ to think His thoughts in us, to form His purposes in us, to feel His emotions and affections in us. It is to renounce all life independent of Christ, and constantly to look to Him for the inflow of His life into us, and the outworking of His life through us. When we do this, and in so far as we do this, our prayers will obtain that which we seek from God.

This must necessarily be so, for our desires will not be our own desires, but Christ's, and our prayers will not in reality be our own prayers, but Christ praying in us. Such prayers will always be in harmony with God's will, and the Father heareth Him always. When our prayers fail it is because they are indeed our prayers. We have conceived the desire and framed the petition of ourselves, instead of looking to Christ to pray through us.

To say that one should be abiding in Christ in all his prayers, looking to Christ to pray through Him rather than praying himself, is simply saying in another way that one should pray "in the Spirit." When we thus abide in Christ, our thoughts are not our own thoughts, but His, our joys are not our own joys, but His, our fruit is not our own fruit, but His; just as the buds, leaves, blossoms and fruit of the branch that abides in the vine are not the buds, leaves, blossoms and fruit of the branch, but of the vine itself whose life is flowing into the branch and manifests itself in these buds, leaves, blossoms and fruit.

To abide in Christ, one must of course already be in Christ through the acceptance of Christ as an atoning Savior from the guilt of sin, a risen Savior from the power of sin, and a Lord and Master over all his life. Being in Christ, all that we have to do to abide (or continue) in Christ is simply to renounce our self-life—utterly renouncing every thought, every purpose, every desire, every affection of our own, and just looking day by day and hour by hour for Jesus Christ to form His thoughts, His purposes, His affections, His desires in us. Abiding in Christ is really a very simple matter, though it is a wonderful life of privilege and of power.

2. But there is another condition stated in this verse, though it is really involved in the first: "And My words abide in you."

If we are to obtain from God all that we ask from Him, Christ's words must abide or continue in us. We must study His words, fairly devour His words, let them sink into our thought and into our heart, keep them in our memory, obey them constantly in our life, let them shape and mold our daily life and our every act.

This is really the method of abiding in Christ. It is through His words that Jesus imparts Himself to us. The words He speaks unto us, they are spirit and they are life. (John 6:33) It is vain to expect power in prayer unless we meditate much upon the words of Christ, and let them sink deep and find a permanent abode in our hearts. There are many who wonder why they are so powerless in prayer, but the very simple explanation of it all is found in their neglect of the words of Christ. They have not hidden His words in their hearts; His words do not abide in them. It is not by seasons of mystical meditation and rapturous experiences that we learn to abide in Christ; it is by feeding upon His word, His written word as found in the Bible, and looking to the Holy Spirit to implant these words in our hearts and to make them a living thing in our hearts. If we thus let the words of Christ abide in us, they will stir us up in prayer. They will be the mold in which our prayers are shaped, and our prayers will be necessarily along the line of God's will, and will prevail with Him. Prevailing prayer is almost an impossibility where there is neglect of the study of the Word of God.

Mere intellectual study of the Word of God is not enough; there must be meditation upon it. The Word of God must be revolved over and over and over in the mind, with a constant looking to God by His Spirit to make that Word a living thing in the heart. The prayer that is born of meditation upon the Word of God is the prayer that soars upward most easily to God's listening ear.

George Muller, one of the mightiest men of prayer of the present generation, when the hour for prayer came would begin by reading and meditating upon God's Word until out of the study of the Word a prayer began to form itself in his heart. Thus God Himself was a real author of the prayer, and God answered the prayers which He Himself had inspired.

The Word of God is the instrument through which the Holy Spirit works, it is the sword of the Spirit in more senses than one; and the one who would know the work of the Holy Spirit in any direction must feed upon the Word. The one who would pray in the Spirit must meditate much upon the Word, that the Holy Spirit may have something through which He can work. The Holy Spirit works His prayers in us through the Word, and neglect of the Word makes praying in the Holy Spirit an impossibility. If we would feed the fire of our prayers with the fuel of God's Word, all our difficulties in prayer would disappear.

Chapter VIII: Praying with Thanksgiving

There are two words often overlooked in the lesson about prayer which Paul gives us in Phil. 4:6, 7, "In nothing be anxious; but in everything by prayer and supplication with thanksgiving let your requests be made known unto God. And the peace of God, which passeth all understanding, shall guard your hearts and your thoughts in Christ Jesus." The two important words often overlooked are, "*with thanksgiving.*"

In approaching God to ask for new blessings, we should never forget to return thanks for blessings already granted. If any one of us would stop and think how many of the prayers which we have offered to God have been answered, and how seldom we have gone back to God to return thanks for the answers thus given, I am sure we would be overwhelmed with confusion. We should be just as definite in returning thanks as we are in prayer. We come to God with most specific petitions, but when we return thanks to Him, our thanksgiving is indefinite and general.

Doubtless one reason why so many of our prayers lack power is because we have neglected to return thanks for blessings already received. If any one were to constantly come to us asking help from us, and should never say "Thank you" for the help thus given, we would soon tire of helping one so ungrateful. Indeed, regard for the one we were helping would hold us back from encouraging such rank ingratitude. Doubtless our heavenly Father out of a wise regard for our highest welfare oftentimes refuses to answer petitions that we send up to Him in order that we may be brought to a sense of our ingratitude and taught to be thankful.

God is deeply grieved by the thanklessness and ingratitude of which so many of us are guilty. When Jesus healed the ten lepers and only one came back to give Him thanks, in wonderment and pain He exclaimed,

"Were not the ten cleansed? But where are the nine?" (Luke 17:17)

How often must He look down upon us in sadness at our forgetfulness of His repeated blessings, and His frequent answer to our prayers.

Returning thanks for blessings already received increases our faith and enables us to approach God with new boldness and new assurance. Doubtless the reason so many have so little faith when they pray, is because they take so little time to meditate upon and thank God for blessings already received. As one meditates upon the answers to prayers already granted, faith waxes bolder and bolder, and we come to feel in the very depths of our souls that there is nothing too hard for the Lord. As we reflect upon the wondrous goodness of God toward us on the one hand, and upon the other hand upon the little thought and strength and time that we ever put into thanksgiving, we may well humble ourselves before God and confess our sin.

The mighty men of prayer in the Bible, and the mighty men of prayer throughout the ages of the church's history have been men who were much given to thanksgiving and praise. David was a mighty man of prayer, and how his Psalms abound with thanksgiving and praise. The apostles were mighty men of prayer; of them we read that "they were continually in the temple, praising and blessing God." Paul was a mighty man of prayer, and how often in his epistles he bursts out in definite thanksgiving to God for definite blessings and definite answers to prayers. Jesus is our model in prayer as in everything else. We find in the study of His life that His manner of returning thanks at the simplest meal was so noticeable that two of His disciples recognized Him by this after His resurrection.

Thanksgiving is one of the inevitable results of being filled with the Holy Spirit and one who does not learn "in everything to give thanks" cannot continue to pray in the Spirit. If we would learn to pray with power we would do well to let these two words sink deep into our hearts: "WITH THANKSGIVING."

Chapter IX: Hindrances to Prayer

We have gone very carefully into the positive conditions of prevailing prayer; but there are some things which hinder prayer. These God has made very plain in His Word.

1. The first hindrance to prayer we will find in James 4:3, "Ye ask and receive not *because ye ask amiss, that ye may spend it in your pleasures.*"

A selfish purpose in prayer robs prayer of power. Very many prayers are selfish. These may be prayers for things for which it is perfectly proper to ask, for things which it is the will of God to give, but the motive of the prayer is entirely wrong, and so the prayer falls powerless to the ground. The true purpose in prayer is that God may be glorified in the answer. If we ask any petition merely that we may receive something to use in our pleasures or in our own gratification in one way or another, we "ask amiss" and need not expect to receive what we ask. This explains why many prayers remain unanswered.

For example, many a woman is praying for the conversion of her husband. That certainly is a most proper thing to ask; but many a woman's motive in asking for the conversion of her husband is entirely improper, it is selfish. She desires that her husband may be converted because it would be so much more pleasant for her to have a husband who sympathized with her; or it is so painful to think that her husband might die and be lost forever. For some such selfish reason as this she desires to have her husband converted. The prayer is purely selfish. Why should a woman desire the conversion of her husband? First of all and above all, that God may be glorified; because she cannot bear the thought that God the Father should be dishonored by her husband trampling underfoot the Son of God.

Many pray for a revival. That certainly is a prayer that is pleasing to God, it is along the line of His will; but many prayers for revivals are purely selfish. The churches desire revivals in order that the membership may be increased, in order that the church may have a position of more power and influence in the community, in order that the church treasury may be filled, in order that a good report may be made at the presbytery or conference or association. For such low purposes as these, churches and ministers oftentimes are praying for a revival, and oftentimes too God does not answer the prayer. Why should we pray for a revival? For the glory of God, because we cannot endure it that God should continue to be dishonored by the worldliness of the church, by the sins of unbelievers, by the proud unbelief of the day; because God's Word is being made void; in order that God may be glorified by the outpouring of His Spirit on the Church of Christ. For these reasons first of all and above all, we should pray for a revival.

Many a prayer for the Holy Spirit is a purely selfish prayer.

It certainly is God's will to give the Holy Spirit to them that ask Him—He has told us so plainly in His Word (Luke 11:13), but many a prayer for the Holy Spirit is hindered by the selfishness of the motive that lies back of the prayer. Men and women pray for the Holy Spirit in order that they may be happy, or in order that they may be saved from the wretchedness of defeat in their lives, or in order that they may have power as Christian workers, or for some other purely selfish motive. Why should we pray for the Spirit? In order that God may no longer be dishonored by the low level of our Christian lives and by our ineffectiveness in service, in order that God may be glorified in the new beauty that comes into our lives and the new power that comes into our service.

2. The second hindrance to prayer we find in Is. 59:1, 2: "Behold, the Lord's hand is not shortened, that it cannot save; neither His ear heavy, that it cannot hear. But *your iniquities have separated between you and your God, and your sins have hid His face from you, that He will not hear.*"

Sin hinders prayer. Many a man prays and prays and prays, and gets absolutely no answer to his prayer. Perhaps he is tempted to think that it is not the will of God to answer, or he may think that the days when God answered prayer, if He ever did, are over. So the Israelites seem to have thought. They thought that the Lord's hand was shortened, that it could not save, and that His ear had become heavy that it could no longer hear.

"Not so," said Isaiah, "God's ear is just as open to hear as ever, His hand just as mighty to save; but there is a hindrance. That hindrance is your own sins. Your iniquities have separated between you and your God, and your sins have hid His face from you that He will not hear."

It is so to-day. Many and many a man is crying to God in vain, simply because of sin in his life. It may be some sin in the past that has been unconfessed and unjudged, it may be some sin in the present that is cherished, very likely is not even looked upon as sin, but there the sin is, hidden away somewhere in the heart or in the life, and God "will not hear."

Any one who finds his prayers ineffective should not conclude that the thing which he asks of God is not according to His will, but should go alone with God with the Psalmist's prayer, "Search me, O God, and know my heart: try me, and know my thoughts: and see if there be any wicked way in me" (Ps. 139:23, 24), and wait before Him until He puts His finger upon the thing that is displeasing in His sight. Then this sin should be confessed and put away.

I well remember a time in my life when I was praying for two definite things that it seemed that I must have, or God would be dishonored; but the answer did not come. I awoke in the middle of the night in great physical suffering and great distress of soul. I cried to God for these things, reasoned with Him as to how necessary it was that I get them, and get them at once; but no answer came. I asked God to show me if there was anything wrong in my own life. Something came to my mind that had often come to it before, something definite but which I was unwilling to confess as sin. I said to God,

"If this is wrong I will give it up"; but still no answer came. In my innermost heart, though I had never admitted it, I knew it was wrong.

At last I said:

"This is wrong. I have sinned. I will give it up."

I found peace. In a few moments I was sleeping like a child. In the morning I woke well in body, and the money that was so much needed for the honor of God's name came.

Sin is an awful thing, and one of the most awful things about it is the way it hinders prayer, the way it severs the connection between us and the source of all grace and power and blessing. Any one who would have power in prayer must be merciless in dealing with his own sins. "If I regard iniquity in my heart, the Lord will not hear me." (Ps. 66:18) So long as we hold on to sin or have any controversy with God, we cannot expect Him to heed our prayers. If there is anything that is constantly coming up in your moments of close communion with God, that is the thing that hinders prayer: put it away.

3. The third hindrance to prayer is found in Ez. 14:3, "Son of man, these men have taken their idols into their heart, and put the stumbling block of their iniquity before their face: should I be inquired of at all by them?" *Idols in the heart cause God to refuse to listen to our prayers.*

What is an idol? An idol is anything that takes the place of God, anything that is the supreme object of our affection. God alone has the right to the supreme place in our hearts. Everything and everyone else must be subordinate to Him.

Many a man makes an idol of his wife. Not that a man can love his wife any too much, but he can put her in the wrong place, he can put her before God; and when a man regards his wife's pleasure before God's pleasure, when he gives her the first place and God the second place, his wife is an idol, and God cannot hear his prayers.

Many a woman makes an idol of her children. Not that we can love our children too much. The more dearly we love Christ, the more dearly we love our children; but we can put our children in the wrong place, we can put them before God, and their interests before God's interests. When we do this our children are our idols.

Many a man makes an idol of his reputation or his business. Reputation or business is put before God. God cannot hear the prayers of such a man.

One great question for us to decide, if we would have power in prayer is, Is God absolutely first? Is He before wife, before children, before reputation, before business, before our own lives? If not, prevailing prayer is impossible.

God often calls our attention to the fact that we have an idol, by not answering our prayers, and thus leading us to inquire as to why our prayers are not answered, and so we discover the idol, put it away, and God hears our prayers.

4. The fourth hindrance to prayer is found in Prov. 21:13, "*Whoso stoppeth his ears at the cry of the poor,* he also shall cry himself, but shall not be heard.*"

There is perhaps no greater hindrance to prayer than stinginess, the lack of liberality toward the poor and toward God's work. It is the one who gives generously to others who receives generously from God. "Give, and it shall be given unto you; good measure, pressed down, shaken together, running over, shall they give into your bosom. For with what measure ye mete it shall be measured to you again." (Luke 6:38) The generous man is the mighty man of prayer. The stingy man is the powerless man of prayer.

One of the most wonderful statements about prevailing prayer (already referred to) 1 John 3:22, "Whatsoever we ask we receive of Him, because we keep His commandments, and do those things that are pleasing in His sight," is made in direct connection with generosity toward the needy. In the context we are told that it is when we love, not in word or in tongue, but in deed and in truth, when we open our hearts toward the brother in need, it is then and only then we have confidence toward God in prayer.

Many a man and woman who is seeking to find the secret of their powerlessness in prayer need not seek far; it is nothing more nor less than downright stinginess. George Muller, to whom reference has already been made, was a mighty man of prayer because he was a mighty giver. What he received from God never stuck to his fingers; he immediately passed it on to others. He was constantly receiving because he was constantly giving. When one thinks of the selfishness of the professing church to-day, how the orthodox churches of this land do not average $1.00 per year per member for foreign missions, it is no wonder that the church has so little power in prayer. If we would get from God, we must give to others. Perhaps the most wonderful promise in the Bible in regard to God's supplying our need is Phil. 4:19, "And my God shall fulfill every need of yours according to His riches in glory in Christ Jesus." This glorious promise was made to the Philippian church, and made in immediate connection with their generosity.

5. The fifth hindrance to prayer is found in Mark 11:25, "And when ye stand praying, *forgive*, if ye have ought against any; that your Father also which is in heaven may forgive you your trespasses."

An unforgiving spirit is one of the commonest hindrances to prayer. Prayer is answered on the basis that our sins are forgiven; and God cannot deal with us on the basis of forgiveness while we are harboring ill-will against those who have wronged us. Any one who is nursing a grudge against another has fast closed the ear of God against his own petition. How many there are crying to God for the conversion of husband, children, friends, and wondering why it is that their prayer is not answered, when the whole secret is some grudge that they have in their hearts against some one who has injured them, or who they fancy has injured them. Many and many a mother and father are allowing their children to go down to eternity unsaved, for the miserable gratification of hating somebody.

6. The sixth hindrance to prayer is found in 1 Peter 3:7, "Ye husbands, in like manner, dwell with your wives according to knowledge, giving honor unto the woman, as unto the weaker vessel as being also joint-heirs of the grace of life; to the end that your prayers be not hindered." Here we are plainly told that *a wrong relation between husband and wife is a hindrance to prayer*.

In many and many a case the prayers of husbands are hindered because of their failure of duty toward their wives. On the other hand, it is also doubtless true that the prayers of wives are hindered because of their failure in duty toward their husbands. If husbands and wives should seek diligently to find the cause of their unanswered prayers, they would often find it in their relations to one another.

Many a man who makes great pretentions to piety, and is very active in Christian work, shows but little consideration in his treatment of his wife, and is oftentimes unkind, if not brutal; then he wonders why it is that his prayers are not answered. The verse that we have just quoted explains the seeming mystery. On the other hand, many a woman who is very devoted to the church, and very faithful in attendance upon all services, treats her husband with the most unpardonable neglect, is cross and peevish toward him, wounds him by the sharpness of her speech, and by her ungovernable temper; then wonders why it is that she has no power in prayer.

There are other things in the relations of husbands and wives which cannot be spoken of publicly, but which doubtless are oftentimes a hindrance in approaching God in prayer. There is much of sin covered up under the holy name of marriage that is a cause of spiritual deadness, and of powerlessness in prayer. Any man or woman whose prayers seem to bring no answer should spread their whole married life out before God, and ask Him to put His finger upon anything in it that is displeasing in His sight.

7. The seventh hindrance to prayer is found in James 1:5-7, "But if any of you lacketh wisdom, let him ask of God, who giveth to all liberally and upbraideth not; and it shall be given him. But let him ask *in faith, nothing doubting*: for he that doubteth is

like the surge of the sea driven by the wind and tossed. For let not that man think that he shall receive anything of the Lord."

Prayers are hindered by unbelief. God demands that we shall believe His Word absolutely. To question it is to make Him a liar. Many of us do that when we plead His promises, and is it any wonder that our prayers are not answered? How many prayers are hindered by our wretched unbelief! We go to God and ask Him for something that is positively promised in His Word, and then we do not more than half expect to get it. "Let not that man think that he shall receive anything of the Lord."

Chapter X: When to Pray

If we would know the fulness of blessing that there is in the prayer life, it is important not only that we pray in the right way, but also that we pray at the right time. Christ's own example is full of suggestiveness as to the right time for prayer.

1. In the 1st chapter of Mark, the 35th verse, we read, "And *in the morning*, rising up *a great while before day,* He went out, and departed into a solitary place, and there prayed."

Jesus chose the early morning hour for prayer. Many of the mightiest men of God have followed the Lord's example in this. In the morning hour the mind is fresh and at its very best. It is free from distraction, and that absolute concentration upon God which is essential to the most effective prayer is most easily possible in the early morning hours. Furthermore, when the early hours are spent in prayer, the whole day is sanctified, and power is obtained for overcoming its temptations, and for performing its duties. More can be accomplished in prayer in the first hours of the day than at any other time during the day. Every child of God who would make the most out of his life for Christ, should set apart the first part of the day to meeting God in the study of His Word and in prayer. The first thing we do each day should be to go alone with God and face the duties, the temptations, and the service of that day, and get strength from God for all. We should get victory before the hour of trial, temptation or service comes. The secret place of prayer is the place to fight our battles and gain our victories.

2. In the 6th chapter of Luke in the 12th verse, we get further light upon the right time to pray. We read, "And it came to pass in those days, that He went out into a mountain to pray, and continued *all night* in prayer to God."

Here we see Jesus praying in the night, spending the entire night in prayer. Of course we have no reason to suppose that this was the constant practice of our Lord, nor do we even know how common this practice was, but there were certainly times when the whole night was given up to prayer. Here too we do well to follow in the footsteps of the Master.

Of course there is a way of setting apart nights for prayer in which there is no profit; it is pure legalism. But the abuse of this practice is no reason for neglecting it altogether. One ought not to say, "I am going to spend a whole night in prayer," with the thought that there is any merit that will win God's favor in such an exercise; that is legalism. But we oftentimes do well to say, "I am going to set apart this night for meeting God, and obtaining His blessing and power; and if necessary, and if He so leads me, I will give the whole night to prayer." Oftentimes we will have prayed things through long before the night has passed, and we can retire and find more refreshing and invigorating sleep than if we had not spent the time in prayer. At other times God doubtless will keep us in communion with Himself away into the morning, and when He does this in His infinite grace, blessed indeed are these hours of night prayer!

Nights of prayer to God are followed by days of power with men. In the night hours the world is hushed in slumber, and we can easily be alone with God and have undisturbed communion with Him. If we set apart the whole night for prayer, there will be no hurry, there will be time for our own hearts to become quiet before God, there will be time for the whole mind to be brought under the guidance of the Holy Spirit, there will be plenty of time to pray things through. A night of prayer should be put entirely under God's control. We should lay down no rules as to how long we will pray, or as to what we shall pray about, but be ready to wait upon God for a short time or a long time as He may lead, and to be led out in one direction or another as He may see fit.

3. Jesus Christ prayed *before all the great crises in his earthly life.*

He prayed before choosing the twelve disciples; before the sermon on the mount; before starting out on an evangelistic tour; before His anointing with the Holy Spirit and His entrance upon His public ministry; before announcing to the twelve His approaching death; before the great consummation of His life at the cross. (Luke 6:12, 13; Luke 9:18, 21, 22; Luke 3:21, 22; Mark 1:35-38; Luke 22:39-46.) He prepared for every important crisis by a protracted season of prayer. So ought we to do also. Whenever any crisis of life is seen to be approaching, we should prepare for it by a season of very definite prayer to God. We should take plenty of time for this prayer.

4. Christ prayed not only before the great events and victories of His life, but He also prayed *after its great achievements and important crises.*

When He had fed the five thousand with the five loaves and two fishes, and the multitude desired to take Him and make Him king, having sent them away He went up into the mountain apart to pray, and spent hours there alone in prayer to God (Matt. 14:23; Jn. 6:15). So He went on from victory to victory.

It is more common for most of us to pray before the great events of life than it is to pray after them, but the latter is as important as the former. If we would pray after the great achievements of life, we might go on to still greater; as it is we are often either puffed up or exhausted by the things that we do in the name of the Lord, and so we advance no further. Many and many a man in answer to prayer has been endued with power and thus has wrought great things in the name of the Lord, and when these great things were accomplished, instead of going alone with God and humbling himself before Him, and giving Him all the glory for what was achieved, he has congratulated himself upon what has been accomplished, has become puffed up, and God has been obliged to lay him aside. The great things done were not followed by humiliation of self, and prayer to God, and so pride has come in and the mighty man has been shorn of his power.

5. Jesus Christ gave a special time to prayer *when life was unusually busy.* He would withdraw at such a time from the multitudes that thronged about Him, and go into the wilderness and pray. For example, we read in Luke 5:15, 16, "But so much the more went abroad the report concerning Him: and great multitudes came together to hear, and to be healed of their infirmities. But He withdrew Himself in the deserts and prayed."

Some men are so busy that they find no time for prayer. Apparently the busier Christ's life was, the more He prayed. Sometimes He had no time to eat (Mark 3:20), sometimes He had no time for needed rest and sleep (Mark 6:31, 33, 46), but He always took time to pray; and the more the work crowded the more He prayed.

Many a mighty man of God has learned this secret from Christ, and when the work has crowded more than usual they have set an unusual amount of time apart for prayer. Other men of God, once mighty, have lost their power because they did not learn this secret, and allowed increasing work to crowd out prayer.

Years ago it was the writer's privilege, with other theological students, to ask questions of one of the most useful Christian men of the day. The writer was led to ask,

"Will you tell us something of your prayer life?"

The man was silent a moment, and then, turning his eyes earnestly upon me, replied:

"Well, I must admit that I have been so crowded with work of late that I have not given the time I should to prayer."

Is it any wonder that that man lost power, and the great work that he was doing was curtailed in a very marked degree? Let us never forget that the more the work presses on us, the more time must we spend in prayer.

6. Jesus Christ prayed *before the great temptations of His life.*

As He drew nearer and nearer to the cross, and realized that upon it was to come the great final test of His life, Jesus went out into the garden to pray. He came "unto a place called Gethsemane, and saith unto the disciples, Sit ye here while I go and pray yonder." (Matt. 26:36) The victory of Calvary was won that night in the garden of Gethsemane. The calm majesty of His bearing in meeting the awful onslaughts of Pilate's Judgment Hall and of Calvary, was the outcome of the struggle, agony and victory of Gethsemane. While Jesus prayed the disciples slept, so He stood fast while they fell ignominiously.

Many temptations come upon us unawares and unannounced, and all that we can do is to lift a cry to God for help then and there; but many of the temptations of life we can see approaching from the distance, and in such cases the victory should be won before the temptation really reaches us.

7. In 1 Thess. 5:17 we read, "Pray *without ceasing,*" and in Eph. 6:18, "praying *at all seasons.*"

Our whole life should be a life of prayer. We should walk in constant communion with God. There should be a constant upward looking of the soul to God. We should walk so habitually in His presence that even when we awake in the night it would be the most natural thing in the world for us to speak to Him in thanksgiving or in petition.

Chapter XI: The Need of a General Revival

If we are to pray aright in such a time as this, much of our prayer should be for a general revival. If there was ever a time in which there was need to cry unto God in the words of the Psalmist, "Wilt Thou not revive us again, that Thy people may rejoice in Thee?" (Ps. 85:6) it is this day in which we live. It is surely time for the Lord to work, for men have made void His law (Ps. 119:126). The voice of the Lord given in the written Word is set at naught both by the world and the church. Such a time is not a time for discouragement—the man who believes in God and believes in the Bible can never be discouraged; but it is a time for Jehovah Himself to step in and work. The intelligent Christian, the wide-awake watchman on the walls of Zion, may well cry with the

Psalmist of old, "It is time for Jehovah to work, for they have made void Thy law." (Ps. 119:126)

The great need of the day is a general revival.

Let us consider first of all what a general revival is.

A revival is a time of quickening or impartation of life. As God alone can give life, a revival is a time when God visits His people and by the power of His Spirit imparts new life to them, and through them imparts life to sinners dead in trespasses and sins. We have religious excitements gotten up by the cunning methods and hypnotic influence of the mere professional evangelist; but these are not revivals and are not needed. They are the devil's imitations of a revival. *New life from God*—that is a revival. A general revival is a time when this new life from God is not confined to scattered localities, but is general throughout Christendom and the earth.

The reason why a general revival is needed is that spiritual dearth and desolation and death is general. It is not confined to any one country, though it may be more manifest in some countries than in others. It is found in foreign mission fields as well as in home fields. We have had local revivals. The life-giving Spirit of God has breathed upon this minister and that, this church and that, this community and that; but we need, we sorely need, a revival that shall be widespread and general.

Let us look for a few moments at the results of a revival. These results are apparent in ministers, in the church and in the unsaved.

1. The results of a revival in a minister are:

(1) The minister has a new love for souls. We ministers as a rule have no such love for souls as we ought to have, no such love for souls as Jesus had, no such love for souls as Paul had. But when God visits His people the hearts of ministers are greatly burdened for the unsaved. They go out in great longing for the salvation of their fellow men. They forget their ambition to preach great sermons and for fame, and simply long to see men brought to Christ.

(2) When true revivals come ministers get a new love for God's Word and a new faith in God's Word. They fling to the winds their doubts and criticisms of the Bible and of the creeds, and go to preaching the Bible and especially Christ crucified. Revivals make ministers who are loose in their doctrines orthodox. A genuine wide-sweeping revival would do more to turn things upside down and thus get them right side up than all the heresy trials ever instituted.

(3) Revivals bring to ministers new liberty and power in preaching. It is no week-long grind to prepare a sermon, and no nerve-consuming effort to preach it after it has been prepared. Preaching is a joy and a refreshment, and there is power in it in times of revival.

2. The results of a revival on Christians generally are as marked as its results upon the ministry.

(1) In times of revival Christians come out from the world and live separated lives. Christians who have been dallying with the world, who have been playing cards and dancing and going to the theater and indulging in similar follies, give them up. These things are found to be incompatible with increasing life and light.

(2) In times of revival Christians get a new spirit of prayer. Prayer-meetings are no longer a duty, but become the necessity of a hungry, importunate heart. Private prayer is

followed with new zest. The voice of earnest prayer to God is heard day and night. People no longer ask, "Does God answer prayer?" They know He does, and besiege the throne of grace day and night.

(3) In times of revival Christians go to work for lost souls.

They do not go to meeting simply to enjoy themselves and get blessed. They go to meeting to watch for souls and to bring them to Christ. They talk to men on the street and in the stores and in their homes. The cross of Christ, salvation, heaven and hell become the subjects of constant conversation. Politics and the weather and new bonnets and the latest novels are forgotten.

(4) In times of revival Christians have new joy in Christ. Life is joy, and new life is new joy. Revival days are glad days, days of heaven on earth.

(5) In times of revival Christians get a new love for the Word of God. They want to study it day and night. Revivals are bad for saloons and theaters, but they are good for bookstores and Bible agencies.

3. But revivals also have a decided influence on the unsaved world.

(1) First of all, they bring deep conviction of sin. Jesus said that when the Spirit was come He would convince the world of sin (Jn. 16:7, 8). Now we have seen that a revival is a coming of the Holy Spirit, and therefore there must be a new conviction of sin, and there always is. If you see something men call a revival, and there is no conviction of sin, you may know at once that it is bogus. It is a sure mark.

(2) Revivals bring also conversion and regeneration. When God refreshes His people, He always converts sinners also. The first result of Pentecost was new life and power to the one hundred and twenty disciples in the upper room; the second result was three thousand conversions in a single day. It is always so. I am constantly reading of revivals here and there, where Christians were greatly helped but there were no conversions. I have my doubts about that kind. If Christians are truly refreshed, they will get after the unsaved by prayer and testimony and persuasion, and there will be conversions.

WHY A GENERAL REVIVAL IS NEEDED

We see what a general revival is, and what it does; let us now face the question why it is needed at the present time.

I think that the mere description of what it is and what it does shows that it is needed, sorely needed, but let us look at some specific conditions that exist to-day that show the need of it. In showing these conditions one is likely to be called a pessimist. If facing the facts is to be called a pessimist, I am willing to be called a pessimist. If in order to be an optimist one must shut his eyes and call black white, and error truth, and sin righteousness, and death life, I don't want to be called an optimist. But I am an optimist all the same. Pointing out the real condition will lead to a better condition.

1. Look first at the ministry.

(1) Many of us who are professedly orthodox ministers are practically infidels. That is plain speech, but it is also indisputable fact. There is no essential difference between the teachings of Tom Paine and Bob Ingersoll and the teachings of some of our theological professors. The latter are not so blunt and honest about it; they phrase it in more elegant and studied sentences; but it means the same. Much of the so-called new learning and higher criticism is simply Tom Paine infidelity sugar-coated. Prof. Howard

Osgood, who is a real scholar and not a mere echo of German infidelity, once read a statement of some positions, and asked if they did not fairly represent the scholarly criticism of to-day, and when it was agreed that they did, he startled his audience by saying:

"I am reading from Tom Paine's 'Age of Reason.'"

There is little new in the higher criticism. Our future ministers oftentimes are being educated under infidel professors, and being immature boys when they enter the college or seminary, they naturally come out infidels in many cases, and then go forth to poison the church.

(2) Even when our ministers are orthodox—as thank God so very many are!—they are oftentimes not men of prayer. How many modern ministers know what it is to wrestle in prayer, to spend a good share of a night in prayer? I do not know how many, but I do know that many do not.

(3) Many of us who are ministers have no love for souls. How many preach because they *must* preach, because they feel that men every where are perishing, and by preaching they hope to save some? And how many follow up their preaching as Paul did, by beseeching men everywhere to be reconciled to God?

Perhaps enough has been said about us ministers; but it is evident that a revival is needed for our sake or some of us will have to stand before God overwhelmed with confusion in an awful day of reckoning that is surely coming.

2. Look now at the church:

(1) Look at the doctrinal state of the church. It is bad enough. Many do not believe in the whole Bible. The book of Genesis is a myth, Jonah is an allegory, and even the miracles of the Son of God are questioned. The doctrine of prayer is old-fashioned, and the work of the Holy Spirit is sneered at. Conversion is unnecessary, and hell is no longer believed in. Then look at the fads and errors that have sprung up out of this loss of faith, Christian Science, Unitarianism, Spiritualism, Universalism, Babism, Metaphysical Healing, etc., etc., a perfect pandemonium of doctrines of devils.

(2) Look at the spiritual state of the church. Worldliness is rampant among church members. Many church members are just as eager as any in the rush to get rich. They use the methods of the world in the accumulation of wealth, and they hold just as fast to it as any when they have gotten it.

Prayerlessness abounds among church members on every hand. Some one has said that Christians on the average do not spend more than five minutes a day in prayer.

Neglect of the Word of God goes hand in hand with neglect of prayer to God. Very many Christians spend twice as much time every day wallowing through the mire of the daily papers as they do bathing in the cleansing laver of God's Holy Word. How many Christians average an hour a day spent in Bible study?

Along with neglect of prayer and neglect of the Word of God goes a lack of generosity. The churches are rapidly increasing in wealth, but the treasuries of the missionary societies are empty. Christians do not average a dollar a year for foreign missions. It is simply appalling.

Then there is the increasing disregard for the Lord's Day. It is fast becoming a day of worldly pleasure, instead of a day of holy service. The Sunday newspaper with its inane twaddle and filthy scandal takes the place of the Bible; and visiting and golf and bicycle, the place of the Sunday-school and church service.

Christians mingle with the world in all forms of questionable amusements. The young man and young woman who does not believe in dancing with its rank immodesties, the card table with its drift toward gambling, and the theater with its ever-increasing appeal to lewdness, is counted an old fogy.

Then how small a proportion of our membership has really entered into fellowship with Jesus Christ in His burden for souls! Enough has been said of the spiritual state of the church.

3. Now look at the state of the world.

(1) Note how few conversions there are. The Methodist church, which has led the way in aggressive work has actually lost more members than it has gained the last year. Here and there a church has a large number of accessions upon confession of faith, but these churches are rare exceptions; and where there are such accessions, in how few cases are the conversions deep, thorough and satisfactory.

(2) There is lack of conviction of sin. Seldom are men overwhelmed with a sense of their awful guilt in trampling under foot the Son of God. Sin is regarded as a "misfortune" or as "infirmity," or even as "good in the making"; seldom as enormous wrong against a holy God.

(3) Unbelief is rampant. Many regard it as a mark of intellectual superiority to reject the Bible, and even faith in God and immortality. It is about the only mark of intellectual superiority many possess, and perhaps that is the reason they cling to it so tenaciously.

(4) Hand in hand with this widespread infidelity goes gross immorality, as has always been the case. Infidelity and immorality are Siamese twins. They always exist and always grow and always fatten together. This prevailing immorality is found everywhere.

Look at the legalized adultery that we call divorce. Men marry one wife after another, and are still admitted into good society; and women do likewise. There are thousands of supposedly respectable men in America living with other men's wives, and thousands of supposedly respectable women living with other women's husbands.

This immorality is found in the theater. The theater at its best is bad enough, but now "Sapphos," and the "Degenerates," and all the unspeakable vile accessories of the stage rule the day, and the women who debauch themselves by appearing in such plays are defended in the newspapers and welcomed by supposedly respectable people.

Much of our literature is rotten, but decent people will read books as bad as "Trilby" because it is the rage. Art is oftentimes a mere covering for shameless indecency. Women are induced to cast modesty to the winds that the artist may perfect his art and defile his morals.

Greed for money has become a mania with rich and poor. The multi-millionaire will often sell his soul and trample the rights of his fellow men under foot in the mad hope of becoming a billionaire, and the laboring man will often commit murder to increase the power of the union and keep up wages. Wars are waged and men shot down like dogs to improve commerce, and to gain political prestige for unprincipled politicians who parade as statesmen.

The licentiousness of the day lifts its serpent head everywhere. You see it in the newspapers, you see it on the bill- boards, you see it on the advertisements of cigars, shoes, bicycles, patent medicines, corsets and everything else. You see it on the streets at night. You see it just outside the church door. You find it not only in the awful cesspools set apart for it in the great cities, but it is crowding further and further up our business streets and into the residence portions of our cities. Alas! now and then you find it, if you look sharp, in supposedly respectable homes; indeed it will be borne to your ears by the confessions of broken-hearted men and women. The moral condition of the world in our day is disgusting, sickening, appalling.

We need a revival, deep, widespread, general, in the power of the Holy Ghost. It is either a general revival or the dissolution of the church, of the home, of the state. A revival, new life from God, is the cure, and the only cure. That will stem the awful tide of immorality and unbelief. Mere argument will not do it; but a wind from heaven, a new outpouring of the Holy Ghost, a true God-sent revival will. Infidelity, higher criticism, Christian Science, Spiritualism, Universalism, all will go down before the outpouring of the Spirit of God. It was not discussion but the breath of God that relegated Tom Paine, Voltaire, Volney and other of the old infidels to the limbo of forgetfulness; and we need a new breath from God to send the Wellhausens and the Kuenens and the Grafs and the parrots they have trained to occupy chairs and pulpits in England and America to keep them company. I believe that breath from God is coming.

The great need of to-day is a general revival. The need is clear. It admits of no honest difference of opinion. What then shall we do? Pray. Take up the Psalmist's prayer, "Revive us again, that Thy people may rejoice in Thee." Take up Ezekiel's prayer, "Come from the four winds, O breath (breath of God), and breathe upon these slain that they may live." Hark, I hear a noise! Behold a shaking! I can almost feel the breeze upon my cheek. I can almost see the great living army rising to their feet. Shall we not pray and pray and pray and pray, till the Spirit comes, and God revives His people?

Chapter XII: The Place of Prayer Before and During Revivals

No treatment of the subject How to Pray would be at all complete if it did not consider the place of prayer in revivals.

The first great revival of Christian history had its origin on the human side in a ten-days' prayer-meeting. We read of that handful of disciples, "These all with one accord continued steadfastly in prayer." (Acts 1:14) The result of that prayer-meeting we read of in the 2nd chapter of the Acts of the Apostles,

"They were all filled with the Holy Ghost, and began to speak with other tongues, as the Spirit gave them utterance." (v.4) Further on in the chapter we read that "there were added unto them in that day about three thousand souls." (v.41) This revival proved genuine and permanent. The converts "continued steadfastly in the apostles' teaching and fellowship, in the breaking of bread and the prayers." (v.42) "And the Lord added to them day by day those that were being saved." (v.47)

Every true revival from that day to this has had its earthly origin in prayer. The great revival under Jonathan Edwards in the 18th century began with his famous call to prayer. The marvelous work of grace among the Indians under Brainerd had its origin in the days and nights that Brainerd spent before God in prayer for an enduement of power from on high for this work.

A most remarkable and widespread display of God's reviving power was that which broke out at Rochester, New York, in 1830, under the labors of Charles G. Finney. It not only spread throughout the State but ultimately to Great Britain as well. Mr. Finney himself attributed the power of this work to the spirit of prayer that prevailed. He describes it in his autobiography in the following words:

"When I was on my way to Rochester, as we passed through a village, some thirty miles east of Rochester, a brother minister whom I knew, seeing me on the canal-boat, jumped aboard to have a little conversation with me, intending to ride but a little way and return. He, however, became interested in conversation, and upon finding where I was going, he made up his mind to keep on and go with me to Rochester. We had been there but a few days when this minister became so convinced that he could not help weeping aloud at one time as we passed along the street. The Lord gave him a powerful spirit of prayer, and his heart was broken. As he and I prayed together, I was struck with his faith in regard to what the Lord was going to do there. I recollect he would say, 'Lord, I do not know how it is; but I seem to know that Thou art going to do a great work in this city.' The spirit of prayer was poured out powerfully, so much so that some persons stayed away from the public services to pray, being unable to restrain their feelings under preaching.

"And here I must introduce the name of a man, whom I shall have occasion to mention frequently, Mr. Abel Clary. He was the son of a very excellent man, and an elder of the church where I was converted. He was converted in the same revival in which I was. He had been licensed to preach; but his spirit of prayer was such, he was so burdened with the souls of men, that he was not able to preach much, his whole time and strength being given to prayer. The burden of his soul would frequently be so great that he was unable to stand, and he would writhe and groan in agony. I was well acquainted with him, and knew something of the wonderful spirit of prayer that was upon him. He was a very silent man, as almost all are who have that powerful spirit of prayer.

"The first I knew of his being in Rochester, a gentleman who lived about a mile west of the city, called on me one day and asked me if I knew a Mr. Abel Clary, a minister. I told him that I knew him well. 'Well,' he said, 'he is at my house, and has been there for some time, and I don't know what to think of him.' I said, 'I have not seen him at any of our meetings.' 'No,' he replied, 'he cannot go to meeting, he says. He prays nearly all the time, day and night, and in such agony of mind that I do not know what to make of it. Sometimes he cannot even stand on his knees, but will lie prostrate on the floor, and groan and pray in a manner that quite astonishes me.' I said to the brother, 'I understand it: please keep still. It will all come out right; he will surely prevail.'

"I knew at the time a considerable number of men who were exercised in the same way. A Deacon P—, of Camden, Oneida county; a Deacon T—, of Rodman, Jefferson county; a Deacon B—, of Adams, in the same county; this Mr. Clary and many others among the men, and a large number of women partook of the same spirit, and spent a great part of their time in prayer. Father Nash, as we called him, who in several of my fields of labor came to me and aided me, was another of those men that had such a powerful spirit of prevailing prayer. This Mr. Clary continued in Rochester as long as I did, and did not leave it until after I had left. He never, that I could learn, appeared in public, but gave himself wholly to prayer.

"I think it was the second Sabbath that I was at Auburn at this time, I observed in the congregation the solemn face of Mr. Clary. He looked as if he was borne down with an agony of prayer. Being well acquainted with him, and knowing the great gift of God that was upon him, the spirit of prayer, I was very glad to see him there. He sat in the pew with his brother, the doctor, who was also a professor of religion, but who had nothing by experience, I should think, of his brother Abel's great power with God.

"At intermission, as soon as I came down from the pulpit, Mr. Clary, with his brother, met me at the pulpit stairs, and the doctor invited me to go home with him and spend the intermission and get some refreshments. I did so.

"After arriving at his house we were soon summoned to the dinner table. We gathered about the table, and Dr. Clary turned to his brother and said, 'Brother Abel, will you ask the blessing?' Brother Abel bowed his head and began, audibly, to ask a blessing. He had uttered but a sentence or two when he broke instantly down, moved suddenly back from the table, and fled to his chamber. The doctor supposed he had been taken suddenly ill, and rose up and followed him. In a few moments he came down and said, 'Mr. Finney, brother Abel wants to see you.' Said I, 'What ails him?' Said he, 'I do not know but he says, you know. He appears in great distress, but I think it is the state of his mind.' I understood it in a moment, and went to his room. He lay groaning upon the bed, the Spirit making intercession for him, and in him, with groanings that could not be uttered. I had barely entered the room, when he made out to say, 'Pray, brother Finney.' I knelt down and helped him in prayer, by leading his soul out for the conversion of sinners. I continued to pray until his distress passed away, and then I returned to the dinner table.

"I understood that this was the voice of God. I saw the spirit of prayer was upon him, and I felt his influence upon myself, and took it for granted that the work would move on powerfully. It did so. The pastor told me afterward that he found that in the six weeks that I was there, five hundred souls had been converted."

Mr. Finney in his lectures on revivals tells of other remarkable awakenings in answer to the prayers of God's people. He says in one place, "A clergyman in W———n told me of a revival among his people, which commenced with a zealous and devoted woman in the church. She became anxious about sinners, and went to praying for them; she prayed, and her distress increased; and she finally came to her minister, and talked with him, and asked him to appoint an anxious meeting, for she felt that one was needed. The minister put her off, for he felt nothing of it. The next week she came again, and besought him to appoint an anxious meeting, she knew there would be somebody to come, for she felt as if God was going to pour out His Spirit. He put her off again. And finally she said to him, 'If you do not appoint an anxious meeting I shall die, for there is certainly going to be a revival.' The next Sabbath he appointed a meeting, and said that if there were any who wished to converse with him about the salvation of their souls, he would meet them on such an evening. He did not know of one, but when he went to the place, to his astonishment he found a large number of anxious inquirers."

In still another place he says, "The first ray of light that broke in upon the midnight which rested on the churches in Oneida county, in the fall of 1825, was from a woman in feeble health, who, I believe had never been in a powerful revival. Her soul was exercised about sinners. She was in agony for the land. She did not know what ailed her, but she kept praying more and more, till it seemed as if her agony would destroy her body. At length she became full of joy and exclaimed, 'God has come! God has come! There is no mistake about it, the work is begun, and is going over all the region!' And sure enough the work began, and her family were almost all converted, and the work spread all over that part of the country."

The great revival of 1857 in the United States began in prayer and was carried on by prayer more than by anything else. Dr. Cuyler in an article in a religious newspaper some years ago said, "Most revivals have humble beginnings, and the fire starts in a few warm hearts. Never despise the day of small things. During all my own long ministry, nearly every work of grace had a similar beginning. One commenced in a meeting gathered at a few hours' notice in a private house. Another commenced in a group gathered for Bible study by Mr. Moody in our mission chapel. Still another—the most powerful of all—was kindled on a bitter January evening at a meeting of young Christians under my roof. Dr. Spencer, in his 'Pastor's Sketches', (the most suggestive book of its kind I have ever read), tells us that a remarkable revival in his church sprang from the fervent prayers of a godly old man who was confined to his room by lameness. That profound Christian, Dr. Thomas H. Skinner, of the Union Theological Seminary, once gave me an account of a remarkable coming together of three earnest men in his study when he was the pastor of the Arch Street Church in Philadelphia. They literally wrestled in prayer. They made a clean breast in confession of sin, and humbled themselves before God. One and another church officer came in and joined them. The heaven-kindled flame soon spread through the whole congregation in one of the most powerful revivals ever known in that city."

In the early part of the seventeenth century there was a great religious awakening in Ulster, Ireland. The lands of the rebel chiefs which had been forfeited to the British crown, were settled up by a class of colonists who for the most part were governed by a spirit of wild adventure. Real piety was rare. Seven ministers, five from Scotland and two from England, settled in that country, the earliest arrivals being in 1613. Of one of these ministers named Blair it is recorded by a contemporary, "He spent many days and nights in prayer, alone and with others, and was vouchsafed great intimacy with God." Mr. James Glendenning, a man of very meager natural gifts, was a man similarly minded as regards prayer. The work began under this man Glendenning. The historian of the time says, "He was a man who never would have been chosen by a wise assembly of ministers nor sent to begin a reformation in this land. Yet this was the Lord's choice to begin with him the admirable work of God which I mention on purpose that all may see how the glory is only the Lord's in making a holy nation in this profane land, and that it was 'not by might, nor by power, nor by man's wisdom, but by My Spirit, saith the Lord.'" In his preaching at Oldstone multitudes of hearers felt in great anxiety and terror of conscience. They looked on themselves as altogether lost and damned, and cried out, "Men and brethren, what shall we do to be saved?" They were stricken into a swoon by the power of His Word. A dozen in one day were carried out of doors as dead. These were not women, but some of the boldest spirits of the neighborhood; "some who had formerly feared not with their swords to put a whole market town into a fray." Concerning one of them, the historian writes, "I have heard one of them, then a mighty strong man, now a mighty Christian, say that his end in coming into church was to consult with his companions how to work some mischief."

This work spread throughout the whole country. By the year 1626 a monthly concert of prayer was held in Antrim. The work spread beyond the bounds of Down and Antrim to the churches of the neighboring counties. So great became the religious interest that Christians would come thirty or forty miles to the communions, and continue from the time they came until they returned without wearying or making use of sleep. Many of them neither ate nor drank, and yet some of them professed that they "went away most fresh and vigorous, their souls so filled with the sense of God."

This revival changed the whole character of northern Ireland.

Another great awakening in Ireland in 1859 had a somewhat similar origin. By many who did not know, it was thought that this marvelous work came without warning and preparation, but Rev. William Gibson, the moderator of the General Assembly of the Presbyterian Church in Ireland in 1860, in his very interesting and valuable history of the work tells how there had been preparation for two years. There had been constant discussion in the General Assembly of the low estate of religion, and of the need of a revival. There had been special sessions for prayer. Finally four young men, who became leaders in the origin of the great work, began to meet together in an old schoolhouse in the neighborhood of Kells. About the spring of 1858 a work of power began to manifest itself. It spread from town to town, and from county to county. The congregations became too large for the buildings, and the meetings were held in the open air, oftentimes attended by many thousands of people. Many hundreds of persons were frequently convicted of sin in a single meeting. In some places the criminal courts and jails were closed for lack of occupation. There were manifestations of the Holy Spirit's power of a most remarkable character, clearly proving that the Holy Spirit is as ready to work to-day as in apostolic days, when ministers and Christians really believe in Him and begin to prepare the way by prayer.

Mr. Moody's wonderful work in England and Scotland and Ireland that afterwards spread to America had its origin on the manward side in prayer. Mr. Moody made little impression until men and women began to cry to God. Indeed his going to England at all was in answer to the importunate cries to God of a bed-ridden saint. While the spirit of prayer continued the revival abode in strength, but in the course of time less and less was made of prayer and the work fell off very perceptibly in power. Doubtless one of the great secrets of the unsatisfactoriness and superficiality and unreality of many of our modern so-called revivals, is that more dependence is put upon man's machinery than upon God's power, sought and obtained by earnest, persistent, believing prayer. We live in a day characterized by the multiplication of man's machinery and the diminution of God's power. The great cry of our day is work, work, work, new organizations, new methods, new machinery; the great need of our day is prayer. It was a master stroke of the devil when he got the church so generally to lay aside this mighty weapon of prayer. The devil is perfectly willing that the church should multiply its organizations, and deftly contrive machinery for the conquest of the world for Christ if it will only give up praying. He laughs as he looks at the church to-day and says to himself:

"You can have your Sunday-schools and your Young People's Societies, your Young Men's Christian Associations and your Women's Christian Temperance Unions, your Institutional Churches and your Industrial Schools, and your Boy's Brigades, your grand choirs and your fine organs, your brilliant preachers and your revival efforts too, if you don't bring the power of Almighty God into them by earnest, persistent, believing, mighty prayer."

Prayer could work as marvelous results today as it ever could, if the church would only betake itself to it.

There seem to be increasing signs that the church is awakening to this fact. Here and there God is laying upon individual ministers and churches a burden of prayer that they have never known before. Less dependence is being put upon machinery and more dependence upon God. Ministers are crying to God day and night for power. Churches and portions of churches are meeting together in the early morning hours and the late night hours crying to God for the latter rain. There is every indication of the coming of a mighty and widespread revival. There is every reason why, if a revival should come in any country at this time, it should be more widespread in its extent than any revival of history. There is the closest and swiftest communication by travel, by letter, and by cable between all parts of the world. A true fire of God kindled in America would soon spread to the uttermost parts of the earth. The only thing needed to bring this fire is prayer.

It is not necessary that the whole church get to praying to begin with. Great revivals always begin first in the hearts of a few men and women whom God arouses by His Spirit to believe in Him as a living God, as a God who answers prayer, and upon whose heart He lays a burden from which no rest can be found except in importunate crying unto God.

May God use this book to arouse many others to pray that the greatly-needed revival may come, and come speedily.

LET US PRAY

Power Through Prayer

~ ※ ~

By *Edward M. Bounds*

The 1922 Edition

~ ※ ~

Recreation to a minister must be as whetting is with the mower—that is, to be used only so far as is necessary for his work. May a physician in plague-time take any more relaxation or recreation than is necessary for his life, when so many are expecting his help in a case of life and death? Will you stand by and see sinners gasping under the pangs of death, and say: "God doth not require me to make myself a drudge to save them?" Is this the voice of ministerial or Christian compassion or rather of sensual laziness and diabolical cruelty?
—Richard Baxter

Misemployment of time is injurious to the mind. In illness I have looked back with self-reproach on days spent in my study; I was wading through history and poetry and monthly journals, but I was in my study! Another man's trifling is notorious to all observers, but what am I doing? Nothing, perhaps, that has reference to the spiritual good of my congregation. Be much in retirement and prayer. Study the honor and glory of your Master. —Richard Cecil

1. Men of Prayer Needed

Study universal holiness of life. Your whole usefulness depends on this, for your sermons last but an hour or two; your life preaches all the week. If Satan can only make a covetous minister a lover of praise, of pleasure, of good eating, he has ruined your ministry. Give yourself to prayer, and get your texts, your thoughts, your words from God. Luther spent his best three hours in prayer.
—Robert Murray McCheyne

WE are constantly on a stretch, if not on a strain, to devise new methods, new plans, new organizations to advance the Church and secure enlargement and efficiency for the gospel. This trend of the day has a tendency to lose sight of the man or sink the man in the plan or organization. God's plan is to make much of the man, far more of him than of anything else. Men are God's method. The Church is looking for better methods; God is looking for better men. "There was a man sent from God whose name was John." The dispensation that heralded and prepared the way for Christ was bound up in that man John. "Unto us a child is born, unto us a son is given." The world's salvation comes out of that cradled Son. When Paul appeals to the personal character of the men who rooted the gospel in the world, he solves the mystery of their success. The glory and efficiency of the gospel is staked on the men who proclaim it. When God declares that "the eyes of the Lord run to and fro throughout the whole earth, to show himself strong in the behalf of them whose heart is perfect toward him," he declares the necessity of men and his dependence on them as a channel through which to exert his power upon the world. This vital, urgent truth is one that this age of machinery is apt to forget. The forgetting of it is as baneful on the work of God as would be the striking of the sun from his sphere. Darkness, confusion, and death would ensue.

What the Church needs to-day is not more machinery or better, not new organizations or more and novel methods, but men whom the Holy Ghost can use—men of prayer, men mighty in prayer. The Holy Ghost does not flow through methods, but through men. He does not come on machinery, but on men. He does not anoint plans, but men—men of prayer.

An eminent historian has said that the accidents of personal character have more to do with the revolutions of nations than either philosophic historians or democratic politicians will allow. This truth has its application in full to the gospel of Christ, the character and conduct of the followers of Christ—Christianize the world, transfigure nations and individuals. Of the preachers of the gospel it is eminently true.

The character as well as the fortunes of the gospel is committed to the preacher. He makes or mars the message from God to man. The preacher is the golden pipe through which the divine oil flows. The pipe must not only be golden, but open and flawless, that the oil may have a full, unhindered, unwasted flow.

The man makes the preacher. God must make the man. The messenger is, if possible, more than the message. The preacher is more than the sermon. The preacher makes the sermon. As the life-giving milk from the mother's bosom is but the mother's life, so all the preacher says is tinctured, impregnated by what the preacher is. The treasure is in earthen vessels, and the taste of the vessel impregnates and may discolor. The man, the whole man, lies behind the sermon. Preaching is not the performance of an hour. It is the outflow of a life. It takes twenty years to make a sermon, because it takes twenty years to make the man. The true sermon is a thing of life. The sermon grows because the man grows. The sermon is forceful because the man is forceful. The sermon is holy because the man is holy. The sermon is full of the divine unction because the man is full of the divine unction.

Paul termed it "My gospel;" not that he had degraded it by his personal eccentricities or diverted it by selfish appropriation, but the gospel was put into the heart and lifeblood of the man Paul, as a personal trust to be executed by his Pauline traits, to be set aflame and empowered by the fiery energy of his fiery soul. Paul's sermons—what were they? Where are they? Skeletons, scattered fragments, afloat on the sea of inspiration! But the man Paul, greater than his sermons, lives forever, in full form, feature and stature, with his molding hand on the Church. The preaching is but a voice. The voice in silence dies, the text is forgotten, the sermon fades from memory; the preacher lives.

The sermon cannot rise in its life-giving forces above the man. Dead men give out dead sermons, and dead sermons kill. Everything depends on the spiritual character of the preacher. Under the Jewish dispensation the high priest had inscribed in jeweled letters on a golden frontlet: "Holiness to the Lord." So every preacher in Christ's ministry must be molded into and mastered by this same holy motto. It is a crying shame for the Christian ministry to fall lower in holiness of character and holiness of aim than the Jewish priesthood. Jonathan Edwards said: "I went on with my eager pursuit after more holiness and conformity to Christ. The heaven I desired was a heaven of holiness." The gospel of Christ does not move by popular waves. It has no self-propagating power. It moves as the men who have charge of it move. The preacher must impersonate the gospel. Its divine, most distinctive features must be embodied in him. The constraining power of love must be in the preacher as a projecting, eccentric, an all-commanding, self-oblivious force. The energy of self-denial must be his being, his heart and blood and bones. He must go forth as a man among men, clothed with humility, abiding in meekness, wise as a serpent, harmless as a dove; the bonds of a servant with the spirit of a king, a king in high, royal, in dependent bearing, with the simplicity and sweetness of a child. The preacher must throw himself, with all the abandon of a perfect, self-emptying faith and a self-consuming zeal, into his work for the salvation of men. Hearty, heroic, compassionate, fearless martyrs must the men be who take hold of and shape a generation for God. If they be timid time servers, place seekers, if they be men pleasers or men fearers, if their faith has a weak hold on God or his Word, if their denial be broken by any phase of self or the world, they cannot take hold of the Church nor the world for God.

The preacher's sharpest and strongest preaching should be to himself. His most difficult, delicate, laborious, and thorough work must be with himself. The training of the twelve was the great, difficult, and enduring work of Christ. Preachers are not sermon makers, but men makers and saint makers, and he only is well-trained for this business who has made himself a man and a saint. It is not great talents nor great learning nor great preachers that God needs, but men great in holiness, great in faith, great in love, great in fidelity, great for God—men always preaching by holy sermons in the pulpit, by holy lives out of it. These can mold a generation for God.

After this order, the early Christians were formed. Men they were of solid mold, preachers after the heavenly type—heroic, stalwart, soldierly, saintly. Preaching with them meant self-denying, self-crucifying, serious, toilsome, martyr business. They applied themselves to it in a way that told on their generation, and formed in its womb a generation yet unborn for God. The preaching man is to be the praying man. Prayer is the preacher's mightiest weapon. An almighty force in itself, it gives life and force to all.

The real sermon is made in the closet. The man—God's man—is made in the closet. His life and his profoundest convictions were born in his secret communion with God. The burdened and tearful agony of his spirit, his weightiest and sweetest messages were got when alone with God. Prayer makes the man; prayer makes the preacher; prayer makes the pastor.

The pulpit of this day is weak in praying. The pride of learning is against the dependent humility of prayer. Prayer is with the pulpit too often only official—a performance for the routine of service. Prayer is not to the modern pulpit the mighty force it was in Paul's life or Paul's ministry. Every preacher who does not make prayer a mighty factor in his own life and ministry is weak as a factor in God's work and is powerless to project God's cause in this world.

2. Our Sufficiency Is of God

But above all he excelled in prayer. The inwardness and weight of his spirit, the reverence and solemnity of his address and behavior, and the fewness and fullness of his words have often struck even strangers with admiration as they used to reach others with consolation. The most awful, living, reverend frame I ever felt or beheld, I must say, was his prayer. And truly it was a testimony. He knew and lived nearer to the Lord than other men, for they that know him most will see most reason to approach him with reverence and fear.
—William Penn of George Fox

THE sweetest graces by a slight perversion may bear the bitterest fruit. The sun gives life, but sunstrokes are death. Preaching is to give life; it may kill. The preacher holds the keys; he may lock as well as unlock. Preaching is God's great institution for the planting and maturing of spiritual life. When properly executed, its benefits are untold; when wrongly executed, no evil can exceed its damaging results. It is an easy matter to destroy the flock if the shepherd be unwary or the pasture be destroyed, easy to capture the citadel if the watchmen be asleep or the food and water be poisoned. Invested with such gracious prerogatives, exposed to so great evils, involving so many grave responsibilities, it would be a parody on the shrewdness of the devil and a libel on his character and reputation if he did not bring his master influences to adulterate the preacher and the preaching. In face of all this, the exclamatory interrogatory of Paul, "Who is sufficient for these things?" is never out of order.

Paul says: "Our sufficiency is of God, who also hath made us able ministers of the new testament; not of the letter, but of the spirit: for the letter killeth, but the spirit giveth life." The true ministry is God-touched, God-enabled, and God-made. The Spirit of God is on the preacher in anointing power, the fruit of the Spirit is in his heart, the Spirit of God has vitalized the man and the word; his preaching gives life, gives life as the spring gives life; gives life as the resurrection gives life; gives ardent life as the summer gives ardent life; gives fruitful life as the autumn gives fruitful life. The life-giving preacher is a man of God, whose heart is ever athirst for God, whose soul is ever following hard after God, whose eye is single to God, and in whom by the power of God's Spirit the flesh and the world have been crucified and his ministry is like the generous flood of a life-giving river.

The preaching that kills is non-spiritual preaching. The ability of the preaching is not from God. Lower sources than God have given to it energy and stimulant. The Spirit is not evident in the preacher nor his preaching. Many kinds of forces may be projected and stimulated by preaching that kills, but they are not spiritual forces. They may resemble spiritual forces, but are only the shadow, the counterfeit; life they may seem to have, but the life is magnetized. The preaching that kills is the letter; shapely and orderly it may be, but it is the letter still, the dry, husky letter, the empty, bald shell. The letter may have the germ of life in it, but it has no breath of spring to evoke it; winter seeds they are, as hard as the winter's soil, as icy as the winter's air, no thawing nor germinating by them. This letter-preaching has the truth. But even divine truth has no life-giving energy alone; it must be energized by the Spirit, with all God's forces at its back. Truth unquickened by God's Spirit deadens as much as, or more than, error. It may be the truth without admixture; but without the Spirit its shade and touch are deadly, its truth error, its light darkness. The letter-preaching is unctionless, neither mellowed nor oiled by the Spirit. There may be tears, but tears cannot run God's machinery; tears may be but summer's breath on a snow-covered iceberg, nothing but surface slush. Feelings and earnestness there may be, but it is the emotion of the actor and the earnestness of the attorney. The preacher may feel from the kindling of his own sparks, be eloquent over his own exegesis, earnest in delivering the product of his own brain; the professor may usurp the place and imitate the fire of the apostle; brains and nerves may serve the place and feign the work of God's Spirit, and by these forces the letter may glow and sparkle like an illumined text, but the glow and sparkle will be as barren of life as the field sown with pearls. The death-dealing element lies back of the words, back of the sermon, back of the occasion, back of the manner, back of the action. The great hindrance is in the preacher himself. He has not in himself the mighty life-creating forces. There may be no discount on his orthodoxy, honesty, cleanness, or earnestness; but somehow the man, the inner man, in its secret places has never broken down and surrendered to God, his inner life is not a great highway for the transmission of God's message, God's power. Somehow self and not God rules in the holy of holiest. Somewhere, all unconscious to himself, some spiritual nonconductor has touched his inner being, and the divine current has been arrested. His inner being has never felt its thorough spiritual bankruptcy, its utter powerlessness; he has never learned to cry out with an ineffable cry of self-despair and self-helplessness till God's power and God's fire comes in and fills, purifies, empowers. Self-esteem, self-ability in some pernicious shape has defamed and violated the temple which should be held sacred for God. Life-giving preaching costs the preacher much—death to self, crucifixion to the world, the travail of his own soul. Crucified preaching only can give life. Crucified preaching can come only from a crucified man.

3. The Letter Killeth

During this affliction I was brought to examine my life in relation to eternity closer than I had done when in the enjoyment of health. In this examination relative to the discharge of my duties toward my fellow creatures as a man, a Christian minister, and an officer of the Church, I stood approved by my own conscience; but in relation to my Redeemer and Savior the result was different. My returns of gratitude and loving obedience bear no proportion to my obligations for redeeming, preserving, and supporting me through the vicissitudes of life from infancy to old age. The coldness of my love to Him who first loved me and has done so much for me overwhelmed and confused me; and to complete my unworthy character, I had not only neglected to improve the grace given to the extent of my duty and privilege, but for want of improvement had, while abounding in perplexing care and labor, declined from first zeal and love. I was confounded, humbled myself, implored mercy, and renewed my covenant to strive and devote myself unreservedly to the Lord.
—Bishop McKendree

THE preaching that kills may be, and often is, orthodox—dogmatically, inviolably orthodox. We love orthodoxy. It is good. It is the best. It is the clean, clear-cut teaching of God's Word, the trophies won by truth in its conflict with error, the levees which faith has raised against the desolating floods of honest or reckless misbelief or unbelief; but orthodoxy, clear and hard as crystal, suspicious and militant, may be but the letter well-shaped, well-named, and well-learned, the letter which kills. Nothing is so dead as a dead orthodoxy, too dead to speculate, too dead to think, to study, or to pray.

The preaching that kills may have insight and grasp of principles, may be scholarly and critical in taste, may have every minutia of the derivation and grammar of the letter, may be able to trim the letter into its perfect pattern, and illume it as Plato and Cicero may be illumined, may study it as a lawyer studies his text-books to form his brief or to defend his case, and yet be like a frost, a killing frost. Letter-preaching may be eloquent, enameled with poetry and rhetoric, sprinkled with prayer spiced with sensation, illumined by genius and yet these be but the massive or chaste, costly mountings, the rare and beautiful flowers which coffin the corpse. The preaching which kills may be without scholarship, unmarked by any freshness of thought or feeling, clothed in tasteless generalities or vapid specialties, with style irregular, slovenly, savoring neither of closet nor of study, graced neither by thought, expression, or prayer. Under such preaching how wide and utter the desolation! how profound the spiritual death!

This letter-preaching deals with the surface and shadow of things, and not the things themselves. It does not penetrate the inner part. It has no deep insight into, no strong grasp of, the hidden life of God's Word. It is true to the outside, but the outside is the hull which must be broken and penetrated for the kernel. The letter may be dressed so as to attract and be fashionable, but the attraction is not toward God nor is the fashion for heaven. The failure is in the preacher. God has not made him. He has never been in the hands of God like clay in the hands of the potter. He has been busy about the sermon, its thought and finish, its drawing and impressive forces; but the deep things of God have never been sought, studied, fathomed, experienced by him. He has never stood before "the throne high and lifted up," never heard the seraphim song, never seen the vision nor felt the rush of that awful holiness, and cried out in utter abandon and despair under the sense of weakness and guilt, and had his life renewed, his heart touched, purged, inflamed by the live coal from God's altar. His ministry may draw people to him, to the Church, to the form and ceremony; but no true drawings to God, no sweet, holy, divine communion induced. The Church has been frescoed but not edified, pleased but not sanctified. Life is suppressed; a chill is on the summer air; the soil is baked. The city of our God becomes the city of the dead; the Church a graveyard, not an embattled army. Praise and prayer are stifled; worship is dead. The preacher and the preaching have helped sin, not holiness; peopled hell, not heaven.

Preaching which kills is prayerless preaching. Without prayer the preacher creates death, and not life. The preacher who is feeble in prayer is feeble in life-giving forces. The preacher who has retired prayer as a conspicuous and largely prevailing element in his own character has shorn his preaching of its distinctive life-giving power. Professional praying there is and will be, but professional praying helps the preaching to its deadly work. Professional praying chills and kills both preaching and praying. Much of the lax devotion and lazy, irreverent attitudes in congregational praying are attributable to professional praying in the pulpit. Long, discursive, dry, and inane are the prayers in many pulpits. Without unction or heart, they fall like a killing frost on all the graces of worship. Death-dealing prayers they are. Every vestige of devotion has perished under their breath. The deader they are the longer they grow. A plea for short praying, live praying, real heart praying, praying by the Holy Spirit—direct, specific, ardent, simple, unctuous in the pulpit—is in order. A school to teach preachers how to pray, as God counts praying, would be more beneficial to true piety, true worship, and true preaching than all theological schools.

Stop! Pause! Consider! Where are we? What are we doing? Preaching to kill? Praying to kill? Praying to God! the great God, the Maker of all worlds, the Judge of all men! What reverence! what simplicity! what sincerity! what truth in the inward parts is demanded! How real we must be! How hearty! Prayer to God the noblest exercise, the loftiest effort of man, the most real thing! Shall we not discard forever accursed preaching that kills and prayer that kills, and do the real thing, the mightiest thing—prayerful praying, life-creating preaching, bring the mightiest force to bear on heaven and earth and draw on God's exhaustless and open treasure for the need and beggary of man?

4. Tendencies to Be Avoided

Let us often look at Brainerd in the woods of America pouring out his very soul before God for the perishing heathen without whose salvation nothing could make him happy. Prayer—secret fervent believing prayer—lies at the root of all personal godliness. A competent knowledge of the language where a missionary lives, a mild and winning temper, a heart given up to God in closet religion—these, these are the attainments which, more than all knowledge, or all other gifts, will fit us to become the instruments of God in the great work of human redemption. —Carrey's Brotherhood, Serampore

THERE are two extreme tendencies in the ministry. The one is to shut itself out from intercourse with the people. The monk, the hermit were illustrations of this; they shut themselves out from men to be more with God. They failed, of course. Our being with God is of use only as we expend its priceless benefits on men. This age, neither with preacher nor with people, is much intent on God. Our hankering is not that way. We shut ourselves to our study, we become students, bookworms, Bible worms, sermon makers, noted for literature, thought, and sermons; but the people and God, where are they? Out of heart, out of mind. Preachers who are great thinkers, great students must be the greatest of prayers, or else they will be the greatest of backsliders, heartless professionals, rationalistic, less than the least of preachers in God's estimate.

The other tendency is to thoroughly popularize the ministry. He is no longer God's man, but a man of affairs, of the people. He prays not, because his mission is to the people. If he can move the people, create an interest, a sensation in favor of religion, an interest in Church work—he is satisfied. His personal relation to God is no factor in his work. Prayer has little or no place in his plans. The disaster and ruin of such a ministry cannot be computed by earthly arithmetic. What the preacher is in prayer to God, for himself, for his people, so is his power for real good to men, so is his true fruitfulness, his true fidelity to God, to man, for time, for eternity.

It is impossible for the preacher to keep his spirit in harmony with the divine nature of his high calling without much prayer. That the preacher by dint of duty and laborious fidelity to the work and routine of the ministry can keep himself in trim and fitness is a serious mistake. Even sermon-making, incessant and taxing as an art, as a duty, as a work, or as a pleasure, will engross and harden, will estrange the heart, by neglect of prayer, from God. The scientist loses God in nature. The preacher may lose God in his sermon.

Prayer freshens the heart of the preacher, keeps it in tune with God and in sympathy with the people, lifts his ministry out of the chilly air of a profession, fructifies routine and moves every wheel with the facility and power of a divine unction.

Mr. Spurgeon says: "Of course the preacher is above all others distinguished as a man of prayer. He prays as an ordinary Christian, else he were a hypocrite. He prays more than ordinary Christians, else he were disqualified for the office he has undertaken. If you as ministers are not very prayerful, you are to be pitied. If you become lax in sacred devotion, not only will you need to be pitied but your people also, and the day cometh in which you shall be ashamed and confounded. All our libraries and studies are mere emptiness compared with our closets. Our seasons of fasting and prayer at the Tabernacle have been high days indeed; never has heaven's gate stood wider; never have our hearts been nearer the central Glory."

The praying which makes a prayerful ministry is not a little praying put in as we put flavor to give it a pleasant smack, but the praying must be in the body, and form the blood and bones. Prayer is no petty duty, put into a corner; no piecemeal performance made out of the fragments of time which have been snatched from business and other engagements of life; but it means that the best of our time, the heart of our time and strength must be given. It does not mean the closet absorbed in the study or swallowed up in the activities of ministerial duties; but it means the closet first, the study and activities second, both study and activities freshened and made efficient by the closet. Prayer that affects one's ministry must give tone to one's life. The praying which gives color and bent to character is no pleasant, hurried pastime. It must enter as strongly into the heart and life as Christ's "strong crying and tears" did; must draw out the soul into an agony of desire as Paul's did; must be an inwrought fire and force like the "effectual, fervent prayer" of James; must be of that quality which, when put into the golden censer and incensed before God, works mighty spiritual throes and revolutions.

Prayer is not a little habit pinned on to us while we were tied to our mother's apron strings; neither is it a little decent quarter of a minute's grace said over an hour's dinner, but it is a most serious work of our most serious years. It engages more of time and appetite than our longest dinings or richest feasts. The prayer that makes much of our preaching must be made much of. The character of our praying will determine the character of our preaching. Light praying will make light preaching. Prayer makes preaching strong, gives it unction, and makes it stick. In every ministry weighty for good, prayer has always been a serious business.

The preacher must be preeminently a man of prayer. His heart must graduate in the school of prayer. In the school of prayer only can the heart learn to preach. No learning can make up for the failure to pray. No earnestness, no diligence, no study, no gifts will supply its lack.

Talking to men for God is a great thing, but talking to God for men is greater still. He will never talk well and with real success to men for God who has not learned well how to talk to God for men. More than this, prayerless words in the pulpit and out of it are deadening words.

5. Prayer, the Great Essential

You know the value of prayer: it is precious beyond all price. Never, never neglect it. —Sir Thomas Buxton

Prayer is the first thing, the second thing, the third thing necessary to a minister. Pray, then, my dear brother: pray, pray, pray. —Edward Payson

PRAYER, in the preacher's life, in the preacher's study, in the preacher's pulpit, must be a conspicuous and an all-impregnating force and an all-coloring ingredient. It must play no secondary part, be no mere coating. To him it is given to be with his Lord "all night in prayer." The preacher, to train himself in self-denying prayer, is charged to look to his Master, who, "rising up a great while before day, went out, and departed into a solitary place, and there prayed." The preacher's study ought to be a closet, a Bethel, an altar, a vision, and a ladder, that every thought might ascend heavenward ere it went manward; that every part of the sermon might be scented by the air of heaven and made serious, because God was in the study.

As the engine never moves until the fire is kindled, so preaching, with all its machinery, perfection, and polish, is at a dead standstill, as far as spiritual results are concerned, till prayer has kindled and created the steam. The texture, fineness, and strength of the sermon is as so much rubbish unless the mighty impulse of prayer is in it, through it, and behind it. The preacher must, by prayer, put God in the sermon. The preacher must, by prayer, move God toward the people before he can move the people to God by his words. The preacher must have had audience and ready access to God before he can have access to the people. An open way to God for the preacher is the surest pledge of an open way to the people.

It is necessary to iterate and reiterate that prayer, as a mere habit, as a performance gone through by routine or in a professional way, is a dead and rotten thing. Such praying has no connection with the praying for which we plead. We are stressing true praying, which engages and sets on fire every high element of the preacher's being—prayer which is born of vital oneness with Christ and the fullness of the Holy Ghost, which springs from the deep, overflowing fountains of tender compassion, deathless solicitude for man's eternal good; a consuming zeal for the glory of God; a thorough conviction of the preacher's difficult and delicate work and of the imperative need of God's mightiest help. Praying grounded on these solemn and profound convictions is the only true praying. Preaching backed by such praying is the only preaching which sows the seeds of eternal life in human hearts and builds men up for heaven.

It is true that there may be popular preaching, pleasant preaching, taking preaching, preaching of much intellectual, literary, and brainy force, with its measure and form of good, with little or no praying; but the preaching which secures God's end in preaching must be born of prayer from text to exordium, delivered with the energy and spirit of prayer, followed and made to germinate, and kept in vital force in the hearts of the hearers by the preacher's prayers, long after the occasion has past.

We may excuse the spiritual poverty of our preaching in many ways, but the true secret will be found in the lack of urgent prayer for God's presence in the power of the Holy Spirit. There are preachers innumerable who can deliver masterful sermons after their order; but the effects are short-lived and do not enter as a factor at all into the regions of the spirit where the fearful war between God and Satan, heaven and hell, is being waged because they are not made powerfully militant and spiritually victorious by prayer.

The preachers who gain mighty results for God are the men who have prevailed in their pleadings with God ere venturing to plead with men. The preachers who are the mightiest in their closets with God are the mightiest in their pulpits with men.

Preachers are human folks, and are exposed to and often caught by the strong driftings of human currents. Praying is spiritual work; and human nature does not like taxing, spiritual work. Human nature wants to sail to heaven under a favoring breeze, a full, smooth sea. Prayer is humbling work. It abases intellect and pride, crucifies vainglory, and signs our spiritual bankruptcy, and all these are hard for flesh and blood to bear. It is easier not to pray than to bear them. So we come to one of the crying evils of these times, maybe of all times—little or no praying. Of these two evils, perhaps little praying is worse than no praying. Little praying is a kind of make-believe, a salvo for the conscience, a farce and a delusion.

The little estimate we put on prayer is evident from the little time we give to it. The time given to prayer by the average preacher scarcely counts in the sum of the daily aggregate. Not infrequently the preacher's only praying is by his bedside in his nightdress, ready for bed and soon in it, with, perchance the addition of a few hasty snatches of prayer ere he is dressed in the morning. How feeble, vain, and little is such praying compared with the time and energy devoted to praying by holy men in and out of the Bible! How poor and mean our petty, childish praying is beside the habits of the true men of God in all ages! To men who think praying their main business and devote time to it according to this high estimate of its importance does God commit the keys of his kingdom, and by them does he work his spiritual wonders in this world. Great praying is the sign and seal of God's great leaders and the earnest of the conquering forces with which God will crown their labors.

The preacher is commissioned to pray as well as to preach. His mission is incomplete if he does not do both well. The preacher may speak with all the eloquence of men and of angels; but unless he can pray with a faith which draws all heaven to his aid, his preaching will be "as sounding brass or a tinkling cymbal" for permanent God-honoring, soul-saving uses.

6. A Praying Ministry Successful

The principal cause of my leanness and unfruitfulness is owing to an unaccountable backwardness to pray. I can write or read or converse or hear with a ready heart; but prayer is more spiritual and inward than any of these, and the more spiritual any duty is the more my carnal heart is apt to start from it. Prayer and patience and faith are never disappointed. I have long since learned that if ever I was to be a minister faith and prayer must make me one. When I can find my heart in frame and liberty for prayer, everything else is comparatively easy. —Richard Newton

IT may be put down as a spiritual axiom that in every truly successful ministry prayer is an evident and controlling force—evident and controlling in the life of the preacher, evident and controlling in the deep spirituality of his work. A ministry may be a very thoughtful ministry without prayer; the preacher may secure fame and popularity without prayer; the whole machinery of the preacher's life and work may be run without the oil of prayer or with scarcely enough to grease one cog; but no ministry can be a spiritual one, securing holiness in the preacher and in his people, without prayer being made an evident and controlling force.

The preacher that prays indeed puts God into the work. God does not come into the preacher's work as a matter of course or on general principles, but he comes by prayer and special urgency. That God will be found of us in the day that we seek him with the whole heart is as true of the preacher as of the penitent. A prayerful ministry is the only ministry that brings the preacher into sympathy with the people. Prayer as essentially unites to the human as it does to the divine. A prayerful ministry is the only ministry qualified for the high offices and responsibilities of the preacher. Colleges, learning, books, theology, preaching cannot make a preacher, but praying does. The apostles' commission to preach was a blank till filled up by the Pentecost which praying brought. A prayerful minister has passed beyond the regions of the popular, beyond the man of mere affairs, of secularities, of pulpit attractiveness; passed beyond the ecclesiastical organizer or general into a sublimer and mightier region, the region of the spiritual. Holiness is the product of his work; transfigured hearts and lives emblazon the reality of his work, its trueness and substantial nature. God is with him. His ministry is not projected on worldly or surface principles. He is deeply stored with and deeply schooled in the things of God. His long, deep communings with God about his people and the agony of his wrestling spirit have crowned him as a prince in the things of God. The iciness of the mere professional has long since melted under the intensity of his praying.

The superficial results of many a ministry, the deadness of others, are to be found in the lack of praying. No ministry can succeed without much praying, and this praying must be fundamental, ever-abiding, ever-increasing. The text, the sermon, should be the result of prayer. The study should be bathed in prayer, all its duties so impregnated with prayer, its whole spirit the spirit of prayer. "I am sorry that I have prayed so little," was the deathbed regret of one of God's chosen ones, a sad and remorseful regret for a preacher. "I want a life of greater, deeper, truer prayer," said the late Archbishop Tait. So may we all say, and this may we all secure.

God's true preachers have been distinguished by one great feature: they were men of prayer. Differing often in many things, they have always had a common center. They may have started from different points, and traveled by different roads, but they converged to one point: they were one in prayer. God to them was the center of attraction, and prayer was the path that led to God. These men prayed not occasionally, not a little at regular or at odd times; but they so prayed that their prayers entered into and shaped their characters; they so prayed as to affect their own lives and the lives of others; they so prayed as to make the history of the Church and influence the current of the times. They spent much time in prayer, not because they marked the shadow on the dial or the hands on the clock, but because it was to them so momentous and engaging a business that they could scarcely give over.

Prayer was to them what it was to Paul, a striving with earnest effort of soul; what it was to Jacob, a wrestling and prevailing; what it was to Christ, "strong crying and tears." They "prayed always with all prayer and supplication in the Spirit, and watching thereunto with all perseverance." "The effectual, fervent prayer" has been the mightiest weapon of God's mightiest soldiers. The statement in regard to Elijah—that he "was a man subject to like passions as we are, and he prayed earnestly that it might not rain: and it rained not on the earth by the space of three years and six months. And he prayed again, and the heaven gave rain, and the earth brought forth her fruit"—comprehends all prophets and preachers who have moved their generation for God, and shows the instrument by which they worked their wonders.

7. Much Time Should Be Given to Prayer

The great masters and teachers in Christian doctrine have always found in prayer their highest source of illumination. Not to go beyond the limits of the English Church, it is recorded of Bishop Andrews that he spent five hours daily on his knees. The greatest practical resolves that have enriched and beautified human life in Christian times have been arrived at in prayer. —Canon Liddon

WHILE many private prayers, in the nature of things, must be short; while public prayers, as a rule, ought to be short and condensed; while there is ample room for and value put on ejaculatory prayer—yet in our private communions with God time is a feature essential to its value. Much time spent with God is the secret of all successful praying. Prayer which is felt as a mighty force is the mediate or immediate product of much time spent with God. Our short prayers owe their point and efficiency to the long ones that have preceded them. The short prevailing prayer cannot be prayed by one who has not prevailed with God in a mightier struggle of long continuance. Jacob's victory of faith could not have been gained without that all-night wrestling. God's acquaintance is not made by pop calls. God does not bestow his gifts on the casual or hasty comers and goers. Much with God alone is the secret of knowing him and of influence with him. He yields to the persistency of a faith that knows him. He bestows his richest gifts upon those who declare their desire for and appreciation of those gifts by the constancy as well as earnestness of their importunity. Christ, who in this as well as other things is our Example, spent many whole nights in prayer. His custom was to pray much. He had his habitual place to pray. Many long seasons of praying make up his history and character. Paul prayed day and night. It took time from very important interests for Daniel to pray three times a day. David's morning, noon, and night praying were doubtless on many occasions very protracted. While we have no specific account of the time these Bible saints spent in prayer, yet the indications are that they consumed much time in prayer, and on some occasions long seasons of praying was their custom.

We would not have any think that the value of their prayers is to be measured by the clock, but our purpose is to impress on our minds the necessity of being much alone with God; and that if this feature has not been produced by our faith, then our faith is of a feeble and surface type.

The men who have most fully illustrated Christ in their character, and have most powerfully affected the world for him, have been men who spent so much time with God as to make it a notable feature of their lives. Charles Simeon devoted the hours from four till eight in the morning to God. Mr. Wesley spent two hours daily in prayer. He began at four in the morning. Of him, one who knew him well wrote: "He thought prayer to be more his business than anything else, and I have seen him come out of his closet with a serenity of face next to shining." John Fletcher stained the walls of his room by the breath of his prayers. Sometimes he would pray all night; always, frequently, and with great earnestness. His whole life was a life of prayer. "I would not rise from my seat," he said, "without lifting my heart to God." His greeting to a friend was always:

"Do I meet you praying?" Luther said: "If I fail to spend two hours in prayer each morning, the devil gets the victory through the day. I have so much business I cannot get on without spending three hours daily in prayer." He had a motto: "He that has prayed well has studied well."

Archbishop Leighton was so much alone with God that he seemed to be in a perpetual meditation. "Prayer and praise were his business and his pleasure," says his biographer. Bishop Ken was so much with God that his soul was said to be God-enamored. He was with God before the clock struck three every morning. Bishop Asbury said: "I propose to rise at four o'clock as often as I can and spend two hours in prayer and meditation." Samuel Rutherford, the fragrance of whose piety is still rich, rose at three in the morning to meet God in prayer. Joseph Alleine arose at four o'clock for his business of praying till eight. If he heard other tradesmen plying their business before he was up, he would exclaim: "O how this shames me! Doth not my Master deserve more than theirs?" He who has learned this trade well draws at will, on sight, and with acceptance of heaven's unfailing bank.

One of the holiest and among the most gifted of Scotch preachers says: "I ought to spend the best hours in communion with God. It is my noblest and most fruitful employment, and is not to be thrust into a corner. The morning hours, from six to eight, are the most uninterrupted and should be thus employed. After tea is my best hour, and that should be solemnly dedicated to God. I ought not to give up the good old habit of prayer before going to bed; but guard must be kept against sleep. When I awake in the night, I ought to rise and pray. A little time after breakfast might be given to intercession." This was the praying plan of Robert McCheyne. The memorable Methodist band in their praying shame us. "From four to five in the morning, private prayer; from five to six in the evening, private prayer."

John Welch, the holy and wonderful Scotch preacher, thought the day ill spent if he did not spend eight or ten hours in prayer. He kept a plaid that he might wrap himself when he arose to pray at night. His wife would complain when she found him lying on the ground weeping. He would reply: "O woman, I have the souls of three thousand to answer for, and I know not how it is with many of them!"

8. Examples of Praying Men

The act of praying is the very highest energy of which the human mind is capable; praying, that is, with the total concentration of the faculties. The great mass of worldly men and of learned men are absolutely incapable of prayer.
—Samuel Taylor Coleridge

BISHOP WILSON says: "In H. Martyn's journal the spirit of prayer, the time he devoted to the duty, and his fervor in it are the first things which strike me."

Payson wore the hard-wood boards into grooves where his knees pressed so often and so long. His biographer says: "His continuing instant in prayer, be his circumstances what they might, is the most noticeable fact in his history, and points out the duty of all who would rival his eminency. To his ardent and persevering prayers must no doubt be ascribed in a great measure his distinguished and almost uninterrupted success."

The Marquis DeRenty, to whom Christ was most precious, ordered his servant to call him from his devotions at the end of half an hour. The servant at the time saw his face through an aperture. It was marked with such holiness that he hated to arouse him. His lips were moving, but he was perfectly silent. He waited until three half hours had passed; then he called to him, when he arose from his knees, saying that the half hour was so short when he was communing with Christ.

Brainerd said: "I love to be alone in my cottage, where I can spend much time in prayer."

William Bramwell is famous in Methodist annals for personal holiness and for his wonderful success in preaching and for the marvelous answers to his prayers. For hours at a time he would pray. He almost lived on his knees. He went over his circuits like a flame of fire. The fire was kindled by the time he spent in prayer. He often spent as much as four hours in a single season of prayer in retirement.

Bishop Andrewes spent the greatest part of five hours every day in prayer and devotion.

Sir Henry Havelock always spent the first two hours of each day alone with God. If the encampment was struck at 6 A.M., he would rise at four.

Earl Cairns rose daily at six o'clock to secure an hour and a half for the study of the Bible and for prayer, before conducting family worship at a quarter to eight.

Dr. Judson's success in prayer is attributable to the fact that he gave much time to prayer. He says on this point: "Arrange thy affairs, if possible, so that thou canst leisurely devote two or three hours every day not merely to devotional exercises but to the very act of secret prayer and communion with God. Endeavor seven times a day to withdraw from business and company and lift up thy soul to God in private retirement. Begin the day by rising after midnight and devoting some time amid the silence and darkness of the night to this sacred work. Let the hour of opening dawn find thee at the same work. Let the hours of nine, twelve, three, six, and nine at night witness the same. Be resolute in his cause. Make all practicable sacrifices to maintain it. Consider that thy time is short, and that business and company must not be allowed to rob thee of thy God." Impossible, say we, fanatical directions! Dr. Judson impressed an empire for Christ and laid the foundations of God's kingdom with imperishable granite in the heart of Burmah. He was successful, one of the few men who mightily impressed the world for Christ. Many men of greater gifts and genius and learning than he have made no such impression; their religious work is like footsteps in the sands, but he has engraven his work on the adamant. The secret of its profundity and endurance is found in the fact that he gave time to prayer. He kept the iron red-hot with prayer, and God's skill fashioned it with enduring power. No man can do a great and enduring work for God who is not a man of prayer, and no man can be a man of prayer who does not give much time to praying.

Is it true that prayer is simply the compliance with habit, dull and mechanical? A petty performance into which we are trained till tameness, shortness, superficiality are its chief elements? "Is it true that prayer is, as is assumed, little else than the half-passive play of sentiment which flows languidly on through the minutes or hours of easy reverie?" Canon Liddon continues: "Let those who have really prayed give the answer. They sometimes describe prayer with the patriarch Jacob as a wrestling together with an Unseen Power which may last, not unfrequently in an earnest life, late into the night hours, or even to the break of day. Sometimes they refer to common intercession with St. Paul as a concerted struggle. They have, when praying, their eyes fixed on the Great Intercessor in Gethsemane, upon the drops of blood which fall to the ground in that agony of resignation and sacrifice. Importunity is of the essence of successful prayer. Importunity means not dreaminess but sustained work. It is through prayer especially that the kingdom of heaven suffereth violence and the violent take it by force. It was a saying of the late Bishop Hamilton that "No man is likely to do much good in prayer who does not begin by looking upon it in the light of a work to be prepared for and persevered in with all the earnestness which we bring to bear upon subjects which are in our opinion at once most interesting and most necessary."

9. Begin the Day with Prayer

I ought to pray before seeing any one. Often when I sleep long, or meet with others early, it is eleven or twelve o'clock before I begin secret prayer. This is a wretched system. It is unscriptural. Christ arose before day and went into a solitary place. David says: "Early will I seek thee"; "Thou shalt early hear my voice." Family prayer loses much of its power and sweetness, and I can do no good to those who come to seek from me. The conscience feels guilty, the soul unfed, the lamp not trimmed. Then when in secret prayer the soul is often out of tune, I feel it is far better to begin with God—to see his face first, to get my soul near him before it is near another. —Robert Murray McCheyne

THE men who have done the most for God in this world have been early on their knees. He who fritters away the early morning, its opportunity and freshness, in other pursuits than seeking God will make poor headway seeking him the rest of the day. If God is not first in our thoughts and efforts in the morning, he will be in the last place the remainder of the day.

Behind this early rising and early praying is the ardent desire which presses us into this pursuit after God. Morning listlessness is the index to a listless heart. The heart which is behindhand in seeking God in the morning has lost its relish for God. David's heart was ardent after God. He hungered and thirsted after God, and so he sought God early, before daylight. The bed and sleep could not chain his soul in its eagerness after God. Christ longed for communion with God; and so, rising a great while before day, he would go out into the mountain to pray. The disciples, when fully awake and ashamed of their indulgence, would know where to find him. We might go through the list of men who have mightily impressed the world for God, and we would find them early after God.

A desire for God which cannot break the chains of sleep is a weak thing and will do but little good for God after it has indulged itself fully. The desire for God that keeps so far behind the devil and the world at the beginning of the day will never catch up.

It is not simply the getting up that puts men to the front and makes them captain generals in God's hosts, but it is the ardent desire which stirs and breaks all self-indulgent chains. But the getting up gives vent, increase, and strength to the desire. If they had lain in bed and indulged themselves, the desire would have been quenched. The desire aroused them and put them on the stretch for God, and this heeding and acting on the call gave their faith its grasp on God and gave to their hearts the sweetest and fullest revelation of God, and this strength of faith and fullness of revelation made them saints by eminence, and the halo of their sainthood has come down to us, and we have entered on the enjoyment of their conquests. But we take our fill in enjoyment, and not in productions. We build their tombs and write their epitaphs, but are careful not to follow their examples.

We need a generation of preachers who seek God and seek him early, who give the freshness and dew of effort to God, and secure in return the freshness and fullness of his power that he may be as the dew to them, full of gladness and strength, through all the heat and labor of the day. Our laziness after God is our crying sin. The children of this world are far wiser than we. They are at it early and late. We do not seek God with ardor and diligence. No man gets God who does not follow hard after him, and no soul follows hard after God who is not after him in early morn.

10. Prayer and Devotion United

There is a manifest want of spiritual influence on the ministry of the present day. I feel it in my own case and I see it in that of others. I am afraid there is too much of a low, managing, contriving, maneuvering temper of mind among us. We are laying ourselves out more than is expedient to meet one man's taste and another man's prejudices. The ministry is a grand and holy affair, and it should find in us a simple habit of spirit and a holy but humble indifference to all consequences. The leading defect in Christian ministers is want of a devotional habit. —Richard Cecil

NEVER was there greater need for saintly men and women; more imperative still is the call for saintly, God-devoted preachers. The world moves with gigantic strides. Satan has his hold and rule on the world, and labors to make all its movements subserve his ends. Religion must do its best work, present its most attractive and perfect models. By every means, modern sainthood must be inspired by the loftiest ideals and by the largest possibilities through the Spirit. Paul lived on his knees, that the Ephesian Church might measure the heights, breadths, and depths of an unmeasurable saintliness, and "be filled with all the fullness of God." Epaphras laid himself out with the exhaustive toil and strenuous conflict of fervent prayer, that the Colossian Church might "stand perfect and complete in all the will of God." Everywhere, everything in apostolic times was on the stretch that the people of God might each and "all come in the unity of the faith, and of the knowledge of the Son of God, unto a perfect man, unto the measure of the stature of the fullness of Christ." No premium was given to dwarfs; no encouragement to an old babyhood. The babies were to grow; the old, instead of feebleness and infirmities, were to bear fruit in old age, and be fat and flourishing. The divinest thing in religion is holy men and holy women.

No amount of money, genius, or culture can move things for God. Holiness energizing the soul, the whole man aflame with love, with desire for more faith, more prayer, more zeal, more consecration—this is the secret of power. These we need and must have, and men must be the incarnation of this God-inflamed devotedness. God's advance has been stayed, his cause crippled: his name dishonored for their lack. Genius (though the loftiest and most gifted), education (though the most learned and refined), position, dignity, place, honored names, high ecclesiastics cannot move this chariot of our God. It is a fiery one, and fiery forces only can move it. The genius of a Milton fails. The imperial strength of a Leo fails. Brainerd's spirit can move it. Brainerd's spirit was on fire for God, on fire for souls. Nothing earthly, worldly, selfish came in to abate in the least the intensity of this all-impelling and all-consuming force and flame.

Prayer is the creator as well as the channel of devotion. The spirit of devotion is the spirit of prayer. Prayer and devotion are united as soul and body are united, as life and the heart are united. There is no real prayer without devotion, no devotion without prayer. The preacher must be surrendered to God in the holiest devotion. He is not a professional man, his ministry is not a profession; it is a divine institution, a divine devotion. He is devoted to God. His aim, aspirations, ambition are for God and to God, and to such prayer is as essential as food is to life.

The preacher, above everything else, must be devoted to God. The preacher's relations to God are the insignia and credentials of his ministry. These must be clear, conclusive, unmistakable. No common, surface type of piety must be his. If he does not excel in grace, he does not excel at all. If he does not preach by life, character, conduct, he does not preach at all. If his piety be light, his preaching may be as soft and as sweet as music, as gifted as Apollo, yet its weight will be a feather's weight, visionary, fleeting as the morning cloud or the early dew. Devotion to God—there is no substitute for this in the preacher's character and conduct. Devotion to a Church, to opinions, to an organization, to orthodoxy—these are paltry, misleading, and vain when they become the source of inspiration, the animus of a call. God must be the mainspring of the preacher's effort, the fountain and crown of all his toil. The name and honor of Jesus Christ, the advance of his cause, must be all in all. The preacher must have no inspiration but the name of Jesus Christ, no ambition but to have him glorified, no toil but for him. Then prayer will be a source of his illuminations, the means of perpetual advance, the gauge of his success. The perpetual aim, the only ambition, the preacher can cherish is to have God with him.

Never did the cause of God need perfect illustrations of the possibilities of prayer more than in this age. No age, no person, will be ensamples of the gospel power except the ages or persons of deep and earnest prayer. A prayerless age will have but scant models of divine power. Prayerless hearts will never rise to these Alpine heights. The age may be a better age than the past, but there is an infinite distance between the betterment of an age by the force of an advancing civilization and its betterment by the increase of holiness and Christlikeness by the energy of prayer. The Jews were much better when Christ came than in the ages before. It was the golden age of their Pharisaic religion. Their golden religious age crucified Christ. Never more praying, never less praying; never more sacrifices, never less sacrifice; never less idolatry, never more idolatry; never more of temple worship, never less of God worship; never more of lip service, never less of heart service (God worshiped by lips whose hearts and hands crucified God's Son!); never more of churchgoers, never less of saints.

It is prayer-force which makes saints. Holy characters are formed by the power of real praying. The more of true saints, the more of praying; the more of praying, the more of true saints.

11. An Example of Devotion

I urge upon you communion with Christ a growing communion. There are curtains to be drawn aside in Christ that we never saw, and new foldings of love in him. I despair that I shall ever win to the far end of that love, there are so many plies in it. Therefore dig deep, and sweat and labor and take pains for him, and set by as much time in the day for him as you can. We will be won in the labor. —Samuel Rutherford

God has now, and has had, many of these devoted, prayerful preachers—men in whose lives prayer has been a mighty, controlling, conspicuous force. The world has felt their power, God has felt and honored their power, God's cause has moved mightily and swiftly by their prayers, holiness has shone out in their characters with a divine effulgence.

God found one of the men he was looking for in David Brainerd, whose work and name have gone into history. He was no ordinary man, but was capable of shining in any company, the peer of the wise and gifted ones, eminently suited to fill the most attractive pulpits and to labor among the most refined and the cultured, who were so anxious to secure him for their pastor. President Edwards bears testimony that he was "a young man of distinguished talents, had extraordinary knowledge of men and things, had rare conversational powers, excelled in his knowledge of theology, and was truly, for one so young, an extraordinary divine, and especially in all matters relating to experimental religion. I never knew his equal of his age and standing for clear and accurate notions of the nature and essence of true religion. His manner in prayer was almost inimitable, such as I have very rarely known equaled. His learning was very considerable, and he had extraordinary gifts for the pulpit."

No sublimer story has been recorded in earthly annals than that of David Brainerd; no miracle attests with diviner force the truth of Christianity than the life and work of such a man. Alone in the savage wilds of America, struggling day and night with a mortal disease, unschooled in the care of souls, having access to the Indians for a large portion of time only through the bungling medium of a pagan interpreter, with the Word of God in his heart and in his hand, his soul fired with the divine flame, a place and time to pour out his soul to God in prayer, he fully established the worship of God and secured all its gracious results. The Indians were changed with a great change from the lowest besotments of an ignorant and debased heathenism to pure, devout, intelligent Christians; all vice reformed, the external duties of Christianity at once embraced and acted on; family prayer set up; the Sabbath instituted and religiously observed; the internal graces of religion exhibited with growing sweetness and strength. The solution of these results is found in David Brainerd himself, not in the conditions or accidents but in the man Brainerd. He was God's man, for God first and last and all the time. God could flow unhindered through him. The omnipotence of grace was neither arrested nor straightened by the conditions of his heart; the whole channel was broadened and cleaned out for God's fullest and most powerful passage, so that God with all his mighty forces could come down on the hopeless, savage wilderness, and transform it into his blooming and fruitful garden; for nothing is too hard for God to do if he can get the right kind of a man to do it with.

Brainerd lived the life of holiness and prayer. His diary is full and monotonous with the record of his seasons of fasting, meditation, and retirement. The time he spent in private prayer amounted to many hours daily. "When I return home," he said, "and give myself to meditation, prayer, and fasting, my soul longs for mortification, self-denial, humility, and divorcement from all things of the world." "I have nothing to do," he said, "with earth but only to labor in it honestly for God. I do not desire to live one minute for anything which earth can afford." After this high order did he pray: "Feeling somewhat of the sweetness of communion with God and the constraining force of his love, and how admirably it captivates the soul and makes all the desires and affections to center in God, I set apart this day for secret fasting and prayer, to entreat God to direct and bless me with regard to the great work which I have in view of preaching the gospel, and that the Lord would return to me and show me the light of his countenance. I had little life and power in the forenoon. Near the middle of the afternoon God enabled me to wrestle ardently in intercession for my absent friends, but just at night the Lord visited me marvelously in prayer. I think my soul was never in such agony before. I felt no restraint, for the treasures of divine grace were opened to me. I wrestled for absent friends, for the ingathering of souls, for multitudes of poor souls, and for many that I thought were the children of God, personally, in many distant places. I was in such agony from sun half an hour high till near dark that I was all over wet with sweat, but yet it seemed to me I had done nothing. O, my dear Savior did sweat blood for poor souls! I longed for more compassion toward them. I felt still in a sweet frame, under a sense of divine love and grace, and went to bed in such a frame, with my heart set on God." It was prayer which gave to his life and ministry their marvelous power.

The men of mighty prayer are men of spiritual might. Prayers never die. Brainerd's whole life was a life of prayer. By day and by night he prayed. Before preaching and after preaching he prayed. Riding through the interminable solitudes of the forests he prayed. On his bed of straw he prayed. Retiring to the dense and lonely forests, he prayed. Hour by hour, day after day, early morn and late at night, he was praying and fasting, pouring out his soul, interceding, communing with God. He was with God mightily in prayer, and God was with him mightily, and by it he being dead yet speaketh and worketh, and will speak and work till the end comes, and among the glorious ones of that glorious day he will be with the first.

Jonathan Edwards says of him: "His life shows the right way to success in the works of the ministry. He sought it as the soldier seeks victory in a siege or battle; or as a man that runs a race for a great prize. Animated with love to Christ and souls, how did he labor? Always fervently. Not only in word and doctrine, in public and in private, but in prayers by day and night, wrestling with God in secret and travailing in birth with unutterable groans and agonies, until Christ was formed in the hearts of the people to whom he was sent. Like a true son of Jacob, he persevered in wrestling through all the darkness of the night, until the breaking of the day!"

12. Heart Preparation Necessary

For nothing reaches the heart but what is from the heart or pierces the conscience but what comes from a living conscience. —William Penn

In the morning was more engaged in preparing the head than the heart. This has been frequently my error, and I have always felt the evil of it especially in prayer. Reform it then, O Lord! Enlarge my heart and I shall preach.
—Robert Murray McCheyne

A sermon that has more head infused into it than heart will not borne home with efficacy to the hearers. —Richard Cecil

PRAYER, with its manifold and many-sided forces, helps the mouth to utter the truth in its fullness and freedom. The preacher is to be prayed for, the preacher is made by prayer. The preacher's mouth is to be prayed for; his mouth is to be opened and filled by prayer. A holy mouth is made by praying, by much praying; a brave mouth is made by praying, by much praying. The Church and the world, God and heaven, owe much to Paul's mouth; Paul's mouth owed its power to prayer.

How manifold, illimitable, valuable, and helpful prayer is to the preacher in so many ways, at so many points, in every way! One great value is, it helps his heart.

Praying makes the preacher a heart preacher. Prayer puts the preacher's heart into the preacher's sermon; prayer puts the preacher's sermon into the preacher's heart.

The heart makes the preacher. Men of great hearts are great preachers. Men of bad hearts may do a measure of good, but this is rare. The hireling and the stranger may help the sheep at some points, but it is the good shepherd with the good shepherd's heart who will bless the sheep and answer the full measure of the shepherd's place.

We have emphasized sermon-preparation until we have lost sight of the important thing to be prepared—the heart. A prepared heart is much better than a prepared sermon. A prepared heart will make a prepared sermon.

Volumes have been written laying down the mechanics and taste of sermon-making, until we have become possessed with the idea that this scaffolding is the building. The young preacher has been taught to lay out all his strength on the form, taste, and beauty of his sermon as a mechanical and intellectual product. We have thereby cultivated a vicious taste among the people and raised the clamor for talent instead of grace, eloquence instead of piety, rhetoric instead of revelation, reputation and brilliancy instead of holiness. By it we have lost the true idea of preaching, lost preaching power, lost pungent conviction for sin, lost the rich experience and elevated Christian character, lost the authority over consciences and lives which always results from genuine preaching.

It would not do to say that preachers study too much. Some of them do not study at all; others do not study enough. Numbers do not study the right way to show themselves workmen approved of God. But our great lack is not in head culture, but in heart culture; not lack of knowledge but lack of holiness is our sad and telling defect—not that we know too much, but that we do not meditate on God and his word and watch and fast and pray enough. The heart is the great hindrance to our preaching. Words pregnant with divine truth find in our hearts nonconductors; arrested, they fall shorn and powerless.

Can ambition, that lusts after praise and place, preach the gospel of Him who made himself of no reputation and took on Him the form of a servant? Can the proud, the vain, the egotistical preach the gospel of him who was meek and lowly? Can the bad-tempered, passionate, selfish, hard, worldly man preach the system which teems with long-suffering, self-denial, tenderness, which imperatively demands separation from enmity and crucifixion to the world? Can the hireling official, heartless, perfunctory, preach the gospel which demands the shepherd to give his life for the sheep? Can the covetous man, who counts salary and money, preach the gospel till he has gleaned his heart and can say in the spirit of Christ and Paul in the words of Wesley: "I count it dung and dross; I trample it under my feet; I (yet not I, but the grace of God in me) esteem it just as the mire of the streets, I desire it not, I seek it not?" God's revelation does not need the light of human genius, the polish and strength of human culture, the brilliancy of human thought, the force of human brains to adorn or enforce it; but it does demand the simplicity, the docility, humility, and faith of a child's heart.

It was this surrender and subordination of intellect and genius to the divine and spiritual forces which made Paul peerless among the apostles. It was this which gave Wesley his power and radicated his labors in the history of humanity. This gave to Loyola the strength to arrest the retreating forces of Catholicism.

Our great need is heart-preparation. Luther held it as an axiom: "He who has prayed well has studied well." We do not say that men are not to think and use their intellects; but he will use his intellect best who cultivates his heart most. We do not say that preachers should not be students; but we do say that their great study should be the Bible, and he studies the Bible best who has kept his heart with diligence. We do not say that the preacher should not know men, but he will be the greater adept in human nature who has fathomed the depths and intricacies of his own heart. We do say that while the channel of preaching is the mind, its fountain is the heart; you may broaden and deepen the channel, but if you do not look well to the purity and depth of the fountain, you will have a dry or polluted channel. We do say that almost any man of common intelligence has sense enough to preach the gospel, but very few have grace enough to do so. We do say that he who has struggled with his own heart and conquered it; who has taught it humility, faith, love, truth, mercy, sympathy, courage; who can pour the rich treasures of the heart thus trained, through a manly intellect, all surcharged with the power of the gospel on the consciences of his hearers—such a one will be the truest, most successful preacher in the esteem of his Lord.

13. Grace from the Heart Rather than the Head

Study not to be a fine preacher. Jerichos are blown down with rams' horns. Look simply unto Jesus for preaching food; and what is wanted will be given, and what is given will be blessed, whether it be a barley grain or a wheaten loaf, a crust or a crumb. Your mouth will be a flowing stream or a fountain sealed, according as your heart is. Avoid all controversy in preaching, talking, or writing; preach nothing down but the devil, and nothing up but Jesus Christ.
—Berridge

THE heart is the Savior of the world. Heads do not save. Genius, brains, brilliancy, strength, natural gifts do not save. The gospel flows through hearts. All the mightiest forces are heart forces. All the sweetest and loveliest graces are heart graces. Great hearts make great characters; great hearts make divine characters. God is love. There is nothing greater than love, nothing greater than God. Hearts make heaven; heaven is love. There is nothing higher, nothing sweeter, than heaven. It is the heart and not the head which makes God's great preachers. The heart counts much every way in religion. The heart must speak from the pulpit. The heart must hear in the pew. In fact, we serve God with our hearts. Head homage does not pass current in heaven.

We believe that one of the serious and most popular errors of the modern pulpit is the putting of more thought than prayer, of more head than of heart in its sermons. Big hearts make big preachers; good hearts make good preachers. A theological school to enlarge and cultivate the heart is the golden desideratum of the gospel. The pastor binds his people to him and rules his people by his heart. They may admire his gifts, they may be proud of his ability, they may be affected for the time by his sermons; but the stronghold of his power is his heart. His scepter is love. The throne of his power is his heart.

The good shepherd gives his life for the sheep. Heads never make martyrs. It is the heart which surrenders the life to love and fidelity. It takes great courage to be a faithful pastor, but the heart alone can supply this courage. Gifts and genius may be brave, but it is the gifts and genius of the heart and not of the head.

It is easier to fill the head than it is to prepare the heart. It is easier to make a brain sermon than a heart sermon. It was heart that drew the Son of God from heaven. It is heart that will draw men to heaven. Men of heart is what the world needs to sympathize with its woe, to kiss away its sorrows, to compassionate its misery, and to alleviate its pain. Christ was eminently the man of sorrows, because he was preeminently the man of heart.

"Give me thy heart," is God's requisition of men. "Give me thy heart!" is man's demand of man.

A professional ministry is a heartless ministry. When salary plays a great part in the ministry, the heart plays little part. We may make preaching our business, and not put our hearts in the business. He who puts self to the front in his preaching puts heart to the rear. He who does not sow with his heart in his study will never reap a harvest for God. The closet is the heart's study. We will learn more about how to preach and what to preach there than we can learn in our libraries. "Jesus wept" is the shortest and biggest verse in the Bible. It is he who goes forth *weeping* (not preaching great sermons), bearing precious seed, who shall come again rejoicing, bringing his sheaves with him.

Praying gives sense, brings wisdom, broadens and strengthens the mind. The closet is a perfect school-teacher and schoolhouse for the preacher. Thought is not only brightened and clarified in prayer, but thought is born in prayer. We can learn more in an hour praying, when praying indeed, than from many hours in the study. Books are in the closet which can be found and read nowhere else. Revelations are made in the closet which are made nowhere else.

14. Unction a Necessity

One bright benison which private prayer brings down upon the ministry is an indescribable and inimitable something—an unction from the Holy One . . . . If the anointing which we bear come not from the Lord of hosts, we are deceivers, since only in prayer can we obtain it. Let us continue instant constant fervent in supplication. Let your fleece lie on the thrashing floor of supplication till it is wet with the dew of heaven. —Charles Haddon Spurgeon

ALEXANDER KNOX, a Christian philosopher of the days of Wesley, not an adherent but a strong personal friend of Wesley, and with much spiritual sympathy with the Wesleyan movement, writes: "It is strange and lamentable, but I verily believe the fact to be that except among Methodists and Methodistical clergyman, there is not much interesting preaching in England. The clergy, too generally have absolutely lost the art. There is, I conceive, in the great laws of the moral world a kind of secret understanding like the affinities in chemistry, between rightly promulgated religious truth and the deepest feelings of the human mind. Where the one is duly exhibited, the other will respond. Did not our hearts burn within us?—but to this devout feeling is indispensable in the speaker. Now, I am obliged to state from my own observation that this *onction*, as the French not unfitly term it, is beyond all comparison more likely to be found in England in a Methodist conventicle than in a parish Church. This, and this alone, seems really to be that which fills the Methodist houses and thins the Churches. I am, I verily think, no enthusiast; I am a most sincere and cordial churchman, a humble disciple of the School of Hale and Boyle, of Burnet and Leighton. Now I must aver that when I was in this country, two years ago, I did not hear a single preacher who taught me like my own great masters but such as are deemed Methodistical. And I now despair of getting an atom of heart instruction from any other quarter. The Methodist preachers (however I may not always approve of all their expressions) do most assuredly diffuse this true religion and undefiled. I felt real pleasure last Sunday. I can bear witness that the preacher did at once speak the words of truth and soberness. There was no eloquence— the honest man never dreamed of such a thing—but there was far better: a cordial communication of vitalized truth. I say vitalized because what he declared to others it was impossible not to feel he lived on himself."

This unction is the art of preaching. The preacher who never had this unction never had the art of preaching. The preacher who has lost this unction has lost the art of preaching. Whatever other arts he may have and retain—the art of sermon-making, the art of eloquence, the art of great, clear thinking, the art of pleasing an audience—he has lost the divine art of preaching. This unction makes God's truth powerful and interesting, draws and attracts, edifies, convicts, saves.

This unction vitalizes God's revealed truth, makes it living and life-giving. Even God's truth spoken without this unction is light, dead, and deadening. Though abounding in truth, though weighty with thought, though sparkling with rhetoric, though pointed by logic, though powerful by earnestness, without this divine unction it issues in death and not in life. Mr. Spurgeon says: "I wonder how long we might beat our brains before we could plainly put into word what is meant by preaching with unction. Yet he who preaches knows its presence, and he who hears soon detects its absence. Samaria, in famine, typifies a discourse without it. Jerusalem, with her feast of fat things, full of marrow, may represent a sermon enriched with it. Every one knows what the freshness of the morning is when orient pearls abound on every blade of grass, but who can describe it, much less produce it of itself? Such is the mystery of spiritual anointing. We know, but we cannot tell to others what it is. It is as easy as it is foolish, to counterfeit it. Unction is a thing which you cannot manufacture, and its counterfeits are worse than worthless. Yet it is, in itself, priceless, and beyond measure needful if you would edify believers and bring sinners to Christ."

15. Unction, the Mark of True Gospel Preaching

Speak for eternity. Above all things, cultivate your own spirit. A word spoken by you when your conscience is clear and your heart full of God's Spirit is worth ten thousand words spoken in unbelief and sin. Remember that God, and not man, must have the glory. If the veil of the world's machinery were lifted off, how much we would find is done in answer to the prayers of God's children.
—Robert Murray McCheyne

UNCTION is that indefinable, indescribable something which an old, renowned Scotch preacher describes thus: "There is sometimes somewhat in preaching that cannot be ascribed either to matter or expression, and cannot be described what it is, or from whence it cometh, but with a sweet violence it pierceth into the heart and affections and comes immediately from the Word; but if there be any way to obtain such a thing, it is by the heavenly disposition of the speaker."

We call it unction. It is this unction which makes the word of God "quick and powerful, and sharper than any two-edged sword, piercing even to the dividing asunder of soul and spirit, and of the joints and marrow, and a discerner of the thoughts and intents of the heart." It is this unction which gives the words of the preacher such point, sharpness, and power, and which creates such friction and stir in many a dead congregation. The same truths have been told in the strictness of the letter, smooth as human oil could make them; but no signs of life, not a pulse throb; all as peaceful as the grave and as dead. The same preacher in the meanwhile receives a baptism of this unction, the divine inflatus is on him, the letter of the Word has been embellished and fired by this mysterious power, and the throbbings of life begin—life which receives or life which resists. The unction pervades and convicts the conscience and breaks the heart.

This divine unction is the feature which separates and distinguishes true gospel preaching from all other methods of presenting the truth, and which creates a wide spiritual chasm between the preacher who has it and the one who has it not. It backs and impregnates revealed truth with all the energy of God. Unction is simply putting God in his own word and on his own preachers. By mighty and great prayerfulness and by continual prayerfulness, it is all potential and personal to the preacher; it inspires and clarifies his intellect, gives insight and grasp and projecting power; it gives to the preacher heart power, which is greater than head power; and tenderness, purity, force flow from the heart by it. Enlargement, freedom, fullness of thought, directness and simplicity of utterance are the fruits of this unction.

Often earnestness is mistaken for this unction. He who has the divine unction will be earnest in the very spiritual nature of things, but there may be a vast deal of earnestness without the least mixture of unction.

Earnestness and unction look alike from some points of view. Earnestness may be readily and without detection substituted or mistaken for unction. It requires a spiritual eye and a spiritual taste to discriminate.

Earnestness may be sincere, serious, ardent, and persevering. It goes at a thing with good will, pursues it with perseverance, and urges it with ardor; puts force in it. But all these forces do not rise higher than the mere human. The *man* is in it—the whole man, with all that he has of will and heart, of brain and genius, of planning and working and talking. He has set himself to some purpose which has mastered him, and he pursues to master it. There may be none of God in it. There may be little of God in it, because there is so much of the man in it. He may present pleas in advocacy of his earnest purpose which please or touch and move or overwhelm with conviction of their importance; and in all this earnestness may move along earthly ways, being propelled by human forces only, its altar made by earthly hands and its fire kindled by earthly flames. It is said of a rather famous preacher of gifts, whose construction of Scripture was to his fancy or purpose, that he "grew very eloquent over his own exegesis." So men grow exceeding earnest over their own plans or movements. Earnestness may be selfishness simulated.

What of unction? It is the indefinable in preaching which makes it preaching. It is that which distinguishes and separates preaching from all mere human addresses. It is the divine in preaching. It makes the preaching sharp to those who need sharpness. It distills as the dew to those who need to he refreshed. It is well described as:

> *"...a two-edged sword*
> *Of heavenly temper keen,*
> *And double were the wounds it made*
> *Wherever it glanced between.*
> *'Twas death to silt; 'twas life*
> *To all who mourned for sin.*
> *It kindled and it silenced strife,*
> *Made war and peace within."*

This unction comes to the preacher not in the study but in the closet. It is heaven's distillation in answer to prayer. It is the sweetest exhalation of the Holy Spirit. It impregnates, suffuses, softens, percolates, cuts, and soothes. It carries the Word like dynamite, like salt, like sugar; makes the Word a soother, an arranger, a revealer, a searcher; makes the hearer a culprit or a saint, makes him weep like a child and live like a giant; opens his heart and his purse as gently, yet as strongly as the spring opens the leaves. This unction is not the gift of genius. It is not found in the halls of learning. No eloquence can woo it. No industry can win it. No prelatical hands can confer it. It is the gift of God—the signet set to his own messengers. It is heaven's knighthood given to the chosen true and brave ones who have sought this anointed honor through many an hour of tearful, wrestling prayer.

Earnestness is good and impressive: genius is gifted and great. Thought kindles and inspires, but it takes a diviner endowment, a more powerful energy than earnestness or genius or thought to break the chains of sin, to win estranged and depraved hearts to God, to repair the breaches and restore the Church to her old ways of purity and power. Nothing but this holy unction can do this.

16. Much Prayer the Price of Unction

All the minister's efforts will be vanity or worse than vanity if he have not unction. Unction must come down from heaven and spread a savor and feeling and relish over his ministry; and among the other means of qualifying himself for his office, the Bible must hold the first place, and the last also must be given to the Word of God and prayer. —Richard Cecil

IN the Christian system unction is the anointing of the Holy Ghost, separating unto God's work and qualifying for it. This unction is the one divine enablement by which the preacher accomplishes the peculiar and saving ends of preaching. Without this unction there are no true spiritual results accomplished; the results and forces in preaching do not rise above the results of unsanctified speech. Without unction the former is as potent as the pulpit.

This divine unction on the preacher generates through the Word of God the spiritual results that flow from the gospel; and without this unction, these results are not secured. Many pleasant impressions may be made, but these all fall far below the ends of gospel preaching. This unction may be simulated. There are many things that look like it, there are many results that resemble its effects; but they are foreign to its results and to its nature. The fervor or softness excited by a pathetic or emotional sermon may look like the movements of the divine unction, but they have no pungent, perpetrating heart-breaking force. No heart-healing balm is there in these surface, sympathetic, emotional movements; they are not radical, neither sin-searching nor sin-curing.

This divine unction is the one distinguishing feature that separates true gospel preaching from all other methods of presenting truth. It backs and interpenetrates the revealed truth with all the force of God. It illumines the Word and broadens and enrichens the intellect and empowers it to grasp and apprehend the Word. It qualifies the preacher's heart, and brings it to that condition of tenderness, of purity, of force and light that are necessary to secure the highest results. This unction gives to the preacher liberty and enlargement of thought and soul—a freedom, fullness, and directness of utterance that can be secured by no other process.

Without this unction on the preacher the gospel has no more power to propagate itself than any other system of truth. This is the seal of its divinity. Unction in the preacher puts God in the gospel. Without the unction, God is absent, and the gospel is left to the low and unsatisfactory forces that the ingenuity, interest, or talents of men can devise to enforce and project its doctrines.

It is in this element that the pulpit oftener fails than in any other element. Just at this all-important point it lapses. Learning it may have, brilliancy and eloquence may delight and charm, sensation or less offensive methods may bring the populace in crowds, mental power may impress and enforce truth with all its resources; but without this unction, each and all these will be but as the fretful assault of the waters on a Gibraltar. Spray and foam may cover and spangle; but the rocks are there still, unimpressed and unimpressible. The human heart can no more be swept of its hardness and sin by these human forces than these rocks can be swept away by the ocean's ceaseless flow.

This unction is the consecration force, and its presence the continuous test of that consecration. It is this divine anointing on the preacher that secures his consecration to

God and his work. Other forces and motives may call him to the work, but this only is consecration. A separation to God's work by the power of the Holy Spirit is the only consecration recognized by God as legitimate.

The unction, the divine unction, this heavenly anointing, is what the pulpit needs and must have. This divine and heavenly oil put on it by the imposition of God's hand must soften and lubricate the whole man—heart, head, spirit—until it separates him with a mighty separation from all earthly, secular, worldly, selfish motives and aims, separating him to everything that is pure and Godlike.

It is the presence of this unction on the preacher that creates the stir and friction in many a congregation. The same truths have been told in the strictness of the letter, but no ruffle has been seen, no pain or pulsation felt. All is quiet as a graveyard. Another preacher comes, and this mysterious influence is on him; the letter of the Word has been fired by the Spirit, the throes of a mighty movement are felt, it is the unction that pervades and stirs the conscience and breaks the heart. Unctionless preaching makes everything hard, dry, acrid, dead.

This unction is not a memory or an era of the past only; it is a present, realized, conscious fact. It belongs to the experience of the man as well as to his preaching. It is that which transforms him into the image of his divine Master, as well as that by which he declares the truths of Christ with power. It is so much the power in the ministry as to make all else seem feeble and vain without it, and by its presence to atone for the absence of all other and feebler forces.

This unction is not an inalienable gift. It is a conditional gift, and its presence is perpetuated and increased by the same process by which it was at first secured; by unceasing prayer to God, by impassioned desires after God, by estimating it, by seeking it with tireless ardor, by deeming all else loss and failure without it.

How and whence comes this unction? Direct from God in answer to prayer. Praying hearts only are the hearts filled with this holy oil; praying lips only are anointed with this divine unction.

Prayer, much prayer, is the price of preaching unction; prayer, much prayer, is the one, sole condition of keeping this unction. Without unceasing prayer the unction never comes to the preacher. Without perseverance in prayer, the unction, like the manna overkept, breeds worms.

17. Prayer Marks Spiritual Leadership

Give me one hundred preachers who fear nothing but sin and desire nothing but God, and I care not a straw whether they be clergymen or laymen; such alone will shake the gates of hell and set up the kingdom of heaven on earth. God does nothing but in answer to prayer. —John Wesley

THE apostles knew the necessity and worth of prayer to their ministry. They knew that their high commission as apostles, instead of relieving them from the necessity of prayer, committed them to it by a more urgent need; so that they were exceedingly jealous else some other important work should exhaust their time and prevent their praying as they ought; so they appointed laymen to look after the delicate and engrossing duties of ministering to the poor, that they (the apostles) might, unhindered, "give themselves continually to prayer and to the ministry of the word." Prayer is put first, and their relation to prayer is put most strongly—"give themselves to it," making a business of it, surrendering themselves to praying, putting fervor, urgency, perseverance, and time in it.

How holy, apostolic men devoted themselves to this divine work of prayer! "Night and day praying exceedingly," says Paul. "We will give ourselves continually to prayer" is the consensus of apostolic devotement. How these New Testament preachers laid themselves out in prayer for God's people! How they put God in full force into their Churches by their praying! These holy apostles did not vainly fancy that they had met their high and solemn duties by delivering faithfully God's word, but their preaching was made to stick and tell by the ardor and insistence of their praying. Apostolic praying was as taxing, toilsome, and imperative as apostolic preaching. They prayed mightily day and night to bring their people to the highest regions of faith and holiness. They prayed mightier still to hold them to this high spiritual altitude. The preacher who has never learned in the school of Christ the high and divine art of intercession for his people will never learn the art of preaching, though homiletics be poured into him by the ton, and though he be the most gifted genius in sermon-making and sermon-delivery.

The prayers of apostolic, saintly leaders do much in making saints of those who are not apostles. If the Church leaders in after years had been as particular and fervent in praying for their people as the apostles were, the sad, dark times of worldliness and apostasy had not marred the history and eclipsed the glory and arrested the advance of the Church. Apostolic praying makes apostolic saints and keeps apostolic times of purity and power in the Church.

What loftiness of soul, what purity and elevation of motive, what unselfishness, what self-sacrifice, what exhaustive toil, what ardor of spirit, what divine tact are requisite to be an intercessor for men!

The preacher is to lay himself out in prayer for his people; not that they might be saved, simply, but that they be mightily saved. The apostles laid themselves out in prayer that their saints might be perfect; not that they should have a little relish for the things of God, but that they "might be filled with all the fullness of God." Paul did not rely on his apostolic preaching to secure this end, but "for this cause he bowed his knees to the Father of our Lord Jesus Christ." Paul's praying carried Paul's converts farther along the highway of sainthood than Paul's preaching did. Epaphras did as much or more by prayer for the Colossian saints than by his preaching. He labored fervently always in prayer for them that "they might stand perfect and complete in all the will of God."

Preachers are preeminently God's leaders. They are primarily responsible for the condition of the Church. They shape its character, give tone and direction to its life.

Much every way depends on these leaders. They shape the times and the institutions. The Church is divine, the treasure it incases is heavenly, but it bears the imprint of the human. The treasure is in earthen vessels, and it smacks of the vessel. The Church of God makes, or is made by, its leaders. Whether it makes them or is made by them, it will be what its leaders are; spiritual if they are so, secular if they are, conglomerate if its leaders are. Israel's kings gave character to Israel's piety. A Church rarely revolts against or rises above the religion of its leaders. Strongly spiritual leaders; men of holy might, at the lead, are tokens of God's favor; disaster and weakness follow the wake of feeble or worldly leaders. Israel had fallen low when God gave children to be their princes and babes to rule over them. No happy state is predicted by the prophets when children oppress God's Israel and women rule over them. Times of spiritual leadership are times of great spiritual prosperity to the Church.

Prayer is one of the eminent characteristics of strong spiritual leadership. Men of mighty prayer are men of might and mold things. Their power with God has the conquering tread.

How can a man preach who does not get his message fresh from God in the closet? How can he preach without having his faith quickened, his vision cleared, and his heart warmed by his closeting with God? Alas, for the pulpit lips which are untouched by this closet flame. Dry and unctionless they will ever be, and truths divine will never come with power from such lips. As far as the real interests of religion are concerned, a pulpit without a closet will always be a barren thing.

A preacher may preach in an official, entertaining, or learned way without prayer, but between this kind of preaching and sowing God's precious seed with holy hands and prayerful, weeping hearts there is an immeasurable distance.

A prayerless ministry is the undertaker for all God's truth and for God's Church. He may have the most costly casket and the most beautiful flowers, but it is a funeral, notwithstanding the charmful array. A prayerless Christian will never learn God's truth; a prayerless ministry will never be able to teach God's truth. Ages of millennial glory have been lost by a prayerless Church. The coming of our Lord has been postponed indefinitely by a prayerless Church. Hell has enlarged herself and filled her dire caves in the presence of the dead service of a prayerless Church.

The best, the greatest offering is an offering of prayer. If the preachers of the twentieth century will learn well the lesson of prayer, and use fully the power of prayer, the millennium will come to its noon ere the century closes. "Pray without ceasing" is the trumpet call to the preachers of the twentieth century. If the twentieth century will get their texts, their thoughts, their words, their sermons in their closets, the next century will find a new heaven and a new earth. The old sin-stained and sin-eclipsed heaven and earth will pass away under the power of a praying ministry.

18. Preachers Need the Prayers of the People

If some Christians that have been complaining of their ministers had said and acted less before men and had applied themselves with all their might to cry to God for their ministers—had, as it were, risen and stormed heaven with their humble, fervent and incessant prayers for them—they would have been much more in the way of success. —Jonathan Edwards

SOMEHOW the practice of praying in particular for the preacher has fallen into disuse or become discounted. Occasionally have we heard the practice arraigned as a disparagement of the ministry, being a public declaration by those who do it of the inefficiency of the ministry. It offends the pride of learning and self-sufficiency, perhaps, and these ought to be offended and rebuked in a ministry that is so derelict as to allow them to exist.

Prayer, to the preacher, is not simply the duty of his profession, a privilege, but it is a necessity. Air is not more necessary to the lungs than prayer is to the preacher. It is absolutely necessary for the preacher to pray. It is an absolute necessity that the preacher be prayed for. These two propositions are wedded into a union which ought never to know any divorce: *the preacher must pray; the preacher must be prayed for.* It will take all the praying he can do, and all the praying he can get done, to meet the fearful responsibilities and gain the largest, truest success in his great work. The true preacher, next to the cultivation of the spirit and fact of prayer in himself, in their intensest form, covets with a great covetousness the prayers of God's people.

The holier a man is, the more does he estimate prayer; the clearer does he see that God gives himself to the praying ones, and that the measure of God's revelation to the soul is the measure of the soul's longing, importunate prayer for God. Salvation never finds its way to a prayerless heart. The Holy Spirit never abides in a prayerless spirit. Preaching never edifies a prayerless soul. Christ knows nothing of prayerless Christians. The gospel cannot be projected by a prayerless preacher. Gifts, talents, education, eloquence, God's call, cannot abate the demand of prayer, but only intensify the necessity for the preacher to pray and to be prayed for. The more the preacher's eyes are opened to the nature, responsibility, and difficulties in his work, the more will he see, and if he be a true preacher the more will he feel, the necessity of prayer; not only the increasing demand to pray himself, but to call on others to help him by their prayers.

Paul is an illustration of this. If any man could project the gospel by dint of personal force, by brain power, by culture, by personal grace, by God's apostolic commission, God's extraordinary call, that man was Paul. That the preacher must be a man given to prayer, Paul is an eminent example. That the true apostolic preacher must have the prayers of other good people to give to his ministry its full quota of success, Paul is a preeminent example. He asks, he covets, he pleads in an impassioned way for the help of all God's saints. He knew that in the spiritual realm, as elsewhere, in union there is strength; that the concentration and aggregation of faith, desire, and prayer increased the volume of spiritual force until it became overwhelming and irresistible in its power. Units of prayer combined, like drops of water, make an ocean which defies resistance. So Paul, with his clear and full apprehension of spiritual dynamics, determined to make his ministry as impressive, as eternal, as irresistible as the ocean, by gathering all the scattered units of prayer and precipitating them on his ministry. May not the solution of Paul's preeminence in labors and results, and impress on the Church and the world, be found in this fact that he was able to center on himself and his ministry more of prayer than others? To his brethren at Rome he wrote: "Now I beseech you, brethren, for the Lord Jesus Christ's sake, and for the love of the Spirit, that ye strive together with me in prayers to God for me." To the Ephesians he says: "Praying always with all prayer and supplication in the Spirit, and watching thereunto with all perseverance and supplication for all saints; and for me, that utterance may be given unto me, that I may open my mouth boldly, to make known the mystery of the gospel." To the Colossians he emphasizes: "Withal praying also for us, that God would open unto us a door of utterance, to speak the mystery of Christ, for which I am also in bonds: that I may make it manifest as I ought to speak." To the Thessalonians he says sharply, strongly:

"Brethren, pray for us." Paul calls on the Corinthian Church to help him: "Ye also helping together by prayer for us." This was to be part of their work. They were to lay to the helping hand of prayer. He in an additional and closing charge to the Thessalonian Church about the importance and necessity of their prayers says: "Finally, brethren, pray for us, that the word of the Lord may have free course, and be glorified, even as it is with you: and that we may be delivered from unreasonable and wicked men." He impresses the Philippians that all his trials and opposition can be made subservient to the spread of the gospel by the efficiency of their prayers for him. Philemon was to prepare a lodging for him, for through Philemon's prayer Paul was to be his guest.

Paul's attitude on this question illustrates his humility and his deep insight into the spiritual forces which project the gospel. More than this, it teaches a lesson for all times, that if Paul was so dependent on the prayers of God's saints to give his ministry success, how much greater the necessity that the prayers of God's saints be centered on the ministry of to-day!

Paul did not feel that this urgent plea for prayer was to lower his dignity, lessen his influence, or depreciate his piety. What if it did? Let dignity go, let influence be destroyed, let his reputation be marred—he must have their prayers. Called, commissioned, chief of the Apostles as he was, all his equipment was imperfect without the prayers of his people. He wrote letters everywhere, urging them to pray for him. Do you pray for your preacher? Do you pray for him in secret? Public prayers are of little worth unless they are founded on or followed up by private praying. The praying ones are to the preacher as Aaron and Hur were to Moses. They hold up his hands and decide the issue that is so fiercely raging around them.

The plea and purpose of the apostles were to put the Church to praying. They did not ignore the grace of cheerful giving. They were not ignorant of the place which religious activity and work occupied an the spiritual life; but not one nor all of these, in apostolic estimate or urgency, could at all compare in necessity and importance with prayer. The most sacred and urgent pleas were used, the most fervid exhortations, the most comprehensive and arousing words were uttered to enforce the all-important obligation and necessity of prayer.

"Put the saints everywhere to praying" is the burden of the apostolic effort and the keynote of apostolic success. Jesus Christ had striven to do this in the days of his personal ministry. As he was moved by infinite compassion at the ripened fields of earth perishing for lack of laborers and pausing in his own praying—he tries to awaken the stupid sensibilities of his disciples to the duty of prayer as he charges them, "Pray ye the Lord of the harvest that he will send forth laborers into his harvest." "And he spake a parable unto them to this end, that men ought always to pray and not to faint."

19. Deliberation Necessary to Largest Results from Prayer

This perpetual hurry of business and company ruins me in soul if not in body. More solitude and earlier hours! I suspect I have been allotting habitually too little time to religious exercises, as private devotion and religious meditation, Scripture-reading, etc. Hence I am lean and cold and hard. I had better allot two hours or an hour and a half daily. I have been keeping too late hours, and hence have had but a hurried half hour in a morning to myself. Surely the experience of all good men confirms the proposition that without a due measure of private devotions the soul will grow lean. But all may be done through prayer—almighty prayer, I am ready to say—and why not? For that it is almighty is only through the gracious ordination of the God of love and truth. O then, pray, pray, pray! —William Wilberforce

OUR devotions are not measured by the clock, but time is of their essence. The ability to wait and stay and press belongs essentially to our intercourse with God. Hurry, everywhere unseeming and damaging, is so to an alarming extent in the great business of communion with God. Short devotions are the bane of deep piety. Calmness, grasp, strength, are never the companions of hurry. Short devotions deplete spiritual vigor, arrest spiritual progress, sap spiritual foundations, blight the root and bloom of spiritual life. They are the prolific source of backsliding, the sure indication of a superficial piety; they deceive, blight, rot the seed, and impoverish the soil.

It is true that Bible prayers in word and print are short, but the praying men of the Bible were with God through many a sweet and holy wrestling hour. They won by few words but long waiting. The prayers Moses records may be short, but Moses prayed to God with fastings and mighty cryings forty days and nights.

The statement of Elijah's praying may be condensed to a few brief paragraphs, but doubtless Elijah, who when "praying he prayed," spent many hours of fiery struggle and lofty intercourse with God before he could, with assured boldness, say to Ahab, "There shall not be dew nor rain these years, but according to my word." The verbal brief of Paul's prayers is short, but Paul "prayed night and day exceedingly." The "Lord's Prayer" is a divine epitome for infant lips, but the man Christ Jesus prayed many an all-night ere his work was done; and his all-night and long-sustained devotions gave to his work its finish and perfection, and to his character the fullness and glory of its divinity.

Spiritual work is taxing work, and men are loath to do it. Praying, true praying, costs an outlay of serious attention and of time, which flesh and blood do not relish. Few persons are made of such strong fiber that they will make a costly outlay when surface work will pass as well in the market. We can habituate ourselves to our beggarly praying until it looks well to us, at least it keeps up a decent form and quiets conscience—the deadliest of opiates! We can slight our praying, and not realize the peril till the foundations are gone. Hurried devotions make weak faith, feeble convictions, questionable piety. To be little with God is to be little for God. To cut short the praying makes the whole religious character short, scrimp, niggardly, and slovenly.

It takes good time for the full flow of God into the spirit. Short devotions cut the pipe of God's full flow. It takes time in the secret places to get the full revelation of God. Little time and hurry mar the picture.

Henry Martyn laments that "want of private devotional reading and shortness of prayer through incessant sermon-making had produced much strangeness between God and his soul." He judged that he had dedicated too much time to public ministrations and too little to private communion with God. He was much impressed to set apart times for fasting and to devote times for solemn prayer. Resulting from this he records: "Was assisted this morning to pray for two hours." Said William Wilberforce, the peer of kings: "I must secure more time for private devotions. I have been living far too public for me. The shortening of private devotions starves the soul; it grows lean and faint. I have been keeping too late hours." Of a failure in Parliament he says: "Let me record my grief and shame, and all, probably, from private devotions having been contracted, and so God let me stumble." More solitude and earlier hours was his remedy.

More time and early hours for prayer would act like magic to revive and invigorate many a decayed spiritual life. More time and early hours for prayer would be manifest in holy living. A holy life would not be so rare or so difficult a thing if our devotions were not so short and hurried. A Christly temper in its sweet and passionless fragrance would not be so alien and hopeless a heritage if our closet stay were lengthened and intensified. We live shabbily because we pray meanly. Plenty of time to feast in our closets will bring marrow and fatness to our lives. Our ability to stay with God in our closet measures our ability to stay with God out of the closet. Hasty closet visits are deceptive, defaulting. We are not only deluded by them, but we are losers by them in many ways and in many rich legacies. Tarrying in the closet instructs and wins. We are taught by it, and the greatest victories are often the results of great waiting—waiting till words and plans are exhausted, and silent and patient waiting gains the crown. Jesus Christ asks with an affronted emphasis, "Shall not God avenge his own elect which cry day and night unto him?"

To pray is the greatest thing we can do: and to do it well there must be calmness, time, and deliberation; otherwise it is degraded into the littlest and meanest of things. True praying has the largest results for good; and poor praying, the least. We cannot do too much of real praying; we cannot do too little of the sham. We must learn anew the worth of prayer, enter anew the school of prayer. There is nothing which it takes more time to learn. And if we would learn the wondrous art, we must not give a fragment here and there—"A little talk with Jesus," as the tiny saintlets sing—but we must demand and hold with iron grasp the best hours of the day for God and prayer, or there will be no praying worth the name.

This, however, is not a day of prayer. Few men there are who pray. Prayer is defamed by preacher and priest. In these days of hurry and bustle, of electricity and steam, men will not take time to pray. Preachers there are who "say prayers" as a part of their programme, on regular or state occasions; but who "stirs himself up to take hold upon God?" Who prays as Jacob prayed—till he is crowned as a prevailing, princely intercessor? Who prays as Elijah prayed—till all the locked-up forces of nature were unsealed and a famine-stricken land bloomed as the garden of God? Who prayed as Jesus Christ prayed as out upon the mountain he "continued all night in prayer to God?" The apostles "gave themselves to prayer"—the most difficult thing to get men or even the preachers to do. Laymen there are who will give their money—some of them in rich abundance—but they will not "give themselves" to prayer, without which their money is but a curse. There are plenty of preachers who will preach and deliver great and eloquent addresses on the need of revival and the spread of the kingdom of God, but not many there are who will do that without which all preaching and organizing are worse than vain—pray. It is out of date, almost a lost art, and the greatest benefactor this age could have is the man who will bring the preachers and the Church back to prayer.

20. A Praying Pulpit Begets a Praying Pew

I judge that my prayer is more than the devil himself; if it were otherwise, Luther would have fared differently long before this. Yet men will not see and acknowledge the great wonders or miracles God works in my behalf. If I should neglect prayer but a single day, I should lose a great deal of the fire of faith.
—Martin Luther

ONLY glimpses of the great importance of prayer could the apostles get before Pentecost. But the Spirit coming and filling on Pentecost elevated prayer to its vital and all-commanding position in the gospel of Christ. The call now of prayer to every saint is the Spirit's loudest and most exigent call. Sainthood's piety is made, refined, perfected, by prayer. The gospel moves with slow and timid pace when the saints are not at their prayers early and late and long.

Where are the Christly leaders who can teach the modern saints how to pray and put them at it? Do we know we are raising up a prayerless set of saints? Where are the apostolic leaders who can put God's people to praying? Let them come to the front and do the work, and it will be the greatest work which can be done. An increase of educational facilities and a great increase of money force will be the direst curse to religion if they are not sanctified by more and better praying than we are doing. More praying will not come as a matter of course. The campaign for the twentieth or thirtieth century fund will not help our praying but hinder if we are not careful. Nothing but a specific effort from a praying leadership will avail. The chief ones must lead in the apostolic effort to radicate the vital importance and *fact* of prayer in the heart and life of the Church. None but praying leaders can have praying followers. Praying apostles will beget praying saints. A praying pulpit will beget praying pews. We do greatly need some body who can set the saints to this business of praying. We are not a generation of praying saints. Non-praying saints are a beggarly gang of saints who have neither the ardor nor the beauty nor the power of saints. Who will restore this breach? The greatest will he be of reformers and apostles, who can set the Church to praying.

We put it as our most sober judgment that the great need of the Church in this and all ages is men of such commanding faith, of such unsullied holiness, of such marked spiritual vigor and consuming zeal, that their prayers, faith, lives, and ministry will be of such a radical and aggressive form as to work spiritual revolutions which will form eras in individual and Church life.

We do not mean men who get up sensational stirs by novel devices, nor those who attract by a pleasing entertainment; but men who can stir things, and work revolutions by the preaching of God's Word and by the power of the Holy Ghost, revolutions which change the whole current of things.

Natural ability and educational advantages do not figure as factors in this matter; but capacity for faith, the ability to pray, the power of thorough consecration, the ability of self-littleness, an absolute losing of one's self in God's glory, and an ever-present and insatiable yearning and seeking after all the fullness of God—men who can set the Church ablaze for God; not in a noisy, showy way, but with an intense and quiet heat that melts and moves everything for God.

God can work wonders if he can get a suitable man. Men can work wonders if they can get God to lead them. The full endowment of the spirit that turned the world upside down would be eminently useful in these latter days. Men who can stir things mightily for God, whose spiritual revolutions change the whole aspect of things, are the universal need of the Church.

The Church has never been without these men; they adorn its history; they are the standing miracles of the divinity of the Church; their example and history are an unfailing inspiration and blessing. An increase in their number and power should be our prayer.

That which has been done in spiritual matters can be done again, and be better done. This was Christ's view. He said "Verily, verily, I say unto you, He that believeth on me, the works that I do shall he do also; and greater works than these shall he do; because I go unto my Father." The past has not exhausted the possibilities nor the demands for doing great things for God. The Church that is dependent on its past history for its miracles of power and grace is a fallen Church.

God wants elect men—men out of whom self and the world have gone by a severe crucifixion, by a bankruptcy which has so totally ruined self and the world that there is neither hope nor desire of recovery; men who by this insolvency and crucifixion have turned toward God perfect hearts.

Let us pray ardently that God's promise to prayer may be more than realized.

The Kneeling Christian

~ ※ ~

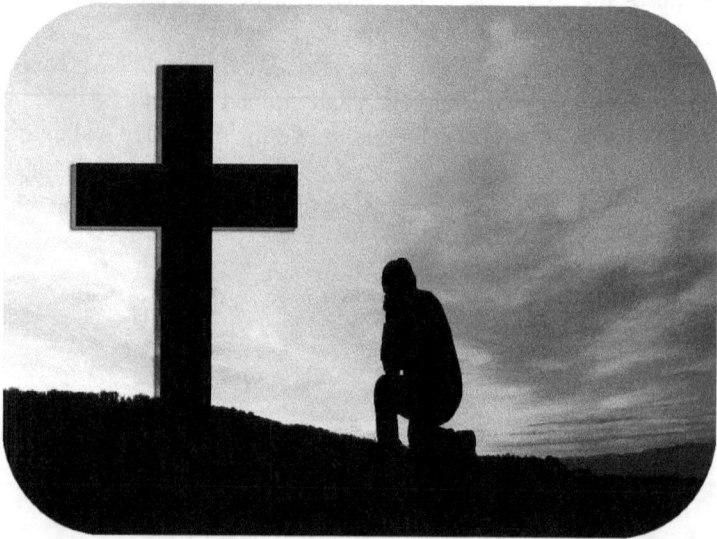

By *Unknown Christian*

(Assumed today to be Albert Richardson)

The 1922 Edition

~ ※ ~

Author Preface

A traveller in China visited a heathen temple on a great feast-day. Many were the worshippers of the hideous idol enclosed in a sacred shrine. The visitor noticed that most of the devotees brought with them small pieces of paper on which prayers had been written or printed. These they would wrap up in little balls of stiff mud and fling at the idol. He enquired the reason for this strange proceeding, and was told that if the mud ball stuck fast to the idol, then the prayer would assuredly be answered; but if the mud fell off, the prayer was rejected by the god.

We may smile at this peculiar way of testing the acceptability of a prayer. But is it not a fact that the majority of Christian men and women who pray to a Living God know very little about real prevailing prayer? Yet prayer is the key which unlocks the door of God's treasure-house.

It is not too much to say that all real growth in the spiritual life—all victory over temptation, all confidence and peace in the presence of difficulties and dangers, all repose of spirit in times of great disappointment or loss, all habitual communion with God— depend upon the practice of secret prayer.

This book was written by request, and with much hesitancy. It goes forth with much prayer. May He Who said, "Men ought always to pray, and not to faint," "teach us to pray."

Chapter 1: God's Great Need

"GOD Wondered." This is a very striking thought! The very boldness of the idea ought surely to arrest the attention of every earnest Christian man, woman and child. A wondering God! Why, how staggered we might well be if we knew the cause of God's "wonder"! Yet we find it to be, apparently, a very little thing. But if we are willing to consider the matter carefully, we shall discover it to be one of the greatest possible importance to every believer on the Lord Jesus Christ. Nothing else is so momentous—so vital—to our spiritual welfare.

God "wondered that there was no intercessor" (Isa. lix. 16)—"none to interpose" (R.V., marg.). But this was in the days of long ago, before the coming of the Lord Jesus Christ "full of grace and truth"—before the outpouring of the Holy Spirit, full of grace and power, "helping our infirmity," "Himself making intercession for us" and in us (Rom. viii. 26). Yes, and before the truly amazing promises of our Savior regarding prayer; before men knew very much about prayer; in the days when sacrifices for their sins loomed larger in their eyes than supplication for other sinners.

Oh, how great must be God's wonder today! For how few there are among us who know what prevailing prayer really is! Every one of us would confess that we believe in prayer, yet how many of us truly believe in the power of, prayer? Now, before we go a step farther, may the writer most earnestly implore you not to read hurriedly what is contained in these chapters. Much—very much—depends upon the way in which every reader receives what is here recorded. For everything depends upon prayer.

Why are many Christians so often defeated? Because they pray so little. Why are many church-workers so often discouraged and disheartened? Because they pray so little.

Why do most men see so few brought "out of darkness to light" by their ministry? Because they pray so little.

Why are not our churches simply on fire for God? Because there is so little real prayer.

The Lord Jesus is as powerful today as ever before. The Lord Jesus is as anxious for men to be saved as ever before. His arm is not shortened that it cannot save: but He cannot stretch forth His arm unless we pray more—and more really.

We may be assured of this—the secret of all failure is our failure in secret prayer.

If God "wondered" in the days of Isaiah, we need not be surprised to find that in the days of His flesh our Lord "marvelled." He marvelled at the unbelief of some—unbelief which actually prevented Him from doing any mighty work in their cities (Mark vi. 6).

But we must remember that those who were guilty of this unbelief saw no beauty in Him that they should desire Him, or believe on Him. What then must His "marvel" be today, when He sees amongst us who do truly love and adore Him, so few who really "stir themselves up to take hold of God" (Isa. lxiv. 7). Surely there is nothing so absolutely astonishing as a practically prayerless Christian? These are eventful and ominous days. In fact, there are many evidences that these are "the last days" in which God promised to pour out His Spirit—the Spirit of supplication—upon all flesh (Joel ii. 28). Yet the vast majority of professing Christians scarcely know what "supplication" means; and very many of our churches not only have no prayer-meeting, but sometimes unblushingly condemn such meetings, and even ridicule them.

The Church of England, recognizing the importance of worship and prayer, expects her clergy to read prayers in Church every morning and evening.

But when this is done, is it not often in an empty church? And are not the prayers frequently raced through at a pace which precludes real worship? "Common prayer," too, often must necessarily be rather vague and indefinite.

And what of those churches where the old-fashioned weekly prayer-meeting is retained? Would not "weakly" be the more appropriate word? C. H. Spurgeon had the joy of being able to say that he conducted a prayer-meeting every Monday night "which scarcely ever numbers less than from a thousand to twelve hundred attendants."

My brothers, have we ceased to believe in prayer? If you still hold your weekly gathering for prayer, is it not a fact that the very great majority of your church members never come near it? Yes, and never even think of coming near it. Why is this? Whose fault is it?

"Only a prayer-meeting"—how often we have heard the utterance! How many of those reading these words really enjoy a prayer-meeting? Is it a joy or just a duty? Please forgive me for asking so many questions and for pointing out what appears to be a perilous weakness and a lamentable shortcoming in our churches. We are not out to criticize—far less to condemn. Anybody can do that. Our yearning desire is to stir up Christians "to take hold of" God, as never before. We wish to encourage, to enhearten, to uplift.

We are never so high as when we are on our knees.

Criticize? Who dare criticize another? When we look back upon the past and remember how much prayerlessness there has been in one's own life, words of criticism of others wither away on the lips.

But we believe the time has come when a clarion call to the individual and to the Church is needed—a call to prayer.

Now, dare we face this question of prayer? It seems a foolish query, for is not prayer a part and parcel of all religions? Yet we venture to ask our readers to look at this matter fairly and squarely. Do I really believe that prayer is a power? Is prayer the greatest power on earth, or is it not? Does prayer indeed "move the Hand that moves the world"?

Do God's prayer-commands really concern Me? Do the promises of God concerning prayer still hold good? We have all been muttering "Yes—Yes—Yes" as we read these questions. We dare not say "No" to any one of them. And yet—!

Has it ever occurred to you that our Lord never gave an unnecessary or an optional command? Do we really believe that our Lord never made a promise which He could not, or would not, fulfil? Our Savior's three great commands for definite action were:—

> *Pray ye*
>> *Do this*
>>> *Go ye!*

Are we obeying Him? How often His command, "Do this," is reiterated by our preachers today! One might almost think it was His only command! How seldom we are reminded of His bidding to "Pray" and to "Go." Yet, without obedience to the "Pray ye," it is of little or no use at all either to "Do this" or to "Go."

In fact, it can easily be shown that all want of success, and all failure in the spiritual life and in Christian work, is due to defective or insufficient prayer. Unless we pray aright we cannot live aright or serve aright. This may appear, at first sight, to be gross exaggeration, but the more we think it over in the light Scripture throws upon it, the more convinced shall we be of the truth of this statement.

Now, as we begin once more to see what the Bible has to say about this mysterious and wonderful subject, shall we endeavor to read some of our Lord's promises, as though we had never heard them before. What will the effect be?

Some twenty years ago the writer was studying in a Theological College. One morning, early, a fellow-student—who is today one of England's foremost missionaries—burst into the room holding an open Bible in his hands. Although he was preparing for Holy Orders, he was at that time only a young convert to Christ.

He had gone up to the University "caring for none of these things." Popular, clever, athletic—he had already won a place amongst the smart set of his college, when Christ claimed him. He accepted the Lord Jesus as a personal Savior, and became a very keen follower of his Master. The Bible was, comparatively, a new book to him, and as a result he was constantly making "discoveries." On that memorable day on which he invaded my quietude he cried excitedly—his face all aglow with mingled joy and surprise—"Do you believe this? Is it really true?" "Believe what?" I asked, glancing at the open Bible with some astonishment. "Why, this—" and he read in eager tones St. Matthew xxi. 21, 22: "'If ye have faith and doubt not . . . all things whatsoever ye shall ask in prayer, believing, ye shall receive.' Do you believe it? Is it true?" "Yes," I replied, with much surprise at his excitement, "of course it's true—of course I believe it."

Yet, through my mind there flashed all manner of thoughts! "Well, that's a very wonderful promise," said he. "It seems to me to be absolutely limitless! Why don't we pray more?" And he went away, leaving me thinking hard. I had never looked at those verses quite in that way. As the door closed upon that eager young follower of the Master, I had a vision of my Savior and His love and His power such as I never had before. I had a vision of a life of prayer—yes, and "limitless" power, which I saw depended upon two things only—faith and prayer. For the moment I was thrilled. I fell on my knees, and as I bowed before my Lord what thoughts surged through my mind—what hopes and aspirations flooded my soul! God was speaking to me in an extraordinary way. This was a great call to prayer. But—to my shame be it said—I heeded not that call.

Where did I fail? True, I prayed a little more than before, but nothing much seemed to happen. Why? Was it because I did not see what a high standard the Savior requires in the inner life of those who would pray successfully?

Was it because I had failed to measure up my life to the "perfect love" standard so beautifully described in the thirteenth chapter of the first Epistle to the Corinthians?

For, after all, prayer is not just putting into action good resolutions "to pray." Like David, we need to cry, "Create in me a clean heart, O God" (Psa. li. 10) before we can pray aright. And the inspired words of the Apostle of Love need to be heeded today as much as ever before: "Beloved, if our heart condemn us not, we have boldness toward God; and [then] whatsoever we ask, we receive of Him" (I John iii. 21).

"True—and I believe it." Yes, indeed, it is a limitless promise, and yet how little we realize it, how little we claim from Christ. And our Lord "marvels" at our unbelief. But if we could only read the Gospels for the first time, what an amazing book it would seem! Should not we "marvel" and "wonder"? And today I pass on that great call to you. Will you give heed to it? Will you profit by it? Or shall it fall on deaf ears and leave you prayerless?

Fellow-Christians, let us awake! The devil is blinding our eyes. He is endeavoring to prevent us from facing this question of prayer. These pages are written by special request. But it is many months since that request came.

Every attempt to begin to write has been frustrated, and even now one is conscious of a strange reluctance to do so. There seems to be some mysterious power restraining the hand. Do we realize that there is nothing the devil dreads so much as prayer? His great concern is to keep us from praying. He loves to see us "up to our eyes" in work—provided we do not pray. He does not fear because we are eager and earnest Bible students—provided we are little in prayer. Someone has wisely said, "Satan laughs at our toiling, mocks at our wisdom, but trembles when we pray." All this is so familiar to us—but do we really pray? If not, then failure must dog our footsteps, whatever signs of apparent success there may be.

Let us never forget that the greatest thing we can do for God or for man is to pray. For we can accomplish far more by our prayers than by our work. Prayer is omnipotent; it can do anything that God can do! When we pray God works. All fruitfulness in service is the outcome of prayer—of the worker's prayers, or of those who are holding up holy hands on his behalf. We all know how to pray, but perhaps many of us need to cry as the disciples did of old, "Lord, teach us to pray."

> O Lord, by Whom ye come to God,
>   The Life, the Truth, the Way,
> The path of prayer Thyself hast trod;
>   Lord, teach us now to pray.

Chapter 2: Almost Incredible Promises

"WHEN we stand with Christ in glory, looking o'er life's finished story," the most amazing feature of that life as it is looked back upon will be its prayerlessness.

We shall be almost beside ourselves with astonishment that we spent so little time in real intercession. It will be our turn to "wonder."

In our Lord's last discourse to His loved ones, just before the most wonderful of all prayers, the Master again and again held out His kingly golden sceptre and said, as it were, "What is your request? It shall be granted unto you, even unto the whole of My kingdom!"

Do we believe this? We must do so if we believe our Bibles. Shall we just read over very quietly and thoughtfully one of our Lord's promises, reiterated so many times? If we had never read them before, we should open our eyes in bewilderment, for these promises are almost incredible. From the lips of any mere man they would be quite unbelievable. But it is the Lord of heaven and earth Who speaks; and He is speaking at the most solemn moment of His life. It is the eve of His death and passion. It is a farewell message. Now listen!

"Verily, verily I say unto you, he that believeth on Me, the works that I do shall he do also; and greater works than these shall he do: because I go unto the Father. And whatsoever ye shall ask in My name, that will I do, that the Father may be glorified in the Son. If ye shall ask anything in My name, that will I do" (John xiv. 13, 14). Now, could any words be plainer or clearer than these? Could any promise be greater or grander? Has anyone else, anywhere, at any time, ever offered so much?

How staggered those disciples must have been! Surely they could scarcely believe their own ears. But that promise is made also to you and to me.

And, lest there should be any mistake on their part, or on ours, our Lord repeats Himself a few moments afterwards. Yes, and the Holy Spirit bids St. John record those words again. "If ye abide in Me, and My words abide in you, ask whatsoever ye will, and it shall be done unto you. Herein is My Father glorified, that ye bare much fruit; and so shall ye be My disciples" (John xv. 7, 8).

These words are of such grave importance, and so momentous, that the Savior of the world is not content even with a threefold utterance of them. He urges His disciples to obey His command "to ask." In fact, He tells them that one sign of their being His "friends" will be the obedience to His commands in all things (verse 14). Then He once more repeats His wishes: "Ye did not choose Me, but I chose you, and appointed you, that ye should go and bear fruit, and that your fruit should abide: that whatsoever ye shall ask the Father, in My name, He may give it you" (John xv. 16).

One would think that our Lord had now made it plain enough that He wanted them to pray; that He needed their prayers, and that without prayer they could accomplish nothing. But to our intense surprise He returns again to the same subject, saying very much the same words.

"In that day ye shall ask Me nothing"—i.e., "ask Me no question" (R.V., marg.)— "Verily, verily I say unto you, if ye ask anything of the Father, He will give it you in My name. Hitherto have ye asked nothing in My name: ask, and ye shall receive, that your joy may be fulfilled" (John xvi. 23, 24).

Never before had our Lord laid such stress on any promise or command—never! This truly marvelous promise is given us six times over. Six times, almost in the same breath, our Savior commands us to ask whatsoever we will. This is the greatest—the most wonderful—promise ever made to man. Yet most men—Christian men—practically ignore it! Is it not so?

The exceeding greatness of the promise seems to over-whelm us. Yet we know that He is "able to do exceeding abundantly above all that we ask or think" (Eph. iii. 20).

So our blessed Master gives the final exhortation, before He is seized, and bound, and scourged, before His gracious lips are silenced on the cross, "Ye shall ask in My name . . . for the Father Himself loveth you" (John xvi. 26-27). We have often spent much time in reflecting upon our Lord's seven words from the cross. And it is well we should do so. Have we ever spent one hour in meditating upon this, our Savior's sevenfold invitation to pray?

Today He sits on the throne of His Majesty on high, and He holds out to us the sceptre of His power. Shall we touch it and tell Him our desires? He bids us take of His treasures. He yearns to grant us "according to the riches of His glory," that we may "be strengthened with power through His Spirit in the inner man." He tells us that our strength and our fruitfulness depend upon our prayers. He reminds us that our very joy depends upon answered prayer (John xvi. 24).

And yet we allow the devil to persuade us to neglect prayer! He makes us believe that we can do more by our own efforts than by our prayers—by our intercourse with men than by our intercession with God. It passes one's comprehension that so little heed should be given to our Lord's sevenfold invitation—command—promise! How dare we work for Christ without being much on our knees? Quite recently an earnest Christian "worker"— a Sunday-school teacher and communicant—wrote me, saying, "I have never had an answer to prayer in all my life." But why? Is God a liar? Is not God trustworthy? Do His promises count for nought. Does He not mean what He says? And doubtless there are many reading these words who in their hearts are saying the same thing as that Christian worker. Payson is right—is Scriptural—when he says: "If we would do much for God, we must ask much of God: we must be men of prayer." If our prayers are not answered— always answered, but not necessarily granted—the fault must be entirely in ourselves, and not in God. God delights to answer prayer; and He has given us His word that He will answer.

Fellow-laborers in His vineyard, it is quite evident that our Master desires us to ask, and to ask much. He tells us we glorify God by doing so! Nothing is beyond the scope of prayer which is not beyond the will of God—and we do not desire to go beyond His will.

We dare not say that our Lord's words are not true. Yet somehow or other few Christians really seem to believe them. What holds us back? What seals our lips? What keeps us from making much of prayer? Do we doubt His love? Never! He gave His life for us and to us. Do we doubt the Father's love? Nay. "The Father Himself loveth you," said Christ when urging His disciples to pray.

Do we doubt His power? Not for a moment. Hath He not said, "All power hath been given unto Me in heaven and on earth. Go ye . . . and lo, I am with you alway . . ."? (Matt. xxviii. 18-20). Do we doubt His wisdom? Do we mistrust His choice for us? Not for a moment. And yet so very few of His followers consider prayer really worth while. Of course, they would deny this—but actions speak louder than words. Are we afraid to put God to the test? He has said we may do so. "Bring Me the whole tithe into the storehouse . . . and prove Me now herewith, saith the Lord of Hosts, if I will not open you the windows of heaven, and pour you out a blessing that there shall not be room enough to receive it" (Mal. iii. 10). Whenever God makes us a promise, let us boldly say, as did St. Paul, I believe God (Acts xxvii. 25), and trust Him to keep His word.

Shall we begin today to be men of prayer, if we have never done so before? Let us not put it off till a more convenient season. God wants me to pray. The dear Savior wants me to pray. He needs my prayers. So much—in fact, everything—depends upon prayer. How dare we hold back? Let every one of us ask on our knees this question: "If no one on earth prayed for the salvation of sinners more fervently or more frequently than I do, how many of them would be converted to God through prayer?"

Do we spend ten minutes a day in prayer? Do we consider it important enough for that?

Ten minutes a day on our knees in prayer—when the Kingdom of Heaven can be had for the asking!

Ten minutes? It seems a very inadequate portion of our time to spend in taking hold of God (Isa. lxiv. 7)!

And is it prayer when we do "say" our prayers, or are we just repeating daily a few phrases which have become practically meaningless, whilst our thoughts are wandering hither and thither?

If God were to answer the words we repeated on our knees this morning should we know it? Should we recognize the answer? Do we even remember what we asked for? He does answer. He has given us His word for it. He always answers every real prayer of faith.

But we shall see what the Bible has to say on this point in a later chapter. We are now thinking of the amount of time we spend in prayer.

"How often do you pray?" was the question put to a Christian woman. "Three times a day, and all the day beside," was the quick reply. But how many are there like that? Is prayer to me just a duty, or is it a privilege—a pleasure—a real joy—a necessity?

Let us get a fresh vision of Christ in all His glory, and a fresh glimpse of all the "riches of His glory" which He places at our disposal, and of all the mighty power given unto Him. Then let us get a fresh vision of the world and all its needs. (And the world was never so needy as it is today.)

Why, the wonder is not that we pray so little, but that we can ever get up from our knees if we realize our own need; the needs of our home and our loved ones; the needs of our pastor and the Church; the needs of our city—of our country—of the heathen and Mohammedan world! All these needs, can be met by the riches of God in Christ Jesus. St. Paul had no doubt about this—nor have we. Yes! "My God shall supply all your need according to His riches in glory, in Christ Jesus" (Phil. iv. 19). But to share His riches we must pray, for the same Lord is rich unto all that call upon Him (Rom. x. 12).

So great is the importance of prayer that God has taken care to anticipate all the excuses or objections we may be likely to make.

Men plead their weakness or infirmity—or they declare they do not know how to pray.

God foresaw this inability long ages ago. Did He not inspire St. Paul to say: "The Spirit also helpeth our infirmity, for we know not how to pray as we ought; but the Spirit Himself maketh intercession for us with groanings which cannot be uttered; and He that searcheth the hearts knoweth what is in the mind of the Spirit, because He maketh intercession for the saints according to the will of God" (Rom. viii. 26, 27).

Yes. Every provision is made for us. But only the Holy Spirit can "stir us up" to "take hold of God." And if we will but yield ourselves to the Spirit's promptings we shall most assuredly follow the example of the apostles of old, who "gave themselves to prayer," and "continued steadfastly in prayer" (R.V., Acts vi. 4).

We may rest fully assured of this—a man's influence in the world can be gauged not by his eloquence, or his zeal, or his orthodox, or his energy, but by his prayers. Yes, and we will go farther and maintain that no man can live aright who does not pray aright.

We may work for Christ from morn till night; we may spend much time in Bible study; we may be most earnest and faithful and "acceptable" in our preaching and in our individual dealing, but none of these things can be truly effective unless we are much in prayer. We shall only be full of good works; and not "bearing fruit in every good work" (Col. i. 10). To be little with God in prayer is to be little for God in service. Much secret prayer means much public power. Yet is it not a fact that whilst our organizing is well nigh perfect, our agonizing in prayer is well nigh lost?

Men are wondering why the Revival delays its coming. There is only one thing that can delay it, and that is lack of prayer. All Revivals have been the outcome of prayer. One sometimes longs for the voice of an archangel, but what would that avail if the voice of Christ Himself does not stir us up to pray? It seems almost impertinence for any man to take up the cry when our Savior has put forth His "limitless" promises. Yet we feel that something should be done, and we believe that the Holy Spirit is prompting men to remind themselves and others of Christ's words and power. No words of mine can impress men with the value of prayer, the need of prayer, and the omnipotence of prayer.

But these utterances go forth steeped in prayer that God the Holy Spirit will Himself convict Christian men and women of the sin of prayerlessness, and drive them to their knees, to call upon God day and night in burning, believing, prevailing intercession! The Lord Jesus, now in the heavenlies, beckons to us to fall upon our knees and claim the riches of His grace.

No man dare prescribe for another how long a time he ought to spend in prayer, nor do we suggest that men should make a vow to pray so many minutes or hours a day. Of course, the Bible command is to "Pray without ceasing." This is evidently the "attitude of prayer"—the attitude of one's life.

Here we are speaking of definite acts of prayer. Have you ever timed your prayers? We believe that most of our readers would be amazed and confounded if they did time themselves!

Some years ago the writer faced this prayer question. He felt that for himself at least one hour a day was the minimum time that he should spend in prayer. He carefully noted down every day a record of his prayer-life. As time went on he met a working-man who was being much used of God.

When asked to what he chiefly attributed his success, this man quietly replied, "Well, I could not get on without two hours a day of private prayer."

Then there came across my path a Spirit-filled missionary from overseas, who told very humbly of the wonderful things God was doing through his ministry. (One could see all along that God was given all the praise and all the glory.) "I find it necessary, oftentimes, to spend four hours a day in prayer," said this missionary.

And we remember how the Greatest Missionary of all used sometimes to spend whole nights in prayer. Why? Our blessed Lord did not pray simply as an example to us: He never did things merely as an example. He prayed because He needed to pray. As perfect Man, prayer to Him was a necessity. Then how much more is it necessary to you and me?

"Four hours a day in prayer!" exclaimed a man who is giving his whole life to Christian work as a medical missionary. "Four hours? Give me ten minutes and I'm done!" That was an honest and a brave confession—even if a sad one. Yet, if some of us were to speak out as honestly—?

Now, it was not by accident that these men crossed my path. God was speaking through them. It was just another "call to prayer" from the "God of patience," who is also a "God of comfort" (Rom. xv. 5). and when their quiet message had sunk into my soul a book came into my hands, "by chance," as people say. It told briefly and simply the story of John Hyde—"Praying Hyde," as he came to be called. Just as God sent St. John the Baptist to prepare the way of our Lord at His first coming, so He sent in these last days St. John the Pray-er, to make straight paths for His coming again. "Praying Hyde"—what a name! As one read of this marvelous life of prayer, one began to ask, "Have I ever prayed?"

I found others were asking the same question. One lady, who is noted for her wonderful intercession, wrote me, saying, "When I laid down this book, I began to think I had never in all my life really prayed!"

But here we must leave the matter. Shall we get on our knees before God and allow His Holy Spirit to search us through and through? Are we sincere? Do we really desire to do God's will? Do we really believe His promises? If so, will it not lead us to spend more time on our knees before God? Do not vow to pray "so much" a day. Resolve to pray much, but prayer, to be of value, must be spontaneous, and not from constraint.

But we must bear in mind that mere resolutions to take more time for prayer, and to conquer reluctance to pray, will not prove lastingly effective unless there is a wholehearted and absolute surrender to the Lord Jesus Christ. If we have never taken this step, we must take it now if we desire to be men of prayer.

I am quite certain of this fact: God wants me to pray: wants you to pray. The question is, are we willing to pray?

Gracious Savior, pour out upon us the fullness of the Holy Spirit, that we may indeed become Kneeling Christians.

> *To God your every want*
> *In instant prayer display.*
> *Pray always; pray and never faint:*
> *Pray! Without ceasing, pray.*

Chapter 3: "Ask of Me and I Will Give"

GOD wants me to pray, to be much in prayer—because all success in spiritual work is dependent on prayer.

A preacher who prays little may see some results of his labors, but if he does it will be because someone, somewhere is praying for him. The "fruit" is the pray-er's—not the preacher's. How surprised some of us preachers will be one day, when the Lord shall "reward every man according to his works." "Lord! Those were my converts! It was I who conducted that mission at which so many were brought into the fold." Ah, yes—I did the preaching, the pleading, the persuading; but was it "I" who did the praying?

Every convert is the result of the Holy Spirit's pleading in answer to the prayers of some believer.

O God, grant that such surprise may not be ours. O Lord, teach us to pray!

We have had a vision of a God pleadingly calling for prayer from His children. How am I treating that call? Can I say, with St. Paul, "I am 'not disobedient to the heavenly vision'"? Again we repeat, if there are any regrets in heaven, the greatest will be that we spent so little time in real intercession whilst we were on earth.

Think of the wide sweep of prayer! "Ask of Me, and I will give thee the heathen for thine inheritance, and the uttermost parts of the earth for thy possession" (Psalm ii. 8). Yet many people do not trouble to bring even the little details of their own lives to God in prayer, and nine out of ten Christian people never think of praying for the heathen!

One is staggered at the unwillingness of Christians to pray. Perhaps it is because they have never experienced, or even heard of, convincing answers to prayer.

In this chapter we are setting out to do the "impossible." What is that? We long to bring home to the heart and conscience of every reader the power of prayer. We venture to describe this as "impossible." For if men will not believe, and act upon, our Lord's promises and commands, how can we expect them to be persuaded by any mere human exhortations?

But do you remember that our Lord, when speaking to His disciples, asked them to believe that He was in the Father and the Father in Him? Then he added: "If you cannot believe My bare word about this, believe Me for the very works' sake" (John xiv. 11). It was as if He said, "If My Person, My sanctified life, and My wonderful words do not elicit belief in Me, then look at My works: surely they are sufficient to compel belief? Believe Me because of what I do."

Then He went on to promise that if they would believe, they should do greater works than these. It was after this utterance that He gave the first of those six wonderful promises in regard to prayer. The inference surely is that those "greater works" are to be done only as the outcome of prayer.

May the disciple therefore follow the Master's method? Fellow-worker, if you fail to grasp, fail to trust our Lord's astounding promises regarding prayer, will you not believe them "for the very works' sake"? That is, because of those "greater works" which men and women are performing today—or, rather, the works which the Lord Jesus is doing, through their prayerful co-operation?

What are we "out for"? What is our real aim in life? Surely we desire most of all to be abundantly fruitful in the Master's service. We seek not position, or prominence, or power. But we do long to be fruitful servants. Then we must be much in prayer. God can do more through our prayers than through our preaching. A. J. Gordon once said, "You can do more than pray, after you have prayed, but you can never do more than pray until you have prayed." If only we would believe this!

A lady in India was cast down through the failure of her life and work. She was a devoted missionary, but somehow or other conversions never resulted from her ministry.

The Holy Spirit seemed to say to her, "Pray more." But she resisted the promptings of the Spirit for some time. "At length," said she, "I set apart much of my time for prayer. I did it in fear and trembling lest my fellow-workers should complain that I was shirking my work. After a few weeks I began to see men and women accepting Christ as their Savior. Moreover, the whole district was soon awakened, and the work of all the other missionaries was blessed as never before. God did more in six months than I had succeeded in doing in six years. And," she added, "no one ever accused me of shirking my duty." Another lady missionary in India felt the same call to pray. She began to give much time to prayer. No opposition came from without, but it did come from within. But she persisted, and in two years the baptized converts increased sixfold!

God promised that He would "pour out the Spirit of grace and supplication upon all flesh" (Joel ii. 28). How much of that Spirit of "supplication" is ours? Surely we must get that Spirit at all costs? Yet if we are not willing to spend time in "supplication," God must perforce withhold His Spirit, and we become numbered amongst those who are "resisting the Spirit," and possibly "quenching" the Spirit. Has not our Lord promised the Holy Spirit to them that ask? (Luke xi. 13).

Are not the very converts from heathendom putting some of us to shame?

A few years ago, when in India, I had the great joy of seeing something of Pandita Ramabai's work. She had a boarding-school of 1,500 Hindu girls. One day some of these girls came with their Bibles and asked a lady missionary what St. Luke xii. 49 meant—"I came to cast fire upon the earth; and what will I, if it is already kindled?" The missionary tried to put them off with an evasive answer, not being very sure herself what those words meant. But they were not satisfied, so they determined to pray for this fire. And as they prayed—and because they prayed—the very fire of heaven came into their souls. A very Pentecost from above was granted them. No wonder they continued to pray!

A party of these girls upon whom God had poured the "Spirit of supplication" came to a mission house where I spent some weeks. "May we stay here in your town and pray for your work?" they asked. The missionary did not entertain the idea with any great enthusiasm. He felt that they ought to be at school, and not "gadding about" the country. But they only asked for a hall or barn where they could pray; and we all value prayers on our behalf. So their request was granted, and the good man sat down to his evening meal, thinking. As the evening wore on, a native pastor came round. He broke down completely. He explained, with tears running down his face, that God's Holy Spirit had convicted him of sin, and that he felt compelled to come and openly confess his wrongdoing. He was quickly followed by one Christian after another, all under deep conviction of sin.

There was a remarkable time of blessing. Back-sliders were restored, believers were sanctified, and heathen brought into the fold—all because a few mere children were praying.

God is no respecter of persons. If anyone is willing to conform to His conditions, He for His part will assuredly fulfill His promises. Does not our heart burn within us, as we hear of God's wonderful power? And that power is ours for the asking. I know there are "conditions." But you and I can fulfill them all through Christ. And those of us who cannot have the privilege of serving God in India or any other overseas mission, may yet take our part in bringing down a like blessing. When the Revival in Wales was at its height, a Welsh missionary wrote home begging the people to pray that India might be moved in like manner. So the coal-miners met daily at the pit-mouth half an hour before dawn to pray for their comrade overseas. In a few weeks' time the welcome message was sent home: "The blessing has come."

Isn't it just splendid to know that by our prayers we can bring down showers of blessing upon India, or Africa, or China, just as readily as we can get the few drops needed for our own little plot?

Many of us will recall the wonderful things which God did for Korea a few years ago, entirely in answer to prayer. A few missionaries decided to meet together to pray daily at noon. At the end of the month one brother proposed that, "as nothing had happened," the prayer-meeting should be discontinued. "Let us each pray at home as we find it convenient," said he. The others, however, protested that they ought rather to spend even more time in prayer each day. So they continued the daily prayer-meeting for four months. Then suddenly the blessing began to be poured out. Church services here and there were broken up by weeping and confessing of sins. At length a mighty revival broke out. At one place during a Sunday evening service the leading man in the church stood up and confessed that he had stolen one hundred dollars in administering a widow's legacy. Immediately conviction of sin swept the audience. That service did not end till 2 o'clock on Monday morning. God's wondrous power was felt as never before. And when the Church was purified, many sinners found salvation.

Multitudes flocked to the churches out of curiosity. Some came to mock, but fear laid hold of them, and they stayed to pray. Amongst the "curious" was a brigand chief, the leader of a robber band. He was convicted and converted. He went straight off to the magistrate and gave himself up. "You have no accuser," said the astonished official, "yet you accuse yourself! We have no law in Korea to meet your case." So he dismissed him.

One of the missionaries declared, "It paid well to have spent several months in prayer, for when God gave the Holy Spirit, He accomplished more in half a day than all the missionaries together could have accomplished in half a year." In less than two months, more than 2,000 heathen were converted. The burning zeal of those converts has become a byword. Some of them gave all they had to build a church, and wept because they could not give more. Needless to say, they realized the power of prayer. Those converts were themselves baptized with the "Spirit of supplication." In one church it was announced that a daily prayer-meeting would be held at 4:30 every morning. The very first day 400 people arrived long before the stated hour—eager to pray! The number rapidly increased to 600 as days went on. At Seoul, 1,100 is the average attendance at the weekly prayer-meeting.

Heathen people came—to see what was happening. They exclaimed in astonishment, "The living God is among you." Those poor heathen saw what many Christians fail to see. Did not Christ say, "Where two or three are gathered together in My name, there am I in the midst of them"? (Matt. xviii. 20). What is possible in Korea is possible here. God is "no respecter" of nations. He is longing to bless us, longing to pour His Spirit upon us.

Now, if we—here in this so-called Christian country—really believed in prayer, i.e., in our Lord's own gracious promises, should we avoid prayer-meetings? If we had any genuine concern for the lost condition of thousands in our own land and tens of thousands in heathen lands, should we withhold our prayers? Surely we do not think, or we should pray more. "Ask of Me—I will give," says an almighty, all-loving God, and we scarcely heed His words!

Verily, converts from heathendom put us to shame. In my journeyings I came to Rawal Pindi, in N.W. India. What do you think happened there? Some of Pandita Ramabai's girls went there to camp. But a little while before this, Pandita Ramabai had said to her girls, "If there is any blessing in India, we may have it. Let us ask God to tell us what we must do in order to have the blessing."

As she read her Bible she paused over the verse, "Wait for the promise of the Father . . . ye shall receive power after that the Holy Ghost is come upon you" (Acts i. 4-8). "'Wait'! Why, we have never done this," she cried. "We have prayed, but we have never expected any greater blessing today than we had yesterday!" Oh, how they prayed! One prayer-meeting lasted six hours. And what a marvelous blessing God poured out in answer to their prayers.

Whilst some of these girls were at Rawal Pindi, a lady missionary, looking out of her tent towards midnight, was surprised to see a light burning in one of the girls' tents—a thing quite contrary to rules. She went to expostulate, but found the youngest of those ten girls—a child of fifteen—kneeling in the farthest corner of the tent, holding a little tallow candle in one hand and a list of names for intercession in the other. She had 500 names on her list—500 out of the 1,500 girls in Pandita Ramabai's school. Hour after hour she was naming them before God. No wonder God's blessing fell wherever those girls went, and upon whomsoever those girls prayed for.

Pastor Ding Li Mei, of China, has the names of 1,100 students on his prayer-list. Many hundreds have been won to Christ through his prayers. And so out-and-out are his converts that many scores of them have entered the Christian ministry.

It would be an easy matter to add to these amazing and inspiring stories of blessing through prayer. But there is no need to do so. I know that God wants me to pray. I know that God wants you to pray.

"If there is any blessing in England we may have it." Nay, more—if there is any blessing in Christ we may have it. "Blessed be the God and Father of our Lord Jesus Christ, who hath blessed us with every spiritual blessing in the heavenly places in Christ" (Eph. i. 3). God's great storehouse is full of blessings. Only prayer can unlock that storehouse. Prayer is the key, and faith both turns the key and opens the door, and claims the blessing. Blessed are the pure in heart, for they shall see God. And to see Him is to pray aright.

Listen! We have come—you and I—once more to the parting of the ways. All our past failure, all our past inefficiency and insufficiency, all our past unfruitfulness in service, can be banished now, once and for all, if we will only give prayer its proper place. Do it today. Do not wait for a more convenient time.

Everything worth having depends upon the decision we make. Truly God is a wonderful God! And one of the most wonderful things about Him is that He puts His all at the disposal of the prayer of faith. Believing prayer from a wholly-cleansed heart never fails. God has given us His word for it. Yet vastly more wonderful is the amazing fact that Christian men and women should either not believe God's word, or should fail to put it to the test.

When Christ is "all in all"—when He is Savior and Lord and King of our whole being, then it is really He Who prays our prayers. We can then truthfully alter one word of a well-known verse and say that the Lord Jesus ever liveth to make intercession in us. Oh, that we might make the Lord Jesus "marvel" not at our unbelief but at our faith! When our Lord shall again "marvel," and say of us, "Verily . . . I have not found so great faith, no, not in Israel" (Matt. viii. 10), then indeed shall "palsy"—paralysis—be transformed into power.

Has not our Lord come to "cast fire" upon us? Are we "already kindled"? Can He not use us as much as he used those mere children of Khedgaon? God is no respecter of persons. If we can humbly and truthfully say, "To me to live is Christ" (Phil. i. 21), will He not manifest forth His mighty power in us?

Some of us have been reading about Praying Hyde. Truly, his intercession changed things. Men tell us that they were thrilled when John Hyde prayed. They were stirred to their inmost being when he just pleaded the name "Jesus!—Jesus!—Jesus!" and a baptism of love and power came upon them.

But it was not John Hyde, it was the Holy Spirit of God whom one consecrated man, filled with that Spirit, brought down upon all around him. May we not all become "Praying Hydes"? Do you say "No! He had a special gift of prayer"? Very well—how did he get it? He was once just an ordinary Christian man—just like any of us.

Have you noticed that, humanly speaking, he owed his prayer-life to the prayers of his father's friend? Now get hold of this point. It is one of greatest importance, and one which may profoundly affect your whole life. Perhaps I may be allowed to tell the story fully, for so much depends upon it. Shall we quote John Hyde himself? He was on board a ship sailing for India, whither he was going as a missionary. He says, "My father had a friend who greatly desired to be a foreign missionary, but was not permitted to go. This friend wrote me a letter directed in care of the ship. I received it a few hours out of New York harbor. The words were not many, but the purport of them was this: 'I shall not cease praying for you, dear John, until you are filled with the Holy Spirit.' When I had read the letter I crumpled it up in anger and threw it on the deck. Did this friend think I had not received the baptism of the Spirit, or that I would think of going to India without this equipment? I was angry. But by and by better judgment prevailed, and I picked up the letter, and read it again. Possibly I did need something which I had not yet received. I paced up and down the deck, a battle raging within. I felt uncomfortable: I loved the writer; I knew the holy life he lived, and down in my heart there was a conviction that he was right, and that I was not fit to be a missionary. . . . This went on for two, or three days, until I felt perfectly miserable. . . . At last, in a kind of despair, I asked the Lord to fill me with the Holy Spirit; and the moment I did this . . . I began to see myself, and what a selfish ambition I had."

But he did not yet receive the blessing sought. He landed in India and went with a fellow-missionary to an open-air service. "The missionary spoke," said John Hyde, "and I was told that he was speaking about Jesus Christ as the real Savior from sin. When he had finished his address, a respectable-looking man, speaking good English, asked the missionary whether he himself had been thus saved? The question went home to my heart; for if it had been asked me, I would have had to confess that Christ had not fully saved me, because I knew there was a sin in my life which had not been taken away. I realized what a dishonor it would be on the name of Christ to have to confess that I was preaching a Christ that had not delivered me from sin, though I was proclaiming to others that He was a perfect Savior. I went back to my room and shut myself in, and told the Lord that it must be one of two things: either He must give me victory over all my sins, and especially over the sin that so easily beset me, or I must return to America and seek there for some other work. I said I could not stand up to preach the Gospel until I could testify of its power in my own life. I . . . realized how reasonable this was, and the Lord assured me that He was able and willing to deliver me from all sin. He did deliver me, and I have not had a doubt of this since."

It was then, and then only, that John Hyde became Praying Hyde. And it is only by such a full surrender and such a definite claiming to be delivered from the power of sin in our lives that you and I can be men of prevailing prayer. The point we wish to emphasize, however, is the one already mentioned. A comparatively unknown man prays for John

Hyde, who was then unknown to the world, and by his prayers brings down such a blessing upon him that everyone knows of him now as "Praying Hyde." Did you say in your heart, dear reader, a little while ago, that you could not hope to be a Praying Hyde? Of course we cannot all give so much time to prayer. For physical or other reasons we may be hindered from long-continued praying. But we may all have his spirit of prayer. And may we not all do for others what the unnamed friend did for John Hyde?

Can we not pray the blessing down upon others—upon your vicar or pastor? Upon your friend? Upon your family? What a ministry is ours, if we will but enter it! But to do so, we must make the full surrender which John Hyde made. Have we done it? Failure in prayer is due to fault in the heart. Only the "pure in heart" can see God. And only those who "call on the Lord out of a pure heart" (II Tim. ii. 22) can confidently claim answers to their prayers.

What a revival would break out, what a mighty blessing would come down if only everyone who read these words would claim the fullness of the Holy Spirit now!

Do you not see why it is that God wants us to pray? Do you now see why everything worth having depends upon prayer? There are several reasons, but one stands out very clearly and vividly before us after reading this chapter. It is just this: if we ask and God does not give, then the fault is with us. Every unanswered prayer is a clarion call to search the heart to see what is wrong there; for the promise is unmistakable in its clearness: "If ye shall ask anything in My name, that will I do" (John xiv. 14).

Truly he who prays puts, not God, but his own spiritual life to the test!

> Let me come closer to Thee, Jesus,
>   Oh, closer every day;
> Let me lean harder on Thee, Jesus,
>   Yes, harder all the way.

Chapter 4: Asking for Signs

"DOES God indeed answer prayer?" is a question often on the lips of people, and oftener still in their inmost hearts. "Is prayer of any real use?" Somehow or other we cannot help praying; but then even pagan savages cry out to someone or something to aid them in times of danger and disaster and distress.

And those of us who really do believe in prayer are soon faced with another question: "Is it right to put God to the test?" Moreover, a further thought flashes into our minds: "Dare we put God to the test?" For there is little doubt that failure in the prayer-life is often—always?—due to failure in the spiritual life. So many people harbor much unbelief in the heart regarding the value and effectiveness of prayer; and without faith, prayer is vain.

Asking for signs? Putting God to the test? Would to God we could persuade Christian men and women to do so. Why, what a test this would be of our own faith in God, and of our own holiness of life. Prayer is the touchstone of true godliness. God asks our prayers, values our prayers, needs our prayers. And if those prayers fail, we have only ourselves to blame. We do not mean by this that effective prayer always gets just what it asks for. Now, the Bible teaches us that we are allowed to put God to the test. The example of Gideon in Old Testament days is sufficient to show us that God honors our faith even when that faith is faltering. He allows us to "prove Him" even after a definite promise from Himself. This is a very great comfort to us.

Gideon said unto God, "If Thou wilt save Israel by mine hand, as Thou hast said, behold, I will put a fleece of wool on the floor; and if the dew be on the fleece only . . . then shall I know that Thou wilt save Israel by mine hand, as Thou has said." Yet, although there was a "bowl full of water" in the fleece the next morning, this did not satisfy Gideon! He dares to put God to the test the second time, and to ask that the fleece should be dry instead of wet the following night. "And God did so that night" (Judges vi. 40).

It is all very wonderful, the Almighty God just doing what a hesitating man asks Him to do! We catch our breath and stand amazed, scarcely knowing which startles us the more—the daring of the man, or the condescension of God! Of course, there is more in the story than meets the eye. No doubt Gideon thought that the "fleece" represented himself, Gideon.

If God would indeed fill him with His Spirit, why, salvation was assured. But as he wrung the fleece out, he began to compare himself with the saturated wool. "How unlike this fleece am I! God promises deliverance, but I do not feel full of the Spirit of God. No inflow of the mighty power of God seems to have come into me. Am I indeed fit for this great feat?" No! But then, it is "Not I, but God." "O God, let the fleece be dry—canst Thou still work? Even if I do not feel any superhuman power, any fullness of spiritual blessing within me: even if I feel as dry as this fleece, canst Thou still deliver Israel by my arm?" (Little wonder that he prefaced his prayer with the words, "Let not Thine anger be hot against me"!) "And God did so that night: for it was dry upon the fleece only, and there was dew on all the ground" (verse 40).

Yes, there is more in the story than can be seen at a glance. And is it not so in our own case? The devil so often assures us that our prayers cannot claim an answer because of the "dryness" of our souls. Answers to prayer, however, do not depend upon our feelings, but upon the trustworthiness of the Promiser.

Now, we are not urging that Gideon's way of procedure is for us, or for anyone, the normal course of action. It seems to reveal much hesitation to believe God's Word. In fact, it looks gravely like doubting God. And surely it grieves God when we show a faith in Him which is but partial.

The higher and better and safer way is to "ask, nothing doubting." But it is very comforting and assuring to us to know that God allowed Gideon to put Him to the test. Nor is this the only such case mentioned in Scripture. The most surprising instance of "proving God" happened on the Sea of Galilee. St. Peter put our Lord Himself to the test. "If it be Thou—" yet our Savior had already said, "It is I." "If it be Thou, bid me come unto Thee on the water." And our Lord said, "Come," and Peter "walked on the water" (Matt. xiv. 28, 29). But this "testing-faith" of Peter's soon failed him. "Little faith" (verse 31) so often and so quickly becomes "doubt." Remember that Christ did not reprove him for coming. Our Lord did not say, "Wherefore didst thou come?" but "Wherefore didst thou doubt?"

To put God to the test is, after all, not the best method. He has given us so many promises contingent on believing prayer, and has so often proved His power and His willingness to answer prayer, that we ought, as a rule, to hesitate very much before we ask Him for signs as well as for wonders!

But, someone may be thinking, does not the Lord God Almighty Himself bid us to put Him to the test? Did He not say, "Bring ye the whole tithe into the storehouse . . . and prove Me now herewith, saith the Lord of Hosts, if I will not open unto you the windows of heaven, and pour you out a blessing, that there shall not be room enough to receive it"? (Mal. iii. 10).

Yes that is true: God does say, "Prove Me: test Me." But it is really we ourselves who are thus tested. If the windows of heaven are not opened when we pray, and this blessing of fullness-to-overflowing is not bestowed upon us, it can only be because we are not whole-tithers. When we are in very deed wholly yielded to God—when we have brought the whole tithe into the storehouse for God—we shall find such a blessing that we shall not need to put God to any test! This is a thing we shall have to speak about when we come to the question of unanswered prayer.

Meanwhile we want every Christian to ask, "Have I ever fairly tested prayer?" How long is it since you last offered up a definite prayer? People pray for "a blessing" upon an address, or a meeting, or a mission; and some blessing is certain to come, for others are also pleading with God about the matter. You ask for relief from pain or healing of sickness: but Godless people, for whom no one appears to be praying, often recover, and sometimes in a seemingly miraculous way. And we may feel that we might have got better even if no prayer had been offered on our behalf. It seems to me that so many people cannot put their finger upon any really definite and conclusive answer to prayer in their own experience. Most Christians do not give God a chance to show His delight in granting His children's petitions; for their requests are so vague and indefinite. If this is so, it is not surprising that prayer is so often a mere form—an almost mechanical repetition, day by day, of certain phrases; a few minutes' "exercise" morning and evening.

Then there is another point. Have you, when in prayer, ever had the witness borne in upon you that your request was granted? Those who know something of the private life of men of prayer are often amazed at the complete assurance which comes over them at times that their prayers are answered, long before the boon they seek is actually in their possession. One prayer-warrior would say, "A peace came over my soul. I was confident my request was granted me." He then just thanked God for what he was quite sure God had done for him. And his assurance would prove to be absolutely well founded.

Our Lord Himself always had this assurance, and we should ever bear in mind that, although He was God, He lived His earthly life as a perfect Man, depending upon the Holy Spirit of God.

When He stood before the opened tomb of Lazarus, before He had actually called upon the dead to come forth, He said, "Father, I thank Thee that Thou hast heard Me. And I know that Thou hearest Me always" (John xi. 41, 42). Why, then, did He utter His thanks? "Because of the people which stand by I said it, that they may believe that Thou hast sent Me." If Christ is dwelling in our hearts by faith: if the Holy Spirit is breathing into us our petitions, and we are "praying in the Holy Ghost," ought we not to know that the Father "hears" us? (Jude 20). And will not those who stand by begin to recognize that we, too, are God-sent?

Men of prayer and women of prayer will agonize before God for something which they know is according to His will, because of some definite promise on the page of Scripture. They may pray for hours, or even for days, when suddenly the Holy Spirit reveals to them in no uncertain way that God has granted their request; and they are confident that they need no longer send up any more petitions to God about the matter. It is as if God said in clear tones: "Thy prayer is heard and I have granted thee the desire of thy heart." This is not the experience of only one man, but most men to whom prayer is the basis of their life will bear witness to the same fact. Nor is it a solitary experience in their lives: it occurs again and again.

Then prayer must give place to action. God taught Moses this: "Wherefore criest thou unto Me? Speak unto the children of Israel that they go forward" (Exod. xiv. 15).

We are not surprised to find that Dr. Goforth, a much-used missionary in China, often has this assurance given him that his petitions are granted. "I knew that God had answered. I received definite assurance that He would open the way." For why should anyone be surprised at this? The Lord Jesus said, "Ye are My friends, if ye do the things I command you. No longer do I call you servants; for the servant knoweth not what his lord doeth: but I have called you friends" (John xv. 14, 15). Do you think it surprising, then, if the Lord lets us, His "friends," know something of His plans and purposes?

The question at once arises, does God mean this to be the experience of only a few chosen saints, or does He wish all believers to exercise a like faith, and to have a like assurance that their prayers are answered?

We know that God is no respecter of persons, and therefore we know that any true believer in Him may share His mind and will. We are His friends if we do the things He commands us. One of those things is "prayer." Our Savior begged His disciples to "have faith in God" (the literal translation is "Have the faith of God"). Then, He declares, you can say to a mountain, "Be thou taken up and cast into the sea," and if you believe and doubt not, it shall come to pass. Then He gives this promise: "All things whatsoever ye pray and ask for, believe that ye have received them [that is, in heaven], and ye shall have them [on earth]" (Mark xi. 24). Now, this is exactly the experience we have been talking about. This is just what real men of prayer do. Such things naturally pass the comprehension of unbelievers. Such things are perplexing to the half-believers. Our Lord, however, desires that men should know that we are His disciples, sent as He was sent (John xvii. 18 and xx. 21). They will know this if we love one another (John xiii. 35). But another proof is provided, and it is this: if we know and they see that "God heareth us always" (John xi. 42).

Some of us at once recall to mind George Müller's wonderful prayer-life. On one occasion, when crossing from Quebec to Liverpool, he had prayed very definitely that a chair he had written to New York for should arrive in time to catch the steamer, and he was quite confident that God had granted his petition. About half an hour before the tender was timed to take the passengers to the ship, the agents informed him that no chair had arrived, and that it could not possibly come in time for the steamer. Now, Mrs. Muller suffered much from sea-sickness, and it was absolutely essential that she should have the chair. Yet nothing would induce Mr. Muller to buy another one from a shop near by. "We have made special prayer that our Heavenly Father would be pleased to provide it for us, and we will trust Him to do so," was his reply; and he went on board absolutely sure that his trust was not misplaced, and would not miscarry. Just before the tender left, a van drove up, and on the top of the load it carried was Mr. Muller's chair. It was hurried on board and placed into the hands of the very man who had urged George Müller to buy another one! When he handed it to Mr. Muller, the latter expressed no surprise, but quietly removed his hat and thanked his Heavenly Father. To this man of God such an answer to prayer was not wonderful, but natural. And do you not think that God allowed the chair to be held back till the very last minute as a lesson to Mr. Muller's friends-and to us? We should never have heard of that incident but for that delay.

God does all He can to induce us to pray and to trust, and yet how slow we are to do so! Oh, what we miss through lack of faith and want of prayer! No one can have very real and deep communion with God who does not know how to pray so as to get answers to prayer.

If one has any doubt as to God's willingness to be put to the test, let him read a little book called Nor Scrip (Marshall, Morgan and Scott, Ltd.). Miss Amy Wilson Carmichael tells us in its pages how again and again she "proved God." One gets the impression from the book that it was no accident that led her to do so. Surely God's hand was in it? For instance, in order to rescue a Hindu child from a life of "religious" shame, it was necessary to spend a hundred rupees. Was she justified in doing so? She could help many girls for such a sum: ought she to spend it on one? Miss Wilson Carmichael felt led to pray that God would send her the round sum of a hundred rupees—no more, no less—if it was His will that the money should be spent in this way. The money came—the exact amount— and the sender of it explained that she had sat down to write a check for a broken sum, but had been impelled to make it just a hundred rupees.

That happened over fifteen years ago, and since that time this same missionary has put God to the test over and over again, and He has never failed her. This is what she says: "Never once in fifteen years has a bill been left unpaid; never once has a man or woman been told when we were in need of help; but never once have we lacked any good thing. Once, as if to show what could be done if it were required, 25 pounds came by telegram! Sometimes a man would emerge from the clamoring crowd at a railway station, and slip some indispensable gift of money into the hand, and be lost in the crowd again before the giver could be identified."

Is it wonderful? Wonderful! Why, what does St. John say, speaking by the Spirit of God? "And this is the boldness which we have towards Him, that if we ask anything, according to His will, He heareth us; and if we know that He heareth us, whatsoever we ask, we know that we have the petitions which we have asked of Him" (I John v. 14, 15). Have you and I such "boldness"? If not, why not?

To call it wonderful is to show our want of faith. It is natural to God to answer prayer: normal, not extraordinary.

The fact is—let us be quite honest and straightforward about it—the fact is so many of us do not believe God. We may just as well be quite candid about it. If we love God we ought to pray, because He wants us to pray, and commands us to pray. If we believe God we shall pray because we cannot help doing so: we cannot get on without it. Fellow-Christian, you believe in God, and you believe on Him (John iii. 16), but have you advanced far enough in the Christian life to believe Him; that is, to believe what He says and all He says? Does it not sound blasphemous to ask such a thing of a Christian man? Yet how few believers really believe God!—God forgive us! Has it ever struck you that we trust the word of our fellow-man more easily than we trust God's word? And yet, when a man does "believe God," what miracles of grace God works in and through him! No man ever lived who has been revered and respected by so many peoples and tongues as that man of whom we are told three times over in the New Testament that "He believed God" (Rom. iv. 3; Gal. iii. 6; James ii. 23). Yes, "Abraham believed God, and it was reckoned unto him for righteousness." And today, Christian and Jew and Moslem vie with each other in honoring his name. We implore every believer on Christ Jesus never to rest till he can say, "I believe God, and will act on that belief" (Acts xxvii. 25).

But before we leave the question of testing God, we should like to point out that sometimes God leads us on "to prove Him." Sometimes God has put it into the heart of Miss Wilson Carmichael to ask for things she saw no need for. Yet she felt impelled by the Holy Spirit to ask. Not only were they granted her, but they also proved an inestimable boon. Yes, God knows what things we have need of, whether we want them or not, before we ask (Matt. vi. 8). Has not God said, "I will in no wise fail thee"?

Oftentimes the temptation would come to Miss Wilson Carmichael to let others know of some special need. But always the inner assurance would come, as in the very voice of God, "I know, and that is enough." And, of course, God was glorified. During the trying days of the war, even the heathen used to say, "Their God feeds them." "Is it not known all the country round," said a worldly heathen, "that your God hears prayer?"

Oh, what glory to God was brought about by their simple faith! Why do not we believe God? Why do we not take God at His word? Do believers or unbelievers ever say of us, "We know your prayers are answered"? Ye missionaries the wide world over, listen! (Oh, that these words might reach every ear, and stir every heart!) It is the yearning desire of God—of our loving Savior Jesus Christ—that every one of us should have the same strong faith as that devoted lady missionary we are speaking about.

Our loving Father does not wish any child of His to have one moment's anxiety or one unsatisfied need. No matter how great our need may be; no matter how numerous our requirements, if we only "prove Him" in the manner He bids us, we shall never have room enough to receive all the blessing He will give (Mal. iii. 10).

> Oh, what peace we often forfeit!
> Oh, what needless pain we bear!
> All because we do not carry
> Everything to God in prayer;

or all because, when we do "carry it," we do not believe God's word. Why is it we find it so hard to trust Him? Has He ever failed us? Has He not said over and over and over again that He will grant all petitions offered out of a pure heart, "in His name"? "Ask of Me"; "Pray ye"; "Prove Me"; "Try Me." The Bible is full of answers to prayer—wonderful answers, miraculous answers; and yet somehow our faith fails us, and we dishonor God by distrusting Him!

> If our faith were but more simple
> We should take Him at His word,
> And our lives would be all sunshine
> In the bounties of our Lord.

But our eye must be "single" if our faith is to be simple and our "whole body full of light" (Matt. vi. 22). Christ must be the sole Master. We cannot expect to be free from anxiety if we are trying to serve God and Mammon (Matt. vi. 24, 25). Again we are led back to the Victorious Life! When we indeed present our bodies "a living sacrifice, holy, acceptable to God" (Rom. xii. 1); when we present our members "as servants to righteousness and sanctification" (Rom. vi. 19); then He presents Himself to us and fills us with all the fullness of God (Eph. iii. 19).

Let us ever bear in mind that real faith not only believes that God can, but that He does answer prayer. We may be slothful in prayer, but "the Lord is not slack concerning His promise" (II Peter iii. 9). Is not that a striking expression?

Perhaps the most extraordinary testing of God which that Dohnavur missionary tells us of is the following. The question arose of purchasing a rest-house in the hills near by. Was it the right thing to do? Only God could decide. Much prayer was made. Eventually the petition was offered up that if it was God's will that the house should be purchased, the exact sum of 100 pounds should be received. That amount came at once. Yet they still hesitated. Two months later they asked God to give them again the same sign of His approval of the purchase. That same day another check for 100 pounds came. Even now they scarcely liked to proceed in the matter. In a few days' time, however, another round sum of 100 pounds was received, earmarked for the purchase of such a house. Does it not flood our hearts with joy to remember that our gracious Savior is so kind? It is St. Luke the physician who tells us that God is kind (Luke vi. 35). Love is always "kind" (I Cor. xiii. 4); and God is Love. Think over it when you pray. Our Lord is "kind." It will help us in our intercessions. He bears so patiently with us when our faith would falter. "How precious is Thy lovingkindness, O God" (Psalm xxxvi. 7); "Thy lovingkindness is better than life" (Psalm lxiii. 3).

The danger is that we read of such simple faith in prayer, and say, "How wonderful!" and forget that God desires every one of us to have such faith and such prayer. God has no favorites! He wants me to pray; He wants you to pray. He allows such things to happen as we have described above, and suffers them to come to our knowledge, not to surprise us, but to stimulate us. One sometimes wishes that Christian people would forget all the man-made rules with which we have hedged prayer about! Let us be simple. Let us be natural. Take God at His word. Let us remember that "the kindness of God our Savior, and His love toward man," has appeared (Titus iii. 4). God sometimes leads men into the prayer-life. Sometimes, however, God has to drive us into such a life.

As some of us look back over our comparatively prayerless life, what a thrill of wonder and of joy comes over us as we think of the kindness and "patience of Christ" (II Thess. iii. 5). Where should we have been without that? We fail Him, but, blessed be His name, He has never failed us, and He never will do so. We doubt Him, we mistrust His love and His providence and His guidance; we "faint because of the way"; we murmur because of the way; yet all the time He is there blessing us, and waiting to pour out upon us a blessing so great that there shall not be room to receive it.

The promise of Christ still holds good: "Whatsoever ye shall ask in My name, that will I do, that the Father may be glorified in the Son" (John xiv. 14).

> *Prayer changes things—and yet how blind*
> *And slow we are to taste and see*
> *The blessedness that comes to those*
>   *Who trust in Thee.*

But henceforth we will just believe God.

Chapter 5: What Is Prayer?

MR. MOODY was once addressing a crowded meeting of children in Edinburgh. In order to get their attention he began with a question: "What is prayer?"—looking for no reply, and expecting to give the answer himself.

To his amazement scores of little hands shot up all over the hall. He asked one lad to reply; and the answer came at once, clear and correct, "Prayer is an offering up of our desires unto God for things agreeable to His will, in the name of Christ, with confession of our sins and thankful acknowledgment of His mercies." Mr. Moody's delighted comment was, "Thank God, my boy, that you were born in Scotland." But that was half a century ago. What sort of answer would he get today? How many English children could give a definition of prayer? Think for a moment and decide what answer you yourself would give.

What do we mean by prayer? I believe the vast majority of Christians would say, "Prayer is asking things from God." But surely prayer is much more than merely "getting God to run our errands for us," as someone puts it. It is a higher thing than the beggar knocking at the rich man's door.

The word "prayer" really means "a wish directed towards," that is, towards God. All that true prayer seeks is God Himself, for with Him we get all we need. Prayer is simply "the turning of the soul to God." David describes it as the lifting up of the living soul to the living God. "Unto Thee, O Lord, do I lift up my soul" (Psa. xxv. 1). What a beautiful description of prayer that is! When we desire the Lord Jesus to behold our souls, we also desire that the beauty of holiness may be upon us.

When we lift up our souls to God in prayer it gives God an opportunity to do what He will in us and with us. It is putting ourselves at God's disposal. God is always on our side, but we are not always on His side. When man prays, it is God's opportunity. The poet says:

> *Prayer is the soul's sincere desire,*
> *Uttered or unexpressed,*
> *The motion of a hidden fire*
> *That trembles in the breast.*

"Prayer," says an old Jewish mystic, "is the moment when heaven and earth kiss each other."

Prayer, then, is certainly not persuading God to do what we want God to do. It is not bending the will of a reluctant God to our will. It does not change His purpose, although it may release His power. "We must not conceive of prayer as overcoming God's reluctance," says Archbishop Trench, "but as laying hold of His highest willingness."

For God always purposes our greatest good. Even the prayer offered in ignorance and blindness cannot swerve Him from that, although, when we persistently pray for some harmful thing, our wilfulness may bring it about, and we suffer accordingly. "He gave them their request," says the Psalmist, "but sent leanness into their soul" (Psa. cvi. 15). They brought this "leanness" upon themselves. They were "cursed with the burden of a granted prayer."

Prayer, in the minds of some people, is only for emergencies! Danger threatens, sickness comes, things are lacking, difficulties arise—then they pray. Like the infidel down a coal mine: when the roof began to fall he began to pray. An old Christian standing by quietly remarked, "Aye, there's nowt like cobs of coal to make a man pray."

Prayer is, however, much more than merely asking God for something, although that is a very valuable part of prayer if only because it reminds us of our utter dependence upon God. It is also communion with God—intercourse with God—talking with (not only to) God. We get to know people by talking with them. We get to know God in like manner. The highest result of prayer is not deliverance from evil, or the securing of some coveted thing, but knowledge of God. "And this is life eternal, that they should know Thee, the only true God" (John xvii. 3). Yes, prayer discovers more of God, and that is the soul's greatest discovery. Men still cry out, "O, that I knew where I might find Him, that I might come even to His seat" (Job xxiii. 3).

The kneeling Christian always "finds" Him, and is found of Him. The heavenly vision of the Lord Jesus blinded the eyes of Saul of Tarsus on his downward course, but he tells us, later on, that when he was praying in the temple at Jerusalem he fell into a trance and saw Jesus. "I . . . saw him" (Acts xxii. 18). Then it was that Christ gave him his great commission to go to the Gentiles. Vision is always a precursor of vocation and venture. It was so with Isaiah. "I saw the Lord high and lifted up, and his train filled the temple" (Isa vi. 1). The prophet was evidently in the sanctuary praying when this happened. This vision also was a prelude to a call to service, "Go . . . ." Now, we cannot get a vision of God unless we pray. And where there is no vision the soul perishes.

A vision of God! Brother Lawrence once said, "Prayer is nothing else than a sense of God's presence"—and that is just the practice of the presence of God.

A friend of Horace Bushnell was present when that man of God prayed. There came over him a wonderful sense of God's nearness. He says: "When Horace Bushnell buried his face in his hands and prayed, I was afraid to stretch out my hand in the darkness, lest I should touch God." Was the Psalmist of old conscious of such a thought when he cried, "My soul, wait thou only upon God"? (Psa. lxii. 5.) I believe that much of our failure in prayer is due to the fact that we have not looked into this question, "What is prayer?" It is good to be conscious that we are always in the presence of God. It is better to gaze upon Him in adoration. But it is best of all to commune with Him as a Friend—and that is prayer.

Real prayer at its highest and best reveals a soul athirst for God—just for God alone. Real prayer comes from the lips of those whose affection is set on things above. What a man of prayer Zinzendorf was. Why? He sought the Giver rather than His gifts. He said: "I have one passion: it is He, He alone." Even the Mohammedan seems to have got hold of this thought. He says that there are three degrees in prayer. The lowest is that spoken only by the lips. The next is when, by a resolute effort, we succeed in fixing our thoughts on Divine things. The third is when the soul finds it hard to turn away from God. Of course, we know that God bids us "ask" of Him. We all obey Him so far; and we may rest well assured that prayer both pleases God and supplies all our need. But he would be a strange child who only sought his father's presence when he desired some gift from him! And do we not all yearn to rise to a higher level of prayer than mere petition? How is it to be done?

It seems to me that only two steps are necessary—or shall we say two thoughts? There must be, first of all, a realization of God's glory, and then of God's grace. We sometimes sing:

Grace and glory flow from Thee;
Shower, O shower them, Lord, on me.

Nor is such a desire fanciful, although some may ask what God's glory has to do with prayer.

But ought we not to remind ourselves Who He is to Whom we pray? There is logic in the couplet:

Thou art coming to a King;
Large petitions with thee bring.

Do you think that any one of us spends enough time in pondering over, yes, and marveling over, God's exceeding great glory? And do you suppose that any one of us has grasped the full meaning of the word "grace"? Are not our prayers so often ineffective and powerless—and sometimes even prayerless—because we rush unthinkingly and unpreparedly into God's presence, without realizing the majesty and glory of the God Whom we are approaching, and without reflecting upon the exceeding great riches of His glory in Christ Jesus, which we hope to draw upon? We must "think magnificently of God."

May we then suggest that before we lay our petitions before God we first dwell in meditation upon His glory and then upon His grace—for He offers us both. We must lift up the soul to God. Let us place ourselves, as it were, in the presence of God and direct our prayer to the King of kings, and Lord of lords, Who only hath immortality, dwelling in light unapproachable . . . to Whom be honor and power eternal (I Tim. vi. 16). Let us then give Him adoration and praise because of His exceeding great glory. Consecration is not enough. There must be adoration.

"Holy, holy, holy, is the Lord of Hosts," cry the seraphim; "the whole earth is full of his glory" (Isa. vi. 3). "Glory to God in the highest," cries the "whole multitude of the heavenly host" (Luke ii. 14). Yet some of us try to commune with God without stopping to "put off our shoes from off our feet" (Exod. iii. 5).

Lips cry "God be merciful"
That ne'er cry "God be praised."

O come let us adore Him!

And we may approach His glory with boldness. Did not our Lord pray that His disciples might behold His glory? (John xvii. 24). Why? And why is "the whole earth full of His glory"? The telescope reveals His infinite glory. The microscope reveals His uttermost glory. Even the unaided eye sees surpassing glory in landscape, sunshine, sea and sky. What does it all mean? These things are but a partial revelation of God's glory. It was not a desire for self-display that led our Lord to pray, "Father, glorify Thy Son" . . . "O Father, glorify Thou Me" (John xvii. 1, 3). Our dear Lord wants us to realize His infinite trustworthiness and unlimited power, so that we can approach Him in simple faith and trust.

In heralding the coming of Christ the prophet declared that "glory of the Lord shall be revealed, and all flesh shall see it together" (Isa. xl. 5). Now we must get a glimpse of that glory before we can pray aright. So our Lord said, "When ye pray, say Our Father, Who art in heaven [the realm of glory], hallowed be Thy name." There is nothing like a glimpse of glory to banish fear and doubt. Before we offer up our petitions may it not help us to offer up our adoration in the words of praise used by some of the saints of old? Some devout souls may not need such help. We are told that Francis of Assisi would frequently spend an hour or two in prayer on the top of Mount Averno, whilst the only word which escaped his lips would be "God" repeated at intervals. He began with adoration—and often stopped there!

But most of us need some help to realize the glory of the invisible God before we can adequately praise and adore Him. Old William Law said, "When you begin to pray, use such expressions of the attributes of God as will make you sensible of His greatness and power."

This point is of such tremendous importance that we venture to remind our readers of helpful words. Some of us begin every day with a glance heavenwards whilst saying, "Glory be to the Father, and to the Son, and to the Holy Ghost." The prayer, "O Lord God most holy, O Lord most mighty, O holy and merciful Savior!" is often enough to bring a solemn awe and a spirit of holy adoration upon the soul. The Gloria in Excelsis of the Communion Service is most uplifting: "Glory be to God on high and in earth peace. . . . We praise Thee; we bless Thee; we worship Thee; we glorify Thee; we give thanks to Thee for Thy great glory, O Lord God, heavenly King, God the Father Almighty." Which of us can from the heart utter praise like that and remain unmoved, unconscious of the very presence and wondrous majesty of the Lord God Almighty? A verse of a hymn may serve the same purpose.

> My God. how wonderful Thou art!
>   Thy majesty how bright.
> How beautiful Thy mercy-seat
>   In depths of burning light!
> How wonderful, how beautiful
>   The sight of Thee must be;
> Thine endless wisdom, boundless power
>   And awful purity.

This carries us into the very heavenlies, as also do the words:

> Holy, holy, holy, Lord God Almighty,
> All Thy works shall praise Thy name
> In earth, and sky, and sea.

We need to cry out, and to cry often, "My soul doth magnify the Lord, and my spirit hath rejoiced in God my Savior" (Luke i. 46, 47). Can we catch the spirit of the Psalmist and sing, "Bless the Lord, O my soul, and all that is within me, bless His holy name"? (Psa. ciii. 1.) "Bless the Lord, O my soul. O Lord my God, Thou art very great; Thou are clothed with honor and majesty" (Psa. civ. 1). When shall we learn that "in His temple everything saith Glory!" (Psa. xxix. 9, R.V.) Let us, too, cry, Glory!

Such worship of God, such adoration and praise and thanksgiving, not only put us into the spirit of prayer, but in some mysterious way they help God to work on our behalf. Do you remember those wonderful words, "Whoso offereth the sacrifice of thanksgiving, glorifyeth Me and prepareth a way that I may show him the salvation of God"?, (Psa. l. 23, R.V., marg.) Praise and thanksgiving not only open the gates of heaven for me to approach God, but also "prepare a way" for God to bless me. St. Paul cries, "Rejoice evermore!" before he says, "Pray without ceasing." So then our praise, as well as our prayers, is to be without ceasing.

At the raising of Lazarus our Lord's prayer had as its first utterance a note of thanksgiving. "Father, I thank Thee that Thou heardest Me" (John xi. 41). He said it for those around to hear. Yes, and for us to hear.

You may perhaps be wondering why it is that we should specially give thanks to God for His great glory when we kneel in prayer; and why we should spend any time in thinking of and gazing upon that glory. But is He not the King of Glory? All He is and all He does is glory. His holiness is "glorious" (Exod. xv. 11). His name is glorious (Deut. xxviii. 58). His work is "glorious" (Psa. cxi. 3). His power is glorious (Col. i. 11). His voice is glorious (Isa. xxx. 30).

> All things bright and beautiful
>   All creatures great and small.
> All things wise and wonderful,
>   The Lord God made them all.

for His glory.

"For of him and through him and unto him are all things; to whom be glory for ever" (Rom. xi. 36). And this is the God who bids us come to Him in prayer. This God is our God, and He has "gifts for men" (Psa. lxviii. 18). God says that everyone that is called by His name has been created for His glory (Isa. xliii. 7). His Church is to be a "glorious" Church—holy and without blemish (Eph. v. 27). Have you ever fully realized that the Lord Jesus desires to share with us the glory we see in Him? This is His great gift to you and me, His redeemed ones. Believe me, the more we have of God's glory, the less shall we seek His gifts. Not only in that day "when he shall come to be glorified in his saints" (II Thess. i. 10) is there glory for us, but here and now—today. He wishes us to be partakers of His glory. Did not our Lord Himself say so? "The glory which thou has given me, I have given unto them," He declares (John xvii. 22). What is God's command? "Arise, shine, for thy light is come, and the glory of the Lord is risen upon thee." Nay, more than this: "His glory shall be seen upon thee," says the inspired prophet (Isa. lx. 1, 2).

God would have people say of us as St. Peter said of the disciples of old: "The Spirit of Glory and the Spirit of God resteth upon you" (I Peter iv. 14). Would not that be an answer to most of our prayers? Could we ask for anything better? How can we get this glory? How are we to reflect it? Only as the result of prayer. It is when we pray, that the Holy Spirit takes of the things of Christ and reveals them unto us (John xvi. 15).

It was when Moses prayed, "Show me, I pray thee, thy glory," that he not only saw somewhat of it, but shared something of that glory, and his own face shone with the light of it (Exod. xxxiii. 18, xxxiv. 29). And when we, too, gaze upon the "glory of God in the face of Jesus Christ" (II Cor. iv. 6), we shall see not only a glimpse of that glory, but we shall gain something of it ourselves.

Now, that is prayer, and the highest result of prayer. Nor is there any other way of securing that glory, that God may be glorified in us (Isa. lx. 21).

Let us often meditate upon Christ's glory—gaze upon it and so reflect it and receive it. This is what happened to our Lord's first disciples. They said in awed tones, "We beheld his glory!" Yes, but what followed? A few plain, unlettered, obscure fishermen companied with Christ a little while, seeing His glory; and lo! they themselves caught something of that glory. And then others marveled and "took knowledge of them that they had been with Jesus" (Acts iv. 13). And when we can declare, with St. John, "Yea, and our fellowship is with the Father and with His Son Jesus Christ" (I John i. 3), people will say the same of us: "They have been with Jesus!"

As we lift up our soul in prayer to the living God, we gain the beauty of holiness as surely as a flower becomes beautiful by living in the sunlight. Was not our Lord Himself transfigured when He prayed? And the "very fashion" of our countenance will change, and we shall have our Mount of Transfiguration when prayer has its rightful place in our lives. And men will see in our faces "the outward and visible sign of an inward and spiritual grace." Our value to God and to man is in exact proportion to the extent in which we reveal the glory of God to others.

We have dwelt so much upon the glory of Him to Whom we pray, that we must not now speak of His grace.

What is prayer? It is a sign of spiritual life. I should as soon expect life in a dead man as spiritual life in a prayerless soul! Our spirituality and our fruitfulness are always in proportion to the reality of our prayers. If, then, we have at all wandered away from home in the matter of prayer, let us today resolve, "I will arise and go unto my Father, and say unto Him, Father—."

At this point I laid down my pen, and on the page of the first paper I picked up were these words: "The secret of failure is that we see men rather than God. Romanism trembled when Martin Luther saw God. The 'great awakening' sprang into being when Jonathan Edwards saw God. The world became the parish of one man when John Wesley saw God. Multitudes were saved when Whitfield saw God. Thousands of orphans were fed when George Müller saw God. And He is 'the same yesterday, today, and forever.' "

Is it not time that we got a new vision of God—of God in all His glory? Who can say what will happen when the Church sees God? But let us not wait for others. Let us, each one for himself, with unveiled face and unsullied heart, get this vision of the glory of the Lord.

"Blessed are the pure in heart, for they shall see God" (Matt. v. 8). No missioner whom it has been my joy to meet ever impressed me quite as much as Dr. Wilbur Chapman. He wrote to a friend: "I have learned some great lessons concerning prayer. At one of our missions in England the audiences were exceedingly small. But I received a note saying that an American missionary . . . was going to pray God's blessing down upon our work. He was known as 'Praying Hyde.' Almost instantly the tide turned. The hall became packed, and at my first invitation fifty men accepted Christ as their Savior. As we were leaving I said, 'Mr. Hyde, I want you to pray for me.' He came to my room, turned the key in the door, and dropped on his knees, and waited five minutes without a single syllable coming from his lips. I could hear my own heart thumping and his beating. I felt the hot tears running down my face. I knew I was with God. Then, with upturned face, down which the tears were streaming, he said 'O God!' Then for five minutes at least he was still again; and then, when he knew that he was talking with God . . . there came up from the depth of his heart such petitions for men as I had never heard before. I rose from my knees to know what real prayer was. We believe that prayer is mighty, and we believe it as we never did before."

Dr. Chapman used to say, "It was a season of prayer with John Hyde that made me realize what real prayer was. I owe to him more than I owe to any man for showing me what a prayer-life is, and what a real consecrated life is. . . . Jesus Christ became a new Ideal to me, and I had a glimpse of His prayer-life; and I had a longing which has remained to this day to be a real praying man." And God the Holy Spirit can so teach us.

> *Oh, ye who sigh and languish*
> *   And mourn your lack of power,*
> *Hear ye this gentle whisper:*
> *   "Could ye not watch one hour?"*
> *For fruitfulness and blessing*
> *   There is no royal road;*
> *The power for holy service*
> *   Is intercourse with God.*

Chapter 6: How Shall I Pray?

How shall I pray? Could there be a more important question for a Christian man to ask? How shall I approach the King of Glory?

When we read Christ's promises regarding prayer we are apt to think that He puts far too great a power into our hands—unless, indeed, we hastily conclude that it is impossible for Him to act as He promises. He says, ask "anything," "whatsoever," "what ye will," and it shall be done.

But then He puts in a qualifying phrase. He says that we are to ask in His name. That is the condition, and the only one, although, as we shall remind ourselves later on, it is sometimes couched in different words.

If, therefore, we ask and do not receive, it can only be that we are not fulfilling this condition. If then, we are true disciples of His—if we are sincere—we shall take pains (infinite pains, if need be) to discover just what it means to ask in His name; and we shall not rest content until we have fulfilled that condition. Let us read the promise again to be quite sure about it. "Whatsoever ye shall ask in my name, that will I do, that the Father may be glorified in the Son. If ye shall ask anything in my name, I will do it" (John xiv. 13, 14).

This was something quite new, for our Lord said so. "Hitherto ye have asked nothing in my name," but now, "ask and ye shall receive, that your joy may be full" (John xvi. 24).

Five times over our Lord repeats this simple condition, "In my name" (John xiv. 13, 14; xv. 16; xvi. 23, 24, 26). Evidently something very important is here implied. It is more than a condition—it is also a promise, an encouragement, for our Lord's biddings are always His enablings. What, then, does it mean to ask in His name? We must know this at all costs, for it is the secret of all power in prayer. And it is possible to make a wrong use of those words. Our Lord said, "Many shall come in my name, saying, 'I am Christ,' and shall deceive many" (Matt. xxiv. 5). He might well have said, "And many shall think they are praying to the Father in my name, whilst deceiving themselves."

Does it mean just adding the words, "and all this we ask in the name of Jesus Christ," at the end of our prayers?

Many people apparently think that it does. But have you never heard—or offered—prayers full of self-will and selfishness which ended up in that way, "for Christ's sake. Amen"?

God could not answer the prayers St. James refers to in his epistle just because those who offered them added, "we ask these things in the name of our Lord Jesus Christ." Those Christians were asking "amiss" (James iv. 3). A wrong prayer cannot be made right by the addition of some mystic phrase!

And a right prayer does not fail if some such words are omitted. No! It is more than a question of words. Our Lord is thinking about faith and facts more than about some formula. The chief object of prayer is to glorify the Lord Jesus. We are to ask in Christ's name "that the Father may be glorified in the Son" (John xiv. 13). Listen! We are not to seek wealth or health, prosperity or success, ease or comfort, spirituality or fruitfulness in service simply for our own enjoyment or advancement or popularity, but only for Christ's sake—for His glory. Let us take three steps to a right understanding of those important words, "in my name."

(1) There is a sense in which some things are done only "for Christ's sake"—because of His atoning death. Those who do not believe in the atoning death of Christ cannot pray "in His name." They may use the words, but without effect. For we are "justified by His blood" (Rom. v. 9), and "we have redemption through His blood, even the forgiveness of sins" (Eph. i. 7; Col. i. 14). In these days when Unitarianism under its guileful name of Modernism has invaded all sects, it is most important to remember the place and work of the shed blood of Christ, or "prayer"—so-called—becomes a delusion and a snare.

Let us illustrate this point by an experience which happened quite early in Mr. Moody's ministry. The wife of an infidel judge—a man of great intellectual gifts—begged Mr. Moody to speak to her husband. Moody, however, hesitated at arguing with such a man, and told him so quite frankly. "But," he added, "if ever you are converted will you promise to let me know?" The judge laughed cynically, and replied, "Oh, yes, I'll let you know quick enough if I am ever converted!" Moody went his way, relying upon prayer. That judge was converted, and within a year. He kept his promise and told Moody just how it came about. "I began to grow very uneasy and miserable one night when my wife was at a prayer-meeting. I went to bed before she came home. I could not sleep all that night. Getting up early the next morning, I told my wife I should not need any breakfast, and went off to my office. Telling the clerks they could take a holiday, I shut myself up in my private room. But I became more and more wretched. Finally, I fell on my knees and asked God to forgive me my sins, but I would not say 'for Jesus' sake,' for I was Unitarian, and I did not believe in the atonement. In an agony of mind I kept praying, 'O God, forgive me my sins,' but no answer came. At last, in desperation, I cried, 'O God, for Christ's sake forgive my sins.' Then I found peace at once."

That judge had no access to the presence of God until he sought it in the name of Jesus Christ. When he came in Christ's name he was at once heard and forgiven. Yes, to pray "in the name" of the Lord Jesus is to ask for things which the blood of Christ has secured—"purchased"—for us. We have "boldness to enter into the holiest by the blood of Jesus" (Heb. x. 19). There is entrance by no other way.

But this is not all that those words "In my Name" mean.

(2) The most familiar illustration of coming "in the name" of Christ is that of drawing money from a bank by means of a check. I can draw from my bank account only up to the amount of my deposit there. In my own name, I can go no farther. In the Bank of England I have no money whatsoever, and can therefore draw nothing therefrom. But suppose a very wealthy man who has a big account there gives me a blank check bearing his signature, and bids me fill it in to any amount I choose. He is my friend. What shall I do? Shall I just satisfy my present need, or shall I draw as much as I dare? I shall certainly do nothing to offend my friend, or to lower myself in his esteem.

Well, we are told by some that heaven is our bank. God is the Great Banker, for "every good gift and every perfect gift is from above, and cometh down from the Father" (James i. 17). We need a "check" wherewith to "draw" upon this boundless store. The Lord Jesus gives us a blank check in prayer. "Fill it in," says He, "to any amount; ask 'anything,' 'what ye will,' and you shall have it. Present your check in My name, and your request will be honored." Let me put this in the words of a well-known evangelist of today. "That is what happens when I go to the bank of heaven-when I go to God in prayer. I have nothing deposited there; I have no credit there; and if I go in my own name I will get absolutely nothing. But Jesus Christ has unlimited credit in heaven, and He has granted me the privilege of going with His name on my checks; and when I thus go my prayers will be honored to any extent. To pray, then, in the name of Christ is to pray, not on the ground of my credit, but His."

This is all very delightful, and, in a sense, very true.

If the check were drawn on a Government account, or upon some wealthy corporation, one might be tempted to get all one could. But remember we are coming to a loving Father to Whom we owe all, and Whom we love with all our heart, and to Whom we may come repeatedly. In cashing our checks at the bank of heaven we desire chiefly His honor and His glory. We wish to do only that which is pleasing in His sight. To cash some of our "checks"—to answer some of our prayers—would only bring dishonor to His name, and discredit and discomfort to us. True, His resources are unlimited; but His honor is assailable.

But experience makes argument unnecessary! Dear reader, have we not—all of us— often tried this method only to fail?

How many of us dare say we have never come away from the bank of heaven without getting what we asked for, although we have apparently asked "in Christ's name"? Wherein do we fail? Is it because we do not seek to learn God's will for us? We must not try to exceed His will.

May I give a personal experience of my own which has never been told in public, and which is probably quite unique? It happened over thirty years ago, and now I see why. It makes such a splendid illustration of what we are now trying to learn about prayer.

A well-to-do friend, and an exceedingly busy one, wished to give me one pound towards a certain object. He invited me to his office, and hastily wrote out a check for the amount. He folded the check and handed it to me, saying, "I will not cross it. Will you kindly cash it at the bank?" On arriving at the bank I glanced at my name on the check without troubling to verify the amount, endorsed it, and handed it to a clerk. "This is rather a big sum to cash over the counter," he said, eyeing me narrowly. "Yes," I replied laughingly, "one pound!" "No," said the clerk: "this is made out for 'one thousand pounds!'"

And so it was! My friend was, no doubt, accustomed to writing big checks; and he had actually written "one thousand" instead of "one" pound. Now, what was my position legally? The check was truly in his name. The signature was all right. My endorsement was all right. Could I not demand the 1,000 pounds, provided there was sufficient in the account? The check was written deliberately, if hurriedly, and freely to me—why should I not take the gift? Why not?

But I was dealing with a friend—a generous friend to whom I owed many deeds of lovingkindness. He had revealed his mind to me. I knew his wishes and desires.

He meant to give me one pound, and no more. I knew his intention, his "mind," and at once took back the all-too-generous check, and in due time I received just one pound, according to his will. Had that donor given me a blank check the result would have been exactly the same. He would have expected me to write in one pound, and my honor would have been at stake in my doing so. Need we draw the lesson? God has His will for each one of us, and unless we seek to know that will we are likely to ask for "a thousand," when He knows that "one" will be best for us. In our prayers we are coming to a Friend—a loving Father. We owe everything to Him. He bids us come to Him whenever we like for all we need. His resources are infinite.

But He bids us to remember that we should ask only for those things that are according to His will—only for that which will bring glory to His name. John says, "If we ask anything according to His will, He heareth us" (I John v. 14). So then our Friend gives us a blank check, and leaves us to fill in "anything"; but He knows that if we truly love Him we shall never put down—never ask for—things He is not willing to give us, because they would be harmful to us.

Perhaps with most of us the fault lies in the other direction. God gives us a blank check and says, Ask for a pound—and we ask for a shilling! Would not my friend have been insulted had I treated him thus? Do we ask enough? Do we dare to ask "according to His riches in glory"?

The point we are dwelling upon, however, is this—we cannot be sure that we are praying "in His name" unless we learn His will for us.

(3) But even now we have not exhausted the meaning of those words, "In my Name." We all know what it is to ask for a thing "in the name" of another. But we are very careful not to allow anyone to use our name who is not to be trusted, or he might abuse our trust and discredit our name. Gehazi, the trusted servant, dishonestly used Elisha's name when he ran after Naaman. In Elisha's name he secured riches, but also inherited a curse for his wickedness.

A trusted clerk often uses his employer's name and handles great sums of money as if they were his own. But this he does only so long as he is thought to be worthy of such confidence in him. And he uses the money for his master, and not for himself. All our money belongs to our Master, Christ Jesus. We can go to God for supplies in His name if we use all we get for His glory.

When I go to cash a check payable to me, the banker is quite satisfied if the signature of his client is genuine and that I am the person authorized to receive the money. He does not ask for references to my character. He has no right whatever to enquire whether I am worthy to receive the money or to be trusted to use it aright. It is not so with the Bank of

Heaven. Now, this is a point of greatest importance. Do not hurry over what is now to be said.

When I go to heaven's bank in the name of the Lord Jesus, with a check drawn upon the unsearchable riches of Christ, God demands that I shall be a worthy recipient. Not "worthy" in the sense that I can merit or deserve anything from a holy God—but worthy in the sense that I am seeking the gift not for my own glory or self-interest, but only for the glory of God.

Otherwise I may pray and not get. "Ye ask and receive not, because ye ask amiss that ye may spend it in your pleasures" (James iv. 3, R.V.).

The great Heavenly Banker will not cash checks for us if our motives are not right. Is not this why so many fail in prayer? Christ's name is the revelation of His character.

To pray "in His name" is to pray in His character, as His representative sent by Him: it is to pray by His Spirit and according to His will; to have His approval in our asking, to seek what He seeks, to ask help to do what He Himself would wish to be done, and to desire to do it not for our own glorification, but for His glory alone. To pray "in His name" we must have identity of interests and purpose. Self and its aims and desires must be entirely controlled by God's Holy Spirit, so that our wills are in complete harmony with Christ's will.

We must reach the attitude of St. Augustine when he cried, "O Lord, grant that I may do Thy will as if it were my will, so that Thou mayest do my will as if it were Thy will."

Child of God, does this seem to make prayer "in His name" quite beyond us? That was not our Lord's intention. He is not mocking us! Speaking of the Holy Spirit our Lord used these words: "The Comforter . . . Whom the Father will send in my name" (John xiv. 26). Now, our Savior wants us to be so controlled by the Holy Spirit that we may act in Christ's name. "As many as are led by the Spirit of God, they are the sons of God" (Rom. viii. 14). And only sons can say, "Our Father."

Our Lord said of Saul of Tarsus: "He is a chosen vessel unto Me to bear My name before the Gentiles and kings, and the children of Israel" (Acts ix. 15). Not to them, but before them. So St. Paul says: "It pleased God to reveal his Son in me." We cannot pray in Christ's name unless we bear that name before people. And this is only possible so long as we "abide in" Him and His words abide in us. So we come to this—unless the heart is right the prayer must be wrong.

Christ said, "If ye abide in Me, and My words abide in you, ye shall ask what ye will, and it shall be done unto you" (John xv. 7).

Those three promises are really identical—they express the same thought in different words. Look at them—

Ask anything in my name, I will do it (John xiv. 13, 14).

Ask what ye will (if ye abide in me and my words abide in you), and it shall be done (John xv. 7).

Ask anything, according to his will, we have the petitions (I John v. 14).

And we could sum them all up in the words of St. John, "Whatsoever we ask, we receive of him, because we keep his commandments and do the things which are pleasing in his sight" (I John iii. 22). When we do what He bids, He does what we ask! Listen to God and God will listen to you. Thus our Lord gives us "power of attorney" over His kingdom, the kingdom of heaven, if only we fulfil the condition of abiding in Him.

Oh, what a wonder is this! How eagerly and earnestly we should seek to know His "mind," His wish, His will!—How amazing it is that any one of us should by our own self-seeking miss such unsearchable riches! We know that God's will is the best for us. We know that He longs to bless us and make us a blessing. We know that to follow our own inclination is absolutely certain to harm us and to hurt us and those whom we love. We know that to turn away from His will for us is to court disaster. O child of God, why do we not trust Him fully and wholly? Here we are, then, once again brought face to face with a life of holiness. We see with the utmost clearness that our Savior's call to prayer is simply a clarion call to holiness. "Be ye holy!" for without holiness no man can see God, and prayer cannot be efficacious.

When we confess that we "never get answers to our prayers," we are condemning not God, or His promises, or the power of prayer, but ourselves. There is no greater test of spirituality than prayer. The man who tries to pray quickly discovers just where he stands in God's sight.

Unless we are living the Victorious Life we cannot truly pray "in the name" of Christ, and our prayer-life must of necessity be feeble, fitful and oft-times unfruitful.

And "in His name" must be "according to His will." But can we know His will? Assuredly we can. St. Paul not only says, "Let this mind be in you which was in Christ Jesus . . ." (Phil. ii. 5); he also boldly declares, "We have the mind of Christ" (I Cor. ii. 16). How, then, can we get to know God's will?

We shall remember that "the secret of the Lord is with them that fear him" (Psa. xxv. 14).

In the first place, we must not expect God to reveal His will to us unless we desire to know that will and intend to do that will. Knowledge of God's will and the performance of that will go together. We are apt to desire to know God's will so that we may decide whether we will obey or not. Such an attitude is disastrous. "If any man willeth to do His will, he shall know of the teaching" (John vii. 17).

God's will is revealed in His Word in Holy Scriptures. What He promises in His Word I may know to be according to His will.

For example, I may confidently ask for wisdom, because His Word says, "If any . . . lack wisdom, let him ask of God . . . and it shall be given him" (James i. 5). We cannot be men of prevailing prayer unless we study God's Word to find out His will for us.

But it is the Holy Spirit of God Who is prayer's great Helper. Read again those wonderful words of St. Paul: "In the same way the Spirit also helps us in our weakness; for we do not know what prayers to offer nor in what way to offer them, but the Spirit Himself pleads for us in yearnings that can find no words, and the Searcher of hearts knows what the Spirit's meaning is, because His intercessions for God's people are in harmony with God's will" (Rom. viii. 26, 27; Weymouth).

What comforting words! Ignorance and helplessness in prayer are indeed blessed things if they cast us upon the Holy Spirit. Blessed be the name of the Lord Jesus! We are left without excuse. Pray we must: pray we can.

Remember our Heavenly Father is pledged to give the Holy Spirit to them that ask Him (Luke xi. 13)—and any other "good thing" too (Matt. vii. 11).

Child of God, you have often prayed. You have, no doubt, often bewailed your feebleness and slackness in prayer. But have you really prayed in His name?

It is when we have failed and know not "what prayers to offer" or "in what way," that the Holy Spirit is promised as our Helper.

Is it not worth while to be wholly and whole-heartedly yielded to Christ? The half-and-half Christian is of very little use either to God or man. God cannot use him, and man has no use for him, but considers him a hypocrite. One sin allowed in the life wrecks at once our usefulness and our joy, and robs prayer of its power.

Beloved, we have caught a fresh glimpse of the grace and the glory of our Lord Jesus Christ. He is willing and waiting to share with us both His glory and His grace. He is willing to make us channels of blessing. Shall we not worship God in sincerity and truth, and cry eagerly and earnestly, "Lord, what shall I do?" (Acts xxii. 10, R.V.) and then, in the power of His might, do it?

St. Paul once shot up that prayer to heaven; "What shall I do?" What answer did he get? Listen! He tells us in his counsel to believers everywhere just what it meant to him, and should mean to us: "Beloved, put on . . . a heart of compassion, kindness, humility, long-suffering; . . . above all things put on love and let the peace of Christ rule in your hearts. . . . Let the word of Christ dwell in you richly in all wisdom. . . . And whatsoever ye do, in word or deed, do all in the name of the Lord Jesus, giving thanks to God the Father through him" (Col. iii. 12-17).

It is only when whatsoever we do is done in His name that He will do whatsoever we ask in His name.

Chapter 7: Must I Agonize?

PRAYER is measured, not by time, but by intensity. Earnest souls who read of men like Praying Hyde are today anxiously asking, "Am I expected to pray like that?"

They hear of others who sometimes remain on their knees before God all day or all night, refusing food and scorning sleep, whilst they pray and pray and pray. They naturally wonder, "Are we to do the same? Must all of us follow their examples?" We must remember that those men of prayer did not pray by time. They continued so long in prayer because they could not stop praying.

Some have ventured to think that in what has been said in earlier chapters I have hinted that we must all follow in their train. Child of God, do not let any such thought—such fear?—distress you. Just be willing to do what He will have you do—what He leads you to do. Think about it; pray about it. We are bidden by the Lord Jesus to pray to our loving Heavenly Father. We sometimes sing, "Oh, how He loves!" And nothing can fathom that love.

Prayer is not given us as a burden to be borne, or an irksome duty to fulfil, but to be a joy and power to which there is no limit. It is given us that we "may find grace to help us in time of need" (Heb. iv. 16, R.V.). And every time is a "time of need." "Pray ye" is an invitation to be accepted rather than a command to be obeyed. Is it a burden for a child to come to his father to ask for some boon? How a father loves his child, and seeks its highest good! How he shields that little one from any sorrow or pain or suffering! Our heavenly Father loves us infinitely more than any earthly father. The Lord Jesus loves us infinitely more than any earthly friend. God forgive me if any words of mine, on such a precious theme as prayer, have wounded the hearts or consciences of those who are yearning to know more about prayer. "Your heavenly Father knoweth," said our Lord: and if He knows, we can but trust and not be afraid.

A schoolmaster may blame a boy for neglected homework, or unpunctual attendance, or frequent absence; but the loving father in the home knows all about it. He knows all about the devoted service of the little laddie in the home circle, where sickness or poverty throws so many loving tasks in his way. Our dear, loving Father knows all about us. He sees. He knows how little leisure some of us have for prolonged periods of prayer.

For some of us God makes leisure. He makes us lie down (Psa. xxiii. 2) that He may make us look up. Even then, weakness of body often prevents prolonged prayer. Yet I question if any of us, however great and reasonable our excuses, spend enough thought over our prayers. Some of us are bound to be much in prayer. Our very work demands it. We may be looked upon as spiritual leaders; we may have the spiritual welfare or training of others. God forbid that we should sin against the Lord in ceasing to pray enough for them (I Sam. xii. 23). Yes, with some it is our very business—almost our life's work-to pray, Others—

> *Have friends who give them pain,*
> *Yet have not sought a friend in Him.*

For them they cannot help praying. If we have the burden of souls upon us we shall never ask, "How long need I pray?"

But how well we know the difficulties which surround the prayer-life of many! A little pile of letters lies before me as I write. They are full of excuses, and kindly protests, and reasonings it is true. But is that why they are written? No! No! Far from it. In every one of them there is an undercurrent of deep yearning to know God's will, and how to obey the call to prayer amid all the countless claims of life.

Those letters tell of many who cannot get away from others for times of secret prayer; of those who share even bedrooms; of busy mothers, and maids, and mistresses who scarcely know how to get through the endless washing and cooking, mending and cleaning, shopping and visiting; of tired workers who are too weary to pray when the day's work is done.

Child of God, our heavenly Father knows all about it. He is not a taskmaster. He is our Father. If you have no time for prayer, or no chance of secret prayer, why, just tell Him all about it—and you will discover that you are praying!

To those who seem unable to get any solitude at all, or even the opportunity of stealing into a quiet church for a few moments, may we point to the wonderful prayer-life of St. Paul ? Did it ever occur to you that he was in prison when he wrote most of those marvelous prayers of his which we possess? Picture him. He was chained to a Roman soldier day and night, and was never alone for a moment. Epaphias was there part of the time, and caught something of his master's passion for prayer. St. Luke may have been there. What prayer-meetings! No opportunity for secret prayer. No! but how much we owe to the uplifting of those chained hands! You and I may be never, or rarely ever, alone, but at least our hands are not fettered with chains, and our hearts are not fettered, nor our lips.

Can we make time for prayer? I may be wrong, but my own belief is that it is not God's will for most of us—and perhaps not for any of us—to spend so much time in prayer as to injure our physical health through getting insufficient food or sleep. With very many it is a physical impossibility, because of bodily weakness, to remain long in the spirit of intense prayer.

The posture in which we pray is immaterial. God will listen whether we kneel, or stand, or sit, or walk, or work.

I am quite aware that many have testified to the fact that God sometimes gives special strength to those who curtail their hours of rest in order to pray more. At one time the writer tried getting up very early in the morning—and every morning—for prayer and communion with God. After a time he found that his daily work was suffering in intensity and effectiveness, and that it was difficult to keep awake during the early evening hours! But do we pray as much as we might do? It is a lasting regret to me that I allowed the days of youth and vigor to pass by without laying more stress upon those early hours of prayer.

Now, the inspired command is clear enough: "Pray without ceasing" (I Thess. v. 17). Our dear Lord said, "Men ought always to pray, and not to faint"—"and never lose heart" (Weymouth) (Luke xviii. 1).

This, of course, cannot mean that we are to be always on our knees. I am convinced that God does not wish us to neglect rightful work in order to pray. But it is equally certain that we might work better and do more work if we gave less time to work and more to prayer.

Let us work well. We are to be "not slothful in business" (Rom. xii. 11). St. Paul says, "We exhort you, brethren, that ye abound more and more; and that ye. . . do your own business, and to work with your hands. . . that ye may walk honestly . . . and have need of nothing" (I Thess. iv. 11, 12). "If any will not work, neither let him eat" (II Thess. iii. 10).

But are there not endless opportunities during every day of "lifting, up holy hands"—or at least holy hearts—in prayer to our Father? Do we seize the opportunity, as we open our eyes upon each new day, of praising and blessing our Redeemer? Every day is an Easter day to the Christian. We can pray as we dress. Without a reminder we shall often forget. Stick a piece of stamp-paper in the corner of your looking-glass, bearing the words,—"Pray without ceasing." Try it. We can pray as we go from one duty to another. We can often pray at our work. The washing and the writing, the mending and the minding, the cooking and the cleaning will be done all the better for it.

Do not children, both young and old, work better and play better when some loved one is watching? Will it not help us ever to remember that the Lord Jesus is always with us, watching? Aye, and helping. The very consciousness of His eye upon us will be the consciousness of His power within us.

Do you not think that St. Paul had in his mind this habitual praying rather than fixed seasons of prayer when he said, "The Lord is at hand"—i.e., is near (Weymouth). "In nothing be anxious, but in everything, by prayer and supplication, with thanksgiving, let your requests be made known unto God" (Phil. iv. 5, 6)? Does not "in everything" suggest that, as thing after thing befalls us, moment by moment, we should then and there make it a "thing" of prayer and praise to the Lord Who is near? (Why should we limit this "nearness" to the Second Advent?)

What a blessed thought: prayer is to a near-God. When our Lord sent His disciples forth to work, He said, "Lo, I am with you alway."

Sir Thomas Browne, the celebrated physician, had caught this spirit. He made a vow "to pray in all places where quietness inviteth; in any house, highway or street; and to know no street in this city that may not witness that I have not forgotten God and my

Savior in it; and that no town or parish where I have been may not say the like. To take occasion of praying upon the sight of any church which I see as I ride about. To pray daily and particularly for my sick patients, and for all sick people, under whose care soever. And at the entrance into the house of the sick to say, 'The peace and the mercy of God be upon this house.' After a sermon to make a prayer and desire a blessing, and to pray for the minister."

But we question if this habitual communion with our blessed Lord is possible unless we have times—whether long or brief—of definite prayer. And what of these prayer seasons? We have said earlier that prayer is as simple as a little child asking something of its father. Nor would such a remark need any further comment were it not for the existence of the evil one.

There is no doubt whatever that the devil opposes our approach to God in prayer, and does all he can to prevent the prayer of faith. His chief way of hindering us is to try to fill our minds with the thought of our needs, so that they shall not be occupied with thoughts of God, our loving Father, to Whom we pray. He wants us to think more of the gift than of the Giver. The Holy Spirit leads us to pray for a brother. We get as far as "O God, bless my brother"—and away go our thoughts to the brother, and his affairs, and his difficulties, his hopes and his fears, and away goes prayer!

How hard the devil makes it for us to concentrate our thoughts upon God! This is why we urge people to get a realization of the glory of God, and the power of God, and the presence of God, before offering up any petition. If there were no devil there would be no difficulty in prayer, but it is the evil one's chief aim to make prayer impossible. That is why most of us find it hard to sympathize with those who profess to condemn what they call "vain repetitions" and "much speaking" in prayer—quoting our Lord's words in His sermon on the mount.

A prominent London vicar said quite recently, "God does not wish us to waste either His time or ours with long prayers. We must be business-like in our dealings with God, and just tell Him plainly and briefly what we want, and leave the matter there." But does our friend think that prayer is merely making God acquainted with our needs? If that is all there is in it, why, there is no need of prayer! "For your Father knoweth what things ye have need of before ye ask him," said our Lord when urging the disciples to pray.

We are aware that Christ Himself condemned some "long prayers" (Matt. xxiii. 14). But they were long prayers made "for a pretense," "for a show" (Luke xx. 47). Dear praying people, believe me, the Lord would equally condemn many of the "long prayers" made every week in some of our prayer-meetings—prayers which kill the prayer-meeting, and which finish up with a plea that God would hear these "feeble breathings," or "unworthy utterings."

But he never condemns long prayers that are sincere. Let us not forget that our Lord sometimes spent long nights in prayer. We are told of one of these—we do not know how frequently they were (Luke vi. 12). He would sometimes rise a "great while before day" and depart to a solitary place for prayer (Mark i. 35). The perfect Man spent more time in prayer than we do. It would seem an undoubted fact that with God's saints in all ages nights of prayer with God have been followed by days of power with men.

Nor did our Lord excuse Himself from prayer—as we, in our ignorance, might think He could have done—because of the pressing calls to service and boundless opportunities of usefulness. After one of His busiest days, at a time when His popularity was at its highest, just when everyone sought His company and His counsel, He turned His back upon them all and retired to a mountain to pray (Matt. xiv. 23).

We are told that once "great multitudes came together to hear Him, and to be healed of their infirmities." Then comes the remark, "But Jesus himself constantly withdrew into the desert, and there prayed" (Luke v. 15, 16, Weymouth). Why? Because He knew that prayer was then far more potent than "service."

We say we are too busy to pray. But the busier our Lord was, the more He prayed. Sometimes He had no leisure so much as to eat (Mark iii. 20); and sometimes He had no leisure for needed rest and sleep (Mark vi. 31). Yet He always took time to pray. If frequent prayer, and, at times, long hours of prayer, were necessary for our Savior, are they less necessary for us?

I do not write to persuade people to agree with me: that is a very small matter. We only want to know the truth. Spurgeon once said: "There is no need for us to go beating about the bush, and not telling the Lord distinctly what it is that we crave at His hands. Nor will it be seemly for us to make any attempt to use fine language; but let us ask God in the simplest and most direct manner for just the things we want. . . . I believe in business prayers. I mean prayers in which you take to God one of the many promises which He has given us in His Word, and expect it to be fulfilled as certainly as we look for the money to be given us when we go to the bank to cash a check. We should not think of going there, lolling over the counter chattering with the clerks on every conceivable subject except the one thing for which we had gone to the bank, and then coming away without the coin we needed; but we should lay before the clerk the promise to pay the bearer a certain sum, tell him in what form we wished to take the amount, count the cash after him, and then go on our way to attend to other business. That is just an illustration of the method in which we should draw supplies from the Bank of Heaven." Splendid!

But—? By all means let us be definite in prayer; by all means let us put eloquence aside—if we have any! By all means let us avoid needless "chatter," and come in faith, expecting to receive.

But would the bank clerk pass me the money over the counter so readily if there stood by my side a powerful, evil-countenanced, well-armed ruffian whom he recognized to be a desperate criminal waiting to snatch the money before my weak hands could grasp it? Would he not wait till the ruffian had gone? This is no fanciful picture. The Bible teaches us that, in some way or other, Satan can hinder our prayers and delay the answer. Does not St. Peter urge certain things upon Christians, that their "prayers be not hindered"? (I Peter iii. 7.) Our prayers can be hindered. "Then cometh the evil one and snatcheth away that which hath been sown in the heart" (Matt. xiii. 19, R.V.).

Scripture gives us one instance—probably only one out of many—where the evil one actually kept back—delayed—for three weeks an answer to prayer. We only mention this to show the need of repeated prayer, persistence in prayer, and also to call attention to the extraordinary power which Satan possesses. We refer to Daniel x. 12, 13: "Fear not, Daniel, for from the first day that thou didst set thine heart to understand, and to humble thyself before God, thy words were heard: and I am come for thy word's sake. But the prince of the kingdom of Persia withstood me one and twenty days. But lo, Michael, one of the chief princes, came to help me."

We must not overlook this Satanic opposition and hindrance to our prayers. If we were to be content to ask God only once for some promised thing or one we deemed necessary, these chapters would never have been written. Are we never to ask again? For instance, I know that God willeth not the death of a sinner. So I come boldly in prayer: "O God, save my friend." Am I never to ask for his conversion again? George Müller prayed daily—and oftener—for sixty years for the conversion of a friend. But what light does the Bible throw upon "business-like" prayers? Our Lord gave two parables to teach persistence and continuance in prayer. The man who asked three loaves from his friend at midnight received as many as he needed "because of his importunity"—or persistency (Weymouth), i.e., his "shamelessness," as the word literally means (Luke xi. 8). The widow who "troubled" the unjust judge with her "continual coming" at last secured redress. Our Lord adds "And shall not God avenge his elect which cry unto him day and night, and he is long-suffering over them?" (Luke xviii. 7, R.V.)

How delighted our Lord was with the poor Syro-Phoenician woman who would not take refusals or rebuffs for an answer! Because of her continual request He said: "O woman, great is thy faith: be it unto thee even as thou wilt" (Matt. xv. 28). Our dear Lord, in His agony in Gethsemane, found it necessary to repeat even His prayer. "And he left them and went away and prayed a third time, saying again the same words" (Matt. xxvi. 44). And we find St. Paul, the apostle of prayer, asking God time after time to remove his thorn in the flesh. "Concerning this thing," says he, "I besought the Lord thrice that it might depart from me" (II Cor. xii. 8).

God cannot always grant our petitions immediately. Sometimes we are not fitted to receive the gift. Sometimes He says "No" in order to give us something far better. Think, too, of the days when St. Peter was in prison. If your boy was unjustly imprisoned, expecting death at any moment, would you—could you—be content to pray just once, a "business-like" prayer: "O God, deliver my boy from the hands of these men"? Would you not be very much in prayer and very much in earnest?

This is how the Church prayed for St. Peter. "Long and fervent prayer was offered to God by the Church on his behalf" (Acts xii. 5, Weymouth). Bible students will have noticed that the A.V. rendering, "without ceasing," reads "earnestly" in the R.V. Dr. Torrey points out that neither translation gives the full force of the Greek. The word means literally "stretched-out-ed-ly." It represents the soul on the stretch of earnest and intense desire. Intense prayer was made for St. Peter. The very same word is used of our Lord in Gethsemane: "And being in an agony he prayed more earnestly, and his sweat became as it were great drops of blood falling down upon the ground" (Luke xxii. 44).

Ah! there was earnestness, even agony in prayer. Now, what about our prayers? Are we called upon to agonize in prayer? Many of God's dear saints say "No!" They think such agonizing in us would reveal great want of faith. Yet most of the experiences which befell our Lord are to be ours. We have been crucified with Christ, and we are risen with Him. Shall there be, with us, no travailing for souls?

Come back to human experience. Can we refrain from agonizing in prayer over dearly beloved children who are living in sin? I question if any believer can have the burden of souls upon him—a passion for souls—and not agonize in prayer.

Can we help crying out, like John Knox, "O God, give me Scotland or I die"? Here again the Bible helps us. Was there no travail of soul and agonizing in prayer when Moses cried out to God, "O, this people have sinned a great sin, and have made gods of gold. Yet now, if thou wilt forgive their sin—; and if not, blot, me, I pray thee, out of thy book"? (Exod. xxxii. 32.)

Was there no agonizing in prayer when St. Paul said, "I could wish"—("pray," R.V. marg.)—"that I myself were anathema from Christ for my brethren's sake"? (Rom. ix. 3.)

We may, at all events, be quite sure that our Lord, Who wept over Jerusalem, and Who "offered up prayers and supplications with strong crying and tears" (Heb. v. 7), will not be grieved if He sees us weeping over erring ones. Nay, will it not rather gladden His heart to see us agonizing over the sin which grieves Him? In fact, may not the paucity of conversions in so many a ministry be due to lack of agonizing in prayer?

We are told that "As soon as Zion travailed she brought forth her children" (Isa. lxvi. 8). Was St. Paul thinking of this passage when he wrote to the Galatians, "My little children, of whom I am again in travail until Christ be formed in you"? (Gal. iv. 19.) And will not this be true of spiritual children? Oh, how cold our hearts often are! How little we grieve over the lost! And shall we dare to criticise those who agonize over the perishing? God forbid! No; there is such a thing as wrestling in prayer. Not because God is unwilling to answer, but because of the opposition of the "world-rulers of this darkness" (Eph. vi. 12, R.V.).

The very word used for "striving" in prayer means "a contest." The contest is not between God and ourselves. He is at one with us in our desires. The contest is with the evil one, although he is a conquered foe (I John iii. 8). He desires to thwart our prayers.

"We wrestle not against flesh and blood, but against principalities, against the world-rulers of this darkness, against the spiritual hosts of wickedness in the heavenly places" (Eph. vi. 12). We, too, are in these "heavenly places in Christ" (Eph. i. 3); and it is only in Christ that we can be victorious. Our wrestling may be a wrestling of our thoughts from thinking Satan's suggestions, and keeping them fixed on Christ our Savior—that is, watching as well as praying (Eph. vi. 18); "watching unto prayer."

We are comforted by the fact that "the Spirit helpeth our infirmities: for we know not how to pray as we ought" (Rom. viii. 26) How does the Spirit "help" us, teach us, if not by example as well as by precept? How does the Spirit "pray"? "The Spirit Himself maketh intercession for us with groanings which cannot be uttered (Rom. viii. 26). Does the Spirit "agonize" in prayer as the Son did in Gethsemane?

If the Spirit prays in us, shall we not share His "groanings" in prayer? And if our agonizing in prayer weakens our body at the time, will angels come to strengthen us, as they did our Lord? (Luke xxii. 43.) We may, perhaps, like Nehemiah, weep, and mourn, and fast when we pray before God (Neh. i. 4). "But," one asks, "may not a godly sorrow for sin and a yearning desire for the salvation of others induce in us an agonizing which is unnecessary, and dishonoring to God?"

May it not reveal a lack of faith in God's promises? Perhaps it may do so. But there is little doubt that St. Paul regarded prayer—at least sometimes—as a conflict (see Rom. xv. 30). In writing to the Colossian Christians he says: "I would have you know how greatly I strive for you . . . and for as many as have not seen my face in the flesh; that their hearts may be comforted" (Col. ii. 1, 2). Undoubtedly he refers to his prayers for them.

Again, he speaks of Epaphras as one who is "always striving for you in his prayers, that ye may stand perfect, and fully assured in all the will of God" (Col. iv. 12).

The word for "strive" is our word "agonize," the very word used of our Lord being "in an agony" when praying Himself (Luke xxii. 44).

The apostle says again, Epaphras "hath much labor for you," that is, in his prayers. St. Paul saw him praying there in prison, and witnessed his intense striving as he engaged in a long, indefatigable effort on behalf of the Colossians. How the Praetorian guard to whom St. Paul was chained must have wondered—yes, and have been deeply touched—to see these men at their prayers. Their agitation, their tears, their earnest supplications as they lifted up chained hands in prayer must have been a revelation to him! What would they think of our prayers?

No doubt St. Paul was speaking of his own custom when he urged the Ephesian Christians and others "to stand," "with all prayer and supplication, praying at all seasons in the Spirit, and watching thereunto in all perseverance and supplication for all saints, and on my behalf . . . an ambassador in chains." (Eph. vi. 18-20). That is a picture of his own prayer-life, we may be sure.

So then prayer meets with obstacles, which must be prayed away. That is what men mean when they talk about praying through. We must wrestle with the machinations of Satan. It may be bodily weariness or pain, or the insistent claims of other thoughts, or doubt, or the direct assaults of spiritual hosts of wickedness. With us, as with St. Paul, prayer is something of a "conflict," a "wrestle," at least sometimes, which compels us to "stir" ourselves up "to lay hold on God" (Isa. lxiv. 7). Should we be wrong if we ventured to suggest that very few people ever wrestle in prayer? Do we? But let us never doubt our Lord's power and the riches of His grace.

The author of The Christian's Secret of a Happy Life told a little circle of friends, just before her death, of an incident in her own life. Perhaps I may be allowed to tell it abroad. A lady friend who occasionally paid her a visit for two or three days was always a great trial, a veritable tax upon her temper and her patience. Every such visit demanded much prayer-preparation. The time came when this "critical Christian" planned a visit for a whole week! She felt that nothing but a whole night of prayer could fortify her for this great testing. So, providing herself with a little plate of biscuits, she retired in good time to her bedroom, to spend the night on her knees before God, to beseech Him to give her grace to keep sweet and loving during the impending visit. No sooner had she knelt beside her bed than there flashed into her mind the words of Phil. iv. 19: "God shall supply all your need according to His riches in glory by Christ Jesus." Her fears vanished. She said, "When I realized that, I gave Him thanks and praised Him for His goodness. Then I jumped into bed and slept the night through. My guest arrived the next day, and I quite enjoyed her visit."

No one can lay down hard and fast rules of prayer, even for himself. God's gracious Holy Spirit alone can direct us moment by moment. There, however, we must leave the matter. God is our judge and our Guide. But let us remember that prayer is a many-sided thing. As Bishop Moule says, "True prayer can be uttered under innumerable circumstances." Very often

> *Prayer is the burden of a sigh*
> *The falling of a tear,*
> *The upward glancing of an eye*
> *When none but God is near.*

It may be just letting your request be made known unto God (Phil. iv. 6). We cannot think that prayer need always be a conflict and a wrestle. For if it were, many of us would soon become physical wrecks, suffering from nervous breakdown, and coming to an early grave.

And with many it is a physical impossibility to stay any length of time in a posture of prayer. Dr. Moule says: "Prayer, genuine and victorious, is continually offered without the least physical effort or disturbance. It is often in the deepest stillness of soul and body that it wins its longest way. But there is another side of the matter. Prayer is never meant to be indolently easy, however simple and reliant it may be. It is meant to be an infinitely important transaction between man and God. And therefore, very often . . . it has to be viewed as a work involving labor, persistence, conflict, if it would be prayer indeed."

No one can prescribe for another. Let each be persuaded in his own mind how to pray, and the Holy Spirit will inspire us and guide us how long to pray. And let us all be so full of the love of God our Savior that prayer, at all times and in all places, may be a joy as well as a means of grace.

> *Shepherd Divine, our wants relieve*
> *In this and every day;*
> *To all Thy tempted followers give*
> *The power, to watch and pray.*

> *The spirit of interceding grace*
> *Give us the faith to claim;*
> *To wrestle till we see Thy face*
> *And know Thy hidden Name.*

Chapter 8: Does God Always Answer Prayer?

WE now come to one of the most important questions that any man can ask. Very much depends upon the answer we are led to give. Let us not shrink from facing the question fairly and honestly. Does God always answer prayer? Of course, we all grant that He does answer prayer—some prayers, and sometimes. But does He always answer true prayer. Some so-called prayers He does not answer, because He does not hear them. When His people were rebellious, He said, "When ye make many prayers, I will not hear" (Isa. i. 15).

But a child of God ought to expect answers to prayer. God means every prayer to have an answer; and not a single real prayer can fail of its effect in heaven.

And yet that wonderful declaration of St. Paul: "All things are yours, for ye are Christ's" (I Cor. iii. 21), seems so plainly and so tragically untrue for most Christians. Yet it is not so. They are ours, but so many of us do not possess our possessions. The owners of Mount Morgan, in Queensland, toiled arduously for years on its barren slopes, eking out a miserable existence, never knowing that under their feet was one of the richest sources of gold the world has ever known. There was wealth, vast, undreamt of, yet unimagined and unrealized. It was "theirs," yet not theirs.

The Christian, however, knows of the riches of God in glory in Christ Jesus, but he does not seem to know how to get them.

Now, our Lord tells us that they are to be had for the asking. May He indeed give us all a right judgment in "prayer-things." When we say that no true prayer goes unanswered we are not claiming that God always gives just what we ask for. Have you ever met a parent so foolish as to treat his child like that? We do not give our child a red-hot poker because he clamors for it! Wealthy people are the most careful not to allow their children much pocket-money.

Why, if God gave us all we prayed for, we should rule the world, and not He! And surely we would all confess that we are not capable of doing that. Moreover, more than one ruler of the world is an absolute impossibility!

God's answer to prayer may be "Yes," or it may be "No." It may be "Wait," for it may be that He plans a much larger blessing than we imagined, and one which involves other lives as well as our own.

God's answer is sometimes "No." But this is not necessarily a proof of known and wilful sin in the life of the suppliant, although there may be sins of ignorance. He said "No" to St. Paul sometimes (II Cor. xii. 8, 9). More often than not the refusal is due to our ignorance or selfishness in asking. "For we know not how to pray as we ought" (Rom. viii. 26). That was what was wrong with the mother of Zebedee's children. She came and worshipped our Lord and prayed to Him. He quickly replied, "Ye know not what ye ask" (Matt. xx. 22). Elijah, a great man of prayer, sometimes had "No" for an answer. But when he was swept up to glory in a chariot of fire, did he regret that God said "No" when he cried out "O Lord, take away my life"?

God's answer is sometimes "Wait." He may delay the answer because we are not yet fit to receive the gift we crave—as with wrestling Jacob. Do you remember the famous prayer of Augustine—"O God, make me pure, but not now"? Are not our prayers sometimes like that? Are we always really willing to "drink the cup"—to pay the price of answered prayer? Sometimes He delays so that greater glory may be brought to Himself.

God's delays are not denials. We do not know why He sometimes delays the answer and at other times answers "before we call" (Isa. lxv. 24). George Muller, one of the greatest men of prayer of all time, had to pray over a period of more than sixty-three years for the conversion of a friend! Who can tell why? "The great point is never to give up until the answer comes," said Muller. "I have been praying for sixty-three years and eight months for one man's conversion. He is not converted yet, but he will be! How can it be otherwise? There is the unchanging promise of Jehovah, and on that I rest." Was this delay due to some persistent hindrance from the devil? (Dan. x. 13). Was it a mighty and prolonged effort on the part of Satan to shake or break Muller's faith? For no sooner was Muller dead than his friend was converted—even before the funeral.

Yes, his prayer was granted, though the answer tarried long in coming. So many of George Müller's petitions were granted him that it is no wonder that he once exclaimed, "Oh, how good, kind, gracious and condescending is the One with Whom we have to do! I am only a poor, frail, sinful man, but He has heard my prayers ten thousands of times."

Perhaps some are asking, How can I discover whether God's answer is "No" or "Wait"? We may rest assured that He will not let us pray sixty-three years to get a "No"! Muller's prayer, so long repeated, was based upon the knowledge that God "willeth not the death of a sinner"; "He would have all men to be saved" (I Tim. ii. 4).

Even as I write, the postman brings me an illustration of this. A letter comes from one who very rarely writes me, and did not even know my address—one whose name is known to every Christian worker in England. A loved one was stricken down with illness. Is he to continue to pray for her recovery? Is God's answer "No," or is it, "Go on praying—wait"? My friend writes: "I had distinct guidance from God regarding my beloved . . . that it was the will of God she should be taken . . . I retired into the rest of surrender and submission to His will. I have much to praise God for." A few hours later God took that loved one to be with Him in glory.

Again may we urge our readers to hold on to this truth: true prayer never goes unanswered.

If we only gave more thought to our prayers we should pray more intelligently. That sounds like a truism. But we say it because some dear Christian people seem to lay their common sense and reason aside before they pray. A little reflection would show that God cannot grant some prayers. During the war every nation prayed for victory. Yet it is perfectly obvious that all countries could not be victorious. Two men living together might pray, the one for rain and the other for fine weather. God cannot give both these things at the same time in the same place!

But the truthfulness of God is at stake in this matter of prayer. We have all been reading again those marvelous prayer-promises of our Lord, and have almost staggered at those promises—the wideness of their scope, the fullness of their intent, the largeness of the one word "Whatsoever." Very well! "Let God be found true" (Rom. iii. 4). He certainly will always be "found true."

Do not stop to ask the writer if God has granted all his prayers. He has not. To have said "Yes" to some of them would have spelt curse instead of blessing. To have answered others was, alas! a spiritual impossibility—he was not worthy of the gifts he sought. The granting, of some of them would but have fostered spiritual pride and self-satisfaction. How plain all these things seem now, in the fuller light of God's Holy Spirit!

As one looks back and compares one's eager, earnest prayers with one's poor, unworthy service and lack of true spirituality, one sees how impossible it was for God to grant the very things He longed to impart! It was often like asking God to put the ocean of His love into a thimble-heart! And yet, how God just yearns to bless us with every spiritual blessing! How the dear Savior cries again and again, "How often would I . . . but ye would not"! (Matt. xxiii. 37.) The sadness of it all is that we often ask and do not receive because of our unworthiness—and then we complain because God does not answer our prayers! The Lord Jesus declares that God gives the Holy Spirit—who teaches us how to pray—just as readily as a father gives good gifts to his children. But no gift is a "good gift" if the child is not fit to use that gift. God never gives us something that we cannot, or will not, use for His glory (I am not referring to talents, for we may abuse or "bury" those, but to spiritual gifts).

Did you ever see a father give his baby boy a razor when he asked for it, because he hoped the boy would grow into a man and then find the razor useful? Does a father never say to his child, "Wait till you are older, or bigger, or wiser, or better, or stronger"? May not our loving heavenly Father also say to us, "Wait"? In our ignorance and blindness we must surely sometimes say,

> *In very love refuse*
>   *Whate'er Thou seest*
> *Our weakness would abuse.*

Rest assured that God never bestows tomorrow's gift today. It is not unwillingness on His part to give. It is not that God is ever straitened in Himself. His resources are infinite, and His ways are past finding out. It was after bidding His disciples to ask that our Lord goes on to hint not only at His providence, but at His resources. "Look at the wild birds" (Matt. vi. 26, Moffatt); "your heavenly Father feedeth them." How simple it sounds. Yet have you ever reflected that not a single millionaire, the wide world over, is wealthy enough to feed all "the birds of the air," even for one day? Your heavenly Father feedeth them every day, and is none the poorer for it. Shall He not much more feed you, clothe you, take care of you?

Oh, let us rely more upon prayer! Do we not know that "He is a Rewarder of them that diligently seek Him"? (Hebrews xi. 6.) The "oil" of the Holy Spirit will never cease to flow so long as there are empty vessels to receive it (II Kings iv. 6). It is always we who are to blame when the Spirit's work ceases. God cannot trust some Christians with the fullness of the Holy Spirit. God cannot trust some workers with definite spiritual results in their labors. They would suffer from pride and vainglory. No! we do not claim that God grants every Christian everything he prays for.

As we saw in an earlier chapter, there must be purity of heart, purity of motive, purity of desire, if our prayers are to be in His name. God is greater than His promises, and often gives more than either we desire or deserve—but He does not always do so. So, then, if any specific petition is not granted, we may feel sure that God is calling us to examine our hearts. For He has undertaken to grant every prayer that is truly offered in His name. Let us repeat His blessed words once more—we cannot repeat them too often—"Whatsoever ye shall ask in My name, that will I do, that the Father may be glorified in the Son. If ye shall ask anything in My name, that will I do" (John xiv. 13, 14).

Remember that it was impossible for Christ to offer up any prayer which was not granted. He was God—He knew the mind of God—He had the mind of the Holy Spirit.

Does He once say, "Father, if it be possible, let. . ." as He kneels in agony in Gethsemane's garden, pouring out strong crying and tears? Yes, and "He was heard for His reverential awe" (Heb. v. 7, Dr. Moule). Surely not the "agony," but the son-like fear, gained the answer? Our prayers are heard not so much because they are importunate but because they are filial.

Brother Christian, we cannot fully understand that hallowed scene of dreadful awe and wonder. But this we know—that our Lord never yet made a promise which He cannot keep, or does not mean to fulfil. The Holy Spirit maketh intercession for us (Rom. viii. 26), and God cannot say Him "Nay." The Lord Jesus makes intercession for us (Hebrews vii. 25), and God cannot say Him "Nay." His prayers are worth a thousand of ours, but it is He who bids us pray!

"But was not St. Paul filled with the Holy Spirit?" you ask, "and did he not say, 'We have the mind of Christ?' Yet he asked thrice over that God would remove the 'thorn' in his flesh—and yet God distinctly tells him He would not do so."

It is a very singular thing, too, that the only petition recorded of St. Paul seeking something for his own individual need was refused! The difficulty, however, is this: Why did St. Paul, who had the "mind" of Christ, ask for something which he soon discovered was contrary to God's wishes? There are doubtless many fully-consecrated Christians reading these words who have been perplexed because God has not given some things they prayed for.

We must remember that we may be filled with the Spirit and yet err in judgment or desire. We must remember, too, that we are never filled with God's Holy Spirit once for all. The evil one is always on the watch to put his mind into us, so as to strike at God through us. At any moment we may become disobedient or unbelieving, or may be betrayed into some thought or act contrary to the Spirit of love.

We have an astonishing example of this in the life of St. Peter. At one moment, under the compelling influence of God's Holy Spirit, he cries, "Thou art the Christ, the Son of the living God!" Our Lord turns, and with words of high commendation says, "Blessed art thou, Simon, for flesh and blood hath not revealed it unto thee, but My Father, which is in heaven." Yet, a very little while after, the devil gets his mind into St. Peter, and our Lord turns and says unto him, "Get thee behind me, Satan!" (Matt. xvi. 17, 23.) St. Peter was now speaking in the name of Satan! Satan still "desires to have" us.

St. Paul was tempted to think that he could do far better work for his beloved Master if only that "thorn" could be removed. But God knew that Paul would be a better man with the "thorn" than without it.

Is it not a comfort to us to know that we may bring more glory to God under something which we are apt to regard as a hindrance or handicap, than if that undesired thing was removed? "My grace is sufficient for thee: for My power is made perfect in weakness" (II Cor. xii. 9). Remember that

> God nothing does, nor suffers to be done,
> But what thou would'st thyself
> Did'st thou but see
> The end of all He does as well as He.

St. Paul was not infallible—nor was St. Peter, or St. John; nor is the Pope or any other man. We may—and do—offer up mistaken prayers. The highest form of prayer is not, "Thy way, O God, not mine," but "My way, O God, is Thine!" We are taught to pray, not "Thy will be changed," but "Thy will be done."

May we, in conclusion, give the testimony of two who have proved that God can be trusted?

Sir H. M. Stanley, the great explorer, wrote: "I for one must not dare to say that prayers are inefficacious. Where I have been in earnest, I have been answered. When I prayed for light to guide my followers wisely through the perils that beset them, a ray of light has come upon the perplexed mind, and a clear road to deliverance has been pointed out. You may know when prayer is answered, by the glow of content which fills one who has flung his cause before God, as he rises to his feet. I have evidence, satisfactory to myself, that prayers are granted."

Mary Slessor, the story of whose life in West Africa has surely thrilled us all, was once asked what prayer meant to her. She replied, "My life is one long, daily, hourly record of answered prayer for physical health, for mental overstrain, for guidance given marvelously, for errors and dangers averted, for enmity to the Gospel subdued, for food provided at the exact hour needed, for everything that goes to make up life and my poor service. I can testify with a full and often wonder-stricken awe that I believe God answers prayer. I know God answers prayer!"

Chapter 9: Answers to Prayer

MERE human nature would choose a more startling title to this chapter. Remarkable answers—wonderful answers—amazing answers. But we must allow God to teach us that it is as natural to Him to answer prayer as it is for us to ask. How He delights to hear our petitions, and how He loves to answer them! When we hear of some wealthy person giving a treat to poverty-stricken people, or wiping out some crushing deficit in a missionary society, we exclaim, "How nice to be able to do a thing like that!" Well, if it is true that God loves us—and we know it is true—do you not think it gives Him great joy to give us what we ask? We should like, therefore, to recount one or two answers to prayer out of very many which have come to our notice, so that we may have greater boldness in coming to the Throne of Grace. God saves men for whom we pray. Try it.

In talking over this question with a man of prayer a few days ago, he suddenly asked me, "Do you know St. M—'s Church, L—?"

"Quite well—have been there several times."

"Let me tell you what happened when I lived there. We had a prayer-meeting each Sunday before the 8 o'clock communion service. As we rose from our knees one Sunday a sidesman said, 'Vicar, I wish you would pray for my boy. He is twenty-two years old now, and has not been to church for years.' 'We can spare five minutes now,' replied the vicar. They knelt down again and offered up earnest supplication on behalf of that man. Although nothing was said to him about this, that youth came to church that same evening. Something in the sermon convicted him of sin. He came into the vestry broken-hearted, and accepted Jesus Christ as, his Savior."

On Monday morning my friend, who was working as a Church Army captain in the parish, was present at the weekly meeting of the staff. He said to the vicar, "That conversion last night is a challenge to prayer—a challenge from God. Shall we accept it?" "What do you mean?" asked the vicar. "Well," said he, "shall we single out the worst man in the parish and pray for him?" By unanimous consent they fixed upon K—as the worst man they knew. So they "agreed" in prayer for his conversion. At the end of that week, as they were conducting a Saturday night prayer-meeting in the mission hall, and whilst his very name was on their lips, the door swung open and in staggered K—, much the worse for liquor. He had never been in that mission hall before. Without thinking of removing his cap he sank on a chair near the door and buried his face in his hands. The prayer-meeting suddenly became an enquiry-room. Even as he was—in drink—he sought the Lord Who was seeking him. Nor did he ever go back. Today he is one of the finest dockyard missioners in the land.

Oh, why do we not pray for our unconverted friends? They may not listen to us when we plead with them, but they cannot hold out if we pray for them. Let two or three agree in prayer over the salvation of the worst, and then see what God will do! Tell God and then trust God. God works in a wonderful way, as well as in a "mysterious" way, His wonders to perform.

Dan Crawford told us recently that when returning to his mission field after a furlough, it was necessary to make all possible haste. But a deep stream, which had to be crossed, was in flood, and no boats were available, or usable, for that matter. So he and his party camped and prayed. An infidel might well have laughed aloud. How could God get them across that river! But, as they prayed, a tall tree which had battled with that river for scores of years began to totter and fall. It fell clear across the stream! As Mr. Crawford says, "The Royal Engineers of heaven had laid a pontoon bridge for God's servants."

Many young people will be reading these prayer-stories. May we remind them that God still hears the voice of the lad—yes, and the lass? (Gen. xxi. 17.) For them may we be allowed to add the following story, with the earnest desire that prayer may be their heritage, their very life; and that answered prayer may be their daily experience.

Some little time ago, a Chinese boy of twelve years old, named Ma-Na-Si, a boarder in the mission school at Chefoo, went home for the holidays. He is the son of a native pastor.

Whilst standing on the doorstep of his father's house he espied a horseman galloping towards him. The man—a heathen—was in a great state of perturbation. He eagerly enquired for the "Jesus-man"—the pastor. The boy told him that his father was away from home. The poor man was much distressed, and hurriedly explained the cause of his visit. He had been sent from a heathen village some miles away to fetch the "holy man" to cast a devil out of the daughter-in-law of a heathen friend. He poured out his sad story of this young woman, torn by devils, raving and reviling, pulling out her hair, clawing her face, tearing her clothes, smashing up furniture, and dashing away dishes of food. He told of her spirit of sacrilege, and outrageous impiety, and brazen blasphemy, and how these outbursts were followed by foaming at the mouth, and great exhaustion, both physical and mental. "But my father is not at home," the boy kept reiterating. At length the frenzied man seemed to understand. Suddenly he fell on his knees, and, stretching out his hands in desperation, cried, "You, too, are a Jesus-man; will you come ?"

Think of it—a boy of twelve! Yes, but even a lad, when fully yielded to his Savior, is not fearful of being used by that Savior. There was but one moment of surprise, and a moment of hesitation, and then the laddie put himself wholly at his Master's disposal. Like little Samuel of old he was willing to obey God in all things. He accepted the earnest entreaty as a call from God. The heathen stranger sprang into the saddle, and, swinging the Christian boy up behind him, he galloped away.

Ma-Na-Si began to think over things. He had accepted an invitation to cast out a devil in the name of Christ Jesus. But was he worthy to be used of God in this way? Was his heart pure and his faith strong? As they galloped along he carefully searched his own heart for sin to be confessed and repented of. Then he prayed for guidance what to say and how to act, and tried to recall Bible instances of demoniacal possession and how they were dealt with. Then he simply and humbly cast himself upon the God of power and of mercy, asking His help for the glory of the Lord Jesus. On arrival at the house they found that some of the members of the family were by main force holding down the tortured woman upon the bed. Although she had not been told that a messenger had gone for the native pastor, yet as soon as she heard footsteps in the court outside she cried, "All of you get out of my way quickly, so that I can escape. I must flee! A 'Jesus-man' is coming. I cannot endure him. His name is Ma-Na-Si."

Ma-Na-Si entered the room, and after a ceremonial bow knelt down and began to pray. Then he sang a Christian hymn to the praise of the Lord Jesus. Then, in the name of the Risen Lord, glorified and omnipotent, he commanded the demon to come out of the woman. At once she was calm, though prostrate with weakness. From that day she was perfectly whole. She was amazed when they told her that she had uttered the name of the Christian boy, for she had never heard of it or read of it before, for the whole of that village was heathen. But that day was veritably a "beginning of days" to those people, for from it the Word of the Lord had free course and was glorified.

Beloved reader, I do not know how this little narrative affects you. It is one that moves me to the very depths of my being. It seems to me that most of us know so little of the power of God—so little of His overwhelming, irresistible love. Oh, what love is His! Now, every time we pray, that wonderful love envelops us in a special way.

If we really loved our blessed Savior, should we not oftener seek communion with Him in prayer? Fellow Christian, is it because we pray so little that we criticise so much? Oh, let us remember that we, like our dear Savior, are not sent into the world to condemn, to judge, the world, "but that the world should be saved through Him" (John iii. 17).

Will any thoughtless word of criticism of anyone move anyone nearer to Christ? Will it even help the utterer of that fault-finding to be more like the Master? Oh, let us lay aside the spirit of criticism, of blaming, of fault-finding, of disparaging others or their work. Would not St. Paul say to us all, "And such were some of you, but ye are washed"? (I Cor. vi. 11.)

Do you see what we are aiming at? All the evil dispositions and failings we detect in others are due to the devil. It is the evil one in the heart who causes those words and deeds which we are so ready to condemn and to exaggerate. Demon-possession is not unknown in England, but it takes a different form, perhaps. Our very friends and acquaintances, so kindly and lovable, are often tied and bound by some besetting sin—"whom Satan hath bound, lo, these many years."

We may plead with them in vain. We may warn them in vain. Courtesy and charity— and our own failings and shortcomings—forbid us standing over them like Ma-Na-Si and exercising the evil spirit! But have we tried prayer—prayer always backed up by love which cannot be "provoked"? (I Cor. xiii. 5.)

God answers prayer from old and young, when there is a clean heart, a holy life, and a simple faith. God answers prayer. We are but frail and faulty servants at the best. Sincere as we may be, we shall sometimes ask amiss. But God is faithful that promised, and He will guard us from all harm and supply every need.

> *Can I have the things I pray for?*
> *God knows best;*
> *He is wiser than His children.*
> *I can rest.*

"Beloved, if our heart condemn us not, we have boldness toward God; and whatsoever we ask we receive of him, because we keep his commandments, and do those things that are pleasing in his sight" (I John iii. 21.)

Chapter 10: How God Answers Prayer

FOR man fully to understand God and all His dealings with us is an utter impossibility. "O the depth of the riches both of the wisdom and the knowledge of God! How unsearchable are his judgments, and his ways past tracing out!" (Rom. xi. 33.) True, but we need not make difficulties where none exists. If God has all power and all knowledge, surely prayer has no difficulties, though occasionally there may be perplexities. We cannot discover God's method, but we know something of His manner of answering prayer.

But at the very outset may we remind ourselves how little we know about ordinary things? Mr. Edison, whose knowledge is pretty profound, wrote in August, 1921, "We don't know the millionth part of one per cent about anything. We don't know what water is. We don't know what light is. We don't know what gravitation is. We don't know what enables us to keep on our feet to stand up. We don't know what electricity is. We don't know what heat is. We don't know anything about magnetism. We have a lot of hypotheses, but that is all." But we do not allow our ignorance about all these things to deprive us of their use! We do not know much about prayer, but surely this need not prevent us from praying! We do know what our Lord has taught us about prayer. And we do know that He has sent the Holy Spirit to teach us all things (John xiv. 26). How, then, does God answer prayer? One way is just this:—

He reveals His mind to those who pray. His Holy Spirit puts fresh ideas into the minds of praying people. We are quite aware that the devil and his angels are busy enough putting bad thoughts into our minds. Surely, then, God and His holy angels can give us good thoughts? Even poor, weak, sinful men and women can put good thoughts into the minds of others. That is what we try to do in writing! We do not stop to think what a wonderful thing it is that a few peculiar-shaped black marks on this white paper can uplift and inspire, or depress and cast down, or even convict of sin! But, to an untutored savage, it is a stupendous miracle. Moreover, you and I can often read people's thoughts or wishes from an expression on the face or a glance of the eye. Even thought transference between man and man is a commonplace today. And God can in many ways convey His thoughts to us. A remarkable instance of this was related by a speaker last year at Northfield. Three or four years ago, he met an old whaling captain who told him this story.

"A good many years ago, I was sailing in the desolate seas off Cape Horn, hunting whales. One day we were beating directly south in the face of a hard wind. We had been tacking this way and that all the morning, and were making very little headway. About 11 o'clock, as I stood at the wheel, the idea suddenly came into my mind, 'Why batter the ship against these waves? There are probably as many whales to the north as to the south. Suppose we run with the wind instead of against it? In response to that sudden idea I changed the course of the ship, and began to sail north instead of south. One hour later, at noon, the look-out at the masthead shouted 'Boats ahead!' Presently we overtook four lifeboats, in which were fourteen sailors, the only survivors of the crew of a ship which had burned to the water's edge ten days before. Those men had been adrift in their boats ever since, praying God frantically for rescue; and we arrived just in time to save them. They could not have survived another day."

Then the old whaler added, "I don't know whether you believe in religion or not, but I happen to be a Christian. I have begun every day of my life with prayer that God would use me to help someone else, and I am convinced that God, that day, put the idea into my mind to change the course of my ship. That idea was the means of saving fourteen lives."

God has many things to say to us. He has many thoughts to put into our minds. We are apt to be so busy doing His work that we do not stop to listen to His Word. Prayer gives God the opportunity of speaking to us and revealing His will to us. May our attitude often be: "Speak, Lord, Thy servant heareth."

God answers other prayers by putting new thoughts into the minds of those we pray for. At a series of services dealing with the Victorious Life, the writer one afternoon urged the congregation to "make up" their quarrels if they really desired a holy life. One lady went straight home, and after very earnest prayer wrote to her sister, with whom, owing to some disagreement, she had had nothing to do for twenty years! Her sister was living thirty miles away. The very next morning the writer of that note received a letter from that very sister asking forgiveness and seeking reconciliation. The two letters had crossed in the post. While the one sister was praying to God for the other, God was speaking to that other sister, putting into her mind the desire for reconciliation.

You may say, Why did not God put that desire there before? It may be that He foresaw that it would be useless for the distant sister to write asking forgiveness until the other sister was also willing to forgive. The fact remains that, when we pray for others, somehow or other it opens the way for God to influence those we pray for. God needs our prayers, or He would not beg us to pray.

A little time back, at the end of a weekly prayer-meeting, a godly woman begged those present to pray for her husband, who would never go near a place of worship. The leader suggested that they should continue in prayer then and there. Most earnest prayers were offered up. Now, the husband was devoted to his wife, and frequently came to meet her. He did so that night, and arrived at the hall while the prayer-meeting was still in progress. God put it into his mind to open the door and wait inside—a thing he had never done before. As he sat on a chair near the door, leaning his head upon his hand, he overheard those earnest petitions. During the homeward walk he said, "Wife, who was the man they were praying for tonight?" "Oh," she replied, "it is the husband of one of our workers." "Well, I am quite sure he will be saved," said he; "God must answer prayers like that." A little later in the evening he again asked, "Who was the man they were praying for?" She replied in similar terms as before. On retiring to rest he could not sleep. He was under deep conviction of sin. Awaking his wife, he begged her to pray for him.

How clearly this shows us that when we pray, God can work! God could have prompted that man to enter that prayer-meeting any week. But had he done so it is a question whether any good at all would have come from it. When once those earnest, heartfelt petitions were being offered up on his behalf God saw that they would have a mighty influence upon that poor man.

It is when we pray that God can help us in our work and strengthen our resolves. For we can answer many of our own prayers. One bitter winter a prosperous farmer was praying that God would keep a neighbor from starving. When the family prayers were over, his little boy said, "Father, I don't think I should have troubled God about that." "Why not?" he asked. "Because it would be easy enough for you to see that they don't starve!" There is not the slightest doubt that if we pray for others we shall also try to help them.

A young convert asked his vicar to give him some Christian work. "Have you a chum?" "Yes," replied the boy. "Is he a Christian?" "No, he is as careless as I was." "Then go and ask him to accept Christ as his Savior." "Oh, no!" said the lad, "I could never do that. Give me anything but that." "Well," said the vicar, "promise me two things: that you will not speak to him about his soul, and that you will pray to God twice daily for his conversion." "Why, yes, I'll gladly do that," answered the boy. Before a fortnight was up he rushed round to the vicarage. "Will you let me off my promise? I must speak to my chum!" he cried. When he began to pray God could give him strength to witness. Communion with God is essential before we can have real communion with our fellow-man. My belief is that men so seldom speak to others about their spiritual condition because they pray so little for them.

The writer has never forgotten how his faith in prayer was confirmed when, as a lad of thirteen, he earnestly asked God to enable him on a certain day to secure twenty new subscribers for missions overseas. Exactly twenty new names were secured before night closed in. The consciousness that God would grant that prayer was an incentive to eager effort, and gave an unwonted courage in approaching others.

A cleric in England suggested to his people that they should each day pray for the worst man or woman and then go to them and tell them about Jesus. Only six agreed to do so. On arrival home he began to pray. Then he said, "I must not leave this to my people. I must take it up myself. I don't know the bad people. I'll have to go out and enquire." Approaching a rough-looking man at a street corner, he asked, "Are you the worst man in this district?" "No, I'm not." "Would you mind telling me who is?" "I don't mind. You'll find him at No. 7, down that street."

He knocked at No. 7 and entered. "I'm looking for the worst man in my parish. They tell me it might be you?" "Whoever told you that? Fetch him here, and I'll show him who's the worst man! No, there are lots worse than me." "Well, who is the worst man you know?" "Everybody knows him. He lives at the end house in that court. He's the worst man." So down the court he went and knocked at the door. A surly voice cried, "Come in!"

There were a man and his wife. "I hope you'll excuse me, but I'm the minister of the chapel along the round. I'm looking for the worst man in my district, because I have something to tell him. Are you the worst man?" The man turned to his wife and said, "Lass, tell him what I said to you five minutes ago." "No, tell him yourself." "What were you saying?" enquired the visitor. "Well, I've been drinking for twelve weeks. I've had the D.T.'s and have pawned all in the house worth pawning. And I said to my wife a few minutes ago, 'Lass, this thing has to stop, and if it doesn't, I'll stop it myself—I'll go and drown myself.' Then you knocked at the door! Yes, sir, I'm the very worst man. What have you got to say to me?" "I'm here to tell you that Jesus Christ is the greatest Savior, and that He can make out of the worst man one of the best. He did it for me, and He will do it for you." "D'you think He can do it even for me?" "I'm sure He can. Kneel down and ask Him."

Not only was the poor drunkard saved from his sins, but he is today a radiant Christian man, bringing other drunken people to the Lord Jesus Christ.

Surely none of us finds it difficult to believe that God can, in answer to prayer, heal the body, send rain or fair weather, dispel fogs, or avert calamities?

We have to do with a God whose knowledge is infinite. He can put it into the mind of a doctor to prescribe a certain medicine, or diet, or method of cure. All the doctor's skill is from God. "He knoweth our frame"—for He made it. He knows it far better than the cleverest doctor or surgeon. He made, and He can restore. We believe that God desires us to use medical skill, but we also believe that God, by His wonderful knowledge, can heal, and sometimes does heal, without human co-operation. And God must be allowed to work in His own way. We are so apt to tie God down to the way we approve of. God's aim is to glorify His name in answering our prayers. Sometimes He sees that our desire is right, but our petition wrong. St. Paul thought he could bring more glory to God if only the thorn in the flesh could be removed. God knew that he would be a better man and do better work with the thorn than without it. So God said No-No-No to his prayer, and then explained why!

So it was with Monica, who prayed so many years for the conversion of Augustine, her licentious son. When he was determined to leave home and cross the seas to Rome she prayed earnestly, even passionately, that God would keep him by her side, and under her influence. She went down to a little chapel on the seashore to spend the night in prayer close by where the ship lay at anchor. But, when morning came, she found that the ship had sailed even while she prayed! Her petition was refused, but her real desire was granted.

For it was in Rome that Augustine met the sainted Ambrose, who led him to Christ. How comforting it is to know that God knows what is best!

But we should never think it unreasonable that God should make some things dependent upon our prayers. Some people say that if God really loves us He would give us what is best for us whether we ask Him or not. Dr. Fosdick has so beautifully pointed out that God has left man many things to do for himself. He promises seedtime and harvest. Yet man must prepare the soil, sow, and till, and reap in order to allow God to do His share. God provides us with food and drink. But He leaves us to take, and eat, and drink. There are some things God cannot, or at least will not, do without our help. God cannot do some things unless we think. He never emblazons His truth upon the sky. The laws of science have always been there. But we must think, and experiment, and think again if we would use those laws for our own good and God's glory.

God cannot do some things unless we work. He stores the hills with marble, but He has never built a cathedral. He fills the mountains with iron ore, but He never makes a needle or a locomotive. He leaves that to us. We must work.

If, then, God has left many things dependent upon man's thinking and working, why should He not leave some things dependent upon man's praying? He has done so. "Ask and ye shall receive." And there are some things God will not give us unless we ask. Prayer is one of the three ways in which man can co-operate with God; and the greatest of these is prayer.

Men of power are without exception men of prayer. God bestows His Holy Spirit in His fullness only on men of prayer. And it is through the operation of the Spirit that answers to prayer come. Every believer has the Spirit of Christ dwelling in him. For "if any have not the Spirit of Christ, he is none of his." But a man of prevailing prayer must be filled with the Spirit of God.

A lady missionary wrote recently that it used to be said of Praying Hyde that he never spoke to an unconverted man but that he was soundly converted. But if he ever did fail at first to touch a heart for God, he went back to his room and wrestled in prayer till he was shown what it was in himself that had hindered his being used by God. Yes, when we are filled with the Spirit of God, we cannot help influencing others God-ward. But, to have power with men, we must have power with God.

The momentous question for you and me is not, however, "How does God answer prayer?" The question is, "Do I really pray?" What a marvelous power God places at our disposal! Do we for a moment think that anything displeasing to God is worth our while holding on to? Fellow-Christian, trust Christ wholly, and you will find Him wholly true.

Let us give God the chance of putting His mind into us, and we shall never doubt the power of prayer again.

Chapter 11: Hindrances to Prayer

THE poet said, and we often sing—

What various hindrances we meet
In coming to the mercy-seat.

Yes, indeed, they are various. But here again, most of those hindrances are our own making.

God wants me to pray. The devil does not want me to pray, and does all he can to hinder me. He knows that we can accomplish more through our prayers than through our work. He would rather have us do anything else than pray.

We have already referred to Satan's opposition to prayer:

> *Angels our march oppose*
> *Who still in strength excel*
> *Our secret, sworn, relentless foes,*
> *Countless, invisible.*

But we need not fear them, nor heed them, if our eyes are ever unto the Lord. The holy angels are stronger than fallen angels, and we can leave the celestial hosts to guard us. We believe that to them—the hosts of evil—we owe those wandering thoughts which so often wreck prayer. We no sooner kneel than we "recollect" something that should have been done, or something which had better be seen to at once.

These thoughts come from without, and are surely due to the promptings of evil spirits. The only cure for wandering thoughts is to get our minds fixed upon God. Undoubtedly a man's worst foe is himself. Prayer is for a child of God—and one who is living as a child of God should pray.

The great question is: Am I harboring any foes in my heart? Are there traitors within? God cannot give us His best spiritual blessings unless we fulfil conditions of trust, obedience and service. Do we not often ask earnestly for the highest spiritual gifts, without even any thought of fulfilling the necessary requirements? Do we not often ask for blessings we are not fitted to receive? Dare we be honest with ourselves, alone in the presence of God? Dare we say sincerely, "Search me, O God, and see—"? Is there anything in me which is hindering God's blessing for me and through me? We discuss the "problem of prayer"; we are the problem that needs discussing or dissecting! Prayer is all right! There is no problem in prayer to the heart which is absolutely stayed on Christ.

Now, we shall not quote the usual Bible texts which show how prayer may be frustrated. We merely desire that everyone should get a glimpse of his own heart. No sin is too small to hinder prayer, and perhaps to turn the very prayer itself into sin, if we are not willing to renounce that sin. The Moslems in West Africa have a saying, "If there is no purity, there is no prayer; if there is no prayer, there is no drinking of the water of heaven." This truth is so clearly taught in Scripture that it is amazing that any should try to retain both sin and prayer. Yet very many do this. Even David cried, long ages ago, "If I regard iniquity in my heart, the Lord will not hear" (Psa. lxvi. 18).

And Isaiah says, "Your iniquities have separated between you and your God, and your sins have hid his face from you" (Isa. lix. 2). Surely we must all agree that it is sin in us, and not the unwillingness of Christ to hear, that hinders prayer. As a rule, it is some little sin, so-called, that mars and spoils the prayer-life. There may be:

(1) Doubt. Now, unbelief is possibly the greatest hindrance to prayer. Our Lord said that the Holy Spirit would convict the world of sin—"of sin because they believe not on Me" (St. John xvi. 9). We are not "of the world," yet is there not much practical unbelief in many of us? St. James, writing to believers, says: "Ask in faith, nothing doubting; for he that doubteth . . . let not that man think he shall receive anything of the Lord" (St. James i. 6-8). Some have not because they ask not. Others "have not" because they believe not.

Did you think it a little strange that we spent so much time over adoration and thanksgiving before we came to the "asking"? But surely, if we get a glimpse of the glorious majesty of our Lord, and the wonders of His love and grace, unbelief and doubt will vanish away as mists before the rising sun? Was this not the reason that Abraham "staggered not," "wavered not through unbelief," in that he gave God the glory due unto His name, and was therefore "fully assured that what He had promised He was able also to perform"? (Rom. iv. 20, 21). Knowing what we do of God's stupendous love, is it not amazing that we should ever doubt?

(2) Then there is Self—the root of all sin. How selfish we are prone to be even in our "good works"! How we hesitate to give up anything which "self" craves for. Yet we know that a full hand cannot take Christ's gifts. Was this why the Savior, in the prayer He first taught, coupled us with everything else? "Our" is the first word. "Our Father . . . give us . . . forgive us . . . deliver us . . ."

Pride prevents prayer, for prayer is a very humbling thing. How hateful pride must be in the sight of God! It is God who gives us all things "richly to enjoy." "What hast thou that thou didst not receive?" asks St. Paul (I Cor. iv. 7). Surely, surely we are not going to let pride, with its hateful, ugly sister, jealousy, ruin our prayer-life? God cannot do great things for us whereby we may be glad if they are going to "turn our heads." Oh, how foolish we can be! Sometimes, when we are insistent, God does give us what we ask, at the expense of our holiness. "He gave them their request, but sent leanness into their soul" (Psa. cvi. 15). O God, save us from that—save us from self! Again, self asserts itself in criticising others. Let this thought burn itself into your memory—the more like Jesus Christ a man becomes, the less he judges other people. It is an infallible test. Those who are always criticising others have drifted away from Christ. They may still be His, but have lost His Spirit of love. Beloved reader, if you have a criticising nature, allow it to dissect yourself and never your neighbor. You will be able to give it full scope, and it will never be unemployed! Is this a harsh remark? Does it betray a tendency to commit the very sin—for it is sin—it condemns? It would do so were it spoken to any one individual. But its object is to pierce armor which is seemingly invulnerable. And no one who, for one month, has kept his tongue "from picking and stealing" the reputation of other people will ever desire to go back again to back-biting. "Love suffereth long and is kind" (I Cor. xiii. 4). Do we? Are we?

We are ourselves no better because we have managed to paint other people in worse colors than ourselves. But, singularly enough, we enhance our own spiritual joy and our own living witness for Christ when we refuse to pass on disparaging information about others, or when we refrain from "judging" the work or lives of other people. It may be hard at first, but it soon brings untold joy, and is rewarded by the love of all around. It is most hard to keep silent in the face of "modern" heresies. Are we not told to "contend earnestly for the faith which was once for all delivered unto the saints"? (Jude 3.) Sometimes we must speak out—but let it always be in the spirit of love. "Rather let error live than love die."

Even in our private prayers fault-finding of others must be resolutely avoided. Read once more the story of John Hyde praying for the "cold brother." Believe me, a criticising spirit destroys holiness of life more easily than anything else, because it is such an eminently respectable sin, and makes such easy victims of us. We need scarcely add that when a believer is filled with the Spirit of Christ—who is Love—he will never tell others of the un-Christian behavior he may discern in his friends. "He was most rude to me"; "He is too conceited"; "I can't stand that man"; and such-like remarks are surely unkind, unnecessary, and often untrue.

Our dear Lord suffered the contradiction of sinners against Himself, but He never complained or published abroad the news to others. Why should we do so? Self must be dethroned if Christ is to reign supreme. There must be no idols in the heart. Do you remember what God said of some leaders of religion? "These men have taken their idols into their heart . . . ; should I be inquired of at all by them?" (Ezek. xiv. 3.)

When our aim is solely the glory of God, then God can answer our prayers. Christ Himself rather than His gifts should be our desire. "Delight thyself in the Lord and He shall give thee the petitions of thine heart" (Psa. xxxvii. 4, R.V., marg.).

"Beloved, if our heart condemn us not, we have boldness toward God; and whatsoever we ask we receive of him, because we keep his commandments and do the things that are pleasing in his sight" (I John iii. 21, 22).

It is as true today as in the early days of Christianity that men ask, and receive not, because they ask amiss that they may spend it on their pleasures—i.e., self (James iv. 3).

(3) Unlove in the heart is possibly the greatest hindrance to prayer. A loving spirit is a condition of believing prayer. We cannot be wrong with man and right with God. The spirit of prayer is essentially the spirit of love. Intercession is simply love at prayer.

> *He prayeth best who loveth best*
> *All things both great and small;*
> *For the great God Who loveth us,*
> *He made and loveth all.*

Dare we hate or dislike those whom God loves? If we do, can we really possess the Spirit of Christ? We really must face these elementary facts in our faith if prayer is to be anything more than a mere form. Our Lord not only says, "And pray for those that persecute you; that ye may be sons of your Father who is in heaven" (Matt. v. 44, 45).

We venture to think that large numbers of so-called Christians have never faced this question. To hear how many Christian workers—and prominent ones, too—speak of others from whom they disagree, one must charitably suppose they have never heard that command of our Lord!

Our daily life in the world is the best indication of our power in prayer. God deals with my prayers not according to the spirit and tone which I exhibit when I am praying in public or private, but according to the spirit I show in my daily life.

Hot-tempered people can make only frigid prayers. If we do not obey our Lord's command and love one another, our prayers are well-nigh worthless. If we harbor an unforgiving spirit it is almost wasted time to pray. Yet a prominent Dean of one of our cathedrals was recently reported to have said that there are some people we can never forgive! If so, we trust that he uses an abridged form of the Lord's prayer. Christ taught us to say "Forgive us . . . as we forgive." And He goes farther than this. He declares, "If ye forgive not men their trespasses, neither will your heavenly Father forgive your trespasses" (Matt. vi. 15). May we ever exhibit the Spirit of Christ, and not forfeit our own much-needed forgiveness. How many of our readers who have not the slightest intention of forgiving their enemies, or even their offending friends, repeated the Lord's prayer today?

Many Christians have never given prayer a fair chance. It is not through conscious insincerity, but from want of thought. The blame for it really rests upon those of us who preach and teach. We are prone to teach doctrines rather than doings. Most men desire to do what is right, but they regard the big things rather than the little failings in the life of love.

Our Lord goes so far as to say that even our gifts are not to be presented to God if we remember that our brother "hath aught against us" (Matt. v. 23). If He will not accept our gifts, is it likely He will answer our prayers? It was when Job ceased contending with his enemies (whom the Bible calls his "friends") that the Lord "turned his captivity" and gave him twice as much as he had before (Job xlii. 10).

How slow we are—how unwilling we are—to see that our lives hinder our prayers! And how unwilling we are to act on love-lines. Yes, we desire to "win" men. Our Lord shows us one way. Don't publish abroad his wrongdoings. Speak to him alone, and "thou hast gained thy brother" (Matt. xviii. 15). Most of us have rather pained our brothers!

Even the home-life may hinder the prayer-life. See what Peter says about how we should so live in the home that our "prayers be not hindered" (I Peter iii. 1-10). We would venture to urge every reader to ask God to search his heart once again and to show him if there is "any root of bitterness" towards anyone. We all desire to do what is pleasing to God. It would be an immense gain to our spiritual life if we would resolve not to attempt to pray until we had done all in our power to make peace and harmony between ourselves and any with whom we have quarreled. Until we do this as far as lies in our power, our prayers are just wasted breath. Unkindly feelings towards another hinder God from helping us in the way He desires.

A loving life is an essential condition of believing prayer. God challenges us again, today, to become fit persons to receive His superabundant blessings. Many of us have to decide whether we will choose a bitter, unforgiving spirit, or the tender mercies and loving-kindness of our Lord Jesus Christ. Is it not amazing that any man can halt between two opinions with such a choice in the balance? For bitterness harms the bitter more than anyone else.

"Whensoever ye stand praying, forgive if ye have aught against anyone; that your Father also, who is in heaven, may forgive you" (Mark xi. 25). So said the blessed Master. Must we not then either forgive, or cease trying to pray? What shall it profit a man if he gain all his time to pretend to pray, if he harbors unlove in his heart to prevent real prayer? How the devil laughs at us because we do not see this truth!

We have God's word for it that eloquence, knowledge, faith, liberality, and even martyrdom profit a man nothing—get hold of it—nothing, unless his heart is filled with love (I Cor. xiii.). "Therefore give us love."

(4) Refusal to do our part may hinder God answering our prayers. Love calls forth compassion and service at the sight of sin and suffering, both here and overseas. Just as St. Paul's heart was "stirred"—"provoked"—within him as he beheld the city full of idols (Acts xvii. 16). We cannot be sincere when we pray "Thy kingdom come" unless we are doing what we can to hasten the coming of that kingdom—by our gifts, our prayers and our service.

We cannot be quite sincere in praying for the conversion of the ungodly unless we are willing to speak a word, or write a letter, or make some attempt to bring him under the influence of the Gospel. Before one of Moody's great missions he was present at a meeting for prayer asking for God's blessing. Several wealthy men were there. One began to pray that God would send sufficient funds to defray the expenses. Moody at once stopped him. "We need not trouble God about that," he said quietly, "we are able to answer that prayer!"

(5) Praying only in secret may be a hindrance. Children of a family should not always meet their father separately. It is remarkable how often our Lord refers to united prayer— "agreed" prayer. "When ye pray, say, Our Father"; "If two of you shall agree on earth as touching anything they shall ask, it shall be done for them. . . . For where two or three are gathered together in my name, there am I in the midst of them" (Matt. xviii. 19, 20).

We feel sure that the weakness in the spiritual life of many churches is to be traced to an inefficient prayer-meeting, or the absence of meetings for prayer. Daily matins and evensong, even when reverent and without the unseemly haste which is so often associated with them, cannot take the place of less formal gatherings for prayer, in which everyone may take part. Can we not make the weekly prayer-meeting a live thing and a living force?

(6) Praise is as important as prayer. We must enter into His gates with thanksgiving, and into His courts with praise, and give thanks unto Him and bless His name (Ps. c. 4). At one time in his life Praying Hyde was led to ask for four souls a day to be brought into the fold by his ministry. If on any day the number fell short of this, there would be such a weight on his heart that it was positively painful, and he could neither eat nor sleep. Then, in prayer he would ask the Lord to show him what was the obstacle in himself. He invariably found that it was the want of praise in his life. He would confess his sinfulness and pray for a spirit of praise. He said that as he praised God seeking souls would come to him. We do not imply that we, too, should limit God to definite numbers or ways of working; but we do cry: "Rejoice! Praise God with heart and mind and soul."

It is not by accident that we are so often bidden to "rejoice in the Lord." God does not want miserable children; and none of His children has cause for misery. St. Paul, the most persecuted of men, was a man of song. Hymns of praise came from his lips in prison and out of prison: day and night he praised His Savior. The very order of his exhortations is significant. "Rejoice evermore; pray without ceasing; in everything give thanks: for this is the will of God in Christ Jesus to you" (I Thess. v. 16-18).

The will of God. Get that thought into your mind. It is not an optional thing.

REJOICE: PRAY: GIVE THANKS

That is the order, according to the will of God—for you, and for me. Nothing so pleases God as our praises—and nothing so blesses the man who prays as the praises he offers! "Delight thyself also in the Lord; and he shall give thee the petitions of thine heart" (Ps. xxxvii. 4, R.V., marg.).

A missionary who had received very bad news from home, was utterly cast down. Prayer availed nothing to relieve the darkness of his soul. He went to see another missionary, no doubt seeking comfort. There on the wall was a motto-card: "Try Thanksgiving!" He did; and in a moment every shadow was gone, never to return.

Do we praise enough to get our prayers answered? If we truly trust Him, we shall always praise Him. For

> *God nothing does nor suffers to be done*
> *But thou would'st do thyself*
> *Could'st thou but see*
> *The end of all events as well as He.*

One who once overheard Luther praying said, "Gracious God! What spirit and what faith is there in his expressions! He petitions God with as much reverence as if he were in the Divine presence, and yet with as firm a hope and confidence as he would address a father or a friend." That child of God seemed quite unconscious that "hindrances to prayer" existed!

After all that has been said, we see that everything can be summed up under one head. All hindrance to prayer arises from ignorance of the teaching of God's Holy Word on the life of holiness He has planned for all His children, or from an unwillingness to consecrate ourselves fully to Him.

When we can truthfully say to our Father, "All that I am and have is thine," then He can say to us, "All that is mine is thine."

Chapter 12: Who May Pray?

IT is only two centuries ago that six undergraduates were expelled from the University of Oxford solely because they met together in each other's rooms for extempore prayer! Whereupon George Whitefield wrote to the Vice-Chancellor, "It is to be hoped that, as some have been expelled for extempore praying, we shall hear of some few others of a contrary stamp being expelled for extempore swearing." Today, thank God, no man in our land is hindered by his fellow-men from praying. Any man may pray—but has every man a right to pray? Does God listen to anyone ?

Who may pray? Is it the privilege—the right—of all men? Not everyone can claim the right to approach the King of our realm. But there are certain persons and bodies of people who have the privilege of immediate access to our sovereign. The Prime Minister has that privilege. The ancient Corporation of the City of London can at anytime lay its petition at the feet of the King. The ambassador of a foreign power may do the same. He has only to present himself at the gate of the palace of the King, and no power can stand between him and the monarch. He can go at once into the royal presence and present his request. But none of these has such ease of access and such loving welcome as the Kings own son.

But there is the King of kings—the God and Father of us all. Who may go to Him? Who may exercise this privilege—yes, this power—with God? We are told—and there is much truth in the remark—that in the most skeptical man or generation prayer is always underneath the surface, waiting. Has it the right to come forth at any time? In some religions it has to wait. Of all the millions in India living in the bondage of Hinduism, none may pray except the Brahmins! A millionaire merchant of any other caste must perforce get a Brahmin—often a mere boy at school!—to say his prayers for him.

The Mohammedan cannot pray unless he has learned a few phrases in Arabic, for his "god" only hears prayers offered in what they believe to be the holy language. Praise be to God, no such restrictions of caste or language stand between us and our God. Can any man, therefore, pray?

Yes, you reply, anyone. But the Bible does not say so. Only a child of God can truly pray to God. Only a son can enter His presence. It is gloriously true that anyone can cry to Him for help—for pardon and mercy. But that is scarcely prayer. Prayer is much more than that. Prayer is going into "the secret place of the Most High," and abiding under the shadow of the Almighty (Ps. xci. 1). Prayer is a making known to God our wants and desires, and holding out the hand of faith to take His gifts. Prayer is the result of the Holy Spirit dwelling within us. It is communion with God. Now, there can scarcely be communion between a king and a rebel. What communion hath light with darkness? (II Cor. vi. 14.) In ourselves we have no right to pray. We have access to God only through the Lord Jesus Christ (Eph. ii. 18, iii. 12).

Prayer is much more than the cry of a drowning man—of a man sinking in the whirlpool of sin: "Lord, save me! I am lost! I am undone! Redeem me! Save me!" Anyone can do this, and that is a petition which is never unanswered, and one, if sincere, to which the answer is never delayed. For "man cannot be God's outlaw if he would." But that is not prayer in the Bible sense. Even the lions, roaring after their prey, seek their meat from God; but that is not prayer.

We know that our Lord said, "Everyone that asketh receiveth" (Matt. vii. 8). He did say so, but to whom? He was speaking to His disciples (Matt. v. 1, 2). Yes, prayer is communion with God: the "home-life" of the soul, as one describes it. And I much question whether there can be any communion with Him unless the Holy Spirit dwells in the heart, and we have "received" the Son, and so have the right to be called "children of God" (John i. 12).

Prayer is the privilege of a child. Children of God alone can claim from the heavenly Father the things which He hath prepared for them that love Him. Our Lord told us that in prayer we should call God "our Father." Surely only children can use that word? St. Paul says that it is "because ye are sons God sent forth the Spirit of His Son into our hearts, crying, 'Abba, Father'" (Gal. iv. 6). Is this what was in God's mind when, in dealing with Job's "comforters," He said, "My servant Job shall pray for you; for him will I accept"? (Job xlii. 8.) It looked as if they would not have been "accepted" in the matter of prayer. But as soon as one becomes a "son of God" he must enter the school of prayer. "Behold, he prayeth," said our Lord of a man as soon as he was converted. Yet that man had "said" prayers all his life (Acts ix. 11). Converted men not only may pray, but must pray—each man for himself, and, of course, for others. But, unless and until we can truthfully call God "Father," we have no claim to be treated as children—as "sons," "heirs of God and joint heirs with Christ"—no claim at all. Do you say this is hard? Nay, surely it is natural. Has a "child" no privileges?

But do not misunderstand me. This does not shut any man out of the kingdom of heaven. Anyone, anywhere, can cry, "God be merciful to me, a sinner!" Any man who is outside the fold of Christ, outside the family of God, however bad he may be, or however good he thinks he is, can this very moment become a child of God, even as he reads these words. One look to Christ in faith is sufficient; "Look and live." God did not even say "see"—He says just look! Turn your face to God.

How did those Galatian Christians become "sons of God"? By faith in Christ. "For ye are all sons of God through faith in Christ Jesus" (Gal. iii. 26). Christ will make any man a son of God by adoption and grace the moment he turns to Him in true repentance and faith. But we have no rightful claim even upon God's providence unless we are His children. We cannot say with any confidence or certainty, "I shall not want," unless we can say, with confidence and certainty, "The Lord is my Shepherd."

A child, however, has a right to his father's care, and love, and protection, and provision. Now, a child can only enter a family by being born into it. We become children of God by being "born again," "born from above" (John iii. 3, 5). That is, by believing on the Lord Jesus Christ (John iii. 16).

Having said all this as a warning, and perhaps as an explanation why some people find prayer an utter failure, we hasten to add that God often hears and answers prayer even from those who have no legal right to pray—from those who are not His "children," and may even deny that He exists! The Gospels tell us of not a few unbelievers who came to Christ for healing; and He never sent one away without the coveted blessing—never. They came as "beggars," not as "children." And even if "the children must first be fed," these others received the crumbs—yea, and more than crumbs—that were freely given.

So today God often hears the cry of unbelievers for temporal mercies. One case well known to the writer may be given as an illustration. My friend told me that he had been an atheist many years. Whilst an infidel, he had been singing for forty years in a church choir because he was fond of music. His aged father became seriously ill two or three years ago, and lay in great pain. The doctors were helpless to relieve the sufferer. In his distress for his father, the infidel choirman fell on his knees and cried, "O God, if there is a God, show Thy power by taking away my father's pain!" God heard the man's piteous cry, and removed the pain immediately. The "atheist" praised God, and hurried off to his vicar to find out the way of salvation! Today he is out-and-out for Christ, giving his whole time to work for his newly-found Savior. Yes, God is greater than His promises, and is more willing to hear than we are to pray.

Perhaps the most striking of all "prayers" from the lips of unbelievers is that recorded of Caroline Fry, the author of *Christ Our Example*. Although possessed of beauty, wealth, position and friends, she found that none of them satisfied, and at length, in her utter misery, she sought God. Yet her first utterance to Him was an expression of open rebellion to and hatred of Him! Listen to it—it is not the prayer of a "child":—

"O God, if Thou art a God: I do not love Thee; I do not want Thee; I do not believe there is any happiness in Thee: but I am miserable as I am. Give me what I do not seek; give me what I do not want. If Thou canst, make me happy. I am miserable as I am. I am tired of this world; if there is anything better, give it me."

What a "prayer"! Yet God heard and answered. He forgave the wanderer and made her radiantly happy and gloriously fruitful in His service.

> *In even savage bosoms*
> *There are longings, strivings, yearnings*
> *For the good they comprehend not.*
> *And their feeble hands and helpless.*
> *Groping blindly in the darkness,*
> *Touch God's right hand in the darkness,*
> *And are lifted up and strengthened.*

Shall we, then, alter our question a little, and ask, who has a right to pray?" Only children of God in whom the Holy Spirit dwells. But, even so, we must remember that no man can come unashamed and with confidence to his Father in heaven unless he is living as a son of God should live. We cannot expect a father to lavish his favors upon erring children. Only a faithful and sanctified son can pray with the Spirit and pray with the understanding also (I Cor. xiv. 15).

But if we are sons of God, nothing but sin can hinder our prayers. We, His children, have the right of access to God at any time, in any place. And He understands any form of prayer. We may have a wonderful gift of speech pouring itself out in a torrent of thanksgiving, petition, and praise like St. Paul; or we may have the quiet, deep, lover-like communion of a St. John. The brilliant scholar like John Wesley and the humble cobbler like William Carey are alike welcome at the throne of grace. Influence at the court of heaven depends not upon birth, or brilliancy, or achievement, but upon humble and utter independence upon the Son of the King.

Moody attributed his marvelous success to the prayers of an obscure and almost unknown invalid woman! And truly the invalid saints of England could bring about a speedy revival by their prayers. Oh, that all the shut-ins" would speak out!

Do we not make a mistake in supposing that some people have a "gift" of prayer? A brilliant Cambridge undergraduate asked me if the life of prayer was not a gift, and one which very few possessed? He suggested that, just as not everyone was musical, so not everyone is expected to be prayerful! George Müller was exceptional not because he had a gift of prayer, but because he prayed. Those who cannot "speak well," as God declared Aaron could, may labor in secret by intercession with those that speak the word. We must have great faith if we are to have great power with God in prayer, although God is very gracious, and oftentimes goes beyond our faith.

Henry Martyn was a man of prayer, yet his faith was not equal to his prayers. He once declared that he "would as soon expect to see a man rise from the dead as to see a Brahmin converted to Christ." Would St. James say, "Let not that man think he shall receive anything of the Lord"? (James i. 7.) Now, Henry Martyn died without seeing one Brahmin accepting Christ as his Savior. He used to retire, day by day, to a deserted pagoda for prayer. Yet he had not faith for the conversion of a Brahmin. A few months back there knelt in that very pagoda Brahmins and Mohammedans from all parts of India, Burma and Ceylon, now fellow-Christians. Others had prayed with greater faith than Henry Martyn.

Who may pray? We may; but do we? Does our Lord look at us with even more pathos and tenderness than when He first uttered the words, and say, "Hitherto ye have asked nothing in My name? Ask, and ye shall receive, that your joy may be full" (John xvi. 24). If the dear Master was dependent on prayer to make His work a power, how much more are we? He sometimes prayed with "strong crying and tears" (Heb. v. 7). Do we? Have we ever shed a prayerful tear? Well might we cry, "Quicken us, and we will call upon Thy name" (Ps. lxxx. 18).

St. Paul's exhortation to Timothy may well be made to us all: "Stir up the gift of God which is in thee" (II Tim. i. 6). For the Holy Spirit is prayer's great Helper. We are incapable of ourselves to translate our real needs into prayer. The Holy Spirit does this for us. We cannot ask as we ought. The Holy Spirit does this for us. It is possible for unaided man to ask what is for our ill. The Holy Spirit can check this. No weak or trembling hand dare put in motion any mighty force. Can I—dare I—move the Hand that moves the universe? No! Unless the Holy Spirit has control of me.

Yes, we need Divine help for prayer—and we have it! How the whole Trinity delights in prayer! God the Father listens: the Holy Spirit dictates: the eternal Son presents the petition—and Himself intercedes; and so the answer comes down.

Believe me, prayer is our highest privilege, our gravest responsibility, and the greatest power God has put into our hands. Prayer, real prayer, is the noblest, the sublimest, the most stupendous act that any creature of God can perform.

It is, as Coleridge declared, the very highest energy of which human nature is capable. To pray with all your heart and strength—that is the last, the greatest achievement of the Christian's warfare on earth.

"LORD, TEACH US TO PRAY!"

Answers to Prayer

~ ※ ~

George Müller

By *George Müller*

Selections From George Müller's "Narratives" 1898

Compiled by A. E. C. Brooks.

~ ※ ~

"I never remember, in all my Christian course, a period now (in March, 1895) of sixty-nine years and four months, that I ever SINCERELY and PATIENTLY sought to know the will of God by *the teaching of the Holy Ghost*, through the instrumentality of the *Word of God*, but I have been ALWAYS directed rightly. But if *honesty of heart* and *uprightness before God* were lacking, or if I did not *patiently* wait upon God for instruction, or if I preferred *the counsel of my fellow men* to the declarations of *the Word of the living God*, I made great mistakes."

GEORGE MÜLLER.

PREFACE

Mr. Brooks, in this compilation, has endeavored to select those incidents and practical remarks from Mr. Müller's Narratives, that show in an unmistakeable[1] way, both to believers and unbelievers, the secret of believing prayer, the manifest hand of a living God, and His unfailing response, in His own time and way, to every petition which is according to His will.

The careful perusal of these extracts will thus further the great object which Mr. Müller had in view, without the necessity of reading through the various details of his "Narratives,"[2] details which Mr. Müller felt bound to give when writing periodically the account of God's dealings with him.

For those who have the opportunity, an examination of the "Autobiography of George Müller, or, a Million and a Half in Answer to Prayer" will richly repay the time spent upon it.

Mr. Müller's permission for the compilation of this volume is shown by his following words:

"If the extracts are given exactly as printed, and the punctuation exactly as in the book and in the connection in which the facts stand, I have no objection."

---

[1] Original British spelling kept throughout.

[2] The reference is to several volumes, written by Mr. Müller, all entitled "A Narrative of Some of the Lord's Dealings with George Müller."

HOW TO ASCERTAIN THE WILL OF GOD

I seek at the beginning to get my heart into such a state that it has no will of its own in regard to a given matter. Nine-tenths of the trouble with people generally is just here. Nine-tenths of the difficulties are overcome when our hearts are ready to do the Lord's will, whatever it may be. When one is truly in this state, it is usually but a little way to the knowledge of what His will is.

2. Having done this, I do not leave the result to feeling or simple impression. If so, I make myself liable to great delusions.

3. I seek the Will of the Spirit of God through, or in connection with, the Word of God. The Spirit and the Word must be combined. If I look to the Spirit alone without the Word, I lay myself open to great delusions also. If the Holy Ghost guides us at all, He will do it according to the Scriptures and never contrary to them.

4. Next I take into account providential circumstances. These often plainly indicate God's Will in connection with His Word and Spirit.

5. I ask God in prayer to reveal His Will to me aright.

6. Thus, through prayer to God, the study of the Word, and reflection, I come to a deliberate judgment according to the best of my ability and knowledge, and if my mind is thus at peace, and continues so after two or three more petitions, I proceed accordingly. In trivial matters, and in transactions involving most important issues, I have found this method always effective.

GEORGE MÜLLER.

CHAPTER I:
BEGINNING AND EARLY DAYS OF THE ORPHAN WORK.

"That the trial of your faith, being much more precious than of gold that perisheth,
though it be tried with fire, might be found unto praise and honour and glory
at the appearing of Jesus Christ."—1 Peter, i. 7.

Mr. George Müller, the founder of the New Orphan-Houses, Ashley Down, Bristol (institutions that have been for many years the greatest monuments of modern times to a prayer-answering God), gives in that most valuable and instructive book, "A Narrative of Some of the Lord's Dealings with George Müller," Vol. I., among other reasons for establishing an Orphan-House, the following:—

"Sometimes I found children of God tried in mind by the prospect of old age, when they might be unable to work any longer, and therefore were harassed by the fear of having to go into the poor-house. If in such a case I pointed out to them, how their Heavenly Father has always helped those who put their trust in Him, they might not, perhaps, always say, that times have changed; but yet it was evident enough, that God was not looked upon by them as the Living God. My spirit was ofttimes bowed down by this, and I longed to set something before the children of God, whereby they might see, that He does not forsake, even in our day, those who rely upon Him.

"Another class of persons were brethren in business, who suffered in their souls, and brought guilt on their consciences, by carrying on their business, almost in the same way as unconverted persons do. The competition in trade, the bad times, the over-peopled country, were given as reasons why, if the business were carried on simply according to the word of God, it could not be expected to do well. Such a brother, perhaps, would express the wish, that he might be differently situated; but very rarely did I see *that there was a stand made for God, that there was the holy determination to trust in the living God, and to depend on Him, in order that a good conscience might be maintained.* To this class likewise I desired to show, by a visible proof, that God is unchangeably the same.

"Then there was another class of persons, individuals who were in professions in which they could not continue with a good conscience, or persons who were in an unscriptural position with reference to spiritual things; but both classes feared, on account of the consequences, to give up the profession in which they could not abide with God, or to leave their position, lest they should be thrown out of employment. My spirit longed to be instrumental in strengthening their faith, by giving them not only instances from the word of God, of His willingness and ability to help all those who rely upon Him, but *to show them by proofs*, that He is the same in our day. I well knew *that the Word of God ought to be enough*, and it was, by grace, enough, to me; but still, I considered that I ought to lend a helping hand to my brethren, if by any means, by this visible proof to the unchangeable faithfulness of the Lord, I might strengthen their hands in God; for I remembered what a great blessing my own soul had received through the Lord's dealings with His servant A. H. Franke, who in dependence upon the living God alone, established an immense Orphan-House, which I had seen many times with my own eyes. I, therefore, judged myself bound to be the servant of the Church of God, in the particular point on which I had obtained mercy: namely, *in being able to take God by His word and to rely upon it.* All these exercises of my soul, which resulted from the fact that so many believers, with whom I became acquainted, were harassed and distressed in mind, or brought guilt on their consciences, on account of not trusting in the Lord; were used by God to awaken in my heart the desire of setting before the church at large, and before the world, a proof that He has not in the least changed; and this seemed to me best done, by the establishing of an Orphan-House. It needed to be something which could be seen, even by the natural eye. Now, if I, a poor man, simply by prayer and faith, obtained *without asking any individual*, the means for establishing and carrying on an Orphan-House, there would be something which, with the Lord's blessing, might be instrumental in strengthening the faith of the children of God, besides being a testimony to the consciences of the unconverted, of the reality of the things of God. This, then, was the primary reason for establishing the Orphan-House. I certainly did from my heart desire to be used by God to benefit the bodies of poor children, bereaved of both parents, and seek in other respects, with the help of God, to do them good for this life;—I also particularly longed to be used by God in getting the dear orphans trained up in the fear of God;—but still, the first and primary object of the work was (and still is:) that God might be magnified by the fact, that the orphans under my care are provided with all they need, only by *prayer and faith* without anyone being asked by me or my fellow-laborers whereby it may be seen, that God is FAITHFUL STILL, and HEARS PRAYER STILL. That I was not mistaken, has been abundantly proved since November, 1835, both by the conversion of many sinners who have read the accounts, which have been published in connection with this work, and also by the abundance of fruit that has followed in the hearts of the saints, for which from my inmost soul, I desire to be grateful to God, and the honor and glory of which not only is due to Him alone, but, which I, by His help, am enabled to ascribe to Him."

"OPEN THY MOUTH WIDE."

In the account written by Mr. Müller dated Jan. 16, 1836, respecting the Orphan-House intended to be established in Bristol in connection with the Scriptural Knowledge Institution for Home and Abroad, we read:—

"When, of late, the thoughts of establishing an Orphan-House, in dependence upon the Lord, revived in my mind, during the first two weeks I only prayed that if it were of the Lord, he would bring it about, but if not that He graciously would be pleased to take all thoughts about it out of my mind. My uncertainty about knowing the Lord's mind did not arise from questioning whether it would be pleasing in His sight, that there should be an abode and Scriptural education provided for destitute fatherless and motherless children; but whether it were His will that I should be the instrument of setting such an object on foot, as my hands were already more than filled. My comfort, however, was, that, if it were His will, He would provide not merely the means, but also suitable individuals to take care of the children, so that my part of the work would take only such a portion of my time, as, considering the importance of the matter, I might give, notwithstanding my many other engagements. The whole of those two weeks I never asked the Lord for money or for persons to engage in the work.

"On December 5th, however, the subject of my prayer all at once became different. I was reading Psalm lxxxi., and was particularly struck, more than at any time before, with verse 10: *"Open thy month wide, and I will fill it."* I thought a few moments about these words, and then was led to apply them to the case of the Orphan-House. It struck me that I had never asked the Lord for anything concerning it, except to know His will, respecting its being established or not; and I then fell on my knees and opened my mouth wide, asking Him for much. I asked in submission to His will, and without fixing a time when He should answer my petition. I prayed that He would give me a house, *i.e.*, either as a loan, or that someone might be led to pay the rent for one, or that one might be given permanently for this object; further, I asked Him for £1000; and likewise for suitable individuals to take care of the children. Besides this, I have been since led to ask the Lord, to put into the hearts of His people to send me articles of furniture for the house, and some clothes for the children. When I was asking the petition, I was fully aware what I was doing, *i.e.*, that I was asking for something which I had no natural prospect of obtaining from the brethren whom I know, but which was not too much for the Lord to grant."

"December 10, 1835.—This morning I received a letter, in which a brother and sister wrote thus:—'We propose ourselves for the service of the intended Orphan-House, if you think us qualified for it; also to give up all the furniture, &c., which the Lord has given us, for its use; and to do this without receiving any salary whatever; believing that if it be the will of the Lord to employ us, He will supply all our needs, &c.'"

"Dec. 13.—A brother was influenced this day to give 4s. per week, or £10 8s. yearly, as long as the Lord gives the means; 8s. was given by him as two weeks' subscriptions. To-day a brother and sister offered themselves, with all their furniture, and all the provisions which they have in the house, if they can be usefully employed in the concerns of the Orphan-House."

A GREAT ENCOURAGEMENT.

"Dec. 17.—I was rather cast down last evening and this morning about the matter, questioning whether I ought to be engaged in this way, and was led to ask the Lord to give me some further encouragement. Soon after were sent by a brother two pieces of print, the one seven and the other 23¾ yards, 6¾ yards of calico, four pieces of lining, about four yards altogether, a sheet, and a yard measure. This evening another brother brought a clothes horse, three frocks, four pinafores, six handkerchiefs, three counterpanes, one blanket, two pewter salt cellars, six tin cups, and six metal tea spoons; he also brought 3s. 6d. given to him by three different individuals. At the same time he told me that it had been put into the heart of an individual to send to-morrow £100."

ONE THOUSAND POUNDS.

"June 15, 1837.—To-day I gave myself once more earnestly to prayer respecting the remainder of the £1000. This evening £5 was given, so that now the whole sum is made up. To the Glory of the Lord, whose I am, and whom I serve, I would state again, that every shilling of this money, and all the articles of clothing and furniture, which have been mentioned in the foregoing pages, have been given to me, *without one single individual having been asked by me for anything.*"

ORPHANS FOR THE BUILDING.

In a third statement, containing the announcement of the opening of the Orphan-House, for destitute female children, and a proposal for the establishment of an Infant Orphan-House, which was sent to the press on May 18, 1836, Mr. Müller wrote:—

"So far as I remember, I brought even the most minute circumstances concerning the Orphan-House before the Lord in my petitions, being conscious of my own weakness and ignorance. There was, however, one point I never had prayed about, namely that the Lord would send children; for I naturally took it for granted that there would be plenty of applications. The nearer, however, the day came which had been appointed for receiving applications, the more I had a secret consciousness, that the Lord might disappoint my natural expectations, and show me that I could not prosper in one single thing without Him. The appointed time came, and not even one application was made. I had before this been repeatedly tried, whether I might not, after all, against the Lord's mind, have engaged in the work. This circumstance now led me to lie low before my God in prayer the whole of the evening, February 3, and to examine my heart once more as to all the motives concerning it; and being able, as formerly, to say, that His glory was my *chief aim, i.e.,* that it might be seen that it is not a vain thing to trust in the living God,—and that my *second aim* was the spiritual welfare of the orphan-children,—and the *third* their bodily welfare; and still continuing in prayer, I was at last brought to this state, that I could say *from my heart,* that I should rejoice in God being glorified in this matter, though it were by *bringing the whole to nothing.* But as still, after all, it seemed to me more tending to the glory of God, to establish and prosper the Orphan-House, I could then ask Him heartily, to send applications. I enjoyed now a peaceful state of heart concerning the subject, and was also more assured than ever that God would establish it. *The very next day,* February 4, the first application was made, and since then 42 more have been made."

"JUST FOR TO-DAY."

Later on, when there were nearly 100 persons to be maintained, and the funds were reduced to about £20, Mr. Müller writes:—

"July 22 [1838].—This evening I was walking in our little garden, meditating on Heb. xiii. 8, "Jesus Christ the same yesterday, and to-day, and for ever." Whilst meditating on His unchangeable love, power, wisdom, &c.—and turning all, as I went on, into prayer respecting myself; and whilst applying likewise His unchangeable love, and power and wisdom, &c., both to my present spiritual and temporal circumstances:—all at once the present need of the Orphan-House was brought to my mind. Immediately I was led to say to myself, Jesus in His love and power has hitherto supplied me with what I have needed for the Orphans, and in the same unchangeable love and power He will provide me with what I may need for the future. A flow of joy came into my soul whilst realising thus the unchangeableness of our adorable Lord. About one minute after, a letter was brought me, enclosing a bill for £20. In it was written: "Will you apply the amount of the enclosed bill to the furtherance of the objects of your Scriptural Knowledge Society, or of your Orphan Establishment, or in the work and cause of our Master in any way that He Himself, on your application to Him, may point out to you. It is not a great sum, but it is a sufficient provision for the exigency of to-day; and it is for *to-day's* exigencies, that, ordinarily, the Lord provides. To-morrow, as it brings its demands, will find its supply, etc."

"[Of this £20 I took £10 for the Orphan fund, and £10 for trip other objects, and was thus enabled to meet the expenses of about £34 which, in connection with the Orphan-Houses, came upon me within four days afterwards, and which I knew beforehand would come.]"

WAITING FOR HELP.

"Nov. 21, 1838.—Never were we so reduced in funds as to-day. There was not a single halfpenny in hand between the matrons of the three houses. Nevertheless there was a good dinner, and by managing so as to help one another with bread, etc., there was a prospect of getting over this day also; but for none of the houses had we the prospect of being able to take in bread. When I left the brethren and sisters at one o'clock, after prayer, I told them that we must wait for help, and see how the Lord would deliver us this time. I was sure of help, but we were indeed straitened. When I came to Kingsdown, I felt that I needed more exercise, being very cold; wherefore I went not the nearest way home, but round by Clarence Place. About twenty yards from my house, I met a brother who walked back with me, and after a little conversation gave me £10 to be handed over to the brethren, the deacons, towards providing the poor saints with coals, blankets and warm clothing; also £5 for the Orphans, and £5 for the other objects of the Scriptural Knowledge Institution. The brother had called twice while I was gone to the Orphan-Houses, and had I now been *one half minute* later, I should have missed him. But the Lord knew our need, and therefore allowed me to meet him. I sent off the £5 immediately to the matrons."

BEYOND DISAPPOINTMENT.

"Sept. 21 [1840], Monday. By what was in hand for the Orphans, and by what had come in yesterday, the need of to-day is more than supplied, as there is enough for to-morrow also. To-day a brother from the neighbourhood of London gave me £10, to be laid out as it might be most needed. As we have been praying many days for the School,—Bible,—and Missionary Funds, I took it all for them. This brother knew nothing about our work, when he came three days since to Bristol. Thus the Lord, to show His continued care over us, raises up new helpers. They that trust in the Lord shall never be confounded! Some who helped for a while may fall asleep in Jesus; others may grow cold in the service of the Lord; others may be as desirous as ever to help, but have no longer the means; others may have both a willing heart to help, and have also the means, but may see it the Lord's will to lay them out in another way;—and thus, from one cause or another, were we to lean upon man, we should surely be confounded; but, in leaning upon the living God alone, we are *BEYOND disappointment, and BEYOND being forsaken because of death,* or *want of means*, or *want of love*, or *because of the claims of other work*. How precious to have learned in any measure to stand with God alone in the world, and yet to be happy, and to know that surely no good thing shall be withheld from us whilst we walk uprightly!"

A GREAT SINNER CONVERTED.

In his REVIEW OF THE YEAR 1841, Mr. Müller writes:—

"During this year I was informed about the conversion of one of the very greatest sinners, that I ever heard of in all my service for the Lord. Repeatedly I fell on my knees with his wife, and asked the Lord for his conversion, when she came to me in the deepest distress of soul, on account of the most barbarous and cruel treatment that she received from him, in his bitter enmity against her for the Lord's sake, and because he could not provoke her to be in a passion, and *she would not* strike him again, and the like. At the time when it was at its worst I pleaded especially on his behalf the promise in Matthew xviii. 19: 'Again I say unto you, that if two of you shall agree on earth as touching anything that they shall ask, it shall be done for them of my father which is in heaven.' And now this awful persecutor is converted."

PRAYER FOR SPIRITUAL BLESSING AMONG THE SAINTS.

"On May 25th, I began to ask the Lord for greater real spiritual prosperity among the saints, among whom I labour in Bristol, than there ever yet had been among them; and now I have to record to the praise of the Lord that truly He has answered this request; for, considering all things, at no period has there been more manifestation of grace and truth, and spiritual power among us, than there is now while I am writing this for the press (1845). Not that we have attained to what we might; we are far, very far from it; but the Lord has been very, very good to us, and we have most abundant cause for thanksgiving."

WITHHOLDING THE REPORT.

"Dec. 9 [1841].—To-day came in for the Orphans by the sale of stockings 10s. 10d.— We are now brought to the close of the sixth year of this part of the work, *having only in hand the money which has been put by for the rent*; but during the whole of this year we have been supplied with all that was needed.

"During the last three years we had closed the accounts on this day, and had, a few days after, some public meetings, at which, for the benefit of the hearers, we stated how the Lord had dealt with us during the year, and the substance of what had been stated at these meetings was afterwards printed for the benefit of the church at large. This time, however, it appeared to us better to delay for a while both the public meetings and the publishing of the Report. Through grace we had learned to lean upon the Lord only, being assured, that, if we were never to speak or write one single word more about this work, yet should we be supplied with means, as long as He should enable us to depend on Himself alone. But whilst we neither had had those public meetings for the purpose of exposing our necessity, nor had had the account of the Lord's dealings with us published for the sake of working thereby upon the feelings of the readers, and thus inducing them to give money, but only that we might by our experience benefit other saints; yet it might have appeared to some that, in making known our circumstances, we were actuated by some such motives. What better proof, therefore, could we give of our depending upon the living God alone, and not upon public meetings or printed Reports, than that, *in the midst of our deep poverty*, instead of being glad for the time to have come when we could make known our circumstances, we still went on quietly for some time longer, without saying anything. We therefore determined, as we sought and still seek in this work to act for the profit of the saints generally, to delay both the public meetings and the Report for a few months. *Naturally* we should have been, of course, as glad as anyone to have exposed our poverty at that time; but *spiritually* we were unable to delight even then in the prospect of the increased benefit that might be derived by the church at large from our acting as we did.

~ ※ ~

"Dec. 18. Saturday morning. There is now the greatest need, and only 4d. in hand, which I found in the box at my house; yet I fully believe the Lord will supply us this day also with all that is required.—Pause a few moments, dear reader! Observe two things! We acted *for God* in delaying the public meetings and the publishing of the Report; but *God's way leads always into trial, so far as sight and sense are concerned. Nature* always will be tried *in God's ways*. The Lord was saying by this poverty, 'I will now see whether you truly lean upon me, and whether you truly look to me.' Of all the seasons that I had ever passed through since I had been living in this way, *up to that time*, I never knew any period in which my faith was tried so sharply, as during the four months from Dec. 12, 1841, to April 12, 1842. But observe further: We might even now have altered our minds with respect to the public meetings and publishing the Report; *for no one knew our determination, at this time*, concerning the point. Nay, on the contrary, we knew with what delight very many children of God were looking forward to receive further accounts. But the Lord kept us steadfast to the conclusion, at which we had arrived under His guidance."

"HE ABIDETH FAITHFUL."

Under the date Jan. 25, 1842, Mr. Müller writes:—

"Perhaps, dear reader, you have said in your heart before you have read thus far: 'How would it be, suppose the funds for the Orphans were reduced to nothing, and those who are engaged in the work had nothing of their own to give, and a meal time were come, and you had no food for the children.'

"Thus indeed it may be, for our hearts are desperately wicked. If ever we should be so left to ourselves, as that either we depend no more upon the living God, or that 'we regard iniquity in our hearts,' then such a state of things, we have reason to believe, would occur. But so long as we shall be enabled to trust in the living God, and so long as, though falling short in every way of what we might be, and ought to be, we are at least kept from living in sin, such a state of things cannot occur. Therefore, dear reader, if you yourself walk with God, and if, on that account, His glory is dear to you, I affectionately and earnestly entreat you to beseech Him to uphold us; for how awful would be the disgrace brought upon His holy name if we, who have so publicly made our boast in Him, and have spoken well of Him, should be left to disgrace Him, either by unbelief in the hour of trial, or by a life of sin in other respects."

DELAYED BUT SURE.

"March 9 [1842].—At a time of the greatest need, both with regard to the Day-Schools and the Orphans, so much so that we could not have gone on any longer without help, I received this day £10 from a brother who lives near Dublin. The money was divided between the Day-Schools and the Orphan-Houses. The following little circumstance is to be noticed respecting this donation:—As our need was so great, and my soul was, through grace, truly waiting upon the Lord, I looked out for supplies in the course of this morning. The post, however, was out, and no supplies had come. This did not in the least discourage me. I said to myself, the Lord can send means without the post, or even now, though the post is out, by this very delivery of letters He may have sent means, though the money is not yet in my hands. It was not long after I had thus spoken to myself, when, according to my hope in God, we were helped; for the brother who sent us the £10, had this time directed his letter to the Boys' Orphan-House, whence it was sent to me."

"LIKE AS A FATHER."

"March 17.—From the 12th to the 16th had come in £4 5s. 11½d. for the Orphans. This morning our poverty, which now has lasted more or less for several months, had become exceedingly great. I left my house a few minutes after seven to go to the Orphan-Houses, to see whether there was money enough to take in the milk, which is brought about eight o'clock. On my way it was specially my request that the Lord would be pleased to pity us, even as a father pitieth his children, and that He would not lay more upon us than He would enable us to bear, I especially entreated Him that He would now be pleased to refresh our hearts by sending us help. I likewise reminded Him of the consequences that would result, both in reference to believers and unbelievers, if we should have to give up the work because of want of means, and that He therefore would not permit of its coming to nought. I moreover again confessed before the Lord that I deserved not that He should continue to use me in this work any longer. While I was thus in prayer, about two minutes' walk from the Orphan-Houses, I met a brother who was going at this early hour to his business. After having exchanged a few words with him, I went on; but he presently ran after me, and gave me £1 for the Orphans. Thus the Lord speedily answered my prayer. Truly, it is worth being poor and greatly tried in faith, for the sake of having day by day such precious proofs of the loving interest which our kind Father takes in everything that concerns us. And how should our Father do otherwise? He that has given us the greatest possible proof of His love which He could have done, in giving us His own Son, surely He will with Him also freely give us all things."

TRUST IN THE LORD BETTER THAN MAN'S PROMISES.

"May 6 [1845].—About six weeks ago intimation was kindly given by a brother that he expected a certain considerable sum of money, and that, if he obtained it, a certain portion of it should be given to the Lord, so that £100 of it should be used for the work in my hands, and the other part for Brother Craik's and my own personal expenses. However, day after day passed away, and the money did not come. I did not trust in this money, yet, as during all this time, with scarcely any exception, we were more or less needy, I thought again and again about this brother's promise; though I did not, by the grace of God, trust in the brother who had made it, but in the Lord. Thus week after week passed away, and the money did not come. Now this morning it came to my mind, that such promises ought to be valued, in a certain sense, as nothing, i.e., that the mind ought never for a moment to be directed to them, but to the living God, and to the living God only. I saw that such promises ought not to be of the value of one farthing, so far as it regards thinking about them for help. I therefore asked the Lord, when, as usual, I was praying with my beloved wife about the work in my hands that He would be pleased to take this whole matter, about that promise, completely out of my mind, and to help me, not to value it in the least, yea, to treat it as if not worth one farthing, but to keep my eye directed only to Himself. I was enabled to do so. We had not yet finished praying when I received the following letter:

May 5, 1845

Beloved Brother,

Are your bankers still Messrs. Stuckey and Co. of Bristol, and are their bankers still Messrs. Robarts and Co. of London? Please to instruct me on this; and if the case should be so, please to regard this as a letter of advice that £70 are paid to Messrs. Robarts and Co., for Messrs. Stuckey and Co., for you. This sum apply as the Lord may give you wisdom. I shall not send to Robarts and Co. until I hear from you.

Ever affectionately yours,

* * * *

"Thus the Lord rewarded at once this determination to endeavour not to look in the least to that promise from a brother, but only to Himself. But this was not all. About two o'clock this afternoon I received from the brother, who had more than forty days ago, made that promise, £166 18s., as he this day received the money, on the strength of which he had made that promise. Of this sum £100 are to be used for the work in my hands, and the remainder for brother Craik's and my own personal expenses."

Under date 1842 Mr. Müller writes:—

"I desire that all the children of God, who may read these details, may thereby be lead to increased and more simple confidence in God for everything which they may need under any circumstances, and that these many answers to prayer may encourage them to pray, particularly as it regards the conversion of their friends and relatives, their own progress in grace and knowledge, the state of the saints whom they may know personally, the state of the church of God at large, and the success of the preaching of the Gospel. Especially I affectionately warn them against being led away by the device of Satan, to think that these things are peculiar to me, and cannot be enjoyed by all the children of God; for though, as has been stated before, every believer is not called upon to establish Orphan-Houses, Charity Schools, etc., and trust in the Lord for means; yet all believers are called upon, in the simple confidence of faith, to cast all their burdens upon Him, to trust in Him for everything, and not only to make every thing a subject of prayer, but to expect answers to their petitions which they have asked according to His will, and in the name of the Lord Jesus.—Think not, dear reader, that I have *the gift of faith*, that is, that gift of which we read in 1 Cor. xii. 9, and which is mentioned along with 'the gifts of healing,' 'the working of miracles,' 'prophecy,' and that on that account I am able to trust in the Lord. *It is true* that the faith, which I am enabled to exercise, is altogether God's own gift; it is true that He alone supports it, and that He alone can increase it; it is true that, moment by moment, I depend upon Him for it, and that, if I were only one moment left to myself, my faith would utterly fail; but *it is not true* that my faith is that gift of faith which is spoken of in 1 Cor. xii. 9 for the following reasons:—

"1. The faith which I am enabled to exercise with reference to the Orphan-Houses and my own temporal necessities, is not that 'faith' of which it is said in 1 Cor. xiii. 2 (evidently in allusion to the faith spoken of in 1 Cor. xii. 9), 'Though I have all faith, so that I could remove mountains, and have not charity (love), I am nothing'; but it is the self-same faith which is found in *every believer*, and the growth of which I am most sensible of to myself; for, by little and little, it has been increasing for the last sixty-nine years.

"2. This faith which is exercised respecting the Orphan-Houses and my own temporal necessities, shows itself in the same measure, for instance concerning the following points: I have never been permitted to doubt during the last sixty-nine years that my sins are forgiven, that I am a child of God, that I am beloved of God, and that I shall be finally saved; because I am enabled, by the grace of God, to exercise faith upon the word of God, and believe what God says in those passages which settle these matters (1 John v. 1—Gal. iii. 26—Acts x. 43—Romans x. 9, 10—John iii. 16, etc.).... Further, when sometimes all has been dark, exceedingly dark, with reference to my service among the saints, judging from natural appearances; yea, when I should have been overwhelmed indeed in grief and despair, had I looked at things after the outward appearance; at such times I have sought to encourage myself in God, by laying hold in faith on His mighty power, His unchangeable love, and His infinite wisdom, and I have said to myself: God is able and willing to deliver me, if it be good for me; for it is written: "He that spared not His own Son, but delivered Him up for us all, how shall He not with Him also freely give us all things?" Rom. viii. 32. This, this it was which, being believed by me through grace, kept my soul in peace.—Further, when in connection with the Orphan-Houses, Day Schools, etc., trials have come upon me which were far heavier than the want of means when lying reports were spread that the Orphans had not enough to eat, or that they were cruelly treated in other respects, and the like; or when other trials, still greater, but which I cannot mention, have befallen me in connexion with this work, and that at a time when I was nearly a thousand miles absent from Bristol, and had to remain absent week after week: at such times my soul was stayed upon God; I believed His word of promise which was applicable to such cases; I poured out my soul before God, and arose from my knees in peace, because the trouble that was in the soul was in believing prayer cast upon God, and thus I was kept in peace, though I saw it to be the will of God to remain far away from the work.—Further, when I needed houses, fellow-labourers, masters and mistresses for the Orphans or for the Day Schools, I have been enabled to look for all to the Lord and trust in Him for help.—Dear reader, I may seem to boast; but, by the grace of God, I do not boast in thus speaking. From my inmost soul I do ascribe it to God alone that He has enabled me to trust in Him, and that hitherto He has not suffered my confidence in Him to fail. But I thought it needful to make these remarks, lest anyone should think that my depending upon God was a particular gift given to me, which other saints have no right to look for; or lest it should be thought that this my depending upon Him had *only to do with the obtaining of MONEY by prayer and faith*. By the grace of God I desire that my faith in God should extend towards EVERY thing, the smallest of my own temporal and spiritual concerns, and the smallest of the temporal and spiritual concerns of my family, towards the saints among whom I labour, the church at large, everything that has to do with the temporal and spiritual prosperity of the Scriptural Knowledge Institution, etc. Dear reader, do not think that I have attained in faith (and how much less in other respects!) to that degree to which I might and ought to attain; but thank God for the faith which He has given me, and ask Him to uphold and increase it. And lastly, once more, let not Satan deceive you in making you think that you could not have the same faith but that it is only for persons who are situated as I am. When I lose such a thing as a key, I ask the Lord to direct me to it, and I look for an answer to my prayer; when a person with whom I have made an appointment does not come, according to the fixed time, and I begin to be inconvenienced by it, I ask the Lord to be pleased to hasten him to me and I look for an answer; when I do not understand a passage of the word of God, I lift up my heart to the

Lord, that He would be pleased, by His Holy Spirit to instruct me, and I expect to be taught, though I do not fix the time when, and the manner how it should be; when I am going to minister in the Word, I seek help from the Lord, and while I, in the consciousness of natural inability as well as utter unworthiness begin this His service, I am not cast down, but of good cheer, because I look for His assistance, and believe that He, for His dear Son's sake will help me. And thus in other of my temporal and spiritual concerns I pray to the Lord, and expect an answer to my requests; and may not *you* do the same, dear believing reader? Oh! I beseech you, do not think me an extraordinary believer, having privileges above other of God's dear children, which they cannot have; nor look on my way of acting as something that would not do for other believers. Make but trial! Do but stand still in the hour of trial, and you will see the help of God, if you trust in Him. But there is so often a forsaking the ways of the Lord in the hour of trial, and thus the *food of faith*, the means whereby our faith may be increased, is lost. This leads me to the following important point. You ask, How may I, a true believer, have my faith strengthened? The answer is this:—

"I. Every good gift and every perfect gift is from above, and cometh down from the Father of lights, with whom is no variableness, neither shadow of turning." James i. 17. As the increase of faith is a good gift, it must come from God, and therefore He ought to be asked for this blessing.

"II. The following means, however, ought to be used:

1. *The careful reading of the word of God, combined with meditation on it.* Through reading of the word of God, and especially through meditation on the word of God, the believer becomes more and more acquainted with the nature and character of God, and thus sees more and more, besides His holiness and justice, what a kind, loving, gracious, merciful, mighty, wise, and faithful Being He is, and, therefore, in poverty, affliction of body, bereavement in his family, difficulty in his service, want of a situation or employment, he will repose upon the *ability* of God to help him, because he has not only learned from His word that He is of almighty power and infinite wisdom, but he has also seen instance upon instance in the Holy Scriptures in which His almighty power and infinite wisdom have been actually exercised in helping and delivering His people; and he will repose upon the *willingness* of God to help him, because he has not only learned from the Scriptures what a kind, good, merciful, gracious, and faithful being God is, but because he has also seen in the word of God how, in a great variety of instances He has proved Himself to be so. And the consideration of this, if *God has become known to us through prayer and meditation on His own word*, will lead us, in general at least, with a measure of confidence to rely upon Him: and thus the reading of the word of God, together with meditation on it, will be one especial means to strengthen our faith.

2. As with reference to the growth of every grace of the Spirit, it is of the utmost importance that we seek to maintain an upright heart and a good conscience, and, therefore, do not knowingly and habitually indulge in those things which are contrary to the mind of God, so it is also particularly the case with reference to the *growth in faith*. How can I possibly continue to act faith upon God, concerning anything, if I am habitually grieving Him, and seek to detract from the glory and honour of Him in whom I profess to trust, upon whom I profess to depend? All my confidence towards God, all my leaning upon Him in the hour of trial will be gone, if I have a guilty conscience, and do not seek to put away this guilty conscience, but still continue to do the things which are contrary to the mind of God. And if, in any particular instance, I cannot trust in God, because of the

guilty conscience, then my faith is weakened by that instance of distrust; for faith with every fresh trial of it either increases by trusting God, and thus getting help, or it decreases by not trusting Him; and then there is less and less power of looking simply and directly to Him, and a habit of self-dependence is begotten or encouraged. One or the other of these will always be the case in each particular instance. Either we trust in God, and in that case we neither trust in ourselves, nor in our fellow-men, nor in circumstances, nor in anything besides; or we DO trust in one or more of these, and in that case do NOT trust in God.

3. If we, indeed, desire our faith to be strengthened, we should not shrink from opportunities where our faith may be tried, and, therefore, through the trial, be strengthened. In our natural state we dislike dealing with God alone. Through our natural alienation from God we shrink from Him, and from eternal realities. This cleaves to us more or less, even after our regeneration. Hence it is, that more or less, even as believers, we have the same shrinking from standing with God alone,—from depending upon Him alone,—from looking to Him alone:—and yet this is the very position in which we ought to be, if we wish our faith to be strengthened. The more I am in a position to be tried in faith with reference to my body, my family, my service for the Lord, my business, etc., the more shall I have opportunity of seeing God's help and deliverance; and every fresh instance, in which He helps and delivers me, will tend towards the increase of my faith. On this account, therefore, the believer should not shrink from situations, positions, circumstances, in which his faith may be tried; but should cheerfully embrace them as opportunities where he may see the hand of God stretched out on his behalf, to help and deliver him, and whereby he may thus have his faith strengthened.

4. The last important point for the strengthening of our faith is, that we let God work for us, when the hour of the trial of our faith comes, and do not work a deliverance of our own. Wherever God has given faith, it is given, among other reasons, for the very purpose of being tried.

"Yea, however weak our faith may be, God will try it; only with this restriction, that as in every way, He leads on gently, gradually, patiently, so also with reference to the trial of our faith. At first our faith will be tried very little in comparison with what it may be afterwards; for God never lays more upon us that He is willing to enable us to bear. Now when the trial of faith comes, we are naturally inclined to distrust God, and to trust rather in ourselves, or in our friends, or in circumstances.

"We will rather work a deliverance of our own somehow or other, than simply look to God and wait for His help. But if we do not patiently wait for God's help, if we work a deliverance of our own, then at the next trial of our faith it will be thus again, we shall be again inclined to deliver ourselves; and thus with every fresh instance of that kind, our faith will decrease; whilst on the contrary, were we to stand still, in order to see the salvation of God, to see His hand stretched out on our behalf, trusting in Him alone, then our faith would be increased, and with every fresh case in which the hand of God is stretched out on our behalf in the hour of the trial of our faith, our faith would be increased yet more.

"Would the believer, therefore, have his faith strengthened, he must especially, *give time to God*, who tries his faith in order to prove to His child, in the end, how willing He is to help and deliver him, the moment it is good for him."

In the early years of the Institution Mr. Müller and his fellow labourers had to endure many severe trials of faith, as some of these instances show.

Mr. Müller when writing of this period says:—

"Though now (July, 1845) for about seven years our funds have been so exhausted, that it has been a *rare* case that there have been means in hand to meet the necessities of more than 100 persons for *three days* together; yet I have been only once tried in spirit, and that was on September 18, 1838, when, for the first time the Lord seemed not to regard our prayer. But when He did send help at that time, and I saw that it was only for the trial of our faith, and not because He had forsaken the work, that we were brought so low, my soul was so strengthened and encouraged, that I have not only not been allowed to distrust the Lord, but *I have not been even cast down when in the deepest poverty* since that time."

A GIFT OF £12.

"Aug. 20 [1838].—The £5 which I had received on the 18th. had been given for house-keeping, so that to-day I was again penniless. But my eyes were up to the Lord. I gave myself to prayer this morning, knowing that I should want again this week at least £13, if not above £20. To-day I received £12 in answer to prayer, from a lady who is staying at Clifton, whom I had never seen before. Adorable Lord, grant that this may be a fresh encouragement to me!"

A SOLEMN CRISIS.

Regarding one of the sharpest times of trial Mr. Müller writes:—

"Sept. 10 [1838]. Monday morning. Neither Saturday nor yesterday had any money come in. It appeared to me now needful to take some steps on account of our need, *i.e.*, to go to the Orphan-Houses, call the brethren and sisters together, (who, except brother T—, had never been informed about the state of the funds), state the case to them, see how much money was needed for the present, tell them that amidst all this trial of faith I still believed that God would help, and to pray with them. Especially, also, I meant to go for the sake of telling them that no more articles must be purchased than we have the means to pay for, but to let there be nothing lacking in any way to the children as it regards nourishing food and needful clothing; for I would rather at once send them away than that they should lack. I meant to go for the sake also of seeing whether there were still articles remaining which had been sent for the purpose of being sold, or whether there were any articles really needless, that we might turn them into money. I felt that the matter was now come to a solemn crisis. About half-past nine sixpence came in, which had been put anonymously into the box at Gideon Chapel. This money seemed to me like an earnest, that God would have compassion and send more. About ten, after I had returned from brother Craik, to whom I had unbosomed my heart again, whilst once more in prayer for help, a sister called who gave two sovereigns to my wife for the Orphans, stating that she had felt herself stirred up to come and that she had delayed coming already too long. A few minutes after, when I went into the room where she was, she gave me two sovereigns more, and all this without knowing the least about our need. Thus the Lord most mercifully has sent us a little help, to the great encouragement of my faith. A few minutes after I was called on for money from the Infant Orphan-House, to which I sent £2, and £1 0s. 6d. to the Boys' Orphan-House, and £1 to the Girls' Orphan-House."

A PRECIOUS DELIVERANCE.

"Sept. 17 [1838].—The trial still continues. It is now more and more trying, even to faith, as each day comes. Truly, the Lord has wise purposes in allowing us to call so long upon Him for help. But I am sure God will send help, if we can but wait. One of the labourers had had a little money come in of which he gave 12s. 6d.; another labourer gave 11s. 8d., being all the money she had left; this, with 17s. 6d., which, partly, had come in, and, partly was in hand, enabled us to pay what needed to be paid, and to purchase provisions, so that nothing yet, in any way, has been lacking. This evening I was rather tired respecting the long delay of larger sums coming; but being led to go to the Scriptures for comfort, my soul was greatly refreshed, and my faith again strengthened, by the xxxivth Psalm, so that I went very cheerfully to meet with my dear fellow-labourers for prayer. I read to them the Psalm, and sought to cheer their hearts through the precious promises contained in it."

"Sept. 18.—Brother T. had 25s. in hand, and I had 3s. This £1 8s. enabled us to buy the meat and bread, which was needed; a little tea for one of the houses, and milk for all; no more than this is needed. Thus the Lord has provided not only for this day; for there is bread for two days in hand. Now, however, we are come to an extremity. The funds are exhausted. The labourers, who had a little money, have given as long as they had any left. Now observe how the Lord helped us! A lady from the neighbourhood of London who brought a parcel with money from her daughter, arrived four or five days since in Bristol, and took lodgings next door to the Boys' Orphan-House. This afternoon she herself kindly brought me the money, amounting to £3 2s. 6d. We had been reduced so low as to be on the point of selling those things which could be spared; but this morning I had asked the Lord, if it might be, to prevent the necessity, of our doing so. That the money had been so near the Orphan-Houses for several days without being given, is a plain proof that it was from the beginning in the heart of God to help us; but because He delights in the prayers of His children, He had allowed us to pray so long; also to try our faith, and to make the answer so much the sweeter. It is indeed a precious deliverance. I burst out into loud praises and thanks the first moment I was alone, after I had received the money. I met with my fellow-labourers again this evening for prayer and praise; their hearts were not a little cheered. This money was this evening divided, and will comfortably provide for all that will be needed to-morrow."

CHAPTER II:
THE NEW ORPHAN HOUSES, ASHLEY DOWN.

A complaint having been received from a gentleman in October, 1845, that some of the inhabitants of Wilson Street were inconvenienced by the Orphan-Houses being in that street, Mr. Müller ultimately decided for that and other reasons, after much prayerful meditation, to build an Orphan-House elsewhere to accommodate 300 children, and commenced to ask the Lord for means for so doing:—

"Jan. 31 [1846].—It is now 89 days since I have been daily waiting upon God about the building of an Orphan-House. The time seems to me now near when the Lord will give us a piece of ground, and I told the brethren and sisters so this evening, after our usual Saturday evening prayer meeting at the Orphan-Houses.

"Feb. 1.—A poor widow sent to-day 10s.

"Feb. 2.—To-day I heard of suitable and cheap land on Ashley Down.

"Feb. 3.—Saw the land. It is the most desirable of all I have seen.—There was anonymously put in an Orphan-box at my house a sovereign, in a piece of paper, on which was written, 'The New Orphan-House.'

"Feb. 4.—This evening I called on the owner of the land on Ashley Down, about which I had heard on the 2nd, but he was not at home. As I, however, had been informed that I should find him at his house of business, I went there, but did not find him there either, as he had *just before* left. I might have called again at his residence, at a later hour having been informed by one of the servants that he would be sure to be at home about eight o'clock; but I did not do so, judging that there was the hand of God in my not finding him at either place: and I judged it best therefore not to force the matter, but to 'let patience have her perfect work.'

"Feb. 5.—Saw this morning the owner of the land. He told me that he awoke at three o'clock this morning and could not sleep again till five. While he was thus lying awake, his mind was all the time occupied about the piece of land, respecting which inquiry had been made of him for the building of an Orphan-House, at my request; and he determined that if I should apply for it, he would not only let me have it, but for £120 per acre, instead of £200; the price which he had previously asked for it. How good is the Lord! The agreement was made this morning, and I purchased a field of nearly seven acres, at £120 per acre.

"Observe the hand of God in my not finding the owner at home last evening! The Lord meant to speak to His servant first about this matter, during a sleepless night, and to lead him *fully* to decide, before I had seen him."

"BECAUSE OF HIS IMPORTUNITY."

"Nov. 19 [1846].—I am now led more and more to importune the Lord to send me the means, which are requisite in order that I may be able to commence the building. Because (1) it has been for some time past publicly stated in print, that I allow it is not without ground that some of the inhabitants of Wilson Street consider themselves inconvenienced by the Orphan-Houses being in that street, and I long therefore to be able to remove the Orphans from thence as soon as possible. (2) I become more and more convinced, that it would be greatly for the benefit of the children, both physically and morally, with God's blessing, to be in such a position as they are intended to occupy, when the New Orphan-House shall have been built. And (3) because the number of very poor and destitute Orphans, that are waiting for admission, is so great, and there are constantly fresh applications made. Now whilst, by God's grace, I would not wish the building to be begun one single day sooner than is His will; and whilst I firmly believe, that He will give me, in His own time every shilling which I need; yet I also know, that He delights in being earnestly entreated, and that He takes pleasure in the continuance in prayer, and in the importuning Him, which so clearly is to be seen from the parable of the widow and the unjust judge, Luke xviii. 1-8. For these reasons I gave myself again particularly to prayer last evening, that the Lord would send further means, being also especially led to do so, in addition to the above reasons, because there had come in but little comparatively, since the 29th of last month. This morning, between five and six o'clock I prayed again, among other points, about the Building Fund, and then had a long season for the reading of the word of God. In the course of my reading I came to Mark xi. 24, 'What things soever ye desire, when ye pray, believe that ye receive them, and ye shall have them.' The importance of the truth contained in this portion I have often felt and spoken about; but this morning I felt it again most particularly, and, applying it to the New Orphan-House, said to the Lord: 'Lord I believe that Thou wilt give me all I need for this work. I am sure that I shall have all, because I believe that I receive in answer to my prayer.' Thus, with the heart full of peace concerning this work, I went on to the other part of the chapter, and to the next chapter. After family prayer I had again my usual season for prayer with regard to all the many parts of the work, and the various necessities thereof, asking also blessings upon my fellow-labourers, upon the circulation of Bibles and Tracts, and upon the precious souls in the Adult School, the Sunday Schools, the Six Day Schools, and the four Orphan-Houses. Amidst all the many things I again made my requests about means for the Building. And now observe: About five minutes, after I had risen from my knees, there was given to me a registered letter, containing a cheque for £300, of which £280 are for the Building Fund, £10 for my own personal expenses, and £10 for Brother Craik. The Lord's holy name be praised for this precious encouragement, by which the Building Fund is now increased to more than six thousand pounds."

MR. MÜLLER'S FIRST ORPHAN-HOUSE.

"Jan. 25 [1847].—The season of the year is now approaching, when building may be begun. Therefore with increased earnestness I have given myself unto prayer, importuning the Lord that He would be pleased to appear on our behalf, and speedily send the remainder of the amount which is required, and I have increasingly, of late, felt that the time is drawing near, when the Lord will give me all that which is requisite for commencing the building. All the various arguments which I have often brought before God, I brought also again this morning before Him. It is now 14 months and 3 weeks since day by day I have uttered my petitions to God on behalf of this work. I rose from my knees this morning in full confidence, not only that God *could*, but also *would*, send the means, and that soon. Never, during all these 14 months and 3 weeks, have I had the least doubt, that I should have all that which is requisite.—And now, dear believing reader, rejoice and praise with me. About an hour, after I had prayed thus, there was given to me the sum of Two Thousand Pounds for the Building Fund. Thus I have received altogether £9,285 3s. 9½d. towards this work.—I cannot describe the joy I had in God when I received this donation. It must be known from experience, in order to be felt. 447 days I have had day by day to wait upon God, before the sum reached the above amount. How great is the blessing which the soul obtains by *trusting in God*, and *by waiting patiently*. Is it not manifest how precious it is to carry on God's work in this way, even with regard to the obtaining of means?"

The total amount which came in for the Building Fund was £15,784 18s. 10d.

ORPHAN-HOUSES NOS. 2 & 3.

"March 12, 1862.—It was in November, 1850, that my mind became exercised about enlarging the Orphan Work from 300 Orphans to 1000, and subsequently to 1150; and it was in June, 1851, that this my purpose became known, having kept it secret for more than seven months, whilst day by day praying about it. From the end of November, 1850, to this day, March 12, 1862, not one single day has been allowed to pass, without this contemplated enlargement being brought before God in prayer, and generally more than once a day. But only now, this day, the New Orphan-House No. 3 was so far advanced, that it could be opened. Observe then, first, esteemed Reader, how long it may be, before a full answer to our prayers, even to thousands and tens of thousands of prayers, is granted; yea, though those prayers may be believing prayers, earnest prayers, and offered up in the name of the Lord Jesus, and though we may only for the sake of the honour of our Lord desire the answer: for I did, by the grace of God, without the least doubt and wavering look for more than eleven years for the full answer;… and I sought only in this matter the glory of God."

PRAYING THREE TIMES DAILY FOR HELPERS.

"As in the case of No. 2, so also in the case of the New Orphan-House No. 3, I had daily prayed for the needed helpers and assistants for the various departments. Before a stone was laid, I began to pray for this; and, as the building progressed, I continued day by day to bring this matter before God, feeling assured, that, as in everything else, so in this particular also, He would graciously be pleased to appear on our behalf and help us, as the whole work is intended for His honour and glory.

"At last the time was near when the house could be opened, and the time therefore near when the applications, which had been made in writing during more than two years previously, should be considered, for the filling up of the various posts. It now, however, was found that, whilst there had been about 50 applications made for the various situations, some places could not be filled up, because either the individuals, who had applied for them, were married, or were, on examination, found unsuitable. This was no small trial of faith; for day by day, for years, had I asked God to help me in this particular, even as He had done in the case of the New Orphan-House No. 2; I had also expected help, confidently expected help: and yet now, when help *seemed* needed, it was wanting. What was now to be done, dear Reader? Would it have been right to charge God with unfaithfulness? Would it have been right to distrust Him? Would it have been right to say, it is useless to pray? By no means. This, on the contrary, I did; I thanked God for all the help, He had given me in connection with the whole of the enlargement; I thanked Him for enabling me to overcome so many and such great difficulties; I thanked Him for the helpers He had given me for No. 2; I thanked Him, also, for the helpers He had given me already for No. 3; and instead of distrusting God, I looked upon this delay of the full answer to prayer, only as a trial of faith, and therefore resolved, that, instead of praying *once* a day with my dear wife about this matter, as we had been doing day by day for years, we should now meet daily *three* times, to bring this before God. I also brought the matter before the whole staff of my helpers in the work requesting their prayers. Thus I have now continued for about four months longer in prayer, day by day calling upon God three times on account of this need, and the result has been, that one helper after the other has been given, without the help coming *too* late, or the work getting into confusion; or the reception of the children being hindered; and I am fully assured, that the few who are yet needed will also be found, when they are *really* required."

DIFFICULTIES REMOVED AFTER PRAYER AND PATIENCE.

Mr. Müller relates the following incidents in connection with the purchase of the land for the Fourth and Fifth Orphan-Houses, after receiving five thousand pounds for the Building Fund:

"I had now, through all that had come in since May 26th, 1864, including this last-mentioned donation, above Twenty-Seven Thousand Pounds in hand. I had patiently waited God's time. I had determined to do nothing, until I had the full half of the sum needed for the two houses. But now, having above Two Thousand Pounds beyond the half, I felt, after again seeking counsel from God, quite happy, in taking steps for the purchase of land.

"My eyes had been for years directed to a beautiful piece of land, only separated by the turnpike road from the ground on which the New Orphan-House No. 3 is erected. The land is about 18 acres, with a small house and outhouses built on one end thereof. Hundreds of times had I prayed, within the last years, that God for Jesus' sake would count me worthy, to be allowed to erect on this ground two more Orphan-Houses; and hundreds of times I had with a prayerful eye looked on this land, yea, as it were, bedewed it with my prayers. I might have bought it years ago; but that would have been going before the Lord. I had money enough in hand to have paid for it years ago; but I desired patiently, submissively, to wait God's own time, and for Him to mark it clearly and distinctly that His time was come, and that I took the step according to His will; for whatever I might apparently accomplish, if the work were mine, and not the Lord's, I could expect no blessing. But now the Lord's mind was clearly and distinctly made manifest. I had enough money in hand to pay for the land and to build one house, and therefore I went forward, after having still asked the Lord for guidance, and being assured that it was His will I should take active steps. The first thing I did was, to see the agent who acted for the owner of the land, and to ask him, whether the land was for sale. He replied that it was, but that it was let till March 25th, 1867. He said that he would write for the price. Here a great difficulty at once presented itself, that the land was let for two years and four months longer, whilst it appeared desirable that I should be able to take possession of it in about six months, viz., as soon as the conveyance could be made out, and the plans be ready for the New Orphan-House No. 4, and arrangements be made with contractors. But I was not discouraged by this difficulty; for I expected, through prayer, to make happy and satisfactory arrangements with the tenant, being willing to give him a fair compensation for leaving before his time had expired. But, before I had time to see about this, two other great difficulties presented themselves: the one was, that the owner asked £7,000 for the land, which I judged to be considerably more than its value; and the other, that I heard that the Bristol Waterworks Company intended to make an additional reservoir for their water, on this very land, and to get an Act of Parliament passed to that effect.

"Pause here for a few moments, esteemed Reader. You have seen, how the Lord brought me so far, with regard to pecuniary means, that I felt now warranted to go forward; and I may further add, that I was brought to this point as the result of thousands of times praying regarding this object; and that there were, also, many hundreds of children waiting for admission; and yet, after the Lord Himself so manifestly had appeared on our behalf, by the donation of £5,000, He allows this apparent death-blow to come upon the whole. But thus I have found it hundreds of times since I have known the Lord. The difficulties, which He is pleased to allow to arise, are only allowed, under such circumstances, for the exercise of our faith and patience; and more prayer, more patience, and the exercise of faith, will remove the difficulties. Now, as I knew the Lord, these difficulties were no insurmountable difficulties to me, for I put my trust in Him, according to that word: "The Lord also will be a refuge for the oppressed, a refuge in times of trouble. And they that know Thy name will put their trust in Thee: for Thou, Lord, hast not forsaken them that seek Thee." (Psalm ix. 9, 10). I gave myself, therefore, earnestly to prayer concerning all these three especial difficulties which had arisen regarding the land. I prayed several times daily about the matter, and used the following means:

1. I saw the Acting Committee of the Directors of the Bristol Waterworks Company regarding their intended reservoir on the land, which I was about to purchase, and stated to them, what I had seen in print concerning their intentions. They courteously stated to

me, that only a small portion of the land would be required, not enough to interfere with my purpose; and that, if it could be avoided, even this small portion should not be taken.

2. This being settled, I now saw the tenant, after many prayers; for I desired, as a Christian, that if this land were bought, it should be done under amicable circumstances with regard to him. At the first interview, I stated my intentions to him, at the same time expressing my desire that the matter should be settled pleasantly with regard to himself. He said that he would consider the matter, and desired a few days for that purpose. After a week I saw him again, and he then kindly stated, that, as the land was wanted for such an object, he would not stand in the way; but that, as he had laid out a good deal on the house and land, he expected a compensation for leaving it before his time was up. As I, of course, was quite willing to give a *fair* and *reasonable* compensation, I considered this a very precious answer to prayer.

3. I now entered upon the third difficulty, the price of the land. I knew well how much the land was worth to the Orphan Institution; but its value to the Institution was not the market value. I gave myself, therefore, day by day to prayer, that the Lord would constrain the owner to accept a considerably lower sum than he had asked; I also pointed out to him why it was not worth as much as he asked. At last he consented to take £5,500 instead of £7,000, and I accepted the offer; for I knew that by the level character of the land we should save a considerable sum for the two houses, and that by the new sewer, which only a few months before had been completed, running along under the turnpike road near the field, we should be considerably benefited. In addition to these two points I had to take into the account, that we can have gas from Bristol, as in the three houses already in operation. And lastly, the most important point of all, the nearness of this piece of land to the other three houses, so that all could easily be under the same direction and superintendence. In fact, no other piece of land, near or far off, would present so much advantage to us, as this spot, which the Lord thus so very kindly had given to us. All being now settled, I proceeded to have the land conveyed to the same trustees who stood trustees for the New Orphan-Houses No. 1, No. 2, and No. 3.—I have thus minutely dwelt on these various matters for the encouragement of the reader, that he may not be discouraged by difficulties, however great and many and varied, but give himself to prayer, trusting in the Lord for help, yea, expecting help, which, in His own time and way, He will surely grant."

ORPHAN-HOUSES NOS. 4 & 5.

"March 5, 1874.—Both houses, No. 4 and No. 5, have now been for years in operation, No. 4 since Nov. 1868 and No. 5 since the beginning of the year 1870, and above 1,200 Orphans have been already received into them, and month after month more are received, as the Orphans are sent out from them as apprentices or servants. Moreover all the expenses in connection with their being built, fitted up and furnished were met to the full, as the demands arose, and, after all had been paid, there was left a balance of several thousand pounds, which is being used for keeping the houses in repair. See, esteemed Reader, how abundantly God answered our prayers, and how plain it is, that we were not mistaken, after we had patiently and prayerfully sought to ascertain His will. Be encouraged, therefore, yet further and further to confide in the Living God."

CHAPTER III:
PRECIOUS ANSWERS TO PRAYER

In remarkable ways God helped Mr. Müller as "The Narratives" show:—

THE ARTIST'S FIRST RETURN.

"April 30 [1859].—Received the following letter from a considerable distance: 'My dear Christian Brother, I am the husband of Mrs. —— who sends you by this post the two Sovereign piece. How can we better dispose of this relic of affectionate remembrance, than by depositing it in the bank of Christ, who always pays the best interest, and never fails.—Now, my best and spiritual counsellor, I cannot express to you the exceeding great joy I feel, in relating what follows. I am an artist, a *poor* artist, a landscape painter. About two weeks ago I sent a picture to Bristol for exhibition, just as I finished your book that was lent us. I most humbly and earnestly prayed to God to enable me, by the sale of my Bristol picture, to have the blessed privilege of sending you *half the proceeds*. The price of the picture is £20. Now mark. Immediately the exhibition is open, God, in His mercy, mindful of my prayer, sends me a purchaser. I have exhibited in Bristol before, *but never sold* a picture. Oh! my dear friend, my very heart leaps for joy. I have never been so near God before. Through your instrumentality I have been enabled to draw nearer to God, with more earnestness, more faith, more holy desires.—This is the *first return* God has blessed me with for the whole of my last year's labours. What a blessing to have it so returned!—Oh, with what joy I read your book!—The picture I speak of is now being exhibited in the academy of arts at Clifton, numbered in the Catalogue ——, the title is ——. I cannot pay you till the close of the exhibition, as I shall not be paid till then, &c.' Of such letters I have had thousands during the last 40 years."

THE NORTH WIND CHANGED INTO A SOUTH WIND.

"It was towards the end of November of 1857, when I was most unexpectedly informed that the boiler of our heating apparatus at No. 1 leaked very considerably, so that it was impossible to go through the winter with such a leak.—Our heating apparatus consists of a large cylinder boiler, inside of which the fire is kept, and with which boiler the water pipes, that warm the rooms, are connected. Hot air is also connected with this apparatus. The boiler had been considered suited for the work of the winter. To suspect that it was worn out, and not to do anything towards replacing it by a new one, and to have said, I will trust in God regarding it, would be careless presumption, but not faith in God. It would be the counterfeit of faith.

"The boiler is entirely surrounded by brickwork; its state, therefore, could not be known without taking down the brickwork; this, if needless, would be rather injurious to the boiler, than otherwise; and as for eight winters we had had no difficulty in this way, we had not anticipated it now. But suddenly, and most unexpectedly, at the commencement of the winter, this difficulty occurred. What then was to be done? For the children, especially the younger infants, I felt deeply concerned, that they might not suffer, through want of warmth. But how were we to obtain warmth? The introduction of a *new* boiler would, in all probability, take many weeks. The *repairing* of the boiler was a questionable matter, on account of the greatness of the leak; but, if not, nothing could be said of it, till the brick-chamber in which it is enclosed, was, at least in part, removed; but that would, at least, as far as we could judge, take days; and what was to be done in the meantime, to find warm rooms for 300 children? It naturally occurred to me, to introduce temporary gas-stoves; but on further weighing the matter, it was found, that we should be unable to heat our very large rooms with gas, except we had many stoves, which we could not introduce, as we had not a sufficient quantity of gas to spare from our lighting apparatus. Moreover, for each of these stoves we needed a small chimney, to carry off the impure air. This mode of heating, therefore, though applicable to a hall, a staircase, or a shop, would not suit our purpose. I also thought of the temporary introduction of Arnott's stoves; but they would have been unsuitable, requiring long chimneys (as they would have been of a temporary kind) to go out of the windows. On this account, the uncertainty of their answering in our case, and the disfigurement of the rooms, led me to give up this plan also. But what was to be done? Gladly would I have paid £100, if thereby the difficulty could have been overcome, and the children not be exposed to suffer for many days from being in cold rooms. At last I determined on falling entirely into the hands of God, who is very merciful and of tender compassion, and I decided on having the brick-chamber opened, to see the extent of the damage, and whether the boiler might be repaired, so as to carry us through the winter.

"The day was fixed, when the workmen were to come, and all the necessary arrangements were made. The fire, of course, had to be let out while the repairs were going on. But now see. After the day was fixed for the repairs a bleak North wind set in. It began to blow either on Thursday or Friday before the Wednesday afternoon, when the fire was to be let out. Now came the first really cold weather, which we had in the beginning of that winter, during the first days of December. What was to be done? The repairs could not be put off. I now asked the Lord for two things, viz., that He would be pleased to change the north wind into a south wind, and that He would give to the workmen 'a mind to work'; for I remembered how much Nehemiah accomplished in 52 days, whilst building the walls of Jerusalem, because 'the people had a mind to work.' Well, the memorable day came. The evening before, the bleak north wind blew still: but, on the Wednesday, the south wind blew: exactly as I had prayed. The weather was so mild that no fire was needed. The brickwork is removed, the leak is found out very soon, the boiler makers begin to repair in good earnest. About half-past eight in the evening, when I was going home, I was informed at the lodge, that the acting principal of the firm, whence the boiler makers came, had arrived to see how the work was going on, and whether he could in any way speed the matter. I went immediately, therefore, into the cellar, to see him with the men, to seek to expedite the business. In speaking to the principal of this, he said in their hearing, 'the men will work late this evening, and come very early again to-morrow.'

"'We would rather, Sir,' said the leader, 'work all night.' Then remembered I the second part of my prayer, that God would give the men 'a mind to work.' Thus it was: by the morning the repair was accomplished, the leak was stopped, though with great difficulty, and within about 30 hours the brickwork was up again, and the fire in the boiler; and all the time the south wind blew so mildly, that there was not the least need of a fire.

"Here, then, is one of our difficulties which was overcome by prayer and faith."

CONVERSION OF THE ORPHANS.

"May 26, 1860.—Day after day, and year after year, by the help of God, we labour in prayer for the spiritual benefit of the Orphans under our care. These our supplications, which have been for 24 years brought before the Lord concerning them, have been abundantly answered, in former years, in the conversion of hundreds from among them. We have, also, had repeated seasons in which, within a short time, or even all at once, *many* of the Orphans were converted. Such a season we had about three years since, when, within a few days, about 60 were brought to believe in the Lord Jesus; and such seasons we have had again twice during the first year. The first was in July, 1859, when the Spirit of God wrought so mightily in one school of 120 girls, as that very many, yea more than one-half, were brought under deep concern about the salvation of their souls. This work, moreover, was not a mere momentary excitement; but, after more than eleven months have elapsed, there are 31 concerning whom there is *full* confidence as to their conversion, and 32 concerning whom there is like-wise a goodly measure of confidence, though not to the same amount, as regarding the 31. There are therefore 63 out of the 120 Orphans in that one School who are considered to have been converted in July, 1859. This blessed and mighty work of the Holy Spirit cannot be traced to any particular cause. It was however, a most precious answer to prayer. As such we look upon it, and are encouraged by it to further waiting upon God. The second season of the mighty working of the Holy Spirit among the Orphans, during the past year, was at the end of January and the beginning of February, 1860. The particulars of it are of the deepest interest; but I must content myself by stating, that this great work of the Spirit of God in January and February, 1860, began among the younger class of the children under our care, little girls of about 6, 7, 8 and 9 years old; then extended to the older girls; and then to the boys, so that within about 10 days above 200 of the Orphans were stirred up to be anxious about their souls, and in *many* instances found peace *immediately*, through faith in our Lord Jesus. They at once requested to be allowed to hold prayer-meetings among themselves, and have had these meetings ever since. Many of them also manifested a concern about the salvation of their companions and relations, and spoke or wrote to them, about the way to be saved."

APPRENTICING THE ORPHANS.

"In the early part of the summer, 1862, it was found that we had several boys ready to be apprenticed; but there were no applications made by masters for apprentices. As all our boys are invariably sent out as indoor apprentices, this was no small difficulty; for we not only look for Christian masters, but consider their business, and examine into their position, to see whether they are suitable; and the master must also be willing to receive the apprentice into his own family. Under these circumstances, we again gave ourselves to prayer, as we had done for more than twenty years before, concerning this thing, instead of advertising, which, in all probability, would only bring before us masters who desire apprentices for the sake of the premium. We remembered how good the Lord had been to us, in having helped us hundreds of times before, in this very matter. Some weeks passed, but the difficulty remained. We continued, however, in prayer, and then one application was made, and then another; and since we first began to pray about this matter, last summer, we have been able to send out altogether 18 boys up to May 26, 1863; the difficulty was thus again entirely overcome by prayer, as every one of the boys, whom it was desirable to send out, has been sent out."

SICKNESS AT THE ORPHANAGE.

Sickness at times visited the houses.

"During the summer and autumn of 1866 we had also the measles at all the three Orphan-Houses. After they had made their appearance, our especial prayer was:

1. That there might not be too many children ill at one time in this disease, so that our accommodation in the Infirmary rooms or otherwise might be sufficient. This prayer was answered to the full; for though we had at the New Orphan-House No. 1 not less than 83

cases, in No. 2 altogether 111, and in No. 3 altogether 68; yet God so graciously was pleased to listen to our supplications, as that when our spare rooms were filled with the invalids, He so long stayed the spreading of the measles till a sufficient number were restored, so as to make room for others, who were taken ill.

2. Further we prayed, that the children, who were taken ill in the measles, might be safely brought through and not die. Thus it was. We had the full answer to our prayers; for though 262 children altogether had the measles, not one of them died.

3. Lastly we prayed, that no evil physical consequences might follow this disease, as is so often the case; this was also granted. All the 262 children not only recovered, but did well afterwards. I gratefully record this signal mercy and blessing of God, and this full and precious answer to prayer, to the honour of His name."

HELP FOR NEEDY BRETHREN.

1863.—"The end of the year was now at hand, and, in winding up the accounts, it was my earnest desire, to do once more all I could, in sending help to needy labourers in the gospel. I went therefore through the list, writing against the various names of those to whom I had not already recently sent, what amount it appeared desirable to send; and I found, when these sums were added together, the total was £476, but £280 was all I had in hand. I wrote therefore a cheque for £280, though I would have gladly sent £476, yet felt thankful, at the same time, that I had this amount in hand for these brethren. Having written the cheque, as the last occupation of the day, then came my usual season for prayer, for the many things which I daily, by the help of God, bring before Him; and then again, I brought also the case of these preachers of the Gospel before the Lord, and besought Him that He would even now be pleased to give me yet a goodly sum for them, though there remained but three days to the close of our year. This being done, I went home about nine o'clock in the evening, and found there had arrived from a great distance £100 for Missions, with £100 left at my disposal, and £5 for myself. I took, therefore, the whole £200 for Missions, and thus had £480 in hand to meet the £476 which I desired for this object. Those who know the blessedness of really trusting in God, and getting help from Him, as in this case, in answer to prayer, will be able to enter into the spiritual enjoyment I had in the reception of that donation, in which both the answer to prayer was granted, and with it the great enjoyment of gladdening the hearts of many devoted servants of Christ."

THE HEART'S DESIRE GIVEN TO HELP MISSION WORK IN CHINA.

"Sept. 30 [1869].—From Yorkshire £50.—Received also One Thousand Pounds to-day for the Lord's work in China. About this donation it is especially to be noticed, that for months it had been my earnest desire to do more than ever for Mission Work in China, and I had already taken steps to carry out this desire, when this donation of One Thousand Pounds came to hand. This precious answer to prayer for means should be a particular encouragement to all who are engaged in the Lord's work, and who may need means for it. It proves afresh, that, if our work is His work, and we honour Him, by waiting upon and looking to Him for means, He will surely, in His own time and way, supply them."

THE JOY OF ANSWERS TO PRAYER.

"The joy which answers to prayer give, cannot be described; and the impetus which they afford to the spiritual life is exceedingly great. The experience of this happiness I desire for all my Christian readers. If you believe indeed in the Lord Jesus for the salvation of your soul, if you walk uprightly and do not regard iniquity in your heart, if you continue to wait patiently, and believingly upon God; then answers will surely be given to your prayers. You may not be called upon to serve the Lord in the way the writer does, and therefore may never have answers to prayer respecting such things as are recorded here; but, in your various circumstances, your family, your business, your profession, your church position, your labour for the Lord, etc., you may have answers as distinct as any here recorded."

THE GREAT NEED OF BEING SAVED BY FAITH IN CHRIST JESUS.

"Should this, however, be read by any who are not believers in the Lord Jesus, but who are going on in the carelessness or self-righteousness of their unrenewed hearts, then I would affectionately and solemnly beseech such, first of all to be reconciled to God by faith in the Lord Jesus. You are sinners. You deserve punishment. If you do not see this, ask God to show it unto you. Let this now be your first and especial prayer. Ask God also to enlighten you not merely concerning your state by nature, but especially to reveal the Lord Jesus to your heart. God sent Him, that He might bear the punishment, due to us guilty sinners. God accepts the obedience and sufferings of the Lord Jesus, in the room of those who depend upon Him for the salvation of their souls; and the moment a sinner believes in the Lord Jesus, he obtains the forgiveness of all his sins. When thus he is reconciled to God, by faith in the Lord Jesus, and has obtained the forgiveness of his sins, he has boldness to enter into the presence of God, to make known his requests unto Him; and the more he is enabled to realize that his sins are forgiven, and that God, for Christ's sake, is well pleased with those who believe on Him, the more ready he will be to come with all his wants, both temporal and spiritual, to his Heavenly Father, that He may supply them. But as long as the consciousness of unpardoned guilt remains, so long shall we be kept at a distance from God, especially as it regards prayer. Therefore, dear reader, if you are an unforgiven sinner, let your first and especial prayer be, that God would be pleased to reveal to your heart the Lord Jesus, His beloved Son."

A DOUBLE ANSWER.

"July 25 [1865].—From the neighbourhood of London £100, with the following letter: 'My dear Sir, I believe that it is through the Lord's actings upon me, that I enclose you a cheque on the Bank of England, Western Branch, for £100. I hope that your affairs are going on well. Yours in the Lord * * * *.' This Christian gentleman, whom I have never seen, and who is engaged in a very large business in London, had sent me several times before a similar sum. A day or two before I received this last kind donation, I had asked the Lord, that He would be pleased to influence the heart of this donor to help me again, which I had never done before regarding him; and thus I had the double answer to prayer, in that not only money came in, but money from *him*. The reader will now see the meaning in the donor's letter, when he wrote 'I believe that it is through the Lord's actings upon me that I enclose you a cheque, &c.' Verily it was the Lord who acted upon this gentleman, to send me this sum. Perhaps the reader may think, that in acknowledging the receipt of the donation, I wrote to the donor what I have here stated. I did not. My reason for not doing so was, lest he should have thought I was in especial need, and might have been thus influenced to send more. In truly knowing the Lord, in really relying upon Him and upon Him alone, there is no need of giving hints directly or indirectly, whereby individuals may be induced further to help. I might have written to the donor (as was indeed the case), I need a considerable sum day by day for the current expenses of the various objects of the Institution, and also might have with truth told him, at that time, that I yet needed about Twenty Thousand Pounds, to enable me to meet all the expenses connected with the contemplated enlargement of the Orphan work. But my practice is, never to allude to any of these things in my correspondence with donors. When the Report is published, every one can see, who has a desire to see, how matters stand; and thus I leave things in the hands of God, to speak for us to the hearts of His stewards. And this He does. Verily we do not wait upon God in vain!"

CHRISTIANS IN BUSINESS.

"Jan. 1 [1869].—From Scotland £50 for Missions, £25 for the circulation of the Holy Scriptures and £25 for the circulation of Tracts. Received also from a considerable distance £10 for these objects, with £10 for the Orphans. About this latter donation I make a few remarks. At the early part of the year 1868, a Christian business man wrote to me for advice in his peculiar difficult business affairs. His letter showed that he had a desire to walk in the ways of the Lord, and to carry on his business to the glory of God; but his circumstances were of the most trying character. I therefore wrote to him to come to Bristol, that I might be able to advise him. Accordingly he undertook the long journey, and I had an interview with him, through which I saw his most trying position in business. Having fully conversed with him, I gave him the following counsel:

1. That he should day by day, expressly for the purpose, retire with his Christian wife, that they might unitedly spread their business difficulties before God in prayer, and do this, if possible, twice a day.

2. That he should look out for answers to his prayers, and expect that God would help him.

3. That he should avoid all business trickeries, such as exposing for sale two or three articles, marked below cost price, for the sake of attracting customers, because of its being unbecoming a disciple of the Lord Jesus to use such artifices; and that, if he did so, he could not reckon on the blessing of God.

4. I advised him further, to set apart; out of his profits, week by week, a certain proportion for the work of God, whether his income was much or little, and use this income faithfully for the Lord.

5. Lastly, I asked him, to let me know, month after month, how the Lord dealt with him.—The reader will feel interested to learn, that from that time the Lord was pleased to prosper the business of this dear Christian brother, so that his returns from the 1st of March, 1868, up to March 1, 1869, were £9,138 13s. 5d., while during the same period the previous year they had been only £6,609 18s. 3d., therefore £2,528 15s. 2d. more than the year before. When he sent me the donation above referred to, he also writes, that he had been enabled to put aside during the previous year £123 13s. 3d. for the work of God or the need of the poor.—I have so fully dwelt on this, because Christians in business may be benefited by it."

REVIVAL IN THE ORPHAN-HOUSES.

"In giving the statistics of the previous year [1871-72], I referred already to the great spiritual blessing, which it pleased the Lord to grant to the Orphan Work at the end of that year and the beginning of this; but, as this is so deeply important a subject, I enter somewhat further and more fully into it here. It was stated before, that the spiritual condition of the Orphans generally gave to us great sorrow of heart, because there were so few, comparatively, among them, who were in earnest about their souls, and resting on the atoning death of the Lord Jesus for salvation. This our sorrow led us to lay it on the whole staff of assistants, matrons and teachers, to seek earnestly the Lord's blessing on the souls of the children. This was done in our united prayer meetings, and, I have reason to believe, in secret also; and in answer to these our secret and united prayers, in the year 1872, there were, as the result of this, more believers by far among the Orphans than ever. On Jan. 8, 1872, the Lord began to work among them, and this work was going on more or less afterwards. In the New Orphan-House No. 3, it showed itself least, till it pleased the Lord to lay His hand heavily on that house, by the small-pox; and, from that time the working of the Holy Spirit was felt in that house also, particularly in one department. At the end of July, 1872, I received the statements of all the matrons and teachers in the five houses, who reported to me, that, after careful observation and conversation, they had good reason to believe that 729 of the Orphans then under our care, were believers in the Lord Jesus. This number of believing Orphans is by far greater than ever we had, for which we adore and praise the Lord! See how the Lord overruled the great trial, occasioned by the small-pox, and turned it into a great blessing! See, also, how, after so low a state, comparatively, which led us to prayer, earnest prayer, the working of the Holy Spirit was more manifest than ever!"

MR. MÜLLER'S MISSION TOURS.

In the year 1875, when seventy years of age, Mr. Müller was led to start on his Missionary Tours, and during the next twenty years preached to more than three million people, in forty-two countries of the world.

"On August 8th, 1882," Mr. Müller says, "we began our ninth Missionary Tour. The first place at which I preached was Weymouth, where I spoke in public four times. From Weymouth we went, by way of Calais and Brussels, to Düsseldorf on the Rhine, where I preached many times six years before. During this visit, I spoke there in public eight times. Regarding my stay at Düsseldorf, for the encouragement of the reader, I relate the following circumstance. During our first visit to that city, in the year 1876, a godly City Missionary came to me one day, greatly tried, because he had six sons, for whose conversion he had been praying many years, and yet they remained unconcerned about their souls, and he desired me to tell him what to do. My reply was, '*Continue* to pray for your sons, and *expect* an answer to your prayer, and you will have to praise God.' Now, when after six years I was again in the same city, this dear man came to me and said he was surprised he had not seen before himself what he ought to do, and that he had resolved to take my advice and more earnestly than ever give himself to prayer. Two months after he saw me, five of his six sons were converted within eight days, and have for six years now walked in the ways of the Lord, and he had hope that the sixth son also was beginning to be concerned about his state before God. May the Christian reader be encouraged by this, should his prayers not at once be answered; and, instead of ceasing to pray, wait upon God all the more earnestly and perseveringly, and *expect* answers to his petitions."

THE DIVINE PLAN FOR SENDING OUT FOREIGN MISSIONARIES.

The Bristol Church with which Mr. Müller was connected has been privileged to set an example to the Church of God of the way in which Foreign Missionaries (who are so greatly needed) can be sent forth in answer to prayer. Mr. Müller writes on p. 516, Vol. I. of his Narrative:—

"I also mention here, that during the eight years previous to my going to Germany to labour there, it had been laid on my heart, and on the hearts of some other brethren among us, to ask the Lord that he would be pleased to honour us, as a body of believers, by calling forth from our midst brethren, for carrying the truth into foreign lands. But this prayer seemed to remain unanswered. Now, however, the time was come when the Lord was about to answer it, and I, on whose heart particularly this matter had been laid, was to be the first to carry forth the truth from among us. About that very time the Lord called our dear brother and sister Barrington from among us, to go to Demerara, to labour there in connexion with our esteemed brother Strong, and our dear brother and sister Espenett, to go to Switzerland. Both these dear brethren and sisters left very shortly after I had gone to Germany. But this was not all. Our much valued brother Mordal, who had commended himself to the saints by his unwearied faithful service among us for twelve years, had from Aug. 31, 1843, (the day on which brothers Strong and Barrington sailed from Bristol for Demerara), his mind likewise exercised about service there, and went out from among us eleven months after. He, together with myself, had had it particularly laid upon his heart, during the eight years previously, to ask the Lord again and again to call labourers from among us for foreign service. Of all persons he, the father of a large family, and about 50 years of age, seemed the least likely to be called to that work; but God did call him. He went, laboured a little while in Demerara, and then, on January 9, 1845, the Lord took him to his rest.—When we ask God for a thing, such as that He would be pleased to raise up labourers for His harvest, or send means for the carrying on of His work, the honest question to be put to our hearts should be this: Am *I* willing to go, if He should call *me*? Am *I* willing to give according to *my* ability? For we may be the very persons whom the Lord will call for the work, or whose means He may wish to employ."

In the Report of the Scriptural Knowledge Institution for 1896 Mr. Müller shows how greatly this body of believers has been honoured by God.

"From our own midst, as a church sixty brethren and sisters have gone forth to foreign fields of labour, some of whom have finished their labour on earth; but there are still about forty yet engaged in this precious service."

Why should not the great and crying need for workers in Asia, Africa, and other parts of the world be thus met by thousands of churches in Europe and America following this divine plan of praying the Lord of the harvest that He would send forth labourers from among them?

Surely they may expect God to answer their prayers as He did the prayers of this Bristol church.

Look what has been done in China by the faithful use of God's method! We quote Mr. Hudson Taylor's words as given in *China's Millions* for July, 1897:—

"For the obtaining of fellow-workers we took the Master's direction, 'Pray ye the Lord of the Harvest.' As for the first five before the Mission was formed, so for the twenty-four for whom we first asked for the C.I.M.; for further reinforcements when they were needed; for the seventy in three years, for the hundred in one year, and for further additions from time to time, we have ever relied on this plan. Is it possible that in any other way such a band of workers from nearly every denomination, and from many lands, could have been gathered and kept together for thirty years with no other bond save that which the call of God and the love of GOD has proved—a band now numbering over seven hundred men and women, aided by more than five hundred native workers."

THE BEGINNING OF THE 1859 REVIVAL.

"In November, 1856, a young Irishman, Mr. James McQuilkin, was brought to the knowledge of the Lord. Soon after his conversion he saw my Narrative advertised, viz.: the first two volumes of this book. He had a great desire to read it, and procured it accordingly, about January, 1857. God blessed it greatly to his soul, especially in showing to him, what could be obtained by prayer. He said to himself something like this: 'See what Mr. Müller obtains simply by prayer. Thus I may obtain blessing by prayer.' He now set himself to pray, that the Lord would give him a spiritual companion, one who knew the Lord. Soon after he became acquainted with a young man who was a believer. These two began a prayer-meeting in one of the Sunday Schools in the parish of Connor. Having his prayer answered in obtaining a spiritual companion, Mr. James McQuilkin asked the Lord to lead him to become acquainted with some more of His hidden ones. Soon after the Lord gave him two more young men, who were believers previously, as far as he could judge. In Autumn, 1857, Mr. James McQuilkin stated to these three young men, given him in answer to believing prayer, what blessing he had derived from my Narrative, how it had led him to see the power of believing prayer; and he proposed that they should meet for prayer to seek the Lord's blessing upon their various labours in the Sunday Schools, prayer-meetings, and preaching of the Gospel. Accordingly in Autumn, 1857, these four young men met together for prayer in a small school-house near the village of Kells, in the parish of Connor, every Friday evening. By this time the great and mighty working of the Spirit, in 1857, in the United States, had become known, and Mr. James McQuilkin said to himself, 'Why may not we have such a blessed work here, seeing that God did such great things for Mr. Müller, simply in answer to prayer.' On January 1, 1858, the Lord gave them the first remarkable answer to prayer in the conversion of a farm servant. He was taken into the number, and thus there were five who gave themselves to prayer. Shortly after, another young man, about 20 years old, was converted; there were now six. This greatly encouraged the other three who first had met with Mr. James McQuilkin. Others now were converted, who were also taken into the number; but only believers were admitted to these fellowship meetings, in which they read, prayed, and offered to each other a few thoughts from the Scriptures. These meetings and others for the preaching of the Gospel were held in the parish of Connor, Antrim, Ireland. Up to this time all was going on most quietly, though many souls were converted, There were no physical prostrations, as afterwards.

"About Christmas, 1858, a young man, from Ahoghill, who had come to live at Connor, and who had been converted through this little company of believers, went to see his friends at Ahoghill, and spoke to them about their own souls, and the work of God at Connor. His friends desired to see some of these converts. Accordingly Mr. James McQuilkin, with two of the first who met for prayer, went on February 2, 1859, and held a meeting at Ahoghill in one of the Presbyterian Churches. Some believed, some mocked, and others thought there was a great deal of presumption in these young converts; yet many wished to have another meeting. This was held by the same three young men on February 16th, 1859; and now the Spirit of God began to work, and to work mightily. Souls were converted, and from that time conversions multiplied rapidly. Some of these converts went to other places, and carried the spiritual fire, so to speak, with them. The blessed work of the spirit of God spread in *many places*.—On April 5th, 1859, Mr. James McQuilkin went to Ballymena, held a meeting there in one of the Presbyterian Churches; and on April 11th held another meeting in another of the Presbyterian churches. Several were convinced of sin and the work of the Spirit of God went forward in Ballymena.—On May 28th, 1859, he went to Belfast. During the first week there were meetings held in five different Presbyterian Churches, and from that time the blessed work commenced at Belfast. In all these visits he was accompanied and helped by Mr. Jeremiah Meneely, one of the three young men who first met with him, after the reading of my Narrative. From this time the work of the Holy Ghost spread further and further; for the young converts were used by the Lord to carry the truth from one place to another.

"Such was the *beginning* of that mighty work of the Holy Spirit, which has led to the conversion of hundreds of thousands; for some of my readers will remember how in 1859 this fire was kindled in England, Wales and Scotland; how it spread through Ireland, England, Wales and Scotland; how the Continent of Europe was more or less partaking of this mighty working of the Holy Spirit; how it led thousands to give themselves to the work of Evangelists; and how up to the year 1874 not only the effects of this work, first begun in Ireland, are felt, but that still more or less this blessed work is going on in Europe generally. It is almost needless to add, that in no degree the honour is due to the instruments, but to the Holy Spirit alone; yet these facts are stated, in order that it may be seen, what delight God has in answering abundantly the believing prayer of His children."

MR. MÜLLER'S MARRIAGE.

In Vol. 3 of The Narrative, Mr. Müller shows the ordering of God in his meeting with and subsequent marriage to his first wife, Miss Mary Groves.

"In giving her to me, I own the hand of God; nay, His hand was most marked; and my soul says, 'Thou art good, and doest good.'

"I refer to a few particulars for the instruction of others. When at the end of the year 1829, I left London to labour in Devonshire in the Gospel, a brother in the Lord gave to me a card, containing the address of a well-known Christian lady, Miss Paget, who then resided in Exeter, in order that I should call on her, as she was an excellent Christian. I took this address and put it into my pocket, but thought little of calling on her. Three weeks I carried this card in my pocket, without making an effort to see this lady; but at last I was led to do so. This was God's way of giving me my excellent wife. Miss Paget asked me to preach the last Tuesday in the month of January, 1830, at the room which she had fitted up at Poltimore, a village near Exeter, and where Mr. A. N. Groves, afterwards my brother-in-law, had preached once a month, before he went out as a Missionary to Bagdad. I accepted readily the invitation, as I longed, everywhere to set forth the precious truth of the Lord's return, and other deeply important truths, which not long before my own soul had been filled with.

"On leaving Miss Paget, she gave me the address of a Christian brother, Mr. Hake, who had an Infant Boarding School for young ladies and gentlemen, at Northernhay House, the former residence of Mr. A. N. Groves, in order that I might stay there on my arrival in Exeter from Teignmouth. To this place I went at the appointed time. Miss Groves, afterwards my beloved wife, was there; for Mrs. Hake had been a great invalid for a long time, and Miss Groves helped Mr. Hake in his great affliction, by superintending his household matters. My first visit led to my going again to preach at Poltimore, after the lapse of a month, and I stayed again at Mr. Hake's house; and this second visit led to my preaching once a week in a chapel at Exeter; and thus I went, week after week, from Teignmouth to Exeter, each time staying in the house of Mr. Hake. All this time my purpose had been, not to marry at all, but to remain free for travelling about in the service of the Gospel; but after some months I saw, for many reasons, that it was better for me, as a young Pastor, under 25 years of age, to be married. The question now was, to whom shall I be united? Miss Groves was before my mind; but the prayerful conflict was long, before I came to a decision; for I could not bear the thought, that I should take away from Mr. Hake this valued helper, as Mrs. Hake continued still unable to take the responsibility of so large a household. But I prayed again and again. At last this decided me, I had reason to believe that I had begotten an affection in the heart of Miss Groves for me, and that therefore I ought to make a proposal of marriage to her, however unkindly I might appear to act to my dear friend and brother Mr. Hake, and to ask God to give him a suitable helper to succeed Miss Groves. On Aug. 15th, 1830, I therefore wrote to her, proposing to her to become my wife, and on Aug. 19th, when I went over as usual to Exeter for preaching, she accepted me. The first thing we did, after I was accepted, was, to fall on our knees, and to ask the blessing of the Lord on our intended union. In about two or three weeks the Lord, in answer to prayer, found an individual, who seemed suitable to act as housekeeper, whilst Mrs. Hake continued ill; and on Oct. 7, 1830, we were united in marriage. Our marriage was of the most simple character. We walked to church, had no wedding breakfast, but in the afternoon had a meeting of Christian friends in Mr. Hake's house and commemorated the Lord's death; and then I drove off in the stagecoach with my beloved bride to Teignmouth, and the next day we went to work for the Lord. Simple as our beginning was, and unlike the habits of the world, for Christ's sake, so our Godly aim has been, to continue ever since. Now see the hand of God in giving me my dearest wife:—1st, that address of Miss Paget's was given to me under the ordering of God. 2nd, I must at last be made to call on her, though I had long delayed it. 3rd, She might have provided a resting-place with some other Christian friend, where I should not have seen Miss Groves. 4th, My mind might have at last, after all, decided, not to make a proposal to her; but God settled the matter thus in speaking to me through my conscience—you know that you have begotten affection in the heart of this Christian sister, by the way you have acted towards her, and therefore, painful though it may be, to appear to act unkindly towards your friend and brother, you ought to make her a proposal. I obeyed. I wrote the letter in which I made the proposal, and nothing but one even stream of blessing has been the result.

"Let me here add a word of Christian counsel. To enter upon the marriage union is one of the most deeply important events of life. It cannot be too prayerfully treated. Our happiness, our usefulness, our living for God or for ourselves afterwards, are often most intimately connected with our choice. Therefore, in the most prayerful manner, this choice should be made. Neither beauty, nor age, nor money, nor mental powers, should be that which prompt the decision; but 1st, Much waiting upon God for guidance should be used; 2nd, A hearty purpose, to be willing to be guided by Him should be aimed after; 3rd, True godliness without a shadow of doubt, should be the first and absolutely needful qualification, to a Christian, with regard to a companion for life. In addition to this, however, it ought to be, at the same time, calmly and patiently weighed, whether, in other respects, there is a suitableness.

For instance, for an educated man to choose an entirely uneducated woman, is unwise; for however much on his part love might be willing to cover the defect, it will work very unhappily with regard to the children."

DANGEROUS ILLNESS OF MR. MÜLLER'S DAUGHTER.

"In July, 1853, it pleased the Lord to try my faith in a way in which before it had not been tried. My beloved daughter and only child, and a believer since the commencement of the year 1846, was taken ill on June 20th.

"This illness, at first a low fever, turned to typhus. On July 3rd there seemed no hope of her recovery. Now was the trial of faith. But faith triumphed. My beloved wife and I were enabled to give her up into the hands of the Lord. He sustained us both exceedingly. But I will only speak about myself. Though my only and beloved child was brought near the grave, yet was my soul in perfect peace, satisfied with the will of my Heavenly Father, being assured that He would only do that for her and her parents, which in the end would be the best. She continued very ill till about July 20th, when restoration began.

"On Aug. 18th she was so far restored that she could be removed to Clevedon for change of air, though exceedingly weak. It was then 59 days since she was first taken ill.

~ ※ ~

"Parents know what an only child, a beloved child is, and what to believing parents an only child, a believing child must be. Well, the Father in Heaven said, as it were, by this His dispensation, 'Art thou willing to give up this child to me?' My heart responded, As it seems good to Thee, my Heavenly Father. Thy will be done. But as our hearts were made willing to give back our beloved child to Him who had given her to us, so He was ready to leave her to us, and she lived. 'Delight thyself also in the Lord; and He shall give thee the desires of thine heart.' Psalm xxxvii. 4. The desires of my heart were, to retain the beloved daughter if it were the will of God; the means to retain her were to be satisfied with the will of the Lord.

"Of all the trials of faith that as yet I have had to pass through, this was the greatest; and by God's abundant mercy, I own it to His praise, I was enabled to delight myself in the will of God; for I felt perfectly sure, that, if the Lord took this beloved daughter, it would be best for her parents, best for herself, and more for the glory of God than if she lived: this better part I was satisfied with; and thus my heart had peace, perfect peace, and I had not a moment's anxiety. Thus would it be under all circumstances, however painful, were the believer exercising faith."

THE DAILY BREAD.

"Aug. 3, 1844. Saturday. With the 12s. we began the day. My soul said: 'I will now look out for the way in which the Lord will deliver us this day again; for He will surely deliver. Many Saturdays, when we were in need, He helped us, and so He will do this day also.' Between nine and ten o'clock this morning I gave myself to prayer for means, with three of my fellow-labourers, in my house. Whilst we were in prayer, there was a knock at my room-door, and I was informed that a gentleman had come to see me. When we had finished prayer, it was found to be a brother from Tetbury, who had brought from Barnstaple £1 2s. 6d. for the Orphans. Thus we have £1 14s. 6d., with which I must return the letter-bag to the Orphan-Houses, looking to the Lord for more.

"Aug. 6.—Without *one single penny* in my hands the day began. The post brought nothing, nor had I yet received anything, when ten minutes after ten this morning the letter-bag was brought from the Orphan-Houses, for the supplies of to-day.—Now see the Lord's deliverance! In the bag I found a note from one of the labourers in the Orphan-Houses, enclosing two sovereigns, which she sent for the Orphans, stating that it was part of a present which she had just received unexpectedly, for herself.—Thus we are supplied for to-day.

"Sept. 4.—Only one farthing was in my hands this morning. Pause a moment, dear reader! Only one farthing in hand when the day commenced. Think of this, and think of nearly 140 persons to be provided for. You, poor brethren, who have six or eight children and small wages, think of this; and you, my brethren, who do not belong to the working classes, but have, as it is called, very limited means, think of this! May you not do, what we do, under your *trials*? Does the Lord love you less than He loves us? Does He not love all His children with no less love than that, with which He loves His only begotten Son, according to John xvii. 20-23? Or are we better than you? Nay, are we not in ourselves poor miserable sinners as you are; and have any of the children of God any claim upon God, on account of their own worthiness? Is not that, which alone can make us worthy to receive anything from our Heavenly Father, the righteousness of the Lord Jesus, which is imputed to those who believe in Him? Therefore, dear reader, as we pray in our every need, of whatever character it may be, in connection with this work, to our Father in Heaven for help, and as He does help us, so is He willing to help all His children who put their trust in Him.—Well, let us hear then, how God helped when there was only one farthing left in my hands, on the morning of Sept. 4, 1844.

"A little after nine o'clock I received a sovereign from a sister in the Lord, who does not wish the name of the place, where she resides, mentioned. Between ten and eleven o'clock the bag was sent from the Orphan-Houses, in which in a note it was stated that £1 2s. was required for to-day. Scarcely had I read this, when a fly stopped before my house, and a gentleman, Mr. ——, from the neighbourhood of Manchester, was announced. I found that he was a believer, who had come on business to Bristol. He had heard about the Orphan-Houses, and expressed his surprise, that without any regular system of collections, and without personal application to anyone, simply by faith and prayer, I obtained £2,000 and more yearly for the work of the Lord in my hands. This brother, whom I had never seen before; and whose name I did not even know before he came, gave me £2, as an exemplification of what I had stated to him."

"THE POOR WITH YOU ALWAYS."

"Feb. 12, 1845.—After I had sent off this morning the money which was required for the housekeeping of to-day, I had again only 16s. 2½d. left, being only about one-fourth as much as is generally needed for one day, merely for housekeeping, so that there was now again a fresh call for trusting in the Lord. In the morning I met again, as usual, with my dear wife and her sister, for prayer, to ask the Lord for many blessings in connection with this work, and for means also.

"About one hour after, I received a letter from Devonshire, containing an order for £22 of which £10 was for the Orphans, £2 for a poor brother in Bristol, and £10 for myself.—Besides having thus a fresh proof of the willingness of our Heavenly Father to answer our requests on behalf of the Orphans, there is this, moreover, to be noticed. For many months past, the necessities of the poor saints among us have been particularly laid upon my heart. The word of our Lord: 'Ye have the poor with you always,' and 'whensoever ye will ye may do them good,' has again and again stirred me up to prayer on their behalf, and thus it was again in particular this morning. It was the coldest morning we have had the whole winter. In my morning walk for prayer and meditation I thought how well I was supplied with coals, nourishing food, and warm clothing, and how many of the dear children of God might be in need; and I lifted up my heart to God to give me more means for myself, that I might be able, by actions, to show more abundant sympathy with the poor believers in their need; and it was but three hours after when I received this £10 for myself."

THE LORD DIRECTING THE STEPS.

"Feb. 1, 1847.—Before breakfast I took a direction in my usual morning's walk, in which I had not been for many weeks, feeling drawn in that direction, just as if God had an intention in leading me in that way. Returning home I met a Christian gentleman whom formerly I used to meet almost every morning, but whom I had not met for many weeks, because I had not been walking in that direction. He stopped me and gave me £2 for the Orphans. Then I knew why I had been led thus; for there is not yet enough in hand, to supply the matrons to-morrow evening with the necessary means for house-keeping during another week.

"Feb. 4.—Yesterday nothing had come in. This morning, just before I was going to give myself to prayer about the Orphans, a sister in the Lord sent a sovereign, which she had received, as she writes, 'From a friend who had met the Orphan Boys, and was particularly pleased with their neat and orderly appearance.' After having received this £1, I prayed for means for present use, though not confining my prayers to that. About a quarter of an hour after I had risen from my knees, I received a Setter, with an order for £5. The donor writes, that it is 'the proceeds of a strip of land, sold to the railway company.' What various means does the Lord employ to send us help, in answer to our prayers!"

CONTINUED TRIALS OF FAITH AND PATIENCE.

With the enlargement of the work, by which some 330 persons needed to be provided for, the trials of faith continued. Mr. Müller writes:—

"If we formerly had no certain income, so now have we none. We have to look to God for everything in connection with the work, of which often, however, the pecuniary necessities are the smallest matter; but to Him we are enabled to look, and *therefore* it is, that we are not disappointed."

"Oct. 7, 1852.—This evening there was only £8 left in hand for the current expenses for the Orphans. Hitherto we had generally abounded. But though much had come in, since the commencement of this new period, yet our expenses had been greater than our income, as every donation almost of which the disposal was left with me, had been put to the Building Fund. Thus the balance in hand on May 26, 1852, notwithstanding the large income since then, was reduced to about £8. I therefore gave myself particularly to prayer for means, that this small sum might be increased.

"Oct. 9.—This morning Luke vii came in the course of my reading before breakfast. While reading the account about the Centurion and the raising from death the widow's son at Nain, I lifted up my heart to the Lord Jesus thus: 'Lord Jesus, Thou hast the same power now. Thou canst provide me with means for Thy work in my hands. Be pleased to do so.' About half an hour afterwards I received £230 15s.

"The joy which such answers to prayer afford, cannot be described. I was determined to wait upon God only, and not to work an unscriptural deliverance for myself. I have thousands of pounds for the Building Fund; but I would not take of this sum because it was once set apart for that object. There is also a legacy of £100 for the Orphans two months overdue, in the prospect of the payment of which the heart might be naturally inclined to use some money of the Building Fund, to be replaced by the legacy money, when it comes in; but I would not thus step out of God's way of obtaining help. At the very time when this donation arrived, I had packed up £100 which I happened to have in hand; received for the Building Fund, in order to take it to the Bank, as I was determined not to touch it, but to wait upon God. My soul does magnify the Lord for His goodness.

"June 13, 1853.—We were now very poor. Not indeed in debt, nor was even all the money gone; for there was still about £12 in hand; but then there was needed to be bought flour, of which we buy generally 10 sacks at a time, 300 stones of oatmeal, 4 cwt. of soap, and there were many little repairs going on in the house, with a number of workmen, besides the regular current expenses of about £70 per week. Over and above all this, on Saturday, the day before yesterday, I found that the heating apparatus needed to be repaired, which would cost in all probability £25. It was therefore desirable, humanly speaking, to have £100 for these heavy extra expenses, besides means for the current expenses.

"But I had no human prospect whatever of getting even 100 pence, much less £100. In addition to this, to-day was Monday, when generally the income is little. But, in walking to the Orphan-House this morning, and praying as I went, I particularly told the Lord in prayer, that on this day, though Monday, He could send me much. And thus it was. I received this morning £301 for the Lord's service, as might be most needed.—The joy which I had cannot be described. I walked up and down in my room for a long time, tears of joy and gratitude to the Lord raining plentifully over my cheeks, praising and magnifying the Lord for His goodness, and surrendering myself afresh, with all my heart, to Him for His blessed service. I scarcely ever felt more the kindness of the Lord in helping me.

"Nov. 9.—Our need of means is now great, very great. The Lord tries our faith and patience. This afternoon, a brother and sister in the Lord, from Gloucestershire, called to see me at the New Orphan-House, before going through the house. After a few minutes I received from the sister a sovereign, which she had been requested to bring to me for the Building Fund; and she gave me from herself £1 for my own personal expenses, and £1 for the Building Fund, and her husband gave me £5 for the Orphans, and £5 for Foreign Missions.

"Thus the Lord has refreshed my spirit greatly; but I look for more, and need much more.

"Nov. 12.—This evening, while praying for means, came a little parcel, containing ten sovereigns, from a Christian lady, living not far from the New Orphan-House. This was a very great refreshment to my spirit.

"Oct. 17, 1854.—This morning at family prayer, came, in the course of reading, Exodus v, which shows that, just before the deliverance of the Israelites out of Egypt, their trials were greater than ever. They had not only to make the same number of bricks as before, but also to gather stubble, as no straw was given them any longer. This led me, in expounding the portion, to observe that even now the children of God are often in greater trial than ever, just before help and deliverance comes. Immediately after family prayer it was found, that by the morning's post not one penny had come in for the work of the Lord in which I am engaged, though we needed much, and though but very little had come in during the three previous days. Thus I had now to remember Exodus v, and to practice the truths contained therein. In the course of the day nothing was received. In the evening I had, as usual, a season for prayer with my dear wife, respecting the various objects of the Scriptural Knowledge Institution, and then we left the New Orphan-House for our home.

"When we arrived at our house, about nine o'clock, we found that £5 and also 5s. had been sent from Norwich in two Post Office Orders for the Building Fund, and that £8 3s. 11d. had been sent in for Bibles, Tracts, and Reports, which had been sold. This called for thanksgiving. But a little later, between nine and ten o'clock, a Christian gentleman called and gave me £1 for the Orphans and £200 for foreign missions. He had received these sums from an aged Christian woman, whose savings as a servant, during her whole life, made up the £200, and who, having recently had left to her a little annual income of about £30, felt herself constrained, by the love of Christ, to send the savings of her whole life for foreign missions.

~ ※ ~

"Our especial prayer had been again and again, that the Lord would be pleased to send in means for missionary brethren, as I had reason to believe they were in much need of help; and only at eight o'clock this evening I had particularly besought the Lord to send help for this object. By the last mail I had sent off £40 to British Guiana, to help seven brethren there in some measure. This amount took the last pound in hand for this object. How gladly would I have sent assistance to other brethren also, but I had no more. Now I am in some degree supplied for this object.

"July 12, 1854.—Our means were now again reduced to about £30, as only about £150 had come in since June 15. In addition to this, we had very heavy expenses before us. This morning, in reading through the book of Proverbs, when I came to chapter xxii. 19—'That thy trust may be in the Lord, &c.,' I said in prayer to Him: 'Lord, I do trust in Thee; but wilt Thou now be pleased to help me; for I am in need of means for the current expenses of all the various objects of the Institution.' By the first delivery of letters I received an order on a London bank for £100, to be used for all the various objects 'as the present need might require.'"

ARE YOU PREPARED FOR ETERNITY?

"In looking over my account books, I meet again and again with the name of one and another who has finished his course. Soon, dear reader, your turn and mine may come. Are you prepared for eternity? Affectionately I press this question upon you. Do not put it away. Nothing is of greater moment than this point; yea, all other things, however important in their place, are of exceedingly small importance, in comparison with this matter. Do you ask, how you may be prepared for eternity, how to be saved, how to obtain the forgiveness of your sins? The answer is, believe in the Lord Jesus, trust in Him, depend upon Him alone as it regards the salvation of your soul. He was punished by God, in order that we guilty sinners, if we believe in Him, might not be punished. He fulfilled the law of God, and was obedient even unto death, in order that we disobedient, guilty sinners, if we believe in Him, might, on His account, be reckoned righteous by God. Ponder these things, dear reader, should you have never done so before. Through faith in the Lord Jesus alone can we obtain forgiveness of our sins, and be at peace with God; but, believing in Jesus, we become, through this very faith, the children of God; have God as our Father, and may come to Him for all the temporal and spiritual blessings which we need. Thus every one of my readers may obtain answers to prayers, not only to the same extent that we obtain them, but far more abundantly.

"It may be that few, comparatively, of the children of God are called to serve the Lord in the way of establishing Orphan-Houses, &c.; but all of them may, yea, are called upon to trust in God, to rely upon Him, in their various positions and circumstances, and apply the word of God, faith, and prayer to their family circumstances, their earthly occupation, their afflictions and necessities of every kind, both temporally and spiritually; just as we, by God's help, in some little measure seek to apply the word of God, faith and prayer to the various objects of the Scriptural Knowledge Institution for Home and Abroad. Make but trial of it, if you have never done so before, and you will see how happy a life it is.

~ ※ ~

"Truly I prefer by far this life of almost constant trial, if I am only able to roll all my cares upon my Heavenly Father, and thus become increasingly acquainted with Him, to a life of outward peace and quietness, without these constant proofs of His faithfulness, His wisdom, His love, His power, His over-ruling providence, &c."

WAITING ONLY UPON GOD.

"Sept 6, 1854.—Received from Clerkenwell £50 to be used one-half for missions, and the other half as I thought best. I took the one-half for the support of the Orphans, and find the following remark in my journal respecting this donation: 'What a precious answer to prayer!' Since Aug. 26th we have been day by day coming to the Lord for our daily supplies. Precious, also, on account of Missionary brethren, whom I seek to help, for whom there was nothing in hand when this donation was received."

Mr. Müller adds a few remarks to this part of the Narrative:—

"1. Should anyone suppose, on account of its having been stated in the previous pages that we were repeatedly brought low as to means, that the Orphans have not had all that was needful for them; we reply that *never*, since the work has been in existence, has there a meal-time come, but the Orphans have had good nourishing food in sufficient quantity: and never have they needed clothes, but I have had the means to provide them with all they required.

"2. Never since the Orphan work has been in existence have I asked one single human being for any help for this work; and yet, unasked for, simply in answer to prayer, from so many parts of the world, as has been stated, the donations have come in, and that very frequently at a time of the greatest need."

Mr. Müller writes under date, 1859:—

"Every Wednesday evening I meet with my helpers for united prayer; and day by day I have stated seasons, when I seek to bring the work with its great variety of spiritual and temporal necessities, before the Lord in prayer, having perhaps each day 50 or more matters to bring before Him, and thus I obtain the blessing. I ask no human being for help concerning the work. Nay, if I could obtain £10,000 through each application for help; by God's grace, I would not ask. And why not? Because I have dedicated my whole life cheerfully to the precious service of giving to the world and to the church, a clear, distinct, and undeniable demonstration, that it is a blessed thing to trust in, and to wait upon, God; that He is now, as He ever was, the Living God, the same as revealed in the Holy Scriptures, and that if we know and are reconciled to Him through faith in the Lord Jesus, and ask Him in His name for that which is according to His mind, He will surely give it to us, in His own time, provided that we believe that He will.

~ ※ ~

"Nor has God failed me at any time. Forty years have I proved His faithfulness, in this work."

IN THE LORD JEHOVAH IS EVERLASTING STRENGTH.

Under date Nov. 9, 1861, Mr. Müller wrote:—

"Nov. 9. Saturday evening. When this week commenced, I received only £3 19s. by the first delivery. Shortly after there came in the course of my reading, through the Holy Scriptures, Isaiah xxvi, 4, 'Trust ye in the Lord for ever; for in the Lord Jehovah is everlasting strength.'—I laid aside my Bible, fell on my knees, and prayed thus: I believe that there is everlasting strength in the Lord Jehovah, and I do trust in Him; help me, O Lord, for ever to trust in Thee. Be pleased to give me more means this day, and much this week, though only so little now has come in.—That same day, Nov. 3rd, I received £10 from Surbiton, £5 from a donor residing in Clifton, £2 from a Bristol donor, and in the course of the week altogether £457 came in; thus Jehovah again proved, that in Him is everlasting strength, and that He is worthy to be trusted.—Dear believing reader, seek but in the same way to trust in the Lord, if you are not in the habit of doing so already, and you will find as I have found thousands of times, how blessed it is. But if the reader should be yet going on in carelessness about his soul, and therefore be without the knowledge of God and His dear Son, then the first, and most important thing, such a one has to do, is to trust in the Lord Jesus for the salvation of his soul, that he may be reconciled to God, and obtain the forgiveness of his sins."

JESUS CHRIST, THE SAME YESTERDAY, AND TO-DAY, AND FOREVER.

"May 26, 1861.—At the close of the period I find, that the total expenditure for all the various objects was £24,700 16s. 4d., or £67 13s. 5¾d. per day, all the year round. During the coming year I expect the expenses to be considerably greater. But God, who has helped me these many years, will, I believe, help me in future also.

"You see, esteemed reader, how the Lord, in His faithful love helped us year after year. With every year the expenses increased, because the operations of the Institutions were further enlarged; but He never failed us. You may say, however, 'What would you do, if He should fail in helping you?' My reply is, that cannot be, as long as we trust in Him and do not live in sin. But if we were to forsake Him, the fountain of living waters, and to hew out to ourselves broken cisterns, which cannot hold water, by trusting in an arm of flesh; or if we were to live in sin, we should then have to call upon Him in vain, even though we professed still to trust in Him, according to that word: 'If I regard iniquity in my heart, the Lord will not hear me.' Psalm lxvi, 18.

"Hitherto, by God's grace, I have been enabled to continue to trust in Him alone; and hitherto, though failing and weak in many ways, yet, by God's grace, I have been enabled to walk uprightly, hating sin and loving holiness, and longing after increased conformity to the Lord Jesus.

"Oct. 21 1868—As the days come, we make known our requests to Him, for our outgoings have now been for several years at the rate of more than One Hundred Pounds each day; but though the expenses have been so great, He has never failed us. We have indeed, as to the outward appearance, like the 'Burning Bush in the Wilderness;' yet we have not been consumed. Moreover, we are full of trust in the Lord, and therefore of good courage, though we have before us the prospect, that, year by year, our expenses will increase more and more. Did all my beloved fellow disciples, who seek to work for God know the blessedness of looking truly to God alone, and trusting in Him alone, they would soon see how soul refreshing this way is, and how entirely beyond disappointment, so far as He is concerned. Earthly friends may alter their minds regarding the work in which we are engaged; but if indeed we work for God, whoever may alter His mind regarding our service, He will not. Earthly friends may lose their ability to help us, however much they desire so to do; but He remains throughout eternity the infinitely Rich One. Earthly friends may have their minds after a time diverted to other objects, and, as they cannot help everywhere, much as they may desire it, they may, though reluctantly, have to discontinue to help us; but He is able, in all directions, though the requirements were multiplied a million times, to supply all that can possibly be needed, and does it with delight, where His work is carried on, and where He is confided in. Earthly friends may be removed by death, and thus we may lose their help, but He lives for ever, He cannot die. In this latter point of view, I have especially, during the past 40 years, in connection with this Institution, seen the blessedness of trusting in the Living God alone. Not one nor two, nor even five nor ten, but many more, who once helped me much with their means, have been removed by death; but have the operations of the Institution been stopped on that account? No. And how came this? Because I trusted in God, and in God alone."

THOROUGHLY IN HEART PREPARED FOR TRIALS OF FAITH.

Under date July 28, 1874, Mr. Müller wrote:—

"It has for months appeared to me, as if the Lord meant, by His dealings with us, to bring us back to that state of things, in which we were for more than ten years, from August, 1838, to April, 1849, when we had day by day, almost without interruption, to look to Him for our daily supplies, and, for a great part of the time, from meal to meal. The difficulties appeared to me indeed very great, as the Institution is now twenty times larger, than it was then, and our purchases are to be made in a wholesale way; but, at the same time, I am comforted by the knowledge, that God is aware of all this; and that, if this way be for the glory of His name, and for the good of His church and the unconverted world, I am, by His grace, willing to go this way, and to do it to the end of my course. The funds were thus fast expended; but God, our infinitely rich Treasurer, remains to us. It is this which gives me peace. Moreover, if it pleases Him, with a work requiring about £44,000 a year, to make me do again at the evening of my life, what I did from August, 1838, to April, 1849, I am not only prepared for it, but gladly again I would pass through all these trials of faith, with regard to means, if He only might be glorified, and His church and the world be benefited. Often and often this last point has of late passed through my mind, and I have placed myself in the position of having no means at all left, and Two Thousand and One Hundred persons not only daily at the table, but with everything else to be provided for, and all funds gone; 189 Missionaries to be assisted, and nothing whatever left; about one hundred schools, with about nine thousand scholars in them, to be entirely supported, and no means for them in hand; about Four Millions of Tracts and Tens of Thousands of copies of the Holy Scriptures yearly now to be sent out, and all the money expended. Invariably, however, with this probability before me, I have said to myself: 'God, who has raised up this work through me, God who has led me generally year after year to enlarge it, God who has supported this work now for more than forty years, will still help, and will not suffer me to be confounded, because I rely upon Him, I commit the whole work to Him, and He will provide me with what I need, in future also, though I know not, whence the means are to come.'

"Thus I wrote in my journal on July 28, 1874. The reader will now feel interested in learning how we fared under these circumstances.

"When I came home, last evening (July 27), I found letters had arrived, which contained £193, among which there was one from a Missionary in Foreign lands, helped by the funds of this Institution, who, having come into the possession of some money, by the death of a relative, sent £153 0s. 4d. for Foreign Missions. This morning, July 28, came in £24 more, so that, when I met this afternoon with several of my helpers for prayer for means and various other matters, such as spiritual blessing upon the various Objects of the Institution, for more rain in this very dry season, the health of our fellow-labourers, etc., we had received, since yesterday afternoon, altogether £217. We thanked God for it, and asked for more. When the meeting for prayer was over, there was handed to me a letter from Scotland, containing £73 17s. 10d., and a paper with 13s. This was the immediate answer to prayer for more means.

"Aug. 12.—The income for this whole week, since Aug. 5, has been £897 15s. 6½d.

"Sept. 16.—Just after having again prayed for the payment of legacies, which have been left, I had a legacy receipt sent for the payment of a legacy for £1,800.

"Sept. 23.—Income to-day £5,365 13s. 6d., of which there was sent in one donation £5,327 7s. 6d. The Lord be praised!"

STRONG IN FAITH, GIVING GLORY TO GOD.

On March 27, 1881, Mr. Müller found that no money remained in hand for the School, Bible, Missionary and Tract Funds. Nearly £1,400 had been spent for these Objects during the previous month. He writes:—

"What was now to be done, dear reader, under these circumstances, when all the money for the above Objects was again gone? I reply, we did what we have done for 47 years, that is, we waited continually upon God. My dear fellow-labourers in Bristol, and my dear wife and myself in America, brought our necessities again and again before the Lord.

"Here in the United States, besides our habitual daily prayer for help, we had especial seasons 4, 5, and 6 times a day additionally, for pouring out our hearts before our Heavenly Father, and making known our requests unto Him, being assured that help would come: and we have not waited upon the Lord in vain. This plan may be despised by some, ridiculed by others, and considered insufficient by a third class of persons; but, under every trial and difficulty, we find prayer and faith to be our universal remedy; and, after having experienced for half a century their efficacy, we purpose, by God's help, to *continue* waiting upon Him, in order to show to an ungodly world, and to a doubting Church, that the Living God is still able and willing to answer prayer, and that it is the joy of His heart to listen to the supplications of His children. In Psalm ix. 10, the Divine testimony regarding Jehovah is, 'They that know thy name will put their trust in Thee.' We know Him, by His grace, and do therefore put our trust in Him.

"April 27.—On March 27th we had no means at all in hand for these Objects, as stated under that date. We have now been helped through one more month, in answer to prayer, and have been supplied with all we needed, though that amounted to nearly £1000, and have £23 8s. 6¼d. left.

"April 29.—A servant of the Lord Jesus, who, constrained by the love of Christ, seeks to lay up treasure in heaven, having received a legacy of £532 14s. 5d., gave £500 of it for these Objects.

"July 28, 1881.—The income has been for some time past only about the third part of the expenses. Consequently, all we have for the support of the Orphans is nearly gone; and for the first four Objects of the Institution we have nothing at all in hand. The natural appearance now is, that the work cannot be carried on. But I believe that the Lord will help, both with means for the Orphans and also for the other Objects of the Institution, and that we shall not be confounded; also, that the work shall not need to be given up. I am fully expecting help, and have written this to the glory of God, that it may be recorded hereafter for the encouragement of His children. The result will be seen.

"The foregoing was written at 7 a.m. July 28, 1881. As yet we have the means to meet our expenses, and I expect that we shall not be confounded, though for seven years we have not been so poor."

The result has indeed been seen, and will be seen. For more than 20 years since those words were written and Mr. Müller had thus recorded his confidence in the Lord's help, God has sustained the work, and in May, 1902, there was a balance in hand of some thousands of pounds, notwithstanding that more than £500,000 had been received and expended since this entry was made in Mr. Müller's journal on July 28, 1881.

During these 20 years faith and patience were at times greatly tried:

"Aug. 15, 1881.—The balance for the Orphans is now reduced to £332 12s. 7d., lower than it has been for more than twenty-five years. This sum we have in hand to meet the daily expenses in connection with 2,100 persons. It is only enough for the average outgoings of 4½ days. But our eyes are upon the Lord. I look to my heavenly Provider. The total income of to-day has been £28 5s. 2½d.

"Aug. 22.—Part of a legacy, left years ago, £1,000, was paid, as the answer to many prayers.

"Feb. 26, 1882.—The balance in hand to-day for the Orphans is £97 10s. 7½d., viz., £24 more than the average expenses of one single day.

"March 2.—Our position now regarding the Orphan work is, praying day by day 'Give us *this day* our *daily* bread'. For a considerable time we have had day by day to look to the Lord for the supply of our *daily* wants; but God has helped us thus far.

"April 20, 1882.—When in the greatest need we received from Edinburgh £100 with this statement: 'The enclosed was intended as a legacy, but I have sent it in my lifetime.'

"June 3.—From Wottan-under-edge £500. A glorious deliverance was this donation, and a precious earnest of what God would do further for us.

"Oct. 21.—Received from Wottan-under-edge £1,000.... God, in answer to our prayers, spoke to His dear child, and inclined his heart to send to us more than ever. Thus He also gives proof, that during the previous year, when we were so low as to funds, it was only for the trial of our faith and patience, and not in anger; nor did He thereby mean to indicate, that He would not help us any more. For my own part, I *expected* further great help from God, and I have not been confounded.

"Aug. 17, 1883.—Our balance was reduced this afternoon to £10 2s. 7d. Think of this, dear reader! Day by day about 2,100 persons are to be provided for in the Orphan Institution, and £10 2s. 7d. was all that was in hand to do this. You see that we are just in the same position in which we were 46 years since as to funds. God is our banker. In Him we trust, and on Him we draw by faith. This was Saturday. In the evening £30 was received. On Monday we received £129 further, but had to pay out £60. On Tuesday we received £295, but had to pay out £180.

~ ※ ~

"God is pleased continually to vary His mode of dealing with us, in order that we may not be tempted to trust in donors, or in circumstances, but in Him alone, and to keep our eye fixed upon Him. This, by His grace, we are enabled to do, and our hearts are kept in peace."

Some ten months later, when the balance in hand was only £41 10s., a very little more than one-half of the average expenses for the Orphans for one day, and there were sanitary operations advisable to be carried out, the expenses of which would amount to upwards of £2,000, Mr. Müller received a legacy of £11,034 6s.

"June 7, 1884.—This is the largest donation I have *ever* received at *one time*. This legacy had been above six years in Chancery, and year after year its payment was expected, but remained unsettled by the Chancery Court. I kept on praying, however, and for six years prayed day by day that the money might be paid, believing that God in His own time (*which is always the best*), would help at last; for *many* legacies in Chancery I had prayed out of the Court, and the money was eventually paid. In the present case, too, after faith and patience had been sufficiently exercised, God granted this request likewise."

1893.—In the Fifty-fourth Report of the Scriptural Knowledge Institution Mr. Müller says:—

"The readers of the last report will remember, under what particular trials we entered upon the last financial year of the Institution, from May 26th, 1892, to May 26th, 1893; but we trusted in *God*; with unshaken confidence we looked to *Him*, and we *expected* that we should somehow or other be helped.... While thus we went on, my heart was at peace habitually, being assured that all this was permitted by God, to prepare a blessing for thousands, who would afterwards read the record of His dealings with us, during the year from May 26th, 1892, to May 26th, 1893. With reference to our dear fellow-labourers, Mr. Wright and I have seen already, while passing through the trial, how God has blessed it to them.

"Aug. 30, 1892.—This evening, whilst reading in the Psalms, I came to Psalm lxxxi, 10, and remembered the work of the Holy Spirit in my heart, when reading this verse on Dec. 5, 1835, and the effect which this had, not only on leading me to found the greatest Orphan Institution in the world, but I thought also of the blessing which has thus been brought to tens of thousands of believers and unbelievers all over the world. Putting aside the Bible, therefore, I fell on my knees and asked God that He would graciously be pleased to repeat His former kindness, and to supply me again more abundantly with means. Accordingly in less than half an hour, I received £50 from a Bristol Donor and from

Redland a large quantity of fish, in addition to £97 already received to-day as the result of much prayer. By the last delivery, at 9 p. m., I received £5 more also, and had thus £152 in all, this day, as the result of prayer.

"Nov. 11.—There came in to-day, by the first two deliveries, only about £8, but the Lord increased the income to more than £200 this day. I am never discouraged by very little only coming in, but say to myself, and also to my dear helpers, 'More prayer, more patience, and more exercise of faith will bring greater blessing'; for thus I have invariably found it, since October, 1830, now 63 years ago, when I first began this life of entire dependence upon God for everything.

"March 1, 1893.—The income during this week, ending to-day, was £92 8s. 8¾d. for the Orphans, and £9 11s. 2d. for the other Objects, being about the sixth part of our weekly expenses; but now the great trial of our faith was nearly brought to a close, as will presently be seen.

"March 4.—*This very day* God begins to answer our prayers, as we have received a very good offer for the land we have to sell, even £1,000 per acre. The beginning of the day was darker as to outward appearances than ever: but we trusted in God for help. The first three deliveries of letters brought us only £4, and the remaining three brought us so little that the whole day's income was only £8 instead of £90, the amount we require every day to meet all our expenses. But God has now helped us. We have been able this evening to sell ten acres of land and two-fifths of an acre at £1,000 per acre, and shall receive £10,405 altogether for the whole of one field. The contract was signed at 8 o'clock this evening."

MR. MÜLLER'S DEPARTURE TO BE WITH CHRIST.

On the evening of Wednesday, March 9th, 1898, Mr. Müller took part in the usual meeting for prayer held in the Orphan-House No. 3; retired at his usual hour to rest, and early on the following morning (the 10th of March) alone, in his bed-room, breathed his last, realizing what had long been with him a most joyous anticipation, viz., that "to depart and to be with Christ is far better."

March 14.—This day Mr. Müller's earthly remains were laid in the grave of his first and second wives, at Arno' Vale Cemetery. The attendant circumstances, throughout, were very remarkable and interesting to the Christian mind chiefly as illustrating God's eternal principle—"Them that honour Me I will honour." The man who in life sought not his own glory, became in death the one to whom all classes delighted to show respect and honour.

From the masses of sympathizing spectators that lined the streets, from the tearful eyes, and the audible prayerful ejaculations that escaped the lips of bystanders (many of them the poorest of the poor), as the orphans filed past, following the hearse; from the suspension of all traffic in the principal streets, the tolling of muffled bells, and the half-masted flags, and from the dense crowds in the cemetery that awaited the arrival of the funeral company, it seemed as if the whole city had spontaneously resolved to do honour to the man who had not lived for himself, but for the glory of God and the good of his fellows.

For some 21 months before Mr. Müller's death the trials of faith and patience were great. Mr. James Wright, Mr. Müller's successor, writes:

"He who is pleased, sometimes, to teach His servants 'how to *abound*,' sees it *best* for them, at other times 'to be instructed how to suffer need.' For many of the 64 years during which this work has been carried on, the former was our experience; we abounded and richly abounded, latterly, and especially during the last 2 or 3 years it has been the very reverse. *Pressing need* has been the *rule*; a balance in hand, over and above our need, the rare exception. Yet we have never been forsaken."

"Sept. 23, 1897.—Residue of the legacy of the late G. J., Esq., £2,679 18s. 7d. This sum was received when we were in the *deepest need*; and after it had pleased the Lord to allow a very protracted trial of faith and patience; but see, beloved reader, He did not disappoint nor forsake us, as He *never* does those who really trust in Him. The *joy* of *such* a deliverance cannot be tasted without the experience of the previous *trial*.

"Feb. 26, 1898.—The following entry, under this date, is in Mr. Müller's own hand-writing:

"The income to-day, by the two first deliveries, was £7 15s. 11d. Day by day our great trial of faith and patience continues, and thus it has been, more or less, now, for 21 months, yet, by Thy grace, we are sustained."

March 1, 1898.—The following, again, is from a memorandum in Mr. Müller's own hand-writing, under this date:

"For about 21 months with scarcely the least intermission the trial of our faith and patience has continued. Now, to-day, the Lord has refreshed our hearts. This afternoon came in, for the Lord's work, £1,427 1s. 7d. as part payment of a legacy of the late Mrs. E. C. S. For 3 years and 10 months this money had been in the Irish Chancery Court. Hundreds of petitions had been brought before the Lord regarding it, and now at last, this portion of the total legacy has been received."

Thus the Lord, in love and faithfulness, greatly refreshed the heart of His servant, only nine days before taking him home to be with Himself.

APPENDIX A:
FIVE CONDITIONS OF PREVAILING PRAYER

1. Entire dependence upon the merits and mediation of the Lord Jesus Christ, as the only ground of any claim for blessing. (See John xiv. 13, 14; xv. 16, etc.)

2. Separation from all known sin. If we regard iniquity in our hearts, the Lord will not hear us, for it would be sanctioning sin. (Psalm lxvi. 18.)

3. Faith in God's word of promise as confirmed by His oath. Not to believe Him is to make Him both a liar and a perjurer. (Hebrews xi. 6; vi. 13-20.)

4. Asking in accordance with His will. Our motives must be godly: we must not seek any gift of God to consume it upon our lusts. (1 John v. 14; James iv. 3.)

5. Importunity in supplication. There must be waiting on God and waiting for God, as the husbandman has long patience to wait for the harvest. (James v. 7; Luke xviii. 1-8.)

APPENDIX B:
THE CAREFUL AND CONSECUTIVE READING OF THE HOLY SCRIPTURES

Concerning this subject Mr. Müller says: "I fell into the snare, into which so many young believers fall, the reading of religious books in preference to the Scriptures. I could no longer read French and German novels, as I had formerly done, to feed my carnal mind;

but still I did not put into the room of those books the best of all books. I read tracts, missionary papers, sermons, and biographies of godly persons. The last kind of books I found more profitable than others, and had they been well selected, or had I not read too much of such writings, or had any of them tended particularly to endear the Scriptures to me, they might have done me much good.—I never had been at any time in my life in the habit of reading the Holy Scriptures. When under fifteen years of age, I occasionally read a little of them at school; afterwards God's precious book was entirely laid aside, so that I never read one single chapter of it, as far as I remember, till it pleased God to begin a work of grace in my heart. Now the Scriptural way of reasoning would have been: God himself has condescended to become an author, and I am ignorant about that precious book, which His Holy Spirit has caused to be written through the instrumentality of His servants, and it contains that which I ought to know, and the knowledge of which will lead me to true happiness; therefore I ought to read again and again this most precious book, this book of books, most earnestly, most prayerfully, and with much meditation; and in this practice I ought to continue all the days of my life. For I was aware, though I read it but little, that I knew scarcely anything of it. But instead of acting thus, and being led by my ignorance of the word of God to study it more, my difficulty in understanding it, and the little enjoyment I had in it, made me careless of reading it (for much prayerful reading of the Word, gives not merely more knowledge, but increases the delight we have in reading it); and thus, like many believers, I practically preferred, for the first four years of my divine life, the works of uninspired men to the oracles of the living God. The consequence was, that I remained a babe, both in knowledge and grace. In knowledge I say; for all *true* knowledge must be derived, by the Spirit, from the Word. And as I neglected the Word, I was for nearly four years so ignorant, that I did not *clearly* know even the *fundamental* points of our holy faith. And this lack of knowledge most sadly kept me back from walking steadily in the ways of God. For it is the truth that makes us free, (John viii. 31, 32,) by delivering us from the slavery of the lusts of the flesh, the lusts of the eyes, and the pride of life. The Word proves it. The experience of the saints proves it; and also my own experience most decidedly proves it. For when it pleased the Lord in Aug. 1829, to bring me really to the Scriptures, my life and walk became very different. And though even since that I have very much fallen short of what I might and ought to be, yet, by the grace of God, I have been enabled to live much nearer to Him than before.

"If any believers read this, who practically prefer other books to the Holy Scriptures, and who enjoy the writings of men much more than the word of God, may they be warned by my loss. I shall consider this book to have been the means of doing much good, should it please the Lord, through its instrumentality, to lead some of His people no longer to neglect the Holy Scriptures, but to give them that preference, which they have hitherto bestowed on the writings of men. My dislike to increase the number of books would have been sufficient to deter me from writing these pages, had I not been convinced, that this is the only way in which the brethren at large may be benefited through my mistakes and errors, and been influenced by the hope, that in answer to my prayers, the reading of my experience may be the means of leading them to value the Scriptures more highly, and to make them the rule of all their actions.

~ ※ ~

"If anyone should ask me, how he may read the Scriptures most profitably, I would advise him, that:

"I. Above all he should seek to have it settled in his own mind, that God alone, by His Spirit, can teach him, and that therefore, as God will be enquired of for blessings, it becomes him to seek God's blessing previous to reading, and also whilst reading.

"II. He should have it, moreover, settled in his mind, that, although the Holy Spirit is the *best* and *sufficient* teacher, yet that this teacher does not always teach immediately when we desire it, and that, therefore, we may have to entreat Him again and again for the explanation of certain passages; but that He will surely teach us at last, if indeed we are seeking for light prayerfully, patiently, and with a view to the glory of God.

"III. It is of immense importance for the understanding of the word of God, to read it in course, so that we may read every day a portion of the Old and a portion of the New Testament, going on where we previously left off. This is important—

1. Because it throws light upon the connection; and a different course, according to which one *habitually* selects particular chapters, will make it utterly impossible ever to understand much of the Scriptures.

2. Whilst we are in the body, we need a change even in spiritual things; and this change the Lord has graciously provided in the great variety which is to be found in His word.

3. It tends to the glory of God; for the leaving out some chapters here and there, is practically saying, that certain portions are better than others: or, that there are certain parts of revealed truth unprofitable or unnecessary.

4. It may keep us, by the blessing of God, from erroneous views, as in reading thus regularly through the Scriptures we are led to see the meaning of the whole, and also kept from laying too much stress upon certain favourite views.

5. The Scriptures contain the whole revealed will of God, and therefore we ought to seek to read from time to time through the whole of that revealed will. There are many believers, I fear, in our day, who have not read even once through the whole of the Scriptures; and yet in a few months, by reading only a few chapters every day they might accomplish it.

"IV. It is also of the greatest importance to meditate on what we read, so that perhaps a small portion of that which we have read, or, if we have time, the whole may be meditated upon in the course of the day. Or a small portion of a book, or an epistle, or a gospel, through which we go regularly for meditation, may be considered every day, without, however, suffering oneself to be brought into bondage by this plan.

"Learned *commentaries* I have found to store the *head*, with many notions and often also with the truth of God; but when the *Spirit* teaches, through the instrumentality of prayer and meditation, the *heart* is affected. The former kind of knowledge generally puffs up, and is often renounced, when another commentary gives a different opinion, and often also is found good for nothing, when it is to be carried out into practice. The latter kind of knowledge generally humbles, gives joy, leads as nearer to God, and is not easily reasoned away; and having been obtained from God, and thus having entered into the heart, and become our own, is also generally carried out."

APPENDIX C:
PROVING THE ACCEPTABLE WILL OF GOD

It is very instructive and helpful to see the way in which Mr. Müller proved the acceptable will of the Lord, when exercised in heart about the enlargement of the Orphan work, so that not only 300 but 1000 Orphans might be provided for.

"Dec. 11, 1850.—The especial burden of my prayer therefore is, that God would be pleased to teach me His will. My mind has also been especially pondering, how I could know His will satisfactorily concerning this particular. Sure I am, that I shall be taught. I therefore desire patiently to wait for the Lord's time, when He shall be pleased to shine on my path concerning this point.

"Dec. 26.—Fifteen days have elapsed since I wrote the preceding paragraph. Every day since then I have continued to pray about this matter, and that with a goodly measure of earnestness, by the help of God. There has passed scarcely an hour during these days, in which, whilst awake, this matter has not been more or less before me. But all without even a shadow of excitement. I converse with no one about it. Hitherto have I not even done so with my dear wife. From this I refrain still, and deal with God alone about the matter, in order that no outward influence, and no outward excitement may keep me from attaining unto a clear discovery of His will. I have the fullest and most peaceful assurance, that He will clearly show me His will. This evening I have had again an especial solemn season for prayer, to seek to know the will of God. But whilst I continue to entreat and beseech the Lord, that He would not allow me to be deluded in this business, I may say I have scarcely any doubt remaining on my mind as to what will be the issue, even that I should go forward in this matter.

"As this, however, is one of the most momentous steps that I have ever taken, I judge that I cannot go about this matter with too much caution, prayerfulness, and deliberation. I am in no hurry about it. I could wait for years, by God's grace, were this His will, before even taking one single step towards this thing, or even speaking to anyone about it; and, on the other hand, I would set to work to-morrow, were the Lord to bid me do so. This calmness of mind, this having no will of my own in the matter, this only wishing to please my Heavenly Father in it, this only seeking His and not my honour in it; this state of heart, I say, is the fullest assurance to me that my heart is not under a fleshly excitement, and that, if I am helped thus to go on, I shall know the will of God to the full. But, while I write thus, I cannot but add at the same time, that I do crave the honour and the glorious privilege to be more and more used by the Lord. I have served Satan much in my younger years, and I desire now with all my might to serve God, during the remaining days of my earthly pilgrimage. I am forty-five years and three months old. Every day decreases the number of days that I have to stay on earth. I therefore desire with all my might to work. There are vast multitudes of Orphans to be provided for.

~ ※ ~

"I desire that thus it may be more abundantly manifest that God is still the hearer and answerer of prayer, and that He is the living God now, as He ever was and ever will be, when He shall, simply in answer to prayer, have condescended to provide me with a house for 700 Orphans, and with means to support them. This last consideration is the most important point in my mind. The Lord's honour is the principal point with me in this whole matter; and just because that is the case, if He would be more glorified by my not going forward in this business, I should, by His grace, be perfectly content to give up all thoughts about another Orphan-House. Surely, in such a state of mind, obtained by the Holy Spirit, Thou, O my Heavenly Father, will not suffer Thy child to be mistaken, much less to be deluded! By the help of God I shall continue further, day by day, to wait upon Him in prayer concerning this thing, till He shall bid me act.

"Jan. 2, 1851.—A week ago I wrote the preceding paragraph. During this week I have still been helped, day by day, and more than once every day, to seek the guidance of the Lord about another Orphan-House. The burden of my prayer has still been, that He, in His great mercy, would keep me from making a mistake. During the last week the Book of Proverbs has come, in the course of my Scripture reading, and my heart has been refreshed, in reference to this subject, by the following passages: 'Trust in the Lord with all thine heart; and lean not unto thine own understanding. In all thy ways acknowledge Him, and He shall direct thy paths.' Prov. iii. 5, 6. By the grace of God I do acknowledge the Lord in my ways, and in this thing in particular; I have therefore the comfortable assurance that He will direct my paths concerning this part of my service, as to whether I shall be occupied in it or not. Further: 'The integrity of the upright shall preserve them; but the perverseness of fools shall destroy them.' Prov. xi. 3. By the grace of God I am upright in this business. My honest purpose is to get glory to God. Therefore I expect to be guided aright. Further: 'Commit thy works unto the Lord and thy thoughts shall be established.' Prov. xvi. 3. I do commit my works unto the Lord, and therefore expect that my thoughts will be established.—My heart is more and more coming to a calm, quiet, and settled assurance, that the Lord will condescend to use me yet further in the Orphan Work. Here, Lord, is Thy servant!"

Mr. Müller wrote down eight reasons against and eight reasons for establishing another Orphan-House for Seven Hundred Orphans.

The following is his last reason for so doing:

"I am peaceful and happy, spiritually, in the prospect of enlarging the work as on former occasions when I had to do so. This weighs particularly with me as a reason for going forward. After all the calm, quiet, prayerful consideration of the subject for about eight weeks, I am peaceful and happy, spiritually, in the purpose of enlarging the field. This, after all the heart searching which I have had, and the daily prayer to be kept from delusion and mistake in this thing, and the betaking myself to the Word of God, would not be the case, I judge, had not the Lord purposed to condescend to use me more than ever in this service.

"I, therefore, on the ground of the objections answered, and these eight reasons FOR enlarging the work, come to the conclusion that it is the will of the blessed God, that His poor and most unworthy servant should yet more extensively serve Him in this work, which he is quite willing to do."

"May 24.—From the time that I began to write down the exercises of my mind on Dec. 5th, 1850, till this day, ninety-two more Orphans have been applied for, and seventy-eight were already waiting for admission before. But this number increases rapidly as the work becomes more and more known.

"On the ground of what has been recorded above, I purpose to go forward in this service, and to seek to build, to the praise and honour of the living God, another Orphan-House, large enough to accommodate seven hundred Orphans."

A Short and Easy Method of Prayer

~ ※ ~

By *Jeanne Guyon*

Also known as Madame Jeanne Marie Bouvier De La Motte Guyon

Translated by A. W. Marston

1875 Edition

"Walk before me, and be thou perfect." —Gen. xvii. 1.

~ ※ ~

PREFACE TO THE ENGLISH PROTESTANT EDITION.

Some apology is perhaps needed when a Protestant thus brings before Protestant readers the works of a consistent Roman Catholic author. The plea must be, that the doctrine and experience described are essentially Protestant; and so far from their receiving the assent of the Roman Catholic Church, their author was persecuted for holding and disseminating them.

Of the experience of Madame Guyon, it should be borne in mind, that though the glorious heights of communion with God to which she attained may be scaled by the feeblest of God's chosen ones, yet it is by no means necessary that they should be reached by the same apparently arduous and protracted path along which she was led.

The "Torrents" especially needs to be regarded rather as an account of the personal experience of the author, than as the plan which God invariably, or even usually, adopts in bringing the soul into a state of union with Himself. It is true that, in order that we may "live unto righteousness," we must be "dead indeed unto sin;" and that there must be a crucifixion of self before the life of Christ can be made manifest in us. It is only when we can say, "I am crucified with Christ," that we are able to add, "Nevertheless I live, yet not I, but Christ liveth in me." But it does not follow that this inward death must always be as lingering as in the case of Madame Guyon. She tells us herself that the reason was, that she was not wholly resigned to the Divine will, and willing to be deprived of the gifts of God, that she might enjoy the possession of the Giver. This resistance to the will of God implies suffering on the part of the creature, and chastisement on the part of God, in order that He may subdue to Himself what is not voluntarily yielded to Him.

Of the joy of a complete surrender to God, it is not necessary to speak here: thousands of God's children are realising[1] its blessedness for themselves, and proving that it is no hardship, but a joy unspeakable, to present themselves a living sacrifice to God, to live no longer to themselves, but to Him that died for them, and rose again.

A simple trust in a living, personal Saviour; a putting away by His grace of all that is known to be in opposition to His will; and an entire self-abandonment to Him, that His designs may be worked out in and through us; such is the simple key to the hidden sanctuary of communion.

AUTHOR'S PREFACE.

I did not write this little work with the thought of its being given to the public. It was prepared for the help of a few Christians who were desirous of loving God with the whole heart. But so many have requested copies of it, because of the benefit they have derived from its perusal, that I have been asked to publish it.

I have left it in its natural simplicity. I do not condemn the opinions of any: on the contrary, I esteem those which are held by others, and submit all that I have written to the censure of persons of experience and learning. I only ask of all that they will not be content with examining the outside, but that they will penetrate the design of the writer, which is only to lead others to LOVE God, and to serve Him with greater happiness and success,

---

[1] Original spelling has been kept throughout.

by enabling them to do it in a simple and easy way, fit for the little ones who are not capable of extraordinary things, but who truly desire to *give themselves to God.*

I ask all who may read it, to read without prejudice; and they will discover, under common expressions, a hidden unction, which will lead them to seek for a happiness which all ought to expect to possess.

I use the word *facility*, saying that perfection is easy, because it is easy to find God, *when we seek Him within ourselves.* The passage may be quoted which says, "Ye shall seek me, and shall not find me" (John vii. 34). Yet this need not occasion any difficulty; because the same God, who cannot contradict Himself, has said, "He that seeketh findeth" (Matt. vii. 8). *He who seeks God, and who yet is unwilling to forsake sin, will not find Him, because he is seeking Him where He cannot be found;* therefore it is added, "Ye shall die in your sins." *But he who sincerely desires to forsake sin, that he may draw near to God, will find Him infallibly.*

Many people imagine religion so frightful, and prayer so extraordinary, that they are not willing to strive after them, never expecting to attain to them. But as the difficulty which we see in a thing causes us to despair of succeeding in it, and at the same time removes the desire to undertake it; and as, when a thing appears both desirable and easy to be attained, we give ourselves to it with pleasure, and pursue it boldly; I have been constrained to set forth the advantage and the *facility* of this way.

Oh! if we were persuaded of the goodness of God toward His poor creatures, and of the desire which He has to communicate Himself to them, we should not imagine so many obstacles, and despair so easily of obtaining a good which He is so infinitely desirous of imparting to us.

And if He has not spared His own Son, but delivered Him up for us all, is there anything He can refuse us? Assuredly not. We only need a little courage and perseverance. We have so much of both for trifling temporal interests, and we have none for the *"one thing needful."*

As for those who find a difficulty in believing that it is easy to find God in this way, let them not believe all that they are told, but rather let them make trial of it, that they may judge for themselves; and they will find that I say very little in comparison with that which is.

Dear reader, study this little work with a simple and sincere heart, with lowliness of mind, without wishing to criticise it, and you will find it of good to you. Receive it with the same spirit as that in which it is given, which is no other than the longing that you may be led to *give yourself unreservedly to God.* My desire is that it may be the means of leading the simple ones and the children to their Father, who loves their humble confidence, and to whom distrust is so displeasing. Seek nothing but *the love of God;* have a sincere desire for your salvation, and you will assuredly find it, following this little unmethodical method.

I do not pretend to elevate my sentiments above those of others, but I relate simply what has been my own experience as well as that of others, and the advantage which I have found in this simple and natural manner of going to God.

If this book treats of nothing else but the *short and easy method of prayer*, it is because, being written only for that, it cannot speak of other things. It is certain that, if it be read in the spirit in which it has been written, there will be found nothing in it to shock the mind. Those who will make the experience of it will be the most certain of the truth which it contains.

It is to Thee, O Holy Child Jesus, who lovest simplicity and innocence, and who findest Thy delight in the children of men, that is to say, with those amongst men who are willing to become children;—it is to Thee, I say, to give worth and value to this little work, impressing it on the heart, and leading those who read it to seek Thee within themselves, where Thou wilt take Thy rest, receiving the tokens of their love, and giving them proofs of Thine.

It is Thy work, O Divine Child! O uncreated Love! O silent Word! to make Thyself beloved, tasted, and heard. Thou art able to do it; and I even dare to say that Thou wilt do it, by means of this little work, which is all to Thee, all of Thee, and all for Thee.

CHAPTER I.

ALL ARE COMMANDED TO PRAY—PRAYER THE GREAT MEANS OF SALVATION, AND POSSIBLE AT ALL TIMES BY THE MOST SIMPLE.

Prayer is nothing else but the *application of the heart to God*, and the interior exercise of love. St Paul commands us to "pray without ceasing" (1 Thess. v. 17). Our Lord says: "Take ye heed, watch and pray." "And what I say unto you, I say unto all" (Mark xiii. 33, 37). All, then, are capable of prayer, and it is the duty of all to engage in it.

But I do not think that all are fit for meditation; and, therefore, it is not that sort of prayer which God demands or desires of them.

My dear friends, whoever you may be, who desire to be saved, come unto God in prayer. "I counsel thee to buy of me gold tried in the fire, that thou mayest be rich" (Rev. iii. 18). It is easily to be obtained, far more easily than you could ever imagine.

Come, all ye that are athirst, and take this water of life freely (see Rev. xxii. 17). Do not amuse yourselves by hewing out to yourselves "broken cisterns that can hold no water" (Jer. ii. 13). Come, hungry souls, who find nothing that can satisfy you, and you shall be *filled*. Come, poor afflicted ones, weighed down with griefs and sorrows, and you shall be comforted. Come, sick ones, to the great Physician, and do not fear to approach Him because you are so weak and diseased: expose all your diseases to Him, and they shall be healed.

Come, children, to your Father; He will receive you with open arms of love. Come, wandering and scattered sheep, to your Shepherd. Come, sinners, to your Saviour. Come, ignorant and foolish ones, who believe yourselves incapable of prayer; it is you who are the most fitted for it. Come all without exception; Jesus Christ calls you all.

Let those only refuse to come who have no heart. The invitation is not for them; for we must have a heart in order to love. But who is indeed without heart? Oh, come and give that heart to God, and learn in the place of prayer how to do it! All those who long for prayer are capable of it, who have ordinary grace and the gift of the Holy Spirit, which is freely promised to all who ask it.

Prayer is the key of perfection and of sovereign happiness; it is the efficacious means of getting rid of all vices and of acquiring all virtues; for the way to become perfect is to live in the presence of God. He tells us this Himself: "Walk before me, and be thou perfect" (Gen. xvii. 1). Prayer alone can bring you into His presence, and keep you there continually.

What we need, then, is an attitude of prayer, in which we can *constantly* abide, and out of which exterior occupations cannot draw us; a prayer which can be offered alike by princes, kings, prelates, magistrates, soldiers, children, artisans, labourers, women, and the sick. This prayer is not mental, but *of the heart*.

It is not a prayer of thought alone, because the mind of man is so limited, that while it is occupied with one thing it cannot be thinking of another. But it is the PRAYER OF THE HEART, which cannot be interrupted by the occupations of the mind. Nothing can interrupt the prayer of the heart but unruly affections; and when once we have tasted of the love of God, it is impossible to find our delight in anything but Himself.

Nothing is easier than to have God and to live upon Him. He is more truly in us than we are in ourselves. He is more anxious to give Himself to us than we are to possess Him. All that we want is to know the way to seek Him, which is so easy and so natural, that breathing itself is not more so.

Oh, you who imagine yourselves incapable of religious feeling, you may live in prayer and in God as easily and as continuously as you live by the air you breathe. Will you not, then, be inexcusable if you neglect to do it, after you have learned the way?

CHAPTER II.

FIRST DEGREE OF PRAYER—MEDITATION AND MEDITATIVE READING—THE LORD'S PRAYER—PASSAGE FROM THE FIRST DEGREE TO THE SECOND.

There are two means by which we may be led into the higher forms of prayer. One is *Meditation*, the other is *Meditative Reading*. By meditative reading I mean the taking of some truths, either doctrinal or practical—the latter rather than the former—and reading them in this way:—Take the truth which has presented itself to you, and read two or three lines, seeking to enter into the full meaning of the words, and go on no further so long as you find satisfaction in them; leave the place only when it becomes insipid. After that, take another passage, and do the same, not reading more than half a page at once.

It is not so much from the amount read that we derive profit, as from the manner of reading. Those people who get through so much do not profit from it; the bees can only draw the juice from the flowers by resting on them, not by flying round them. Much reading is more for scholastic than for spiritual science; but in order to derive profit from spiritual books, we should read them in this way; and I am sure that this manner of reading accustoms us gradually to prayer, and gives us a deeper desire for it. The other way is *Meditation*, in which we should engage at a chosen time, and not in the hour given to reading. I think the way to enter into it is this:—After having brought ourselves into the presence of God by a definite act of faith, we should read something substantial, not so much to reason upon it, as to fix the attention, observing that the principal exercise should be the presence of God, and that the subject should rather fix the attention than exercise reason.

This *faith in the presence of God within our hearts* must lead us to enter within ourselves, collecting our thoughts, and preventing their wandering; this is an effectual way of getting rid of distracting thoughts, and of losing sight of outward things, in order to draw near to God, who can only be found in the secret place of our hearts, which is the *sancta-sanctorum* in which He dwells.

He has promised that if any one keeps His commandments, He will come to him, and *make His abode* with him (John xiv. 23). St Augustine reproaches himself for the time he lost through not having sought God at first in this way.

When, then, we are thus buried in ourselves, and deeply penetrated with the presence of God within us—when the senses are all drawn from the circumference to the centre, which, though it is not easily accomplished at first, becomes quite natural afterwards—when the soul is thus gathered up within itself, and is sweetly occupied with the truth read, not in reasoning upon it, but in feeding upon it, and exciting the will by the affection rather than the understanding by consideration: the *affection* being thus touched, must be suffered to *repose* sweetly and at peace, *swallowing* what it has tasted.

As a person who only masticated an excellent meat would not be nourished by it, although he would be sensible of its taste, unless he ceased this movement in order to swallow it; so when the affection is stirred, if we seek continually to stir it, we extinguish its fire, and thus deprive the soul of its nourishment. We must swallow by a *loving repose* (full of respect and confidence) what we have masticated and tasted. This method is very necessary, and would advance the soul in a short time more than any other would do in several years.

But as I said that the direct and principal exercise should be the *sense of the presence of God*, we must most faithfully *recall the senses* when they wander.

This is a short and efficacious way of fighting with distractions; because those who endeavour directly to oppose them, irritate and increase them; but by losing ourselves in the thought of a present God, and suffering our thoughts to be drawn to Him, we combat them indirectly, and without thinking of them, but in an effectual manner. And here let me warn beginners not to run from one truth to another, from one subject to another; but to keep themselves to one so long as they feel a taste for it: this is the way to enter deeply into truths, to taste them, and to have them impressed upon us. I say it is difficult at first thus to retire within ourselves, because of the habits, which are natural to us, of being taken up with the outside; but when we are a little accustomed to it, it becomes exceedingly easy; both because we have formed the habit of it, and because God, who only desires to communicate Himself to us, sends us abundant grace, and an experimental sense of His presence, which renders it easy.

Let us apply this method to the Lord's Prayer. We say "Our Father," thinking that God is within us, and will indeed be our Father. After having pronounced this word *Father*, we remain a few moments in silence, waiting for this heavenly Father to make known His will to us. Then we ask this King of Glory *to reign* within us, abandoning ourselves to Him, that He may do it, and yielding to Him the right that He has over us. If we feel here an inclination to peace and silence, we should not continue, but remain thus so long as the condition may last; after which we proceed to the second petition, "Thy will be done on earth, as it is in heaven." We then desire that God may accomplish, in us and by us, all His will; we give up to God our heart and our liberty, that He may dispose of them at His pleasure. Then, seeing that the occupation of the will should be love, we desire to love, and we ask God to give us *His love*. But all this is done quietly, peacefully; and so on with the rest of the prayer.

At other times we hold ourselves in the position of sheep near to the Shepherd, asking of Him our true food. O Divine Shepherd! Thou feedest Thy sheep with Thine own hand, and Thou art their food from day to day. We may also bring before Him our family desires; but it must all be done with the remembrance by faith of the presence of God within us.

We can form no imagination of what God is: a lively faith in His presence is sufficient; for we can conceive no image of God, though we may of Christ, regarding Him as crucified, or as a child, or in some other condition, provided that we always seek Him within ourselves.

At other times we come to Him as to a Physician, bringing our maladies to Him that He may heal them; but always without effort, with a short silence from time to time, that the silence may be mingled with the action, gradually lengthening the silence and shortening the spoken prayer, until at length, as we yield to the operation of God, He gains the supremacy. When the presence of God is given, and the soul begins to taste of silence and repose, this experimental sense of the presence of God introduces it to the second degree of prayer.

CHAPTER III.

SECOND DEGREE OF PRAYER, CALLED HERE "THE PRAYER OF SIMPLICITY."

The second degree has been variously termed *Contemplation*, *The Prayer of Silence*, and *of repose*; while others again have called it the *Prayer of Simplicity*; and it is of this last term that I shall make use here, being more appropriate than that of *Contemplation*, which signifies a degree of prayer more advanced than that of which I speak.

After a time, as I have said, the soul becomes sensible of a facility in recognising the presence of God; it collects itself more easily; prayer becomes natural and pleasant; it knows that it leads to God; and it perceives the smell of His perfumes.

Then it must change its method, and observe carefully what I am about to say, without being astonished at its apparent implausibility.

First of all, when you bring yourself into the presence of God by faith, remain a short time in an attitude of respectful silence. If from the beginning, in making this act of faith, you are sensible of a little taste of the presence of God, remain as you are without troubling yourself on any subject, and keep that which has been given you, so long as it may remain.

If it leaves you, excite your will by means of some tender affection, and if you then find that your former state of peace has returned, remain in it. The fire must be blown softly, and as soon as it is lighted, cease to blow it, or you will put it out. It is also necessary that you should go to God, not so much to obtain something from Him, as to please Him, and to do His will; for a servant who only serves his master in proportion to the recompense he receives, is unworthy of any remuneration.

Go, then, to prayer, not only to enjoy God, but to be as He wills: this will keep you equal in times of barrenness and in times of abundance; and you will not be dismayed by the repulses of God, nor by His apparent indifference.

CHAPTER IV.

ON SPIRITUAL DRYNESS.

As God's only desire is to give Himself to the loving soul who desires to seek Him, He often hides Himself in order to arouse it, and compel it to seek Him with love and fidelity. But how does He reward the faithfulness of His beloved! And how are His apparent flights followed by loving caresses!

The soul imagines that it is a proof of its fidelity and of its increased love that it seeks God with an effort, or that at least such seeking will soon lead to His return.

But no! This is not the way in this degree. With a loving impatience, with deep humility and abasement, with an affection deep and yet restful, with a respectful silence, you must await the return of your Beloved.

You will thus show Him that it is *Himself* alone that you love, and His good pleasure, and not the pleasure that you find in loving Him. Therefore it is said, "Make not haste in time of trouble. Cleave unto Him, and depart not away, that thou mayest be increased at thy last end" (Ecclus. ii. 2, 3). Suffer the suspensions and the delays of the visible consolations of God.

Be patient in prayer, even though you should do nothing all your life but wait in patience, with a heart humbled, abandoned, resigned, and content for the return of your Beloved. Oh, excellent prayer! How it moves the heart of God, and obliges Him to return more than anything else!

CHAPTER V.

ABANDONMENT TO GOD—ITS FRUIT AND ITS IRREVOCABILITY— IN WHAT IT CONSISTS—GOD EXHORTS US TO IT.

It is here that true *abandonment* and consecration to God should commence, by our being deeply convinced that all which happens to us moment by moment is the will of God, and therefore all that is necessary to us.

This conviction will render us contented with everything, and will make us see the commonest events in God, and not in the creature.

I beg of you, whoever you may be, who are desirous of giving yourselves to God, not to take yourselves back when once you are given to Him, and to remember that a thing once given away is no longer at your disposal. *Abandonment* is the key to the inner life: he who is thoroughly abandoned will soon be perfect.

You must, then, hold firmly to your abandonment, without listening to reason or to reflection. A great faith makes a great abandonment; you must trust wholly in God, against hope believing in hope (Rom. iv. 18). *Abandonment* is the casting off of all care of ourselves, to leave ourselves to be guided entirely by God.

All Christians are exhorted to abandonment, for it is said to all, "Take no thought for the morrow; for your Heavenly Father knoweth that ye have need of all these things" (Matt. vi. 32, 34). "In all thy ways acknowledge Him, and He shall direct thy paths" (Prov. iii. 6). "Commit thy works unto the Lord, and thy thoughts shall be established" (Prov. xvi. 3). "Commit thy way unto the Lord; trust also in Him; and He shall bring it to pass" (Ps. xxxvii. 5).

Abandonment, then, ought to be an utter leaving of ourselves, both outwardly and inwardly, in the hands of God, forgetting ourselves, and thinking only of God. By this means the heart is kept always free and contented.

Practically it should be a continual loss of our own will in the will of God, a renunciation of all natural inclinations, however good they may appear, in order that we may be left free to choose only as God chooses: we should be indifferent to all things, whether temporal or spiritual, for the body or the soul; leaving the past in forgetfulness, the future to providence, and giving the present to God; contented with the present moment, which brings with it God's eternal will for us; attributing nothing which happens to us to the creature, but seeing all things in God, and regarding them as coming infallibly from His hand, with the exception only of our own sin.

Leave yourselves, then, to be guided by God as He will, whether as regards the inner or the outward life.

CHAPTER VI.

OF SUFFERING WHICH MUST BE ACCEPTED AS FROM GOD—ITS FRUITS.

Be content with all the suffering that God may lay upon you. If you will love Him purely, you will be as willing to follow Him to Calvary as to Tabor.

He must be loved as much on Calvary as on Tabor, since it is there that He makes the greatest manifestation of His love.

Do not act, then, like those people who give themselves at one time, and take themselves back at another. They give themselves to be caressed, and take themselves back when they are crucified; or else they seek for consolation in the creature.

You can only find consolation in the love of the cross and in complete abandonment. He who has no love for the cross has no love for God (see Matt. xvi. 24). It is impossible to love God without loving the cross; and a heart which has learned to love the cross finds sweetness, joy, and pleasure even in the bitterest things. "To the hungry soul every bitter thing is sweet" (Prov. xxvii. 7), because it is as hungry for the cross as it is hungry for God.

The cross gives God, and God gives the cross. Abandonment and the cross go together. As soon as you are sensible that something is repugnant to you which presents itself to you in the light of suffering, abandon yourself at once to God for that very thing, and present yourself as a sacrifice to Him: you will see that, when the cross comes, it will have lost much of its weight, because you will desire it. This will not prevent your being sensible of its weight. Some people imagine that it is not suffering to feel the cross. The feeling of suffering is one of the principal parts of suffering itself. Jesus Himself was willing to suffer it in its intensity.

Often the cross is borne with weakness, at other times with strength: all should be equal in the will of God.

CHAPTER VII.

ON MYSTERIES—GOD GIVES THEM HERE IN REALITY.

It will be objected that, by this way, mysteries will not be made known. It is just the contrary; they are given to the soul in reality. Jesus Christ, to whom it is abandoned, and whom it follows as the *Way*, whom it hears as the *Truth*, and who animates it as the *Life*, impressing Himself upon it, imparts to it His own condition.

To bear the conditions of Christ is something far greater than merely to consider those conditions. Paul bore the conditions of Christ on his body. "I bear in my body," he says, "the marks of the Lord Jesus" (Gal. vi. 17). But he does not say that he reasoned about them.

Often Christ gives in this state of abandonment views of His conditions in a striking manner. We must receive equally all the dispositions in which He may be pleased to place us, choosing for ourselves to abide near to Him, and to be annihilated before Him, but receiving equally all that He gives us, light or darkness, facility or barrenness, strength or weakness, sweetness or bitterness, temptations or distractions, sorrow, care, uncertainty; none of these things ought to move us.

There are some persons to whom God is continually revealing His mysteries: let them be faithful to them. But when God sees fit to remove them, let them suffer them to be taken.

Others are troubled because no mysteries are made known to them: this is needless, since a loving attention to God includes all particular devotion, and that which is united to God alone, by its rest in Him, is instructed in a most excellent manner in all mysteries. He who loves God loves all that is of Him.

CHAPTER VIII.

ON VIRTUE—ALL VIRTUES GIVEN WITH GOD IN THIS DEGREE OF THE PRAYER OF THE HEART.

This is the short and the sure way of acquiring virtue; because, God being the principle of all virtue, we possess all virtue in possessing God.

More than this, I say that all virtue which is not given inwardly is a mask of virtue, and like a garment that can be taken off, and will wear out. But virtue communicated fundamentally is essential, true, and permanent. "The King's daughter is all glorious within" (Ps. xlv. 13). And there are none who practise virtue more constantly than those who acquire it in this way, though virtue is not a distinct subject of their thought.

How hungry these loving ones are after suffering! They think only of what can please their Beloved, and they begin to neglect themselves, and to think less of themselves. The more they love God, the more they hate themselves.

Oh, if all could learn this method, so easy that it is suited for all, for the most ignorant as for the most learned, how easily the whole Church would be reformed! You only need to love. St Augustine says, "Love, and do as you please;" for when we love perfectly, we shall not desire to do anything that could be displeasing to our Beloved.

CHAPTER IX.

OF PERFECT CONVERSION, WHICH IS AN EFFECT OF THIS METHOD OF PRAYER—TWO OF ITS AIDS, THE ATTRACTION OF GOD, AND THE CENTRAL INCLINATION OF THE SOUL.

"Turn ye unto Him from whom the children of Israel have deeply revolted" (Isa. xxxi. 6). Conversion is nothing else but a turning from the creature to God. Conversion is not perfect, though it is necessary for salvation, when it is merely a turning from sin to grace. To be complete, it must be a turning from without to within.

The soul, being turned in the direction of God, has a great facility for remaining converted to Him. The longer it is converted, the nearer it approaches to God, and attaches itself to Him; and the nearer it approaches to God, the more it becomes necessarily drawn from the creature, which is opposed to God.

But this cannot be done by a violent effort of the creature; all that it can do is to remain turned in the direction of God in a perpetual adherence.

God has an *attracting virtue*, which draws the soul more strongly towards Himself; and in attracting it, He purifies it: as we see the sun attracting a dense vapour, and gradually, without any other effort on the part of the vapour than that of letting itself be drawn, the sun, by bringing it near to himself, refines and purifies it.

There is, however, this difference, that the vapour is not drawn freely, and does not follow willingly, as is the case with the soul.

This manner of turning within is very simple, and makes the soul advance naturally and without effort; because God is its centre. The centre has always a strong attractive power; and the larger the centre, the stronger is its attractive force.

Besides this attraction of the centre, there is given to all natural objects a strong tendency to become united with their centre. As soon as anything is turned in the direction of its centre, unless it be stopped by some invincible obstacle, it rushes towards it with extreme velocity. A stone in the air is no sooner let loose, and turned towards the earth, than it tends to it by its own weight as its centre. It is the same with fire and water, which, being no longer arrested, run incessantly towards their centre.

Now I say that the soul, by the effort it has made in inward recollection, being turned towards its centre, without any other effort, but simply by the weight of love, falls towards its centre; and the more it remains quiet and at rest, making no movement of its own, the more rapidly it will advance, because it thus allows that attractive virtue to draw it.

All the care, then, that we need have is to promote this inward recollection as much as possible, not being astonished at the difficulty we may find in this exercise, which will soon be recompensed with a wonderful co-operation on the part of God, which will render it very easy. When the passions rise, a look towards God, who is present within us, easily deadens them. Any other resistance would irritate rather than appease them.

CHAPTER X.

HIGHER DEGREE OF PRAYER, WHICH IS THAT OF THE SIMPLE PRESENCE OF GOD, OR ACTIVE CONTEMPLATION.

The soul, faithfully exercising itself in the affection and love of its God, is astonished to find Him taking complete possession of it.

His presence becomes so natural, that it would be impossible not to have it: it becomes habitual to the soul, which is also conscious of a great calm spreading over it. Its prayer is all silence, and God imparts to it an intrinsic love, which is the commencement of ineffable happiness.

Oh, if I could describe the infinite degrees which follow! But I must stop here, since I am writing for beginners, and wait till God shall bring to light what may be useful to those more advanced.[2] I can only say, that, at this point, it is most important that all natural operation should cease, that God may act alone: "Be still, and know that I am God," is His own word by David (Ps. xlvi. 10).

But man is so attached to his own works, that he cannot believe God is working, unless he can feel, know, and distinguish His operation. He does not see that it is the speed

---

[2] This subject is pursued in the treatise entitled "Spiritual Torrents."

of his course which prevents his seeing the extent of his advancement; and that the operation of God becoming more abundant, absorbs that of the creature, as we see that the sun, in proportion as he rises, absorbs the light of the stars, which were easily distinguishable before he appeared. It is not the want of light, but an excess of light, which prevents our distinguishing the stars.

It is the same here; man can no longer distinguish his own operation, because the strong light absorbs all his little distinct lights, and makes them fade away entirely, because God's excess surpasses them all. So that those who accuse this degree of prayer of being a state of *idleness*, are greatly deceived; and only speak thus from want of experience. Oh, if they would only prove it! in how short a time they would become experimentally acquainted with this matter!

I say, then, that this failure of work does not spring from scarcity, but from abundance.

Two classes of persons are silent: the one because they have nothing to say, the other because they have too much. It is thus in this degree. We are silent from excess, not from want.

Water causes death to two persons in very different ways. One dies of thirst, another is drowned: the one dies from want, the other from abundance. So here it is abundance which causes the cessation of natural operation. It is therefore important in this degree to remain as much as possible in stillness.

At the commencement of this prayer, a movement of affection is necessary; but when grace begins to flow into us, we have nothing to do but to remain at rest, and take all that God gives. Any other movement would prevent our profiting by this grace, which is given in order to draw us into the *rest of love*.

The soul in this peaceful attitude of prayer falls into a mystic sleep, in which all its natural powers are silenced, until that which had been temporary becomes its permanent condition. You see that the soul is thus led, without effort, without study, without artifice.

The heart is not a fortified place, which must be taken by cannonading and violence: it is a kingdom of peace, which is possessed by love. Gently following in His train, you will soon reach the degree of *intuitive* prayer. God asks nothing extraordinary and difficult: on the contrary, He is most pleased with childlike simplicity.

The grandest part of religion is the most simple. It is the same with natural things. Do you wish to get to the sea? Embark upon a river, and insensibly and without effort you will be taken to it. Do you wish to get to God? Take His way, so quiet, so easy, and in a little while you will be taken to Him in a manner that will surprise you. Oh, if only you would try it! How soon you would see that I am telling you only too little, and that the experience would far surpass any description that could be given! What do you fear? Why do you not throw yourself at once into the arms of Love, who only stretched them out upon the cross in order to take you in? What risk can there be in trusting God, and abandoning yourself to Him? Oh, He will not deceive you, unless it be by giving you far more than you ever expected: while those who expect everything from themselves may well take to themselves the reproach which God utters by the mouth of Isaiah: "Thou art wearied in the greatness of thy way; yet saidst thou not, There is no hope" (Isa. lvii. 10).

CHAPTER XI.

OF REST IN THE PRESENCE OF GOD—ITS FRUITS—INWARD SILENCE—
GOD COMMANDS IT—OUTWARD SILENCE.

The soul, being brought to this place, needs no other preparation than that of repose: for *the presence of God* during the day, which is the great result of prayer, or rather prayer itself, begins to be *intuitive* and *almost continual*. The soul is conscious of a deep inward happiness, and feels that God is in it more truly than it is in itself. It has only one thing to do in order to find God, which is to retire within itself. As soon as the eyes are closed, it finds itself in prayer.

It is astonished at this infinite happiness; there is carried on within it a conversation which outward things cannot interrupt. It might be said of this method of prayer, as was said of Wisdom, "All good things together come to me with her" (Wisdom of Solomon vii. 11), for virtue flows naturally into the soul, and is practised so easily, that it seems to be quite natural to it. It has within it a germ of life and fruitfulness, which gives it a facility for all good, and an insensibility to all evil. Let it then remain faithful, and seek no other frame of mind than that of simple rest. It has only to suffer itself to be filled with this divine effusion.

"The Lord is in His holy temple: let all the earth keep silence before Him" (Hab. ii. 20). The reason why inward silence is so necessary is, that Christ, being the eternal and essential Word, in order that He may be received into the soul, there must be a disposition corresponding with what He is. Now it is certain that in order to receive words we must listen. Hearing is the sense given to enable us to receive the words which are communicated to us. Hearing is rather a passive than an active sense, receiving, and not communicating. Christ being the Word which is to be communicated, the soul must be attentive to this Word which speaks within it.

This is why we are so often exhorted to listen to God, and to be attentive to His voice. Many passages might be quoted. I will be content to mention a few: "Hearken unto me, O my people; and give ear unto me, O my nation" (Isa. li. 4). "Hearken unto me, O house of Jacob, and all the remnant of the house of Israel" (Isa. xlvi. 31). "Hearken, O daughter, and consider, and incline thine ear; forget also thine own people, and thy father's house; so shall the King greatly desire thy beauty" (Ps. xlv. 10, 11).

We must *listen* to God, and be attentive to Him, *forgetting ourselves* and all self-interest. These two actions, or rather passions—for this condition is essentially a passive one—arouse in God a "desire" towards the "beauty" He has Himself communicated.

Outward silence is extremely necessary for the cultivation of inward silence, and it is impossible to acquire inward silence without having a love for silence and solitude.

God tells us by the mouth of His prophet, "I will allure her, and bring her into the wilderness, and speak to her heart" (marginal reading of Hosea ii. 14).

To be inwardly occupied with God, and outwardly occupied with countless trifles, this is impossible.

It will be a small matter to pray, and to retire within ourselves for half an hour or an hour, if we do not retain the unction and the spirit of prayer during the day.

CHAPTER XII.

SELF-EXAMINATION AND CONFESSION.

Self-examination should always precede confession. Those who arrive at this degree should expose themselves to God, who will not fail to enlighten them, and to make known to them the nature of their faults. This examination must be conducted in peace and tranquillity, expecting more from God than from our own research the knowledge of our sins.

When we examine ourselves with an effort, we easily make mistakes. We "call evil good, and good evil;" and self-esteem easily deceives us. But when we remain exposed to the searching gaze of God, that Divine Sun brings to light even the smallest atoms. We must then, for self-examination, abandon ourselves utterly to God.

When we are in this degree of prayer, God is not slow to reveal to us all the faults we commit. We have no sooner sinned than we feel a burning reproach.

It is God Himself who conducts an examination which nothing escapes, and we have only to turn towards God, and suffer the pain and the correction which He gives. As this examination by God is continual, we can no longer examine ourselves; and if we are faithful to our abandonment to God, we shall soon be better examined by the divine light than we could be by all our own efforts. Experience will make this known. One thing which often causes astonishment to the soul is, that when it is conscious of a sin, and comes to confess it to God, instead of feeling regret and contrition, such as it formerly felt, a sweet and gentle love takes possession of it.

Not having experienced this before, it supposes that it ought to draw itself out of this condition to make a definite act of contrition. But it does not see that, by doing this, it would lose true contrition, which is this *intuitive love*, infinitely greater than anything it could create for itself. It is a higher action, which includes the others, with greater perfection, though these are not possessed distinctly.

We should not seek to do anything for ourselves when God acts more excellently in us and for us. It is hating sin as God hates it to hate it in this way. This love, which is the operation of God in the soul, is the purest of all love. All we have to do then is to remain as we are.

Another remarkable thing is, that we often forget our faults, and find it difficult to remember them; but this must not trouble us, for two reasons: The first, that this very forgetfulness is a proof that the sin has been atoned for, and it is better to forget all that concerns ourselves, that we may remember God alone. The second reason is, that God does not fail, whenever confession is needful, to show to the soul its greatest faults, for then it is He Himself who examines it.

CHAPTER XIII.

ON READING—VOCAL PRAYER—REQUESTS.

The proper manner of reading in this degree is, as soon as we feel attracted to meditation, to cease reading, and remain at rest.

The soul is no sooner called to inward silence, than it should cease to utter vocal prayers; saying but little at any time, and when it does say them, if it finds any difficulty, or feels itself drawn to silence, it should remain silent, and make no effort to pray, leaving itself to the guidance of the Spirit of God.

The soul will find that it cannot, as formerly, present definite requests to God. This need not surprise it, for it is now that "the Spirit maketh intercession for the saints, according to the will of God. The Spirit also helpeth our infirmities: for we know not what we should pray for as we ought; but the Spirit itself maketh intercession for us, with groanings which cannot be uttered" (Rom. viii. 26, 27).

We must second the designs of God, which are to strip the soul of its own works, to substitute His in their place.

Let Him work then, and bind yourself to nothing of your own. However good it may appear to you, it cannot be so if it comes in the way of God's will for you. The will of God is preferable to all other good. Seek not your own interests, but live by abandonment and by faith.

It is here that *faith* begins to operate wonderfully in the soul.

CHAPTER XIV.

THE FAULTS COMMITTED IN THIS DEGREE—DISTRACTIONS, TEMPTATIONS— THE COURSE TO BE PURSUED RESPECTING THEM.

As soon as we fall into a fault, or have wandered, we must turn again within ourselves; because this fault having turned us from God, we should as soon as possible turn towards Him, and suffer the penitence which He Himself will give.

It is of great importance that we should not be anxious about these faults, because the anxiety only springs from a secret pride and a love of our own excellence. We are troubled at feeling what we are.

If we become discouraged, we shall grow weaker yet; and reflection upon our faults produces a vexation which is worse than the sin itself.

A truly humble soul does not marvel at its weakness, and the more it perceives its wretchedness, the more it abandons itself to God, and seeks to remain near to Him, knowing how deeply it needs His help. God's own word to us is, "I will instruct thee, and teach thee in the way which thou shalt go: I will guide thee with mine eye" (Ps. xxxii. 8).

In distractions or temptations, instead of combating them directly, which would only serve to augment them, and to wean us from God, with whom alone we ought to be occupied, we should simply turn away from them, and draw nearer to God; as a little child, seeing a fierce animal approaching it, would not stay to fight it, nor even to look at it, but would run for shelter to its mother's arms, where it would be safe. "God is in the midst of her, she shall not be moved: God shall help her, and that right early" (Ps. xlvi. 5).

If we adopt any other course of action, if we attempt to attack our enemies in our weakness, we shall be wounded, even if we are not entirely defeated; but remaining in the simple presence of God, we find ourselves immediately fortified.

This was what David did: he says, "I have set the Lord always before me; because He is at my right hand, I shall not be moved. Therefore my heart is glad, and my glory rejoiceth; my flesh also shall rest in hope." It is also said by Moses, "The Lord shall fight for you, and ye shall hold your peace" (Exod. xiv. 14).

CHAPTER XV.

PRAYER AND SACRIFICE EXPLAINED BY THE SIMILITUDE OF A PERFUME—OUR
ANNIHILATION IN THIS SACRIFICE—SOLIDITY AND FRUITFULNESS OF THIS PRAYER
AS SET FORTH IN THE GOSPEL.

Prayer ought to be both petition and sacrifice.

Prayer, according to the testimony of St John, is an incense, whose perfume rises to God. Therefore it is said in the Revelation (chap. viii. 3), that an angel held a censer, which contained the incense of the prayers of saints.

Prayer is an outpouring of the heart in the presence of God. "I have poured out my soul before the Lord," said the mother of Samuel (1 Sam. i. 15). Thus the prayers of the Magi at the feet of the infant Jesus in the stable of Bethlehem were signified by the incense which they offered.

Prayer is the heat of love, which melts and dissolves the soul, and carries it to God. In proportion as it melts, it gives out its odour, and this odour comes from the love which burns it.

This is what the Bride meant when she said, "While the King sitteth at His table, my spikenard sendeth forth the smell thereof" (Cant. i. 12). The table is the heart. When God is there, and we are kept near to Him, in His presence, this presence of God melts and dissolves the hardness of our hearts, and as they melt, they give forth their perfume. Therefore the Bridegroom, seeing His Bride thus melted by the speech of her Beloved, says, "Who is this that cometh out of the wilderness, perfumed with myrrh and frankincense?" (Cant. iii. 6).

Thus the soul rises up towards its God. But in order to this, it must suffer itself to be destroyed and annihilated by the force of love. This is a state of *sacrifice* essential to the Christian religion, by which the soul suffers itself to be destroyed and annihilated to render homage to the sovereignty of God; as it is written, "The power of the Lord is great, and He is honoured of the lowly" (Ecclus. iii. 20). And the destruction of our own being confesses the sovereign being of God.

We must cease to be, so that the Spirit of the Word may be in us. In order that He may come to us, we must yield our life to Him, and die to self that He may live in us, and that we being dead, our life may be hidden with Christ in God (Col. iii. 3).

"Come unto me," says God, "all ye that be desirous of me, and fill yourselves with my fruits" (Ecclus. xxiv. 19). But how can we be filled with God? Only by being emptied of self, and going out of ourselves in order to be lost in Him.

Now, this can never be brought about except by our becoming nothing. Nothingness is true prayer, which renders to God "honour, and glory, and power, for ever and ever" (Rev. v. 13).

This prayer is the prayer of truth. It is worshipping the Father in spirit and in truth. In *spirit*, because we are by it drawn out of our human and carnal action, to enter into the purity of the Spirit, who prays in us; and in *truth*, because the soul is led into the truth of the ALL of God, and the NOTHING of the creature.

There are but these two truths, the ALL and the NOTHING. All the rest is untruth.

We can only honour the ALL of God by our NOTHINGNESS; and we have no sooner become nothing, than God, who will not suffer us to be empty, fills us with Himself. Oh, if all knew the blessings which come to the soul by this prayer, they would be satisfied with no others: it is the pearl of great price; it is the hidden treasure. He who finds it gladly sells all that he has to buy it (Matt. xiii. 44, 46). It is the well of living water, which springs up into everlasting life (John iv. 14). It is the practice of the pure maxims of the gospel.

Does not Christ Himself tell us that the kingdom of God is within us? (Luke xvii. 21). This kingdom is set up in two ways. The first is, when God is so thoroughly master of us that nothing resists Him: then our heart is truly His kingdom. The other way is, that by possessing God, who is the sovereign Lord, we possess the kingdom of God, which is the height of felicity, and the end for which we were created. As it has been said, *to serve God is to reign.*

The end for which we were created is to enjoy God in this life, and men do not believe it!

CHAPTER XVI.

THIS STATE OF PRAYER NOT ONE OF IDLENESS, BUT OF NOBLE ACTION, WROUGHT BY THE SPIRIT OF GOD, AND IN DEPENDENCE UPON HIM—THE COMMUNICATION OF HIS LIFE AND UNION.

Some people, hearing of the prayer of silence, have wrongly imagined that the soul remains *inactive*, *lifeless*, and *without movement.*

But the truth is, that its action is more noble and more extensive than it ever was before it entered this degree, since it is moved by God Himself, and acted upon by His Spirit. St Paul desires that we should be *led by the Spirit of God* (Rom. viii. 14). I do not say that there must be no action, but that we must act in dependence upon the divine movement. This is admirably set forth by Ezekiel. The prophet saw wheels which had the spirit of life, and wherever this spirit was to go, they went; they went on, or stood, or were lifted up, as they were moved, for the spirit of life was in them: but they never went back (see Ezek. i. 19–21). It should be the same with the soul: it should suffer itself to be moved and guided by the living Spirit who is in it, following His direction, and no other. Now this Spirit will never lead it to go backwards, that is, to reflect upon the creature, or to lean upon itself, but always to go forward, pressing continually towards the mark.

This action of the soul is a restful action. When it acts of itself, it acts with effort; and is therefore more conscious of its action. But when it acts in dependence upon the Spirit of grace, its action is so free, so easy, so natural, that it does not seem to act at all. "He brought me forth also into a large place; He delivered me, because He delighted in me" (Ps. xviii. 19).

As soon as the soul has commenced its course towards its centre,[3] from that moment its action becomes vigorous—that is, its course towards the centre which attracts it, which infinitely surpasses the velocity of any other movement.

It is action then, but an action so *noble*, so *peaceful*, so *tranquil*, that it seems to the soul as though it were not acting at all; because it rests, as it were, naturally. When a wheel is only turning with a moderate speed, it can easily be distinguished; but when it goes quickly, no part of it can be distinctly seen. So the soul which remains at rest in God has an action infinitely noble and exalted, yet very peaceful. The greater its peace, the greater is its velocity, because it is abandoned to the Spirit, who moves it and makes it act. This

---

[3] See Chapter IX.

Spirit is God Himself, who draws us, and in drawing makes us run to Him, as the Bride well knew when she said, "Draw me, we will run" (Cant. i. 4). Draw me, O my Divine Centre, by my inmost heart: my powers and my sensibilities will run at Thy attraction! This attraction alone is a balm which heals me, and a perfume which draws. "We will run," she says, "because of the savour of Thy good ointments." This attracting virtue is *very strong* but the soul follows it *very gladly*; and as it is equally strong and sweet, it attracts by its strength and delights by its sweetness.

The Bride says, "Draw me, we will run." She speaks of herself, and to herself: "Draw *me*;" there is the unity of the object which is attracted: "*We* will run;" there is the correspondence of all the powers and sensibilities which follow in the train of the centre of the heart.

It is not then a question of remaining in idleness, but of acting *in dependence upon the Spirit of God*, who animates us, since it is in Him that "we live, and move, and have our being" (Acts xvii. 23). This calm dependence upon the Spirit of God is absolutely necessary, and causes the soul in a short time to attain the simplicity and unity in which it was created. It was created one and simple, like God. In order, then, to answer the end of our creation, we must quit the multiplicity of our own actions, to enter into the simplicity and unity of God, in whose image we were created (Gen. i. 27). The Spirit of God is "one only," "yet manifold" (Wisdom of Solomon vii. 22), and its unity does not prevent its multiplicity. We enter into God's unity when we are united to His Spirit, because then we have the same Spirit that He has; and we are multiplied outwardly, as regards His dispositions, without leaving the unity.

So that, as God acts infinitely, and we are of one spirit with Him, we act much more than we could do by our own action. We must suffer ourselves to be guided by Wisdom. This "Wisdom" is more moving than any motion (Wisdom of Solomon vii. 24). Let us, then, remain in dependence upon His action, and our action will be vigorous indeed.

"All things were made by (the Word); and without Him was not anything made that was made" (John i. 3). God, in creating us, created us in His image, after His likeness (Gen. i. 26). He gave to us the Spirit of the Word by the breath of life (Gen. ii. 7), which He breathed into us when we were created in the image of God, by the participation of the life of the Word, who is the image of His Father. Now this life is one, simple, pure, intimate, and fruitful.

The devil having disfigured this beautiful image, it became necessary that this same Word, whose breath had been breathed into us at our creation, should come to restore it. It was necessary that it should be He, because He is the image of the Father; and a defaced image cannot be repaired by its own action, but by the action of him who seeks to restore it. Our *action* then should be, to *put ourselves* into a position to suffer the action of God, and to allow the Word to retrace His image in us. An image, if it could move, would by its movement prevent the sculptor's perfecting it. Every movement of our own hinders the work of the Heavenly Sculptor, and produces false features.

We must then remain silent, and only move as He moves us. Jesus Christ has *life in Himself* (John v. 26), and He must communicate life to all who live.

That this action is the most noble cannot be denied. Things are only of value as the principle in which they originate is noble, grand, and elevated. Actions committed by a divine principle are *divine actions*; whereas the actions of the creature, however good they may appear, are *human actions* or at best they are virtuous actions, if they are done with the help of grace.

Jesus says that He has life in Himself; all other beings have but a borrowed life, but the Word has life in Himself; and as He is communicative, He desires to communicate this life to men. We must then give place to this life, that it may flow in us, which can only be done by evacuation, and the loss of the life of Adam and of our own action, as St Paul assures us: "If any man be in Christ, he is a new creature: old things are passed away; behold all things are become new" (2 Cor. v. 17). This can only be brought about by the death of ourselves and of our own action, that the action of God may be substituted for it. We do not profess, then, to be without action, but only to act in dependence upon the Spirit of God, suffering His action to take the place of our own. Jesus shows us this in the gospel. Martha did good things, but because she did them of her own spirit, Christ reproved her for them. The spirit of man is turbulent and boisterous; therefore it does little, though it appears to do much. "Martha, Martha," said Jesus, "thou art careful and troubled about many things; but one thing is needful; and Mary hath chosen that good part, which shall not be taken away from her" (Luke x. 41, 42).

What had she chosen, this Magdalene? Peace, tranquillity, and repose. She apparently ceased to act, that she might be moved by the Spirit of God; she ceased to live, that Christ might live in her.

This is why it is so necessary to renounce ourselves and all our own works to follow Jesus; for we cannot follow Him unless we are animated with His Spirit. In order that the Spirit of Christ may dwell in us, our own spirit must give place to Him. "He that is joined to the Lord," says St Paul, "is one spirit" (1 Cor. vi. 17). "It is good for me to draw near to God: I have put my trust in the Lord God" (Ps. lxxiii. 28). What is this "drawing near"? It is the beginning of union.

Union has its beginning, its continuation, its completion, and its consummation. The commencement of union is an inclination towards God. When the soul is converted in the manner I have described, it has an inclination to its centre, and a strong tendency to union: this tendency is the commencement. Then it adheres, which happens when it approaches nearer to God; then it is united to Him, and finally becomes one with Him—that is, it becomes one spirit with Him; and it is then that this spirit, which proceeded from God, returns to Him as its end.

It is, then, necessary that we should enter this way, which is the divine motion, and the Spirit of Jesus Christ. St Paul says, "If any man have not the Spirit of Christ, he is none of His" (Rom. viii. 9). To be Christ's, then, we must suffer ourselves to be filled with His Spirit, and emptied of our own: our hearts must be evacuated. St Paul, in the same place, proves to us the necessity of this divine motion: he says, "As many as are led by the Spirit of God, they are the sons of God" (Rom. viii. 14).

The divinely-imparted Spirit is the Spirit of divine sonship; therefore, the same apostle continues, "Ye have not received the spirit of bondage again to fear; but ye have received the spirit of adoption, whereby we cry, Abba, Father" (Rom. viii. 15). This spirit is no other than the Spirit of Christ, by whom we participate in His Sonship; and this "Spirit itself beareth witness with our spirit that we are the sons of God."

As soon as the soul leaves itself to be moved by the Spirit of God, it experiences the witness of this divine sonship; and this witness serves the more to increase its joy, as it makes it know *that it is called to the liberty of the sons of God*, and that the spirit it has received is not a spirit of bondage, but of liberty.

The Spirit of the divine motion is so necessary for all things, that Paul founds this necessity upon our ignorance of the things that we ask for. "The Spirit," he says, "helpeth our infirmities; for we know not what we should pray for as we ought; but the Spirit itself maketh intercession for us, with groanings which cannot be uttered." This is conclusive: if we do not know what to pray for, nor how to ask as we ought for what is necessary for us, and if it is needful that the Spirit who is in us, to whose motion we abandon ourselves, should ask it for us, ought we not to leave Him to do it? He does it "with groanings which cannot be uttered."

This Spirit is the Spirit of the Word, who is always heard, as He says Himself: "I know that Thou hearest me always" (John xi. 42). If we leave it to the Spirit within us to ask and to pray, we shall always be answered. Why so? O great apostle, mystic teacher, so deeply taught in the inner life! teach us why. "It is," he adds, "because He that searcheth the hearts knoweth what is the mind of the Spirit, because He maketh intercession for the saints according to the will of God;" that is to say, this Spirit only asks that which it is God's will to give. It is God's will that we should be saved and that we should be perfect. He asks, then, for all that is necessary to our perfection. Why, after this, should we be burdened with superfluous cares, and be wearied in the greatness of our way, without ever saying, There is no hope in ourselves, and therefore resting in God? God Himself invites us to cast all our care upon Him, and He complains, in inconceivable goodness, that we employ our strength, our riches, and our treasure, in countless exterior things, although there is so little joy to be found in them all. "Wherefore do ye spend money for that which is not bread, and your labour for that which satisfieth not? Hearken diligently unto me, and eat ye that which is good, and let your soul delight itself in fatness" (Isa. lv. 2).

Oh, if it were known what happiness there is in thus hearkening unto God, and how the soul is strengthened by it! All flesh must be silent before the Lord (see Zech. ii. 13). All self-effort must cease when He appears. In order still further to induce us to abandon ourselves to Him without reserve, God assures us that we need fear nothing from such abandonment, because He has a special individual care over each of us. He says, "Can a woman forget her sucking-child, that she should not have compassion on the son of her womb? Yea, she may forget, yet will I not forget thee" (Isa. xlix. 15). Ah, words full of consolation! Who on hearing them can fear to abandon himself utterly to the guidance of God?

CHAPTER XVII.

DISTINCTION BETWEEN EXTERIOR AND INTERIOR ACTIONS—THOSE OF THE SOUL IN THIS CONDITION ARE INTERIOR, BUT HABITUAL, CONTINUED, DIRECT, PROFOUND, SIMPLE, AND IMPERCEPTIBLE—BEING A CONTINUAL SINKING IN THE OCEAN OF DIVINITY—SIMILITUDE OF A VESSEL—HOW TO ACT IN THE ABSENCE OF SENSIBLE SUPPORTS.

The actions of men are either exterior or interior. The *exterior* are those which appear outwardly, and have a sensible object, possessing neither good nor evil qualities, excepting as they receive them from the interior principle in which they originate. It is not of these that I intend to speak, but only of interior actions, which are those actions of the soul by which it *applies itself* inwardly to some object, or *turns away* from some other.

When, being applied to God, I desire to commit an action of a different nature from those which He would prompt, I turn away from God, and I turn towards created things more or less according to the strength or weakness of my action. If, being turned towards the creature, I wish to return to God, I must commit the action of turning away from the creature, and turning towards God; and thus the more perfect is this action, the more complete will be the conversion.

Until I am perfectly converted, I need several actions to turn me towards God. Some are done all at once, others gradually; but my action ought to lead me to turn to God, employing all the strength of my soul for Him, as it is written, "Therefore even now, saith the Lord, turn ye even to me with all your heart" (Joel ii. 12). "Thou shalt return unto the Lord thy God … with all thine heart and with all thy soul" (Deut. xxx. 2). God only asks for our heart: "My son, give me thy heart, and let thine eyes observe my ways" (Prov. xxiii. 26). To give the heart to God is to have its gaze, its strength, and its vigour all centred in Him, to follow His will. We must, then, after we have applied to God, remain always turned towards Him.

But as the mind of man is weak, and the soul, being accustomed to turn towards earthly things, is easily turned away from God, it must, as soon as it perceives that it is turned towards outward things, resume its former position in God by a simple act of return to Him.

And as several repeated acts form a habit, the soul contracts a habit of conversion, and from action it passes to a habitual condition.

The soul, then, must not seek by means of any efforts or works of its own to come near to God; this is seeking to perform one action by means of others, instead of by a simple action remaining attached to God alone.

If we believe that we must commit no actions, we are mistaken, for *we are always acting*; but each one must act according to his degree.

I will endeavour to make this point clear, as, for want of understanding it, it presents a difficulty to many Christians.

There are *passing* and *distinct* actions, and *continued* actions; *direct* acts and *reflected* acts. All cannot perform the first, and all are not in a condition to perform the others. The first actions should be committed by those who are turned away from God. They ought to turn to Him by a distinct action, more or less strong according to their distance from Him.

By a *continued* action I understand that by which the soul is completely turned towards its God by a *direct* action, which it does not renew, unless it has been interrupted, but which exists. The soul being altogether turned in this way, is in love, and remains there: "And he that dwelleth in love, dwelleth in God" (1 John iv. 16). Then the soul may be said to be in a habitual act, resting even in this action. But its rest is not idle, for it has an action *always in force*, viz., *a gentle sinking in God*, in which God attracts it more and more strongly; and, following this attraction, and resting in love, it sinks more and more in this love, and has an action infinitely stronger, more vigorous, and more prompt, than that action which forms only the return. Now the soul which is in this *profound and strong action*, being turned towards its God, does not perceive this action, because it is direct, and not reflex; so that persons in this condition, not knowing how rightly to describe it, say that *they have no action*. But they are mistaken; they were never more active. It would be better to say they do not distinguish any action, than that they do not commit any.

The soul does not act of itself, I admit; but it is drawn, and it follows the attracting power. Love is the weight which sinks it, as a person who falls in the sea sinks, and would sink to infinity if the sea were infinite; and without perceiving its sinking, it would sink to the most profound depths with an incredible speed. It is, then, incorrect to say that no actions are committed. All commit actions, but all do not commit them in the same manner; and the abuse arises from the fact, that those who know that action is inevitable wish it to be *distinct* and *sensible*. But sensible action is for beginners, and the other for those more advanced. To stop with the first would be to deprive ourselves of the last; and to wish to commit the last before having passed the first would be an equal abuse.

Everything must be done in its season; each state has its commencement, its progress, and its end. There is no act which has not its beginning. At first we must work with *effort*, but afterwards we enjoy the fruit of our labour.

When a vessel is in the harbour, the sailors have a difficulty in bringing it into the open sea; but once there, they easily turn it in the direction in which they wish to navigate. So, when the soul is in sin, it needs an effort to drag it out; the cords which bind it must be loosened; then, by means of strong and vigorous action, it must be drawn within itself, little by little leaving the harbour, and being turned within, which is the place to which its voyage should be directed.

When the vessel is thus turned, in proportion as it advances in the sea, it leaves the land behind it, and the further it goes from the land, the less effort is needed to carry it along. At last it begins to sail gently, and the vessel goes on so rapidly that the oars become useless. What does the pilot do then? He is contented with spreading the sails and sitting at the helm.

Spreading the sails is simply laying ourselves before God, to be moved by His Spirit. *Sitting at the helm* is preventing our heart from leaving the right way, rowing it gently, and leading it according to the movement of the Spirit of God, who gradually takes possession of it, as the wind gradually fills the sails, and impels the vessel forward. So long as the vessel sails before the wind, the mariners rest from their labour. They voyage farther in an hour, while they rest in this manner and leave the ship to be carried along by the wind, than they would in a much longer time by their own efforts; and if they wished to row, besides the fatigue which would result from it, their labour would be useless, and would only serve to retard the vessel.

This is the conduct we should pursue in our inner life, and in acting thus we shall advance more in a short time by the Divine guidance, than we ever could do by our own efforts. If only you will try this way, you will find it the easiest possible.

When the wind is contrary, if the wind and the tempest are violent, the anchor must be thrown in the sea to stop the vessel. This *anchor* is trust in God and hope in His goodness, waiting in patience for the tempest to cease, and for a favourable wind to return, as David did: "I waited patiently for the Lord," he says, "and He inclined unto me" (Ps. xl. 1).

CHAPTER XVIII.

THE DRYNESS OF PREACHERS, AND THE VARIOUS EVILS WHICH ARISE FROM THEIR FAILING TO TEACH HEART-PRAYER—EXHORTATION TO PASTORS TO LEAD PEOPLE TOWARDS THIS FORM OF PRAYER, WITHOUT AMUSING THEM WITH STUDIED AND METHODICAL DEVOTION.

If all those who are working for the conquest of souls sought to win them *by the heart*, leading them first of all to prayer and to the inner life, they would see many and lasting conversions. But so long as they only address themselves to the outside, and instead of drawing people to Christ by occupying their hearts with Him, they only give them a thousand precepts for outward observances, they will see but little fruit, and that will not be lasting.

When once the heart is won, other defects are easily corrected. This is why God particularly asks for the *heart*. By this means alone would be prevented the drunkenness, blasphemy, lewdness, enmity, and robbery which are prevalent in the world. Jesus Christ would reign universally, and the Church everywhere would be revived.

Error only takes possession of the soul in the absence of faith and prayer. If men could be taught to *believe simply* and to *pray*, instead of disputing amongst themselves, they would be gently led to Christ.

Oh, how inestimable is the loss of those who neglect the inner life! Oh, what an account will they have to render to God who have the charge of souls, for not having discovered this hidden treasure to all those whom they serve in the ministry of the Word!

The excuse given is that there is *danger* in this way, or that ignorant people are incapable of spiritual things. The oracle of truth assures us that God has hid these things from the wise and prudent, and has revealed them to babes. And what danger can there be in walking in the only true way, which is Jesus Christ, in giving ourselves to Him, looking to Him continually, putting all our trust in His grace, and tending, with all the forces of our souls, to His pure love?

Far from the simple ones being *incapable* of this perfection, they are the most suitable for it, because they are more docile, more humble, and more innocent; and as they do not reason, they are not so attached to their own light. Having no science, they more readily suffer themselves to be guided by the Spirit of God: while others who are blind in their own sufficiency resist the divine inspiration.

God tells us, too, that it is to the *simple* He gives understanding by the entrance of His Word (Ps. cxix. 130). "The testimony of the Lord is sure, making wise the *simple*" (Ps. xix. 7). "The Lord preserveth the *simple*: I was brought low, and He helped me" (Ps. cxvi. 6).

O ye who have the oversight of souls! see that you do not prevent the little ones from going to Christ. His words to His disciples were, "Suffer little children to come unto me, and forbid them not; for of such is the kingdom of God" (Luke xviii. 16). Jesus only said this to His disciples, because they wished to keep the children away from Him. Often the remedy is applied to the body, when the disease is at the *heart*. The reason why we have so little success in seeking to reform men, is that we direct our efforts to the outside, and all that we can do there soon passes off. But if we were to give them first *the key of the interior*, the outside would be reformed at once with a natural facility.

And this is very easy. To teach them to seek God in their heart, to think of Him, to return to Him when they find they have turned away, to do all and suffer all for the sake of pleasing Him—this is to direct them to the source of all grace, and to make them find there all that is necessary for their sanctification. O you who serve souls! I conjure you to put them first of all into this way, which is Jesus Christ; and it is He who conjures you to do this by the blood He has shed for the souls He confides to your care. "Speak to the heart of Jerusalem" (Isa. xl. 2, marg.) O dispensers of His grace, preachers of His Word, ministers of sacraments! establish His kingdom; and, in order to establish it truly, make it reign over HEARTS. For as it is the heart alone which can oppose His empire, it is by the subjection of the heart that His sovereignty is most honoured. Alas! we seek to make *studied* prayers; and by wishing to arrange them too much, we render them impossible. We have alienated children from the best of Fathers, in seeking to teach them a polished language. Go, poor children, and speak to your Heavenly Father in your natural language: however uncultivated it may be, it is not so to Him. A father loves best the speech which is put in disorder by love and respect, because he sees that it comes from the heart: it is more to him than a dry harangue, vain and unfruitful though well studied. Oh, how certain glances of love charm and ravish Him! They express infinitely more than all language and reason. By wishing to teach how to love Love Himself with method, much of this love has been lost. Oh! it is not necessary to teach the art of loving. The language of love is barbarous to him who does not love; and we cannot learn to love God better than by loving Him. The Spirit of God does not need our arrangements; He takes shepherds at His pleasure to make them prophets; and, far from closing the palace of prayer to any, as it is imagined, He leaves the doors open to all, and Wisdom is ordered to cry in the public places, "Whoso is simple, let him turn in hither: as for him that wanteth understanding, she saith to him, Come, eat of my bread, and drink of the wine which I have mingled" (Prov. ix. 4, 5). Did not Christ thank His Father that He had hidden these things from the wise and prudent, and had revealed them to babes? (Matt. xi. 25.)

CHAPTER XIX.

AFTER THE PRECEDING WAYS, THERE REMAINS AN AFTER WAY, PREPARATORY TO DIVINE UNION, IN WHICH WISDOM AND JUSTICE MAKE THE PASSIVE PURIFICATION OF THE SOUL, ALL WHICH IS TREATED IN DETAIL IN THE SEPARATE TREATISE, ENTITLED "SPIRITUAL TORRENTS."

It is impossible to attain divine union by the way of meditation alone, or even by the affections, or by any luminous or understood prayer. There are several reasons. These are the principal.

First, according to Scripture, "No man shall see God and live" (Exod. xxxiii. 20). Now all discursive exercises of prayer, or even of *active contemplation*, regarded as an end, and not as a preparation for the *passive*, are exercises of life by which we cannot see God, that is, become united to Him. All that is of man, and of his own industry, however noble and elevated it may be, must die.

St John tells us that "there was silence in heaven." Heaven represents the depths and centre of the soul, where all must be in silence when the majesty of God appears. All that belongs to our own efforts, or to ourselves in any way, must be destroyed, because nothing is opposed to God but appropriation, and all the malignity of man is in this appropriation, which is the source of his evil; so that the more a soul loses its appropriation, the more it becomes pure.

Secondly, in order to unite two things so opposed as the purity of God and the impurity of the creature, the simplicity of God and the multiplicity of the creature, God must operate alone; for this can never be done by the effort of the creature, since two things cannot be united unless there is some relation or resemblance between them, as an impure metal would never unite with one that was pure and refined.

What does God do then? He sends before Him His own Wisdom, as fire will be sent upon the earth to consume by its activity all the impurity that is there. Fire consumes all things, and nothing resists its activity. It is the same with Wisdom; it consumes all impurity in the creature, to prepare him for divine union.

This impurity, so opposed to union, is appropriation and activity. *Appropriation*, because it is the source of the real impurity which can never be united to essential purity; as the sun's rays may touch the mud but cannot unite with it. *Activity*, because God being in an infinite repose, in order that the soul may be united to Him, it must participate in His repose, without which there can be no union, because of the dissemblance; and to unite two things, they must be in a proportionate rest.

It is for this reason that the soul can only attain divine union by the rest of its will; and it can only be united to God when it is in a *central rest* and in the purity of its creation.

To purify the soul God makes use of wisdom as fire is used for the purification of gold. It is certain that gold can only be purified by fire, which gradually consumes all that is earthly and foreign, and separates it from the gold. It is not sufficient that the earth should be changed into gold; it is necessary that the fire should melt and dissolve it, to remove from it all that is earthly; and this gold is put in the fire so many times that it loses its impurity, and all necessity of purification. Then it is fit to be employed in the most excellent workmanship.

And if this gold is impure in the end, it is because it has contracted fresh defilement by coming in contact with other bodies. But this impurity is only superficial, and does not prevent its being used; whereas its former impurity was hidden within it, and, as it were, identified with its nature.

In addition to this, you will remark that gold of an inferior degree of purity cannot mix with that of a superior purity. The one must contract the impurity of the other, or else impart its own purity to it. Put a refined gold with an unrefined one, what can the goldsmith ever do with it? He will have all the impurity taken from the second piece, that it may be able to mix with the first. This is what St Paul tells us, that "the fire shall try every man's work of what sort it is;" he adds, that if any man's work should be found to deserve burning, he should be saved "so as by fire" (1 Cor. iii. 13, 15). That means, that though there are some works which are good, and which God receives, yet, so that he who has done them may be pure, they too must pass through the fire, in order that all appropriation, that is, all that was his own, may be taken from them. God will judge our righteousness, because "by the deeds of the law there shall no flesh be justified," but by "the righteousness of God, which is by faith" (Rom. iii. 20, 22).

This being understood, I say that, in order that man may be united to his God, wisdom and divine justice, like a pitiless and devouring fire, must take from him all appropriation, all that is terrestrial, carnal, and of his own activity; and having taken all this from him, they must unite him to God.

This is never brought about by the labours of the creature; on the contrary, it even causes him regret, because, as I have said, man so loves what is his own, and is so fearful of its destruction, that if God did not accomplish it Himself, and by His own authority, man would never consent to it.

It will be objected to this, that God never deprives man of his liberty, and that therefore he can always resist God; for which reason I ought not to say that *God acts absolutely, without the consent of man.* In explanation I say, that it is sufficient that man should give a *passive consent,* that he may have entire and full liberty; because having at the beginning given himself to God, that He may do as He will both with him and in him, he gave from that time an *active* and general assent to all that God might do. But when God destroys, burns, and purifies, the soul does not see that all this is for its advantage; it rather believes the contrary: and as at first the fire seems to tarnish the gold, so this operation seems to despoil the soul of its purity. So that if an *active* and *explicit* consent were required, the soul would find a difficulty in giving it, and often would not give it. All that it does is to remain in a passive contentment, enduring this operation as well as it can, being neither able nor willing to prevent it.

God then so purifies this soul of all natural, distinct, and perceived operations, that at last He makes it more and more *conformed* to Himself, and then *uniform*, raising the passive capacity of the creature, enlarging it and ennobling it, though in a hidden and unperceived manner, which is termed mystical. But in all these operations the soul must concur passively, and in proportion as the working of God becomes stronger, the soul must continually yield to Him, until He absorbs it altogether. We do not say, then, as some assert, that there must be no *action*; since, on the contrary, this is *the door*; but only that *we must not remain in it*, seeing that man should tend towards the perfection of his end, and that he can never reach it without quitting the first means, which, though they were necessary to introduce him into the way, would greatly hinder him afterwards, if he attached himself obstinately to them. This is what Paul said, "I forget those things which are behind, and reach forth unto those things which are before; I press toward the mark" (Phil. iii. 13, 14).

Should we not consider a person destitute of reason who, after undertaking a journey, stopped at the first inn, because he was assured that several had passed it, that a few had lodged there, and that the landlord lived there? What the soul is required to do, then, is *to advance towards its end*, to take the shortest road, not to stop at the first point, and, following the advice of St Paul, to suffer itself to be "led by the Spirit of God" (Rom. viii. 14), who will lead it to the end for which it was created, which is the enjoyment of God.

It is well known that the sovereign good is God; that essential blessedness consists in union with God, and that this union cannot be the result of our own efforts, since God only communicates Himself to the soul according to its capacity. We cannot be united to God without passivity and simplicity; and this union being bliss, the way which leads to it must be the best, and there can be no risk in walking in it.

This way is not *dangerous*. If it were, Christ would not have represented it as the most perfect and necessary of all ways. All can walk in it; and as all are called to blessedness, all are called to the enjoyment of God, both in this life and in that which is to come, since the enjoyment of God is blessedness. I say the enjoyment of God Himself, not of His gifts, which can never impart essential blessedness, not being able fully to satisfy the soul, which is so constituted that even the richest gifts of God cannot thoroughly content it. The desire of God is to give Himself to us, according to the capacity with which He has endowed us; and yet we fear to leave ourselves to God! We fear to possess Him, and to be prepared for divine union!

You say, *we must not bring ourselves to this condition.* I agree to that; but I say too, that no one ever could bring himself to it, since no man could ever unite himself to God by his own efforts, and God Himself must do the work.

You say that some pretend to have attained it. I say that this state cannot be feigned, any more than a man dying of hunger can for any length of time pretend to be satisfied. It will soon be known whether or no men have attained this end.

Since, then, none can arrive at the end unless he be brought there, it is not a question of introducing people to it, but of showing them the way which leads to it, and begging them not to rest in those practices which must be relinquished at God's command.

Would it not be cruelty to show a fountain to a thirsty man, and then hold him bound, and prevent his going to it, leaving him to die of thirst? That is what is being done now. Let us all be agreed both as to the way and the end. The way has its commencement, its progress, and its terminus. The more we advance towards the terminus, the farther we go from the commencement; and it is impossible to reach the terminus but by constantly going farther from the starting-point, being unable to go from one place to another without passing through all that comes between them: this is incontestable.

Oh, how blind are the majority of men, who pride themselves upon their learning and talent!

O Lord! how true it is that Thou hast hidden Thy secrets from the wise and prudent, and hast revealed them unto babes!

Prayer Availeth Much

~ ※ ~

Daniel's Prayer by Sir Edward John Poynter

By *T. M. Anderson*

The 1896 Edition

". . . The effectual fervent prayer of a righteous man availeth much."
— James 5:16

~ ※ ~

THE FOREWORD

The brief messages on prayer contained in this little book have been written for the purpose of stimulating a greater interest in the importance of praying without ceasing.

I am convinced that the people of God have not explored the boundless possibilities of prayer.

We evidently believe that the effectual fervent prayer of a righteous man availeth much, but we are often aware of the fact that very little has been accomplished by our own prayers.

It has not been possible to present a complete study of the subject of prayer revealed in the Holy Scriptures. For one to undertake such a task would be like an attempt to measure eternity by a span.

It is my sincere desire to encourage God's people to pray without ceasing. When once they understand the fundamental principles of prayer, they will not find it difficult to accomplish some amazing results through effectual fervent intercession.

Your Servant in Christ Jesus,

— *T. M. ANDERSON*

CHAPTER 1: THE FELLOWSHIP OF PRAYER

"Be careful for nothing; but in every thing by prayer and supplication with thanksgiving let your requests be made known unto God." — Phil. 4:6

This timely exhortation stresses the fact that God's people should consult with Him in every matter pertaining to life. Unless they see the imperative necessity of prayer, and give it an important place in daily life, they cannot expect to be maintained by the ample resources of a generous Saviour. It is apparent that we cannot obtain the things essential to life unless we make everything pertaining to life a matter of earnest prayer. It is impossible to live a consistent Christian life in the sight of God by praying occasionally. Praying intermittently is certainly not praying incessantly and importunately. Such careless praying is not consistent with the exhortation to pray without ceasing.

Persons praying spasmodically are like men that gorge themselves with food and drink on special occasions and starve themselves between the feasts. We do not live from feast to famine when we enter into a partnership with Christ in prayer. We are not disturbed by doubts and defeats when we make everything a matter of earnest prayer. We enjoy an unbroken fellowship with Christ when we make our requests known unto Him in daily prayer. He imparts to us the necessary strength to cope with the temptations and trials incident to life in this benighted world when everything relating to life is made known unto Him in prayer. When the inspired Apostle said, ". . . Let your requests be made known unto God," he was obviously emphasizing the importance of revealing to the Lord everything required to sustain us in life. We find it necessary to reveal both our spiritual and our temporal needs unto Him in prayer.

Nothing pertaining to our life in this world is unimportant in the sight of God. He is interested in everything that concerns us in life.

The Lord would have us understand that we obtain rest of soul when we enter into the fellowship of prayer with Him. When Paul said, "Be careful for nothing . . . ," he revealed the true rest of soul to be found in the covenant of prayer. He is urging us to lay aside our troublesome cares and anxieties lest they hinder us in making our requests known unto the Lord. Paul was saying in substance, "Be not anxiously solicitous; do not give place to trouble, no matter what occurs; for anxiety cannot change the condition of things from bad to good, but will certainly injure your soul if you give place to it." It is certainly true that we must cast our burdens and earthly concerns upon the Lord before we can make our requests known unto Him by prayer and supplication with thanksgiving.

Perhaps my personal testimony will enable others to perceive the value of entering into the fellowship of prayer with Christ, for I found true rest of soul and quietness of heart when I entered into the partnership of prayer with Him. "Ask, and ye shall receive, that your joy may be full."

I was teaching in the department of religious education in Asbury College when I entered into the covenant of prayer with Christ. It had been my purpose for several months to prepare some written messages on the Epistle to the Hebrews. In order to have time to devote to this work it was necessary for me to arise early in the morning and do the writing before the hour I was scheduled to meet my classes. I began this work during the first week of 1950.

I was suddenly awakened about midnight on January sixth. Knowing that I had a full day of work before me, I felt it necessary to sleep a few hours lest I be too weary in mind and body to do the writing and teaching. At that moment the Saviour spoke to me. He asked me if I were willing to sacrifice some sleep in order to give Him an opportunity to speak with me in the quiet hours of the morning. He told me that it was necessary to deny myself of sleep in order to prevail in prayer. I realized for the first time that denying myself of sleep was a form of fasting. For five hours I waited before the Lord in sacred worship and holy communion. My soul was greatly revived, and I felt refreshed in mind and rested in body.

After this remarkable manifestation of the Saviour I was constrained to examine my prayer life. I was impressed to consider the time spent in prayer during the average day. I was humbled before the Lord when I discovered how little time had been given to Him in prayer and meditation. It had been my daily practice from the day I was saved to spend some time in prayer morning and evening. I had established the family altar in my home. I had spent time in secret prayer during the years of my ministry. I had never knowingly overlooked the importance of prayer. I am now aware that I had never discovered the possibilities in prayer like they were revealed to me when I waited five delightful hours before the Saviour that memorable morning.

When I entered into the fellowship of prayer with Christ, I solemnly promised Him that I would not allow my plans and pursuits of daily life to infringe on my time to pray. I vowed to take sufficient time to commune with Him in prayer no matter what duties of the day demanded my attention. When I made this covenant with Christ I emptied myself of earthly possessions and concerns. I placed my ministry, my teaching, my writings, my vocation, my travels, and my home in a heap before the Lord. I separated myself from these interests as completely as I ever expect to be separated from them in death. I deliberately put these earthly concerns in a place of secondary importance in my life. I counted all things loss for the excellency of the knowledge of the fellowship with Christ in prayer. I fully realized that Christ was speaking to me when He said, "If any man will come after me, let him deny himself, and take up his cross, and follow me. For whosoever will save his life shall lose it: and whosoever will lose his life for my sake shall find it." I was reminded of how much I had lost through the years because I had not known the value of fellowship with Christ in prayer.

When I entered the fellowship of prayer with the Lord my soul was immediately relieved of the burdens and cares of life. I found the place of His rest in the covenant of prayer. My duties are many, and my body is often weary from my labors in the ministry, but my spirit knows no weariness for my soul dwells at ease in the haven of perfect peace. There were times in the past when the responsibilities of the ministry were almost more than my mind and body could endure. The many concerns of preaching made me restless in the night and disturbed during the day. It is clear to me now that I had not discovered the secret of resting in the Lord. I was pushing and pulling in my own strength. I was not trusting the Spirit to bring things to pass.

I have the same burdens and cares of the ministry today, but I have discovered how to cast my cares upon the Lord in the fellowship of prayer. The yoke of the Meek and Lowly Christ is easy, and His burden is light. He has given me rest of soul and quietness of spirit in the covenant of daily prayer. It is now my daily practice to keep the morning watch with the Saviour.

> *"My voice shalt thou hear in the morning, O Lord; in the morning will I direct my prayer unto thee, and look up." — Psa. 5:3*

The hours between midnight and six o'clock in the morning are the most peaceful. The duties and distractions of the preceding day have ended, and the activities of the new day have not begun.

It is apparent that Jesus made it a practice of His life to pray in the quiet hours of the morning. It is written,

> *"In the morning, rising up a great while before day, he went out, and departed into a solitary place, and there prayed." — Mark 1:35*

The duties of the coming day demanded much from the Saviour. The virtue that went out of Him to heal the hearts and hurts of the people was replenished in the place of prayer. His physical strength was constantly renewed through His ceaseless prayers. Before the dawn of the busy day our Lord went out, and departed into a solitary place, and there prayed. We are not told where He found this peaceful place to pray. He may have found a place of sacred seclusion to pray beneath the overshadowing boughs of a towering tree where nature remained speechless with reverence and the morning star looked down in solemn contemplation. The Lord may have longed to pour out His sinless soul with strong crying and tears in some voiceless valley filled with holy hush. It could be that He sought a solitary place among the friendly hills where the silent shadows of the departing night lingered until hastened into hiding by the light of the approaching dawn. Perhaps He found rest for His burdened heart in a sequestered place in a lonely desert carpeted with shifting sands where the sighing winds ceased to whisper while He prayed.

The example of our Lord enables us to perceive the value of unburdening our hearts in the quiet hours of the morning. It is difficult to pray when the mind is filled with the confusion and rush of the day. We can pray in the quietness of the home while the day is young if we are willing to sacrifice some sleep. The Saviour admonished us to enter into the closet and shut the door. We must shut the door of our mind and exclude the cares and burdens of the day in order to prevail with God in the secret place of prayer.

One will be astonished at the results obtained in the quiet place of prayer. I have seen the Lord work wonders in answer to prayer offered before Him in the early hours of the morning. I have known Him to heal people in homes and hospitals hundreds of miles from the place where I was praying.

CHAPTER 2: OUR REQUESTS MADE KNOWN UNTO GOD

". . . Let your requests be made known unto God." — Phil. 4:6

Paul, the pattern saint, would have us see the value of revealing our needs to God in prayer. We must not presume that the things required to sustain life will be granted without making our requests known unto God. Our requirements on earth and God's resources in heaven are meant for each other. If we ask, we shall receive. When we fail to ask, we fail to receive. The Word declares, "Ye have not, because ye ask not." There would be no point in exhorting Christians to make their requests known unto God unless He had made a sufficient provision to supply all their need. The apostle revealed the abundant riches of God when he said . . .

"My God shall supply all your need according to his riches in glory by Christ Jesus." — Phil. 4:19

This assuring promise discloses the resources God made available to His people in answer to prayer. In the clear light of this certified promise they have no justifiable excuse for spiritual poverty.

We can think of God's promise to be a certified check made payable to us the moment we present it for payment. No matter what gracious spiritual and temporal blessings the promise contains, we cannot receive them until we make our requests known unto God in prayer. It is possible to have an all sufficiency in all things by claiming the riches of God made available to us by prayer and supplication with thanksgiving. When Paul said, "My God shall supply all your need," he is saying, "Christ is all you need." We are enriched in all things pertaining to life in time and in eternity when we possess Him. Christ is all we ever need to cope with the difficulties and dangers confronting us in the path leading to the Father's house of many mansions.

The temporal blessings received from the Lord are not sufficient to supply all our need in this world. Jesus stated this fact when He said,

". . . A man's life consisteth not in the abundance of the things which he possesseth." — Luke 12:14

The fertile fields cannot produce true riches. A man is truly rich toward God when he possesses the resources of Christ contained in His certified promise to supply all our need. When Paul said, "My God . . ." he disclosed the amazing fact that a man can possess God. It is written in the covenant of grace,

". . . I will be their God, and they shall be my people." — 2 Cor. 6:16

The paramount purpose of Christ is achieved the moment He gives Himself to us in the covenant of God. The Scriptures reveal that the Saviour has given everything to redeem us, and provided everything to supply us, and wills to give all that He is in His divine nature to satisfy us. If a man has not received the indwelling Christ in answer to prayer, he has failed to obtain the grand objective of all praying.

We do not find it difficult to make our requests known unto God when we are fully aware of His presence. Paul stated this fact when he said,

". . . The Lord is at hand." — Phil. 4:5

This amazing revelation is evidently an essential part of the admonition to make our requests known unto God. The inspired apostle focused attention on a great truth when he said, ". . . The Lord is at hand." He is saying in substance, "The Lord is handy. The Lord stands ready to give aid and comfort to His praying people." No matter how we interpret the statement, ". . . The Lord is at hand," we are fully aware of His nearness when we make our requests known unto Him. Jesus confirmed this truth when He said, "Lo, I am with you always, even unto the end of the world." He evidently knew that we had the mental and moral capacity to sense His presence at all times and in all places on earth. If we cannot know that He is at hand when we pray, then His promise has no place of value in our profession of faith.

To offer a prayer without realizing the nearness of the Lord would be like speaking meaningless words into empty space. How could we know that our requests had been made known unto God unless He responded by assuring us that our petitions had been heard? I am persuaded that it is not possible to pray with confidence toward the Lord without being aware of His presence. The inspired apostle said,

". . . This is the confidence that we have in him, that, if we ask any thing according to his will, he heareth us: and if we know that he hear us, whatsoever we ask, we know that we have the petitions that we desired of Him." — 1 John 5:14, 15

John is saying in substance, "If you know that God hears you, then you know you have the answer." It is apparent that we must first know that He hears us before we know that we have the answer. Knowing that God hears us when we pray is something vastly more than a beautiful theory about prayer. Spiritual perception in prayer is the norm of spiritual life. We rejoice in prayer when we perceive that the Lord is at hand. Paul said, "Rejoice in the Lord always: and again I say, rejoice." The realization that the Lord is near is the cause of constant praise.

If His abiding presence with us in this troubled world is not the only source of lasting joys, then let us hope that someone will come to guide our footsteps toward the place of endless happiness. God's Word reveals that the Lord will direct our weary feet into the path of praise.

"Thou wilt show me the path of life: in thy presence is fullness of joy; at thy right hand are pleasures for evermore." — Psa. 16:11

It is apparently true that the measure of our joy is always in proportion to the measure of our praying. One must pray without ceasing in order to have joy unspeakable and full of glory. God's praying people discover that the joy of the Lord is their strength, and His abiding presence is their shield. Perhaps Paul was in prison when he uttered the immortal words of praise. The dark and dingy prison was not so carefully guarded, and its rigid bars so firmly fixed that the Lord was prevented from entering its dismal confines to give comfort and courage to His suffering servant.

If Paul had been asked what he had found in the dank cell to cause him to sound such a note of praise, he would have said, ". . . The Lord is at hand." His consoling nearness caused the prisoner to praise, and His assuring presence inspired the suffering saint to sing. The dreary confines of a prison cannot stifle the songs of the soul girded with the gladness of God. The righteous may be incarcerated in dungeons, and the redeemed fastened in the stocks, but their achieving faith is not fettered, and their supplications are not shackled. From the inner cell of the common jail the singing servants of God shook the foundations of the earth, and caused hardened sinners to seek salvation.

The infirmities of the body may imprison a saint like the formidable walls of a federal prison; but the afflictions of the flesh and the trials of life cannot prevent the saints from singing in the shadows like those that sing in the shining. It is written,

> ". . . He that trusteth in the Lord, mercy shall compass him about. Be glad in the Lord, and rejoice, ye righteous: and shout for joy, all ye that are upright in heart." — Psa. 32:11

CHAPTER 3: GOD'S PEACE OBTAINED IN ANSWER TO PRAYER

> ". . . Let your requests be made known unto God. And the peace of God which passeth all understanding, shall keep your hearts and minds through Christ Jesus." — Phil. 4:6, 7

When we make our requests known unto God by prayer and supplication with thanksgiving we are assured of receiving His peace through Christ Jesus. When we enter into the sacred Presence of the Prince of Peace, we enter into the place of perfect peace. The house of prayer is the sanctuary of peace.

Paul would have us understand that Christ imparts a measure of His own peace to our worshipping hearts when we make everything pertaining to life a matter of prayer. We can readily comprehend the possibilities of prayer when we perceive that mortal man can obtain a measure of the peace which the God of Peace possesses in His divine nature. It is not necessary for the children of God to enter heaven in order to enjoy the priceless possession of peace. Christ wills to give the heavenly heritage of His Peace to all the sons of God. He revealed this truth when He said,

> "Peace I leave with you, my peace I give unto you: not as the world giveth, give I unto you. Let not your heart be troubled, neither let it be afraid." — John 14: 27

It is obviously true that Jesus has purposed that His own peace shall give His praying and believing people untroubled hearts in this world of trouble. He would have us understand that His own perfect peace shall confirm us in hope, and comfort us in heart. It is apparent that this heavenly heritage of the heart can be obtained in answer to prayer. God's peace is an essential quality of His divine nature. We saw His peace manifested in Jesus Christ, The Prince of Peace. Jesus was never excited and perturbed by the trickery and hypocrisy of the religious leaders of His day. He never lost His spiritual poise when persecuted and slandered by His enemies.

Jesus was always calm and composed in the time of trial. He was never intimidated by the threats of violence. He had an indomitable courage that confounded His critics. He never compromised truth to gain favor with men. His sublime silence in the hour of His trial caused the multitude to marvel. A faithful witness of the Saviour's sufferings said:

> *". . . Christ also suffered for us, leaving us an example, that we should follow in his steps: who did no sin, neither was guile found in his mouth: who, when he was reviled, reviled not again; when he suffered, he threatened not; but committed himself to him that judgeth righteously." — 1 Peter 2:21-23*

Peter's testimony enables us to see how the peace of God behaves in this world of turmoil and strife. The quality of God's peace was exemplified in the sinless character and conduct of the Saviour. His life revealed the inherent nature of God's peace which passeth all understanding. God has designed that His peace shall keep our hearts and minds. He would have us understand that His peace shall be our guard when we make our requests known unto Him in prayer. When once we grasp the truth about this, and give it an important place in daily life, we will know what it means to possess the peace of God which passeth all understanding.

The heart is the center of man's spiritual being. It is the citadel of his immortal soul. The ambitions, the aspirations, and the affections reside in the heart. The will, the conscience, and the desires dwell in the heart of man. The Word says,

> *"Keep thy heart with all diligence; for out of it are the issues of life."*
> *— Prov. 4:23*

It is God's purpose to expel the indwelling sin of the soul by the power of the indwelling Spirit, and impart peace to man's heart.

> *". . . The work of righteousness shall be peace; and the effect of righteousness quietness and assurance for ever." — Isa. 32:17*

When Jesus said. ". . . Let not your heart be troubled, neither let it be afraid," He implied that it was possible to be delivered from the perplexing troubles and agitating fears incident to life in this world. The peace of God can banish all our burdensome bewilderments and fill our yearning hearts with comfort and contentment. God is willing to make the citadel of our souls the stronghold of His garrison of peace. He wills to make our hearts an impregnable fortress of spiritual power. His peace will mount guard over our hearts and minds like a sentinel appointed to keep watch over a city. Paul added to our comfort when he said,

> *". . . The God of peace shall be with you." — v. 9*

He is saying that we can have the peace of God within, and God of peace without.

When Paul speaks of the mind he is evidently speaking of the intellect, the feelings, and the understanding. We have the capacity to think and to reason about the things of God. We are capable of having the truth of God revealed to us by the Holy Spirit. It is not possible to comprehend the peace of God without the help of the Spirit. We cannot analyze the peace of God in the laboratory of the human mind to ascertain its true nature; neither can we discover the component parts of God's peace by the methods of modern science and philosophy. His peace passeth all human understanding. There are times when our minds are sorely perplexed by the problems confronting us in this uncertain world. There are times when we cannot depend on our reasoning to find the answer to life's trials and tribulations. Jesus said,

> ". . . In the world ye shall have tribulation: but be of good cheer; I have overcome the world." — John 16:33

Life has no fears and death holds no terrors for the soul fortified by the eternal peace of Christ. He is our peace and our protection. The peace received in answer to prayer does not prevent the problems of life from perplexing us; but His peace does prevent these trials from triumphing over us.

There will be times when our feelings will contradict our faith. Sickness can depress our emotions to such an extent that we are disposed to doubt our relationship to Christ. When we are sick, when our nerves are tense, when we are constantly on the verge of tears, our faith will be submerged by our feelings. In such times of trial it seems that the joy of the Lord has departed, and we are tempted to think that for some unknown reason we are suffering the displeasure of the Lord. Our confused state of mind is caused by our illness. The loving Lord has not been grieved by our infirmities of body and mind.

There will be times in life when we seem to stand on the brink of an impassable gulf which the human understanding cannot cross. When we come to the place where reasoning ends and despair begins, we will discover that Christ's protective peace is like a bridge that spans the gulf which our own limited understanding cannot cross. The infirmities of the body can cause the imagination to run wild. Sickness can cause many fantastic ideas and strange impressions to disturb and confuse our minds. Some unhappy people imagine they are being tormented by evil spirits. Some think their nervous disorders are caused by some strange power of Satan. These distressing nervous disorders and groundless fears are caused by their physical condition. A just and holy God will not allow His praying and trusting people to become the unwilling victims of satanic power. He has provided a peace to garrison their hearts and minds through Christ Jesus.

A few devout individuals have been tormented by the fear that they have committed the unpardonable sin. Some have been so completely engulfed by this terrifying thought that they have abandoned all hope. These misguided persons have allowed themselves to become victims of their own confused state of mind. The terrifying thought that they have forfeited all hope of salvation exists only in their overwrought imaginations. If these troubled souls will exercise faith in a merciful and faithful Christ, and humbly ask Him for help and hope, their groundless fears will immediately pass away, and the peace of God will comfort their troubled hearts.

The Saviour has paid a great price to redeem us from all iniquity. He will not withhold His saving mercy and grace from any seeking soul longing with all the heart to please Him in all things. The peace of God will prevent us from becoming the hapless prey of our distraught minds if we will pray without ceasing, and continue to believe on the name of the Son of God. When Jesus said, ". . . Let not your heart be troubled, neither let it be afraid," He intended to impress us with the fact that we can prevent the fears and troubles from entering our hearts and minds. He expects us to keep our minds stayed on Him. The inspired prophet saw this fact when he said,

"Thou wilt keep him in perfect peace, whose mind is stayed on thee; because he trusteth in thee." — Isa. 26:3

The Psalmist said,

"Cast thy burden upon the Lord, and he shall sustain thee: he shall never suffer the righteous to be moved." — Psa. 55:22

If we continue to make our requests known unto God by prayer and supplication with thanksgiving, He will not suffer us to be moved by the forces of evil in this disquieted earth.

CHAPTER 4: THE PRAYING THAT GLORIFIES GOD

"... Whatsoever ye shall ask in my name, that will I do, that the Father may be glorified in the Son." — John 14:13

Jesus revealed His purpose in answering prayer when He said, "... That the Father may be glorified in the Son." In order to achieve His exalted purpose to glorify the Father, the Son has bestowed on His redeemed people the inalienable right to ask anything in His Name. In the clear light of this remarkable truth it is not difficult to perceive that the possibilities in prayer are as great as the purpose of the Son of God. It is likewise apparent that every prayer offered in the Name of the Son must be offered for the specific purpose of obtaining the things which glorify the heavenly Father.

The Saviour was near the close of His public ministry with His disciples when He delivered His parting address preserved for us by John. In His closing address He speaks to the men whose training time has about ended. He instructed His messengers in the "Sermon on the Mount" to pray, believing and trusting the Father to give them all good gifts; but in His closing discourse He points to something higher to be accomplished through prayer and faith. These faithful men were to go and perform His works, even greater works than He had achieved during His ministry in the world. The Master disclosed to them that praying in His Name was to be the channel through which the enabling power was obtained to perform the works which glorify the Father in the Son.

When Jesus said, "... I go to my Father," He was obviously speaking of His ascension to the right hand of God. His exaltation to the right hand of the Majesty on high began a new epoch in the praying and working of the disciples. The Saviour had imparted power to His chosen disciples while with them in the world, and He now purposes to enable them to do greater things for Him. He has promised to impart the power from heaven to accomplish greater works for Him in the world. He ordained His chosen apostles to go and bring forth fruit, saying,

"Herein is my Father glorified, that ye bear much fruit; so shall ye be my disciples." — John 15:8

The indomitable courage they had to witness for Him, the miracles performed in His Name, and the sufferings endured for His sake, were living testimonies of the power received through the fervent prayers offered in His Name.

What is true regarding the Saviour's works achieved by His faithful disciples is likewise true regarding His works to be accomplished by His faithful people in this present age. The same Christ who worked in them and through them in that day, is the same changeless Christ who wills to work in and through His people in these last days. If the people of God expect to perform the works of Christ which shall glorify the Father, they must believe on Him for the very work's sake, and pray in His Name.

We can perceive our responsibilities to Christ when we consider His words regarding the greater works to be accomplished for Him in the world. Apparently the greater works to be performed are not works more excellent in quality, but works greater in quantity. Perhaps the ministry of Jesus did not extend beyond the borders of the land where He lived and died. But it is obvious that He fully intended that the whole world should feel the spiritual impact of His invincible power through the preaching and praying of His ransomed people. Therefore He filled His faithful witnesses with the Holy Ghost and power and sent them unto the uttermost part of the earth to perform the works which glorify the Father in the Son. Let us ever be mindful of the fact that power to achieve the greater works for Christ is obtained through prayer and faith. A man cannot achieve the works of Christ through his eloquence and education; he must fervently pray in the Name of Jesus, and receive power from Him in order to accomplish the works of God in this pleasure loving age.

As long as Jesus was in the world, He performed the works of the Father; devils fled at His word of command, the sick were healed, and the poor had the Gospel preached unto them. When He returned to the Father, His works from the throne of grace must be performed through His praying and trusting people. The oneness between the Lord on His mediatorial throne in heaven and His people on earth is so divinely perfect, that He meant it as the literal truth when He said, ". . . Greater works than these shall he do; because I go unto my Father."

It is for the express purpose of accomplishing the works of Jesus in this present world that such great promises regarding prayer have been given to His people. But His people are not at liberty to claim the Saviour's promise, "If ye shall ask any thing in my name, I will do it," in order to obtain something very special for themselves. His certified promise does not authorize us to make him a servant of our own comforts in life. The Master has assured us that the Father is mindful of our personal needs, and wills to give good things to His children, but our creature comforts are not the things which matter most in this life. Our chief concern should always be to obtain power through prayer to achieve the greater works for Christ.

A careful study of the Saviour's words reveal that it is His purpose to glorify the Father through the life and love and labors of His redeemed people. When once we fully comprehend this amazing truth it will not be difficult to understand the meaning of the praying that glorifies the Father in the Son. When Jesus said, ". . . He that believeth on me, the works that I do shall he do also. . . ," He revealed the obvious fact that a man has both the mental and moral capacity to perform the works of God in this world. It is apparently true that all men do not have the same natural abilities to serve God in this world. The Master disclosed this truth in His parable relating to the Kingdom of heaven.

"Unto one he gave five talents, to another two, and to another one; to every man according to his several ability . . ." — Matt. 25:15

Jesus would have us understand that each man shall be rewarded according to his faithfulness in performing his assigned task. The Master will not require more than any man is capable of doing for Him. It is impossible for any man to accomplish the works of Christ unless he first possesses the works of Christ in his own heart. We must not overlook the fact that moral character and moral conduct are so intimately related that one does not exist apart from the other. A man's character is always exemplified in his conduct. The Saviour said,

"A good man out of the good treasure of his heart bringeth forth that which is good . . ." — Luke 6:45

Jesus revealed the effective cause for achieving His works when He said,

". . . The Father that dwelleth in me, he doeth the works." — John 14:10

Paul stated this sublime truth when he said,

"For it is God which worketh in you both to will and to do of his good pleasure." — Phil. 2:13

It certainly is possible for Almighty God to impart the inherent qualities of His divine nature to a redeemed soul, seeing that He did impart His image and likeness to the first man in the original creation. When Jesus said, ". . . I go to my Father," He was speaking of His death on the cross and His ascension to the throne in heaven. If we sincerely believe in the provisional sacrifice of Christ on the cross, we must believe that the inherent graces of mercy, truth, and holiness together with the fruit of the Spirit can be produced in the heart of mortal man.

When we request Christ to perform His works in our hearts we are devoutly praying that the Father may be glorified in the Son. We must open the doors of our hearts and extend to the Father, the Son and the Holy Spirit the right to rule us for ever, when we truly pray that the Father may be glorified in His Son. Jesus assured us that the heavenly Father would make His abode with us in answer to prayer. Surely a people so signally blessed would be able to exemplify the greater works of Christ in their diligent labors. It is apparent that our Lord has not limited the power made available to His people through prayer in His Name. When He said, ". . . I will do it," He placed His unlimited power at our disposal. He reveals himself to be an Almighty Servant standing ready and willing to do anything and everything pertaining to His works in answer to prayer. While meditating on these amazing promises it is necessary to keep in mind that the primary purpose of Christ in answering prayer is, "That the Father may be glorified in the Son."

The measure of our faith and the fervency of our prayers determine the effectiveness of our labors for Christ. If our faith is weak and our praying passionless we cannot expect to achieve much for Him. A man can ease his accusing conscience by explaining that he failed to accomplish the works of Christ because of adverse conditions where he lives and labors. When a man is willing to face the facts, he may discover that he failed because he had not believed in Christ for the very work's sake, and prayed fervently in His Name. We cannot justify our failures by pleading our lack of natural ability. I am persuaded that God does not impart a greater measure of natural ability to us when we are saved by grace, but I do firmly believe that He releases the powers of our souls when we give ourselves to Him. Only the Creator knows the latent forces and inherent potentialities in an immortal soul. When these spiritual powers are released by the indwelling Spirit of God the whole world can feel the dynamic force of a living Christ.

When Jesus said, ". . . Believe me for the very works' sake," He was pleading for a faith that would not fail to give the message of redeeming love to the whole world. He was thinking of the generations yet unborn when He gave us the right to ask anything in

His Name. While Jesus was in the world, mankind could see His miracles, hear His messages, and be blessed by His ministry. The astonishing fact is that the people of yesterday saw Him crucified, dead and buried, but cared very little about Jesus of Nazareth, the penniless preacher of Palestine. They were too engrossed in their own affairs of life to be impressed by a suffering Saviour. The world of today is too busy to be bothered with thoughts of life eternal. It is God's will to reveal the Son's works to a perishing world. He has willed that the works of His Son shall be accomplished in this present world through the labors and consistent living of His people.

Let us heed the pleadings of the Christ, and believe His promise to answer our prayers that the Father may be glorified in His Son. Let us continue to believe on Him for the very work's sake and pray in His Name for power to achieve the victory for Him on earth. No matter how sorely we are tried, nor how dark the hours may seem in times of sufferings, we must continue to pray that the Father may be glorified in the Son through our services and sacrifices in His work. Let us ever keep in mind that the countless years which have fled into the dateless past have not outmoded the works of Christ, neither shall the oncoming ages overthrow them. His glorious works of grace performed in our hearts and exemplified in our living and labors shall glorify the Father in the Son throughout all ages, world without end.

CHAPTER 5: PRAYING WITHOUT DOUBTING

". . . And shall not doubt in his heart, but shall believe that those things which he saith shall come to pass; he shall have whatsoever he saith." — Mark 11:23

These interesting words are a part of the Saviour's discourse on the power of faith. The disciples were greatly astonished by the power manifested in the Master's words which dried up the fruitless tree from the roots. When Jesus arrested the attention of His disciples by this unusual miracle, He obviously intended to reveal the power of God made available to His people through the prayer of faith. When Peter called the Lord's attention to the withered tree He said, ". . . Have faith in God. For verily I say unto you, That whosoever shall say unto this mountain, Be thou removed, and be thou cast into the sea; and shall not doubt in his heart, but shall believe that those things which he saith shall come to pass; he shall have whatsoever he saith."

In order to understand truth about praying without doubt in our hearts it is necessary to consider the Saviour's opening statement, ". . . Have faith in God." The remarkable discourse following His opening words reveals the fundamental fact relating to the prayer of faith. Our Lord would have us see that we can possess the faith of God. He revealed this fact when He said, "Have faith in God." It would be utterly impossible to believe that those things which we say in prayer shall come to pass unless we had an implicit faith in God. When Jesus said, ". . . Have faith in God," He revealed the Source of the priceless possession of the faith which enables us to pray without a doubt in our hearts. His admonition to have faith in God implies that all men have an inherent faith derived from God when He created the first man in His own image. The quality of inherited faith was not destroyed in the fall although it was greatly impaired as a result of disobedience. Jesus disclosed the amazing fact that we can possess a measure of the faith which Almighty God possesses in His own Divine Nature. This fact should not seem incredible since it is true that God did impart a measure of His own faith to man at the beginning of creation.

We do not hesitate to accept the fact that God imparts a measure of His life and love to His redeemed people. Surely it is not impossible for Him to impart a sufficient measure of His faith to His people to sustain them in life in this world of doubt and disbelief. If His people are not able to accomplish His works in the world because of the littleness of their faith, there is no valid reason to doubt that He can and will increase their measure of achieving faith. When the disciples said, ". . . Lord, Increase our faith," we have reasons to believe that He granted their request. (See Luke 17:5.)

The Saviour did not imply that we could possess the same measureless degree of faith which the infinite God possesses in His Divine Person. But He did encourage us to believe that we can receive a measure of God's faith to enable us to accomplish His purpose in redemption. The Saviour would have us see that we can enter into the faith of God and become workers together with Him in achieving His eternal purpose in His beloved Son. It is obviously true that God works in His people and through them according to the degree of their faith. He cannot do great things unless His people can believe Him for great things. Christ is made invincible in this world through the unwavering faith of His praying people.

The Scriptures reveal that Christ works according to His own faith, and His people enter into His faith and work with Him in accomplishing His purpose in redemption. The fact that He works according to His own faith is as understandable as the fact that a man works according to his own faith. A man can plan to build his house long before he lays the first stone in the foundation. He can plan for the happiness of a family before a child is born to gladden his heart. It is also true that a man's family can enter into his faith and assist him to achieve his purpose in life. Surely it is possible for the redeemed family of Christ to enter into His faith and participate in His eternal purpose to achieve the final victory over sin and death. The Son of God is not limited by circumstances, neither is He lacking in adequate resources to supply the need of His family on earth. Nothing shall prevent Him from bringing many sons unto glory according to the will of the heavenly Father.

We can pray without a doubt regarding the power of God. We can perceive the truth about Christ's eternal verities when we consider His statement about removing the mountain at the word of command. We are aware that the mountain has no power within itself to obey the word of command, ". . . Be thou removed, and be thou cast into the sea. . . " It is also obvious that the mountain is not removed by the efforts of man. Therefore we must conclude that the person speaking the words that remove the mountain has access to a power sufficient to remove the mountain and have it cast into the sea. The words of Jesus warrant us in saying that this power is made available to His praying people through faith. If this is not the truth then we must conclude that the words of Christ have no meaningful application to the perplexing problems of daily life. We are aware that the Master's words are figurative yet they are factual. The mountain evidently represents something that God will remove in answer to the prayer of faith.

Let us assume that the mountain represents the mass of human misery caused by sin in this troubled earth. It is certainly true that no man has power within himself to remove the mass of physical and mental sufferings caused by sin in this world. It is likewise true that no man has the strength of will to remove the mountain of iniquity which stands between himself and a holy God. Sin rests on his guilty soul like the weight of the hills. A man's load of depravity gives him a heavy heart and a burdened spirit. When we look at the mass of human suffering resulting from sin, we can visualize the insurmountable difficulties confronting humanity in this distressed earth. The bewildering sufferings caused by the sins of men constitute a mountain of misery and woe more formidable and forbidding than all the precipitous heights and impregnable rocks of earth's tallest peaks.

Christ is our only hope for deliverance in this disconsolate world. If faith in Him cannot bring the power necessary to surmount these difficulties, then faith has failed utterly to achieve the victory we have a right to expect in the light of God's unfailing promises. The imperishable Word declares, ". . . The just shall live by faith." How can we obey this fundamental law of life unless we can avail ourselves of a power sufficient to overcome every opposing force? We cannot doubt God's willingness to impart to His praying saints a sufficiency of spiritual strength to cope with the trials incident to life. The Scriptures record the victories achieved by the saints of God who were made immortal in sacred history by their dauntless courage and unwavering faith.

Let us pray the prayer of faith, not doubting in our hearts, but believing that strength shall be given day by day to surmount our difficulties in life. Let us not falter in the way as we journey toward fadeless dawn of the eternal day.

We can pray without a doubt regarding the purpose of God. The Scriptures reveal that it is God's eternal purpose in Christ to save all men from all sin on the condition of repentance and faith.

Christ has faith in His own ability to accomplish the Father's purpose by restoring a fallen man to the moral image of God. Nothing shall prevent Him from fulfilling His eternal purpose as revealed in the divine plan of salvation. There is not the remotest possibility that His perfect plan of redemption shall fail. We are assured that the gates of hell shall not prevail against Christ's invincible church, purchased by His blood, endowed, and endued by His Spirit.

We do well to ponder Paul's immortal challenge,

> "What shall we then say to these things? If God be for us, who can be against us?" — Rom. 8:31

When once we have a proper concept of God's immutable purpose as revealed in His Word, it will not be difficult to pray without a doubt. Let us look again at the Saviour's words, ". . . And shall not doubt in his heart, but shall believe that those things which he saith shall come to pass. . ." For the sake of clarity, let us underscore the words, ". . . Shall come to pass . . ." When shall those things which we say in prayer come to pass? When may we reasonably expect every prayer to be answered? The things we have said in prayer shall come to pass when everything spoken by the Lord shall come to pass. When God's plan of salvation has been consummated, then all things spoken by the Son of God, and all things spoken by the mouth of His holy prophets, and all the things spoken in the prayers of His faithful people shall come to pass.

The Scriptures affirm that it is God's purpose to save them to the uttermost that come unto Him through Christ. God's utmost ability was required to save us from the utmost extent of our sin. To be saved to the uttermost according to the purpose of Christ, means to be delivered from all sin in this present life, and delivered from the effects of sin in the body and mind in the life to come.

We can pray without a doubt in our hearts regarding a complete deliverance from sin in this present life, and it shall come to pass. But we must patiently wait until Christ's final triumph over sin and death before we can be delivered from the results of sin in our bodies and minds. We can pray without a doubt in our hearts regarding our final deliverance, and it shall come to pass according to the purpose of God. When Christ has fulfilled His eternal purpose in redemption, then the mountain of human misery and woe shall be removed from the earth. When we perceive this truth as revealed in the Scriptures, we can understand that every prayer offered without a doubt in our hearts shall surely be answered in full.

The things we say in prayer are powerless and meaningless unless we have Christ's authority to say them. But if the things we say in our prayers are the things which He has said, then we can pray without a doubt in our hearts.

We find this truth revealed in the Master's words concerning the mountain being removed at the word of command. Take note of the fact that Jesus first spoke the words, ". . . Be thou removed, and be thou cast into the sea . . ." Assuming that the mountain symbolizes the mass of human woe and suffering caused by sin, we perceive that it is possible to have this mass of human misery removed by speaking the living words of Jesus in our prayer. It is apparent that we can enter in to His faith and engage His omnipotent power to achieve victory over sin and death. When we pray without a doubt in our hearts, we share Christ's faith to achieve the purpose of the Father. When we speak His words, we have a valid reason to expect the things we say to come to pass.

Our prayers can embrace every word of promise and every word of purpose spoken by our Lord. Our faith and prayers can join His faith and prayers and assist Him in the final fulfillment of His Father's will and work. When applying this gracious truth to the things which Christ has spoken in explicit terms of eternal truth, it is not difficult to see that our prayer of faith becomes an integral part of the whole plan of redemption. We are assured that every word spoken in prayer shall be answered in the final restitution of all things. It is written,

> "And He shall send Jesus Christ, which before was preached unto you: Whom the heaven must receive until the times of restitution of all things, which God hath spoken by the mouth of all his holy prophets since the world began."
> — Acts 3:20, 21

Paul vividly revealed the final triumph of Christ when he said,

> "Then cometh the end, when he shall have delivered up the kingdom to God, even the Father; when he shall have put down all rule and all authority and power. For he must reign, till he hath put all enemies under his feet. The last enemy that shall be destroyed is death." — 1 Cor. 15:24-26

Our hope and expectation for final deliverance from all effects of evil in our bodies and minds shall be realized when He shall come to be glorified in His saints, and to be admired in all them that believe in that day. When He shall appear we shall be like Him, for we shall see Him as He is. We shall share in His final victory over disease and death. We shall hear Him say to the mountain of sufferings, ". . . Be thou removed, and be thou cast into the sea. . . ," and it shall come to pass.

In view of this consoling hope let us continue to pray without a doubt in our hearts. Let us rest our faith on the enduring love of Christ, asking nothing more than to be counted worthy of His pleasure throughout all ages, world without end.

CHAPTER 6: PRAYING WITH DESIRE

". . . What things soever ye desire, when ye pray, believe that ye receive them, and ye shall have them." — Mark 11:24

These inspiring words of Jesus disclose that He has obligated Himself to satisfy the incessant and insistent desires of His praying people. His words leave no doubt in our minds regarding His willingness to answer our requests. He makes it plain that whatsoever things are required to satisfy our spiritual and temporal needs shall be granted according to the measure of our faith.

We must obey the fundamental law of faith by sincerely believing that we receive the things desired when we pray, otherwise they shall not be granted. It is necessary to do some clear thinking regarding our Lord's promise to give us the things desired when we pray in faith.

Some unwise persons have interpreted Jesus as saying, "When ye pray, believe that you have the things desired, and you have them." It is difficult to accept this concept of the Master's teaching about the prayer of faith. No intelligent man can believe that he has received the things desired unless he has received them. It would be absurd to make such a claim in the light of truth.

It is misleading to tell a sincere seeker after a pure heart to believe that the blessing has been received when that person knows in his own heart that it is not true. This absurd teaching leaves a man confused and disappointed. A man must receive the witness of the Holy Spirit to confirm the work of grace performed in the heart. An honest man cannot affirm that he has obtained the things desired unless he knows that he has received them from God.

We must not assume that we have the things desired. Our faith does not rest on an assumption; our faith rests on an assurance imparted to us by the spirit of truth. When Jesus revealed His provision to satisfy our desires, He disclosed the incentive to pray. He is saying, "Whatsoever things you desire, when you pray, believe that God has provided them, and you shall have them."

We must first believe that the resources of God are made available to us through prayer. If we entertain the slightest doubt in our hearts regarding this fact, we cannot obtain the things desired to satisfy us in life.

While seriously meditating on the remarkable words of Jesus concerning the things desired in prayer, let us not overlook the fact that He is speaking about the mountain being removed at the word of command. If it is God's purpose to remove all sin and sufferings from the earth at His word of command, then it is likewise true that everything required to accomplish His purpose on behalf of His people is made available to them in the provision of redeeming grace. When we see this truth we can understand God's purpose in establishing the throne of grace. Is it any wonder that we are told to come boldly unto the throne of grace? We can readily understand the real incentive to pray when we know that our legitimate desires will be granted when we pray for things pertaining to the plan of redemption as revealed in Christ. There is no provision made to gratify our desires unless the things desired are directly related to Christ's plan of salvation.

The primary purpose of the Saviour's sacrifice on the cross was to save us from sin and sufferings. It is His purpose to present us faultless before the presence of the Father with exceeding joy. It is our Lord's purpose to dry our tears for ever, open the gates of pearl, and give us an abundant entrance into the City of God. It is permissible to interpret Jesus as saying, "Whatsoever things are required to satisfy you and sustain you in this holy way of life, when you pray, believe that you can obtain them, and you shall have them."

It has not required one tear of sorrow, nor exacted one drop of our blood, nor cost us one night of sleep to provide the things required to save us from sin and sufferings in this world. The unsparing God gave His only Son to provide the things we need for time and eternity.

There are no unholy and selfish desires in the heart of a Christian. A true Christian is motivated to pray by the normal desires of spiritual life like a hungry son is moved to ask bread of his father. The child's desire for food does not spring from force of habit, it is a desire springing from the natural requirements of daily life. The incentive to pray is as normal as the desire for food and drink. The very fact that the desire exists is positive proof that it can be satisfied in a natural and legitimate manner.

There is an intense longing after Christ like the hunger and thirst of a person requiring food and drink. Such a desire cannot be satisfied with anything less than a manifestation of the living Lord. There is a desire to know more about His enduring love. There is a desire to linger long in sacred worship and holy communion with Him in the quiet place of prayer. A Christian says,

"My soul followeth hard after thee . . ." — Psa. 63:8

The inspired writer voiced his desire when he said,

"As the hart panteth after the water brooks, so panteth my soul after thee, O God. My soul thirsteth for God, for the living God: when shall I come and appear before God?" — Psa. 42:1, 2

A man can earn his daily bread by the sweat of his brow, and allay his thirst at the springs flowing out of the earth, but a man that hungers and thirsts after Christ must have the bread from heaven to satisfy his hunger, and drink the living water from the fountain of life to slake his thirst.

We desire a freedom which cannot be obtained while we live in this body. We long to be delivered from our earthly bondage into the glorious liberty of the first resurrection. In this human body we yearn, earnestly desiring to be clothed upon with our house which is from heaven.

"For we that are in this tabernacle do groan, being burdened: not for that we would be unclothed, but clothed upon, that mortality might be swallowed up of life." — 2 Cor. 5:4

When the eternal purpose of Christ has been completed, the saints shall be delivered from the presence of sin and sorrows which have troubled them in this unhappy earth. In that glad hour they shall experience the glorious liberty of the sons of God.

God's redeemed children have no continuing city in this world. They look for a city which hath foundations, whose builder and maker is God. Their citizenship is in heaven; from whence they also look for the Saviour, the Lord Jesus Christ: who shall change their infirm bodies, that they may be fashioned like unto His glorious body, according to the working wherewith He is able even to subdue all things unto Himself. When these things shall come to pass, then shall we obtain the end of our faith, even the salvation of our souls.

CHAPTER 7: A MANIFESTATION OF GOD IN ANSWER TO PRAYER

". . . When they had prayed, the place was shaken where they were assembled together; and they were all filled with the Holy Ghost, and they spake the word of God with boldness." — Acts 4:31

This remarkable manifestation of God reveals the effectiveness of prevailing prayer. It vividly discloses the fact that prayer can accomplish much. It is apparent that neither the apostles, nor the assembled company of devout believers were astonished at the marvelous visitation of God. They had assembled together in one place for the express purpose of achieving victory over the opposition of wicked men, and they fully expected the Lord to answer their united prayers in His own way.

Perhaps the shaking of the place where they were assembled together was an extraordinary occurrence, but receiving a direct answer to their importunate praying was neither unusual nor unexpected. The believers had assembled for the specific purpose of producing a miracle in the spiritual world, and not for the purpose of producing a phenomenon in the natural world. We do not need a manifestation of the supernatural to arrest the attention of a pleasure seeking world. God does not often shake the shackles off His imprisoned saints, and open the doors of the jail with an earthquake. He can do the unusual and the unexpected when necessary. We do not need the Lord to do something to astonish us, but we do need Him to do something to alert us to our dangers.

We cannot ignore the fact that we desperately need a startling manifestation of God to shake us out of our spiritual lethargy and selfish complacency. We cannot substitute a program for power and have the least semblance of hope that the unsaved will be attracted by it.

The believers were praying in a desperate crisis when they said, ". . . Lord, behold their threatenings . . ." We are aware that some of the most enduring results recorded in sacred history were obtained when some devout person prayed in an hour of crisis. Abraham prevailed with God in prayer when the angelic messengers told him about the destruction of Sodom. The holy Scriptures reveal that Moses prayed importunately for the people when they incurred the fierce anger of God by worshipping the golden calf. It was a critical time in Israel when Elijah prayed earnestly on Mount Carmel. Jesus was praying in an hour of crisis when He said, ". . . Father, the hour is come . . ." The believers were confronted by a desperate situation when they said, ". . . Lord, behold their threatenings . . ." With them, it was a case of life or death, victory or defeat. The odds against them were tremendous, but the God that was for them was Almighty.

There is nothing in the sacred records to show that they had the slightest intention of compromising the truth in order to have favor with men. They did not call a meeting of the official board to discuss ways and means of evading the fundamental issues involved. They did not take refuge in a stupefying pessimism saying that nothing could be done to remedy the situation confronting them. Neither did they deceive themselves by saying that things would work out satisfactorily to all parties concerned. They were willing to accept the conflict that challenged their faith and hope in God. They did the most natural thing in the sight of the Lord when they assembled together with one accord in prayer, and lifted up their voice in one concerted petition to Him for help.

The believers in this day of grace should be impressed by the victory achieved by this praying company of saints. There are many things which threaten us today. We are confronted with serious situations that cannot be overcome unless we keep our strength renewed through prevailing prayer.

It is written, ". . . They were all filled with the Holy Ghost, and they spake the word of God with boldness." A gracious infilling with the Spirit of God is the only solution for our spiritual difficulties in this age of the world. The Lord's holy prophet said,

> ". . . When the enemy shall come in like a flood, the Spirit of the Lord shall lift up a standard against him." — Isa. 59:19

We cannot hope to escape the flood of evil which threatens to overwhelm the believers today unless we are constantly refilled and re-invigorated by the Holy Spirit. When Paul said, ". . . Be filled with the Spirit," he was stressing the necessity of continuing in the fullness of the Spirit in order to achieve the victory for Christ in this world. This remarkable filling with the Spirit was evidently different in some respects from the epochal filling received on the day of Pentecost. This gracious enablement of the Spirit was obviously one of the times of refreshing to be expected from the presence of the Lord. (Acts 3:19.)

Unless the believers in the church today have their spiritual strength replenished repeatedly by the Spirit they will not be able to overcome the increasing power of spiritual wickedness threatening them today. The church cannot cope with the menacing threat of worldliness except the company of believers pray for power to meet the insidious threat. The company of believers cannot withstand the subversive teachings of modern Liberalism unless they pray for strength to contend for the faith once delivered to the saints.

It will require much prayer to prevail against the creeping paralysis resulting from meaningless programs and pointless plays promoted by the worldly-minded leaders in the church. Unless the company of believers today are girded with the power of the Holy Spirit they will not be able to cope with the crisis confronting them in this day of formality and unbelief. God did not answer their impassioned prayer in the hour of crisis by miraculously changing the attitude of the determined opposition. He did not remove the threat which endangered them, neither did He destroy the ring-leaders responsible for the persecution of the church. It is interesting to note that the company of believers did not ask the Lord to change the attitude of their enemies. They accepted the fact that such persecution had been foreseen and foretold.

> ". . . Thy servant David hast said, Why did the heathen rage, and the people imagine vain things? The kings of the earth stood up, and the rulers were gathered together against the Lord, and against his Christ." — Acts 4:25 (Psalm 2:1-3)

The Lord would have us understand that suffering persecution for His sake is the price to be paid in blood and tears for the unspeakable pleasure of serving Him in the holy way of life.

Our young people should be impressed with the fact that they cannot expect the Lord to change the attitude of their unsaved friends and associates. When once the young converts discover this truth they will not find it difficult to overcome the hardships of life. Pastors find it difficult to get the young people established in the faith because they apparently believe that God should change their environment in answer to prayer. It is apparently difficult for them to understand that a change in their surroundings is not the solution of their spiritual problem. It is likewise true that a change in the moral conditions which environ the church today is not the solution of its spiritual problem.

The company of believers found the solution of their problem when they lifted up their voice with one accord in prayer to God. The answer they received enabled them to cope with the rising tide of spiritual wickedness in high places. The Lord fortified them with a spiritual power that no combination of evil forces could withstand successfully.

The embattled believers were praying with an unwavering faith when they said, "Lord, thou art God." The indisputable fact of God was the basis of the unshakable confidence which inspired them to pray. It is remarkable how impotent and insignificant the feeble efforts of wicked men appear when we realize that God is our refuge and strength, a very present help in trouble. (Psalm 46:1.)

The imperishable Word declares,

> *"The Lord is on my side; I will not fear: what can man do unto me?"*
> *— Psa. 118:6*

God gave us a certified promise when He said, "I will never leave thee, nor forsake thee." The Lord has never deserted His faithful people in the time of conflict. We need to have this blessed truth imbedded in our consciousness, impressed on our minds, and indelibly inscribed in our hearts by the hand of God. When once we grasp the fact of God it is not difficult to pray.

God's everlasting kingdom will never be destroyed by the combined forces of the ungodly. Almighty God is never in jeopardy. He has no fear of mortal man. He shall remain immutable in purpose and invincible in power for evermore.

Consider what the praying company said about God's enemies,

> *"For of a truth against thy holy child Jesus, whom thou hast anointed, both Herod, and Pontius Pilate, with the Gentiles, and the people of Israel, were gathered together, For to do whatsoever thy hand and thy counsel determined before to be done." — Acts 4:27, 28*

The conscienceless Herod, and the cowardly Pontius Pilate are dead, and their vicious opposition to Christ is dead and buried in the sepulcher of the ages. The aggressive agnosticism and sneering atheism that ran rampant less than a century ago has ceased to occupy a prominent place in the world today. The vicious Liberalism which afflicts the church today will soon be dead, buried together with modern infidels who have advocated its pernicious views.

Perhaps the sands have been washed in the footprints of the Stranger of Galilee, but the world has not forgotten that He lived, loved, and labored to save lost humanity from eternal death. The countless centuries which have hurried into the dateless past have not impaired His strength to save us to the uttermost. The marching millenniums will not erase His matchless Name from the annals of sacred history. The last desolate day of time will not find Him buried in the sepulcher of the ages. The fleeing ghost of eternity will never discover the grave of God. Of Him it is written,

> *"And, Thou, Lord, in the beginning hast laid the foundation of the earth; and the heavens are the works of thine hands: They shall perish; but thou*

remainest; and they all shall wax old as doth a garment; And as a vesture shalt thou fold them up, and they shall be changed: but thou art the same, and thy years shall not fail." — Heb. 1:10-12

When we fortify our faith and underscore our thinking with the words, "Lord, thou art God," we can prevail in prayer and overcome the combined forces of evil which threaten us in these trying times. Almighty God will not abandon His eternal purpose because a few wicked men have lifted up their voices against Him. Our God has assured us that all things work together for good to them that love Him, to them who are the called according to His purpose. His imperishable promises give a strong consolation to lay hold of the hope set before us. Let us hold fast the profession of our faith without wavering; for He is faithful that promised.

The assembled company prayed that the messengers of the Word might have courage. They said,

". . . Grant unto thy servants, that with all boldness they may speak thy word." — Acts 4:29

The voice of prayer was heard in heaven and the answer granted when the assembled company of devout saints prayed this importunate prayer in the time of crisis. God's people were not praying for boldness because they were moral cowards. They were fearfully aware of the danger which threatened them; but they were not too cowardly to face it with God's help.

The rulers of the people, and the elders in Israel had called Peter and John before the council, and commanded them not to speak at all nor teach in the name of Jesus. (Acts 4:18.) God's called servants could not heed this diabolical command and be faithful to the high calling of God in Christ Jesus. To comply with such an unjust demand, not to speak at all nor teach in the Name of Jesus, one must compromise the truth of Christ, and cease to emphasize the central theme of the Gospel message. The very essence of the Gospel is contained in the Name of Jesus.

It is interesting to notice that the believers were praying for the message of divine truth. They said, "With all boldness they may speak thy word." The emphasis is placed on "Thy word." The Christians wanted to hear God's Word declared with firm conviction and unwavering confidence. They evidently wanted to be edified and enlightened by the message of saving truth. They obviously believed that the Gospel was the power of God unto salvation to every one that believed it. It is indeed blessed to discover a people who desire to hear the message of redeeming grace, a people who do not want to be entertained with cheap programs and silly plays in the church, a people hungry for the bread of life which Christ only can give.

The assembled believers prayed for the messengers of the Gospel, saying, "Grant unto thy servants." It is well to notice that the Christians said, "Thy servants." They evidently recognized that the apostles were the servants of God. They were not considered to be servants of an institution, or an organization. They considered the apostles to be the called servants of God, who had commissioned them to serve His redeemed family. These godly men were not hired promoters; they were Christ's holy messengers.

It does not require moral courage to promote a program to entertain a group of nominal Christians. Neither does it require courage to give a book review, or speak on current events; but it does require boldness to press the claims of Christ on men, and demand that they repent of their sins and yield themselves to Him.

It does not require spiritual fortitude to organize a campaign to raise money for the general interests of the church; but it does take much prayer and faithful preaching to precipitate a genuine revival of full salvation.

To raise these issues does not mean that one is indulging in hurtful criticism of God's faithful people and preachers. It does mean that one is gravely concerned about the praying of God's people, who are members of the body of Christ. It is apparent that a devout minister can perform his work for Christ more efficiently when he knows that the Christians want to hear the Word and are supporting him with their prayers and faith. The record shows that Peter and John had joined the company of saints in the fellowship of prayer. This fact discloses that the messengers of Christ realized the necessity of prevailing prayer.

It is not unusual to hear some ministers say they are so burdened with the work of the church that they have very little time to spend in earnest prayer. This is a startling admission for any man to make, especially a minister of the Gospel. It is a serious matter in the life of a preacher when he allows himself to be cumbered with much serving. The results of his neglect of prayer will be revealed by the poverty of his preaching. It is possible for a minister to become so preoccupied with his duties that he will give prayer a place of secondary importance in his life. God's servants should consider that nothing pertaining to the church of Christ is more important than waiting before the Lord in the secret place of prayer. The man of God loses his passion for souls when he willfully neglects to pray. He must wait until his soul is aflame with holy zeal, and his mind stimulated with fresh news from heaven. When he takes proper time to pray, his preaching will edify and enlighten the Christians, and the fruitfulness of his ministry will be increased.

The writer disclosed some remarkable results from this ministry of prayer when he said,

> *"And with great power gave the Apostles witness of the resurrection of the Lord Jesus: and great grace was upon them all." — Acts 4 v. 33*

The assembled company prayed for miracles to be performed in the name of Jesus.

> *"By stretching forth thine hand to heal; and that signs and wonders may be done by the name of thy holy child Jesus." — Acts 4 v. 30*

It is obvious that the Christians expected miracles to accompany the preaching of the Word. It is interesting to note that the prayer for boldness to speak the Word included the petition for healing, and signs and wonders. The order of the prayer places preaching the Word first before the performing of miracles in the name of Jesus.

Our Lord placed more emphasis on preaching and teaching than He did on His gracious ministry of healing the sick, and showing signs and wonders. However, we are not to conclude that such miracles cannot be performed through the power of prayer in this age and generation. The healing of the sick, and the signs and wonders performed in the name of Jesus accompany the preaching of the Word.

This fact is clearly observed when we give thoughtful attention to the import of the prayer. The prayer for miracles reveals the true concept regarding the power of Jesus to heal. They said, "By stretching forth thine hand to heal . . ." The presence of Jesus was so real to praying saints that they asked Him to stretch forth His nail-scarred hand and heal the people.

Jesus did stretch forth His hand and touched the diseased bodies of men, and they were instantly healed. The fact that Christ has ascended to heaven has not changed our concept of His Divine Person. He is willing and able to stretch forth His hand and heal our broken bodies today like He did in the days of His flesh.

I am persuaded to believe that the professing Christians would see more miracles of healings performed by the hand of Jesus if they would spend more time in earnest prayer for the messengers of the Gospel.

I am convinced that the Lord will work wonders in this age of indifference if we will cease to limit Him by unbelief, and accept the fact that miracles can be performed today by the outstretched hand of the Holy Child Jesus.

CHAPTER 8: THE INTERCESSORY PRAYERS OF CHRISTIANS

". . . Friend, lend me three loaves; for a friend of mine in his journey is come to me . . ." — Luke 11:5, 6.

There is evidently a ministry of prayer even as there is a ministry of preaching. The teachings of Jesus contained in the parable show us that praying and preaching are integral parts of the plan of salvation.

Preaching is God's way of speaking to man, and praying is man's way of speaking to God. Preaching is God's way of appealing to the will of man, and praying is man's way of appealing to the will of God.

Our Lord's teachings relating to intercessory prayer are clearly revealed in the Epistles. John's Epistles reveal the amazing power made available to God's people through intercessory prayer. Peter assures us that the eyes of the Lord are over the righteous, and His ears are open unto their prayers. James said, ". . . The prayer of faith shall save the sick, and the Lord shall raise him up . . ." The inspired writings of Paul disclose the astonishing possibilities in the ministry of intercessory prayer. In one of Paul's Epistles the ministry of prayer is connected so closely with the ministry of preaching that it is difficult to tell where the prayer ends and the preaching begins. (Colossians 1:9-17.)

Note the boundless possibilities revealed in the prayers of a faithful minister of Christ.

"Epaphras, who is one of you, a servant of Christ, saluteth you, always labouring fervently for you in prayers, that ye may stand perfect and complete in all the will of God." — Col. 4:12

It is obvious that the fervent prayers of a servant of Christ can enable the believers to stand perfect and complete in all the will of God. Perhaps it is difficult for us to understand how our praying for the children of God can establish them in the faith, nevertheless it is true according to this Scripture. We are convinced that our fervent prayers can obtain power from the throne of grace to preserve some struggling saint in an hour of severe trial.

The man said, ". . . A friend of mine in his journey is come to me . . ." Our Lord focused attention on the responsibility to pray for others when He uttered the stirring words in this parable. It obviously was not the man's own personal need that compelled him to request the three loaves; it was the imperative need of the tired traveler that moved him to ask for bread at midnight.

No man can be a faithful follower of Christ and not recognize his responsibility to pray for others. The spiritual life received from Christ motivates a Christian to present the needs of others at the throne of grace, where mercy is obtained, and the promised grace is found to help others in a time of urgent need.

Our personal responsibility to intercede for others is made more apparent when we emphasize the words, ". . . Is come to me . . ." What strange combination of circumstances caused the man to seek help from his friend?

Perhaps he had taken the wrong road in the confusing darkness of the night. We are aware that the parable does teach the disturbing truth that men are lost in the darkness of sin, and that it is our duty to lead them to Christ. But the pitiful plight of the pilgrim is not the only startling truth contained in our Lord's teachings.

The statement, ". . . A friend of mine in his journey. . . ," persuades one to think that the traveler knew before he started on his journey that he could find rest and comfort in the home of his friend. It was his faith in his friend's reputation for hospitality that encouraged him to continue on his journey through the enveloping darkness of the night.

The parable reveals that men will come to us when they are convinced of our ability to obtain help for them through intercessory prayer. The news that a certain man can prevail with God in prayer will soon reach a multitude of hopeless and helpless people. Some distressed soul will soon be knocking at the man's door seeking help and comfort.

It was the good news that Christ was giving help and comfort to all men that caused the multitudes to seek Him day and night. The disciples had a boldness in their preaching and a power in their praying that drew broken and burdened humanity to seek the Saviour.

Paul expressed his thanks to God for the church when he said,

> ". . . From you sounded out the word of the Lord not only in Macedonia and Achaia, but also in every place your faith to God-ward is spread abroad; so that we need not to speak any thing." — 1 Thess. 1:8

Lost men do not seek Christ by mere chance; He draws them unto Himself through the convicting and convincing power of the Holy Ghost. The Spirit performs His office work in the world through Christ's witnesses. Jesus said,

> ". . . The Spirit of truth, which proceedeth from the Father, he shall testify of me: And ye also shall bear witness, because ye have been with me from the beginning." — John 15:26, 27

It is obvious that the Spirit enables the Christians to attract lost men by faithfully witnessing to the Saviour. Our Lord has not commissioned all of His people to preach, but He called all of them to pray.

The great revivals born in the hours of agonizing prayer attracted the attention of the civilized world. People came for the express purpose of obtaining spiritual help through the preaching and praying of God's servants. The great revival that began at Asbury College in 1950 was born in seasons of importunate praying. Some of the students prayed all night for a great spiritual awakening. Many of the teachers prayed earnestly for a gracious visitation of God. My own soul was in great agony of prayer. The burden was so great that I confessed the sins of the world to God. In some peculiar manner I had been made aware of the condemnation that rested on the souls of lost men.

During the Chapel service I exhorted the students to seek the Lord. I realized that it was God's appointed hour to answer prayer. At that moment the Holy Ghost moved mightily on the entire student body. Wave after wave of deep conviction swept over the audience. Many were moved to seek the Lord with diligence. It was an hour of triumph for the faithful few who had tarried through long seasons of intercessory prayer before the Lord during the quiet hours of the morning. The news of this marvelous visitation of God spread all over the nation. It was broadcast by radio to several foreign countries. People came hundreds of miles to receive spiritual help. Perhaps more than five thousand people were directly influence by this glorious spiritual awakening born in the hours of intercessory prayer.

I am thoroughly convinced that a great spiritual awakening will come to this benighted world if the people of God will deny themselves of sleep and seek God in the peaceful hours of the morning. It is my firm conviction that the great Asbury revival set the pattern to be followed in order to have a great revival in this day and age of the world. God will hear His people when they see the importance of praying for others. Our Lord revealed this fact when He said, "Because of his importunity he will rise and give him as many as he needeth." The man's plea for bread was so insistent that he did not heed the protest of his sleepy friend. The need of the traveler who had come to him out of the night was more important than the rest needed by his friend's entire family.

Is it possible that we are too indolent and indifferent to pray? Is there no passion for souls? Is there no sincere concern for the lost? Can it be that we are too sleepy to watch with Christ in the Gethsemane of prevailing prayer? Are our physical comforts more important than our praying for others?

Perhaps our Lord will draw some weary wayfarers to our door asking for help through our intercessory prayers. If He is pleased to trust us with such a responsibility, let us not fail to feed the famishing soul.

The man made an amazing confession when he said to his friend, ". . . I have nothing to set before him." It is evident that Jesus is not calling attention to the man's embarrassing poverty. He is showing us that our sufficiency is not of ourselves. Paul stated this fact when he said.

> *"Not that we are sufficient of ourselves to think any thing as of ourselves; but our sufficiency is of God." — 2 Cor. 3:5*

We are woefully wanting in natural ability to help others spiritually; we have nothing to set before them. Unless we avail ourselves of the abundant resources of Christ through prayer, we will never have anything of spiritual worth to set before a starving world.

It is not difficult to imagine that the man had an easy chair and a comfortable bed to offer the tired traveler. But furniture is not a substitute for food. The welcome at the door, the furnishing of the house, and the entertaining conversation, cannot satisfy the hunger of the human heart. It requires the bread of life obtained from God to save a famishing soul from death.

Jesus encouraged us to avail ourselves of His resources when He said, ". . . He will rise and give him as many as he needeth." We have nothing of ourselves to save a lost soul, but we have a faithful Friend, who will give us as much as we request in intercessory prayer.

Jesus would have us understand that our importunate praying can overcome our discouragements and difficulties. He disclosed this fact when He said, ". . . He from within shall answer and say, Trouble me not: the door is now shut, and my children are with me in bed; I cannot rise and give thee." He is not saying that our heavenly Father is unwilling to grant our requests for others. The Master is teaching us not to cease praying when we encounter some opposing forces in life. There are times when it seems that our earnest requests have been denied. Let us keep in mind that our heavenly Father is willing to give the bread of life in answer to our intercessory petitions for others.

CHAPTER 9: THE THREE ESSENTIALS OF PRAYER

". . . Every one that asketh receiveth; and he that seeketh findeth; and to him that knocketh it shall be opened." — Luke 11:10

The plain teachings of Jesus accord us a valid reason to believe that every sincere prayer offered by His people shall be answered.

Jesus stated the three essentials of prayer when He said, "Ask, seek, knock." He disclosed these three essentials of prayer in His parable about the man asking his friend for three loaves. It is quite obvious that he was asking, seeking and knocking when he made his request for bread in the middle of the night.

The Master's words revealing the inherent principles of effectual praying confirm our faith, enlarge our understanding, and enable us to appropriate His certified promises. It is apparent that His promises relating to prayer are as vast in scope as the extent of His promises pertaining to salvation. It is written,

> *"He that spared not his own Son, but delivered him up for us all, how shall he not with him also freely give us all things." — Rom. 8:32*

This Scripture reveals the possibilities of prayer to be as great as the boundless measure of redemptive grace. The unsparing God places no limit on our praying because there is no limit placed on His giving. If we believe that Christ was sacrificed to save us to the uttermost, we must likewise believe that He is able to supply our needs to the uttermost.

The lamentable fact is we have been exceedingly slow to comprehend the unlimited possibilities of prayer revealed in Christ's plain words. When we fully understand His instructions about praying, and grasp the promises by faith, we will not find it difficult to pray the effectual fervent prayer of achieving faith. We certainly owe it to ourselves and to all men, to consider seriously the fundamental principles of prayer disclosed to His disciples in answer to their request, ". . . Lord teach us to pray . . ." The very essence of this request is in itself a prayer to know how to pray.

It is necessary to consider Christ's teachings regarding our daily bread in order to understand the three essentials of prayer. He has focused our attention on the requests for bread in His entire discourse on prayer. Our daily bread is contained in the first direct request revealed in the Lord's prayer, "Give us day by day our daily bread." The request for bread follows the prayer of worship. ". . . Hallowed be thy name. Thy kingdom come. Thy will be done . . ." The request for bread also precedes the prayer for pardon and preservation. Bread is obviously the central theme of the Lord's prayer, according to the teachings of Jesus.

Our Lord emphasizes the need of bread in the parable of the man seeking the three loaves at midnight, and concludes His discourse by arresting our attention to the son asking bread of his father.

It is apparent that Christ's teachings about asking for bread contain something much more important than our temporal needs in this life. He evidently intended to stress the fact that we needed spiritual food in order to live in time and in eternity. We recall that Jesus astonished His disciples when He said, "I am the bread of life." When He uttered these words He made it clear that we cannot live without Him, for He is as essential to spiritual life as bread is essential to physical life. (See John 6:48-58.)

The three essentials of prayer are readily understood when applied to the Saviour, who is the living bread from heaven. When we sincerely ask for the Lord Jesus, we shall receive Him; when we earnestly seek Him, we shall find Him; and when we knock at His door, it shall be opened unto us.

The three fundamental principles of prayer apply to the entire scope of life in this world, and in the world to come. I am thoroughly convinced that the redeemed family of God will ask, seek, and knock in prayer throughout all eternity. Their request will not be hindered by their infirmities of body and mind as they are in this world. We are daily aware of the fact that we know not what we should pray for as we ought. We will be able to make our requests known unto God in that holy place with a clear mind and a glorified body.

It is quite evident that our Lord would have us understand this startling fact seeing that He made the request for bread the central theme of family life. It is certainly true that as long as we live in the Father's house we must depend on Him to sustain us. There is no valid reason to believe that this relationship shall end when we enter heaven. There is nothing in the Master's teachings to show us that we ever become self-sustaining in life, either in this world or in the world to come.

I am fully persuaded that the fundamental principle of asking and giving will continue to all eternity. God stated this fundamental rule of His household when He said to the Son,

"Ask of me, and I shall give thee . . ." — Psa. 2:8

This astonishing principle of asking and giving was clearly an integral part of the Saviour's ministry on earth. We find the same basic principle revealed in the amazing fact that He ever lives to make intercession for us.

The three essential principles of prayer are revealed in nature. Every living thing in creation must be fed. Every plant, insect, and living creature on earth must ask, seek, and knock in order to obtain food from nature. We accept this obvious fact without question.

We have no reason to believe that eternal life in heaven will be sustained independent of our relationship to Christ. He supplies our needs in this world in answer to prayer, and He shall continue to supply our eternal requirements in answer to prayer. If this is the rule of the Father's household on earth, it will continue to be the rule for ever.

CHAPTER 10: ASKING AND RECEIVING

". . . Every one that asketh receiveth . . ." — Luke 11:10

When our Lord uttered these immortal words He gave to every child of God the inalienable right to pray. He impressed His disciples with this fact by asking them some pertinent questions:

> *"If a son shall ask bread of any of you that is a father, will he give him a stone? or if he ask a fish, will he for a fish give him a serpent? Or if he shall ask an egg, will he offer him a scorpion? If ye then, being evil, know how to give good gifts unto your children: how much more shall your heavenly Father give the Holy Spirit to them that ask him?" — v. 11-13*

If the father loves his son it would be utterly inconsistent with his nature to give his child a stone, or a snake, or a stinging scorpion instead of bread. The father's answer to his son's request will be granted according to the measure of his love for his child. It is the most natural thing in all the world for a father to listen to the requests of his family. When Jesus said, ". . . Any of you that is a father," he compares a man's love for his children to God's love for His children. He asks us to look up from our earthly fathers, and calculate how much more the heavenly Father will be moved to give good gifts to His children. Jesus is teaching us to understand that as much as God's goodness exceeds the goodness of mortal man, so much greater is our assurance that He will grant our childlike petitions.

Every child of God from the youngest to the oldest has a right to ask the Father for the bread of life. Every child, irrespective of age, sex, or race, can come boldly to the throne of grace, and find grace to help in time of need. There are no underprivileged children in God's family. The crippled, the weak, and the sick children have a right to ask the heavenly Father for the living bread from heaven.

The Saviour would have us perceive the imperishable truth that, ". . . Every one that asketh receiveth . . ." It is utterly unthinkable that our loving Father would ignore our earnest petitions. He will not remain silent and unmoved when His own children are weeping before Him in earnest petitions.

A missionary was telling about the sufferings endured while a prisoner during the war. He said that the crying of his starving family caused him to suffer more than all the cruel and barbarous treatment received at the hands of the savage and inhuman guards. When we understand how this godly man was moved by the constant crying of his famishing family, we can comprehend how our heavenly Father can be moved to answer the unceasing prayers of His family. It was not possible for the faithful missionary to grant the urgent requests of his children, but it is possible for our heavenly Father to grant the requests of His children.

Jesus teaches us that prayer has a human side and a divine side. The human side is the asking, and the divine side is the giving. The two halves which make up the whole of prayer are the asking and the receiving. Our asking and the Father's answering belong to each other. Our requests on earth and the Father's answer in heaven are meant for each other. If we believe that the Father has made an ample provision for the needs of His children, then we must also believe that He will surely give them all good gifts according to the promise.

Jesus teaches us to come to Him day by day to receive the bread of life to sustain us in this world. He wills day by day to do for us what we ask in simple faith.

When the Master said, ". . . Every one that asketh receiveth. . . ," He stressed the fact that we are not to rest without an answer to our petitions. He is saying that it is the Father's will, and the rule of His house to grant the requests of His believing children.

When no answer is received we are often disposed to say that it is not the will of God to give us the answer. We will find it much easier to yield to our own false reasoning about the answer to prayer than it is to shake off our lethargy and seek God until the answer is obtained. There are so many persons who rest content without the distinct experience of answered prayer. This distressing fact reveals the serious deterioration of Christian life in these last days. These unhappy souls pray daily, they ask many things, and devoutly hope that some of their prayers will be answered. They apparently do not know that it is the norm of spiritual life to receive definite answers to prayer. They obviously do not know that the heavenly Father wills day by day to do for us what we ask in faith.

We must take the words of Jesus just as they were spoken. We must not allow human reasoning to weaken the force of His teachings about our asking and receiving. We owe it to ourselves to take sufficient time while praying, to listen to His voice, and believe the truth that "Every one that asketh receiveth."

We should not make our many failures of the past the measure of our faith for the present. We must hold fast the assuring fact that the effectual fervent prayer of God's obedient child availeth much.

The son's request for bread is based on his relationship to the father. It is by virtue of this relationship that the son has the inalienable right to expect his father to answer his requests. When Jesus speaks of the son asking bread of his father, He is speaking of an obedient son. The son that finds no pleasure in obedience to his father and presumes that he can still ask and receive what he desires will certainly be disappointed. A son who loves and honors his father will find it is the father's good pleasure to answer his daily requests.

Consistent living on the part of God's people is the condition for obtaining the answer to prayer. God's precepts requiring obedience in our living, and His promises relating to our praying are inseparable.

We can certainly count on God's fulfilling His promise to answer prayer when we obey His sovereign will in all things. We should take time to meditate on the tenderness and love the heavenly Father has for His obedient children.

Much of our difficulty in praying is removed when we think on the happy relationship existing between an obedient child and a loving heavenly Father. When He sees His child with sincere purpose and steady will seeking diligently in everything to be and live as a child, then our prayers will prevail with Him as the prayer of an obedient child.

It requires considerable time to comprehend fully the teachings of Jesus regarding the inherent principles of effectual praying. If God's people will take sufficient time to meditate on the essentials of prevailing prayer, they will be rewarded richly for the hours spent in the school of Christ. When once we grasp the gracious truth contained in the words of Jesus, and take a firm hold on the promises relating to prayer, we will then realize the meaning of His words, ". . . Every one that asketh receiveth." We firmly believe that the Master stated the truth when He said, ". . . Every one that asketh receiveth . . ." Nevertheless we are confronted frequently with the startling and disconcerting fact that we do not always receive definite answer to our prayers. We find it exceedingly difficult to reconcile these disturbing facts with the explicit statement of Jesus regarding the answer to our prayers.

When we consider the Master's teachings about prayer, we must not strive to make them conform to our wishful thinking regarding the answer to our prayers. It is possible for us to set our heart on obtaining something we greatly desire for our own personal gratification, and then express our keen disappointment because the request was not granted.

The answer to our perplexing questions about prayer will be found when we study the Master's words about the son asking for bread. We are fully aware that the son cannot live without bread; he must have it or perish. However, there are many things the son may ask which are not as important to life as food. He may ask his father for money, or fine clothing, or toys. The father may consider it wise to give his son these good gifts; and again he might deem it best for the son's own good to withhold these things requested; but when the child asks for food it is a different matter of life, because food is a necessity.

There are many good gifts which our heavenly Father may deem it wise to bestow upon us, such as good health, prosperity, and financial security. If He wills to withhold these things we must submit to His sovereign will without complaint. Perfect health, prosperity, and earthly goods are not essential to life in this world. Our relationship to God does not depend on these creature comforts. These things cannot impart to us the moral strength we need to cope with the trials incident to life in this evil world. It requires the "Bread of life" to give the spiritual strength to sustain us in these last days. We are fully assured that our Father will give us the living bread from heaven to keep us strong in faith, undaunted in courage, and invincible in hope.

The grand climax of our Lord's discourse on prayer was reached when He disclosed the Father's promise to give the Holy Spirit to His praying children. He would have us understand that our urgent requests for the bread from heaven are answered by the Father's gift of the Spirit.

He is teaching us that the Spirit is given to the children of God for the express purpose of sustaining and satisfying life. Our incessant demands for spiritual food are supplied by the indwelling Spirit. Our daily prayer should be, "Lord, evermore give us this bread." The answer from heaven is, ". . . Every one that asketh receiveth . . ."

CHAPTER 11: SEEKING AND FINDING

". . . He that seeketh findeth." — Luke 11:10

When Jesus said, "He that seeketh findeth . . . ," He disclosed the second fundamental principle of prevailing prayer. His immortal words assure us that we can make some important discoveries through prayer.

His brief statement presents the greatest challenge known to mortal man. His teachings about prayer are a direct challenge to our profession of faith. If we believe that Christ is the way, the truth, and the life, we must believe that some very important discoveries can be made regarding these essential facts about Him.

It is astonishing what men will do when inspired and motivated by the hope of finding the things of earth they so ardently desire. They sail uncharted seas, endure the scorching heat of the desert, scale the ice-covered mountains, and brave the dangers of a trackless wilderness in hope of discovering the things they diligently seek.

It does not require a chart, or compass, or costly equipment to find the things of God. We have no stormy seas to sail, no blistering sands to cross, no snow-clad mountains to scale, and no pathless wastes to encounter in our efforts to find the things we seek from God. We are not haunted day and night by the tormenting fears that we will not obtain the answer to our sincere petitions. We have not the slightest reason to doubt the validity of Christ's statement, ". . . He that seeketh findeth . . ." Our faith to seek the things of Christ is based on His integrity and veracity.

When Jesus said, "Seek, and ye shall find . . . ," He was evidently speaking about finding the possessions of our heavenly Father. We are assured that His provision is as great as the manifold needs of His children. The weary can seek and find rest. The weak can seek and find strength. The sick can seek and find health. The Father wills to grant the various requests of His praying and trusting children.

When Jesus revealed the Father's promise to give the Holy Spirit in answer to prayer, He obviously intended to impress His trusting children with the fact that the Spirit would enable them to seek and find the treasures of truth. He later confirmed this remarkable fact regarding the ministry of the Spirit, saying,

> ". . . When he, the Spirit of truth, is come, he will guide you into all truth . . ."
> — John 16:13

We do not discover the things of God by mere chance; neither can we find them by a process of human reasoning. The things of God are revealed unto us by His Spirit. The Word declares,

> ". . . Eye hath not seen, nor ear heard, neither have entered into the heart of man, the things which God hath prepared for them that love him. But God hath revealed them unto us by his Spirit: for the Spirit searcheth all things, yea, the deep things of God." — 1 Cor. 2:9, 10

Prayer is like the telescope that enables a man to discover remote stars, blazing suns and whirling worlds in outer space. We may think of prayer as a microscope which enables a man to look into the realm of small things.

The Holy Spirit makes visible the invisible things of God. He enables us to pray so persistently that we can focus the light of Christ on the resources of God, and discover worlds, wealth, and wisdom unknown and unseen by the natural man. The inspired Apostle said,

> ". . .We look not at the things which are seen, but at the things which are not seen: for the things which are seen are temporal; but the things which are not seen are eternal." — 2 Cor. 4:18

We discover the eternal things of God in direct proportion to the measure of our seeking in prayer. The man who seeks diligently to know the things which God has prepared for them that love Him, will be rewarded by a greater measure of knowledge than the man who is casual and indifferent in his seeking.

It is necessary to deny ourselves of many things in order to seek and find the possessions of the Father revealed in His Son. The Apostle disclosed this truth when he said,

> ". . .What things were gain to me, those I counted loss for Christ. Yea doubtless, and I count all things but loss for the excellency of the knowledge of Christ Jesus my Lord . . ." — Phil. 3: 7, 8

It is impossible to obtain a more perfect knowledge of Christ until we count all things loss for Him. We must lay aside the things we count gain. To be aware of Christ in daily life is of greater value than all earthly knowledge to be obtained in this world. It is written,

> *". . . Ye shall seek me, and find me, when ye shall search for me with all your heart." — Jer. 29:13*

We cannot comply with the conditions stated in this promise unless we divest ourselves of all cumbersome cares.

When Jesus gave us the parable about the son asking daily bread of his father, He fully intended to impress us with several salient facts about prayer. The fact that the son seeks and obtains the things provided by his father is not the only truth contained in the parable. A son worthy of such a loving father would consider him to be more than a generous provider; he would rejoice because of his father's presence with his family. The presence of the father means much to an innocent child in this passing world.

Jesus would have us understand that our heavenly Father is present with His family in this world. We know that our Father has provided good things for us, but He means more to us than a generous Provider. The fact that He is present with us at all times, and in all places fills our hearts with joy unspeakable and full of glory.

Philip expressed much in his brief prayer when he said to Jesus, ". . . Shew us the Father, and it sufficeth us." When this faithful disciple made this request, he voiced the deepest longings of the human heart. We cannot be satisfied in this distressed earth without a clear revelation of our heavenly Father. Philip did not ask for the impossible when he made his importunate plea to Jesus. Perhaps he had heard Jesus say, ". . . He that seeketh findeth . . ." The Saviour answered Philip's request when He said, ". . . He that hath seen me hath seen the Father . . ."

If the Father revealed Himself in His Beloved Son in that distant day, we can expect Him to reveal Himself in His Son in this day. Our need is as great as the need of the pleading disciple. When Jesus said, ". . . He that seeketh findeth . . .," He had no intention of leaving us confused and in doubt concerning the things to be discovered through prayer.

The Master's word affords us a valid reason to expect the Father to reveal Himself to us in His Son. This is obviously the truth He would have us see in the parable of the son asking bread. It is absolutely unthinkable that an intelligent child would not be aware that his father was present when he asked him for daily bread. It is likewise contrary to truth to suppose that the child's father would be pleased to remain unknown and unseen by his family.

God's infallible Word reveals that He did manifest Himself to His people in the ages past. If the dateless past is the only time God has revealed Himself, then we in this dispensation of grace have no truth to substantiate our claims that Christ was raised from the dead, and showed Himself alive by many infallible proofs.

We cannot persuade ourselves to believe that Christ has clothed Himself with perpetual silence, and cannot and will not reveal Himself to His people. If a seeking soul cannot be as fully aware of Christ's presence as a child is aware of his father's presence, then the Master's words are utterly meaningless. When Jesus said, ". . . He that seeketh findeth . . . ," He banished for ever our bewildering doubt and confusion of mind concerning the reality of the heavenly Father's abiding presence with His happy family.

If our minds fail to grasp the import of the Saviour's teachings about prayer, we should wait patiently before Him in humble submission and quiet meditation until our minds are clear and our faith strong. The prayer of faith can obtain the substance of things hoped for, and make real to us the evidence of things not seen by the natural eye.

It is not unusual to find reliable witnesses who will testify that Jesus has revealed Himself to them while they were devoutly seeking Him in prayer. These godly people are neither fanatics nor mystics. They consider the recurrent visitations of Jesus to be the norm of spiritual life.

During the peaceful hours of the early morning I was praying and waiting before the Saviour when He suddenly revealed Himself to me. I saw Him as clearly as anyone ever saw Him in the days of His flesh. I ceased to pray, and remained quiet and speechless in His Presence. The moments seemed too sacred for me to break the sweet silence by prayer. What could I have said to Him? Was He not the answer to all prayer?

I do not know how long He lingered with me on that memorable morning. I was not aware of the passing of time. To me, all time had ceased, and eternity had begun. No language can express my boundless joy and happy surprise when He stood before me. I shall never forget the beauty of His face and the glory of His garment. The glory radiating from His Person filled the room with a soft silent light. He spoke not a word to me. His attitude was as One who listens attentively when you speak. I realized as never before in my life that He wanted me to pray. My heart was immediately burdened to pray for a visitation of God. I humbled myself in His Presence and put my head between His feet and poured out my soul in the agony of intercessory prayer.

The vision of Jesus satisfied my heart and gave me perfect contentment of mind regarding His willingness to answer prayer. I realized that He was the end of all seeking and the answer to all problems of life. I bowed low before Him, and opened my inmost being to welcome Him as my Lord and Master. I devoutly worshipped Him in spirit and in truth. To this gladsome hour He is as real as the flesh of my body and the earth beneath my feet. I have never had one doubt regarding His presence.

Perhaps some will ask if there is a scriptural basis for believing that the Saviour will reveal Himself to His seeking people. I was confronted with this question after the Lord manifested Himself to me. Could it be that the vision was nothing more than the result of my wishful thinking? Was I a hopeless victim of an overwrought imagination? Was I suffering from a serious mental disorder? Was it a fanciful dream? These were some of the questions confronting me after the Lord had appeared in answer to my prayer of faith.

In my diligent search for truth, I recalled that the Saviour had said,

> ". . . He that loveth me shall be loved of my Father, and I will love him, and will manifest myself to him." — John 14:21

The gracious words glowed with a new light, and disclosed a new meaning to my rejoicing soul. His assuring words were all I needed to confirm my faith and answer my perplexing questions. I found many promises in the Scriptures, but this one promise was sufficient to satisfy my heart and mind.

Some of my friends firmly believe that I am sick. Certain others are greatly concerned about my mental condition. Perhaps some have devoutly prayed for my immediate healing. I am thankful for their earnest prayers.

I have often wondered how some persons interpret the Saviour's own promise to manifest Himself to them that love Him. I wonder if they believe that such an experience is possible in this present age. I am convinced that many do not believe that the Saviour's promise extends to anyone except the chosen disciples. They evidently consider all reliable testimony as being fantastic and fanatical.

If we allow ourselves to be hindered by the unbelief of this modern age we will surely fail to grasp the fact that frequent visitations of the Lord are to be expected in a normal Christian life.

When Jesus said, ". . . He that seeketh findeth . . . ," He intended to impress us with the fact that an obedient child of God would seek to please Him in all things pertaining to life. This truth is obviously revealed in the parable of the son asking bread. Surely the son would seek to please his father. A son worthy of the heavenly Father would seek to please Him in matters of life. The obedient son would also realize that the father was pleased with him. The perfect example of this is revealed in the Son of God. The Father witnessed to His pleasure in His Son when He said,

> ". . .This is my beloved Son, in whom I am well pleased." — Matt. 3:17

The Beloved Son witnessed to this truth when He said,

> ". . . The Father hath not left me alone; for I do always those things that please him." — John 8:29

We make the greatest discovery in life when we discover the secret of pleasing God. An obedient child of the Father that lives day by day with an awareness of His pleasure has found the pearl of great price.

Our human frailties and infirmities of body and mind will often hinder us in performing always those things which please our heavenly Father, but there is nothing in the world that prevents us from being a pleasure to Him if we are willing to obey Him in all things relating to life. We can be a pleasure to our Father long before we are able to understand how to do the things which are well-pleasing in His sight. The favor of God rests constantly on the people who believe Him and diligently seek Him. It is written,

> ". . . Without faith it is impossible to please him: for he that cometh to God must believe that he is, and that he is a rewarder of them that diligently seek him." — Heb. 11:6

When we obtain His approbation we have received the greatest reward known to mortal man. The earthly pleasures we leave behind when we come to the end of life's journey are not important, but the eternal pleasures received at the end of the way are worth all it costs to obtain them.

CHAPTER 12: THE KNOCKING THAT OBTAINS AN OPENING

> ". . . To him that knocketh it shall be opened." — Luke 11:10

These words of the Master reveal the third fundamental principle of the effectual fervent prayer that availeth much.

The Master disclosed the value of praying persistently in His discourse about the man asking three loaves at midnight. There is something much more encouraging in His teachings about prayer than we find in the words of the reluctant neighbor, who said, ". . . Trouble me not: the door is now shut . . ." Our Lord would have us understand that the goodness of our heavenly Father far exceeds the goodness of the sleepy man. The Master is teaching us that we can prevail in prayer in spite of the discouragements and difficulties confronting us in life.

The bread so desperately needed to satisfy the hunger of the weary wayfarer was on the other side of the closed door. Much depended on the importunate pleading and insistent knocking on the part of the man seeking bread. If he had been discouraged by his friend's gruff words, ". . . Trouble me not . . . ," he would have gone away defeated and empty handed. If he had believed that his drowsy friend had spoken his final word when he said, ". . . The door is now shut . . . ," he would have departed with a deep sense of frustration and failure.

Our heavenly Father will never rebuff his praying children, saying, ". . . The door is now shut . . ." Jesus is teaching us to pray with unwavering faith and firm confidence. He inspired us with dauntless courage to pray persistently when He said, ". . . To him that knocketh it shall be opened."

The Saviour's heartening words imply that a vast realm of truth will be opened unto us when we knock at the door of the Father's house. It will enhance our understanding concerning the possibilities of prayer if we will devote some time to study what the Saviour has said about the open door set before His people.

Jesus identified Himself as being the door when He said,

> *"I am the door: by me if any man will enter in, he shall be saved, and shall go in and out, and find pasture." — John 10:9*

His astonishing words enable us to comprehend more completely the truth about prevailing prayer.

Christ is the door. He is the only entrance to God, and the only entrance to salvation. When we put Him in the promise regarding our persistent knocking in prayer we can perceive the truth. We can interpret the assuring promise as saying, "To him that knocketh, Christ, the Door, shall be opened." In other words, Christ will open Himself to us in answer to prayer. This is a blessed truth to contemplate. Christ opens His loving heart to His praying people. He opens His eternal hope to His praying people. He opens His enduring holiness to His praying people. He opens His invincible strength to His praying people. In the light of this Divine revelation, one is constrained to say,

> *"O the depth of the riches both of the wisdom and knowledge of God! how unsearchable are his judgments, and his ways past finding out!"*
> *— Rom. 11:33*

It has pleased the Lord to open His immutable purpose to His faithful saints and enable them to see His ultimate triumph over sin and death. He opens the gates of eternal life, the greatness of enduring love, and the glory of His likeness to His praying family. Through prayer we can enter into the joys of an uttermost salvation and delight ourselves in the abundance of peace. Through prayer we can escape the snares of Satan, and elude the evil purposes of the foe.

Christ is both an entrance and an exit. We can pray our way into the blessed realities of spiritual life, and pray our way out of the bewildering problems of life. Our Lord revealed these gracious facts to us when He said, ". . . To him that knocketh it shall be opened."

When Jesus opens Himself to His praying people He opens eternity to them, for He fills eternity with Himself and contains eternity in Himself. He is the First Cause and the Final Conclusion of everything in time and in eternity. Our concept of Christ is enlarged when He opens to us. The Psalmist was fully aware of this marvelous truth when he said,

> ". . . Thou hast set my feet in a large room." — Psa. 31:8

Christ wills to open His Word to us in answer to prayer. He stated this fact when He said,

> "I have given unto them the words which thou gavest me; and they have received them, and have known surely that I came out from thee, and they have believed that thou didst send me." — John 17:8

Perhaps my personal testimony will encourage others to pray that Christ will reveal His words to them. During the quiet hour of the morning I was asking the Saviour to enable me to understand His Word. For many years I had made it my practice to study the Scriptures, but I was aware that the Scriptures contained a depth of meaning that I had not perceived. I sincerely desired to understand the Word of God. I realized my need of an enlarged concept of the plan of salvation. It was the one prayer of my heart to know more about God's invincible Word in order to preach the message of life to a perishing world. I was convinced that the Lord had heard my sincere prayer. Not many days after the season of prayer, He began to unfold His Word of truth to my heart and mind with a depth of meaning I had never known.

I was teaching in Asbury College when the Lord began to reveal His Word to me. I listened to my own lecture with great interest. I said things about the Saviour that had not been prepared in my notes for the class. The light of Divine revelation flooding my soul was not the result of my reasoning. The truth about redemption did not come from my own mind; it was coming from the mind of Christ. My soul was enjoying great peace, and His living words were like fire in my spirit. I was constrained to tell others of the Saviour's love for lost humanity. To this happy hour His truth abides within my heart and mind. His Spirit continues to reveal the Words of Christ to me day by day. I can say with the Psalmist,

> "As the hart panteth after the water brooks, so panteth my soul after thee, O God." — Psa. 42:1

God's imperishable truth will glow with a new light when we knock at His door in prayer. If we have failed to grasp the significance of Christ's plain teachings about prayer when He said, ". . . To him that knocketh it shall be opened," we should ask Him to open Himself to us. There is nothing more simple and understandable in life than knocking at a door. Even a little child can knock at a door.

Christ is the Door between the spiritual realm and the physical realm. When we are born of the Spirit we enter a spiritual kingdom, which is a spiritual realm. We live, move, and have our being in a spiritual realm with Christ. We are in the world physically, but we are not of the world spiritually. God's Word declares that a righteous person is like a tree. A tree lives in two realms of nature; it lives in the earth, and it lives above the earth. Paul recognized this amazing fact when he said,

"Set your affection on things above, not on things on the earth." — Col. 3:2

Jesus revealed an amazing truth when He said, "I am the door . . ." We can enter into His presence and pray before Him in the same simple manner that we can go into another room through an open door. When we discover this amazing truth, we find it possible to take others into

His presence and talk with Him about their needs. It has been my pleasure to take others into the presence of Jesus many times. I saw the truth of these things when I entered into a covenant of prayer with Christ. I do not find it difficult to enter into His presence at anytime.

When Jesus said, ". . . To him that knocketh it shall be opened," He meant to show us that it is possible for His praying people to enter the heavenly place where He is seated on the mediatorial throne, and present their petitions to Him. This fact is substantiated by Paul, who said,

> ". . .Seek those things which are above, where Christ sitteth on the right hand of God." — Col. 3:1

The inspired prophet evidently perceived this wonderful truth concerning Christ when he said,

> ". . . He shall be for a glorious throne to his Father's house." — Isa. 22:23

God's children have a glorious throne in the Father's house. They have a perfect right to come boldly to the glorious throne of grace and make their requests known unto their heavenly Father.

Our Lord likewise disclosed a marvelous truth about the door when He said, ". . . And shall go in and out, and find pasture." It is apparent that a saved man can go from one realm to another and find spiritual food. Jesus has made an ample provision to sustain His people in both the physical realm and the spiritual realm. He cares for His people in the natural world and in the spiritual world. The Saviour would have us understand that the Good Shepherd will care for His flock while they are out in the field, even as He cares for them when they are in the fold. In other words, the Saviour will preserve us while we work and witness for Him in the world, like He preserves us when we are resting safely in the fold of His love. It is written,

> "The Lord shall preserve thy going out and thy coming in from this time forth, and even for evermore." — Psa. 121:8

The changeless Christ has spoken with absolute authority concerning the open door.

> ". . . Behold, I have set before thee an open door, and no man can shut it: for thou hast a little strength, and hast kept my word, and hast not denied my name." — Rev. 3:8
> ". . . To him that knocketh it shall be opened." — Matt 7:8

It shall remain open to all eternity.

CHAPTER 13: THE IMMORTAL PRAYERS OF THE SAINTS

". . . Golden vials full of odours, which are the prayers of saints." — Rev. 5:8

Christ frequently chooses some unusual place on earth to reveal Himself to mankind. It is obviously consistent with His Divine Nature and eternal purpose in redemption to disclose Himself in some unusual place and in some unexpected manner.

He revealed Himself to Moses in a burning bush in a desert. He revealed Himself to be the long expected Messiah to a woman of unsavory reputation at Jacob's well. He revealed a measure of His effulgent glory to three chosen disciples on a high mountain. He revealed Himself and His purpose to give the Gentiles the Gospel to Saul of Tarsus on the road to Damascus.

Perhaps the most amazing revelation ever given to mortal man was given to John when the Saviour revealed Himself clothed in His majesty and might standing in the midst of the seven churches. John said,

> ". . . When I saw him, I fell at his feet as dead. . . ." — Rev. 1: 17

Christ chose to reveal Himself to John while in exile on the lonely isle of Patmos. This holy disciple was banished to this wave-washed and wind-swept pile of shattered stones and shifting sands,

> ". . . For the word of God, and for the testimony of Jesus Christ." — Rev. 1:9

The Saviour selected this faithful man to be the human channel through which His sublime truth could be given to His trusting saints. It pleased the blessed Lord to reveal the sublime truth about prayer in John's picturesque language, ". . . Golden vials full of odours . . ."

Our Lord would evidently have us understand that prayer is a part of worship. It is like the odours of sweet incense ascending upward to God. The heavenly Father is pleased with our fervent prayers when we fill them with the fragrance of our sincere worship.

The Saviour would have us understand that our prayers are kept in golden vials in His Holy Place in heaven like the golden censer, and the ark of the covenant overlaid round about with gold, were kept in the most Holy Place in the temple.

Perhaps God's praying people have not fully grasped the fact that all sincere prayers are immortal, and the Lord preserves these prayers like a sweet incense kept in golden vials.

We surely are aware that Christ's prayers are living petitions preserved for us in His plan of eternal salvation. He breathed the power of His endless life into His prayers. His prayers are immortal because He is immortal. His prayers will be answered because He is the answer to all prayer.

The prayers recorded in the Holy Scriptures are an immortal part of the Divine plan of salvation. These petitions were made immortal by the power of the indwelling Holy Spirit. The Spirit enables God's people to pray with yearnings which cannot be uttered.

> "And he that searcheth the hearts knoweth what is the mind of the Spirit, because he maketh intercession for the saints according to the will of God." — Rom. 8:27

It is clearly disclosed in this remarkable Scripture that every prayer empowered by the indwelling Spirit becomes an integral and immortal part of the entire economy of God as disclosed in the plan of redemption.

I am thoroughly convinced that every prayer offered according to the will of God shall be answered either in our lifetime on earth, or after we have entered our heavenly home. However, I cannot discover anything revealed in the Word of God to warrant anyone in believing that the translated saints can pray for persons living on the earth. Praying to the translated saints, and asking them to pray for us, is a modified form of idolatry. Jesus Christ is the only mediator between God and man. All prayers must be offered to Him, and in His Name only.

When I affirm that every prayer offered in the Name of Jesus shall be answered, I am not saying that God will overrule the human will in order to answer our prayers. He cannot and will not save any man against his will, but He will convict a man of sin against his will.

Perhaps an incident will disclose what I mean when I speak of an immortal prayer. One night during a camp meeting, a man came to the altar weeping with deep conviction for sin. After a season of earnest prayer, he was converted and gave a glowing testimony. His faithful father had preached for many years and had prayed often during those years for his unsaved son. He never lived to see his son saved, but on this particular night in the camp meeting, the loving Lord answered prayer and saved this erring son of the preacher.

It helps me to imagine that the Saviour called His sainted servant and said, "My child, I have many of your prayers in golden vials. They are like sweet odours poured out before Me. I have the prayers you offered for your erring son during your lifetime on earth. I am now ready to answer your prayers during the camp meeting where you preached My Gospel many years ago. My child, I have just now granted your son a pardon in answer to your prayers and prayers of My people." It encourages my heart to believe that God will answer every prayer.

While praying during the quiet hours of the morning in a hotel room some years ago, I was burdened to pray for a woman slowly dying with a cancer of the throat. She had been a successful missionary for many years and had returned home from the field broken in health, bitter and resentful in spirit. I knew her saintly mother during her lifetime, and I knew how she had prayed for her daughter.

While praying for this dying missionary, the Lord said to me, "I am ready and willing to answer a mother's prayer, and give her suffering daughter peace of heart and mind." I was so sure that the Lord had spoken to me about this dying woman, and about His willingness to answer her mother's prayers, that I wrote a letter urging certain women to go and pray with this suffering missionary. She found peace and comfort of heart and mind, and went home within a few weeks to be with her faithful Saviour and her rejoicing mother.

Many of the Lord's redeemed children will live and die without receiving the answers to many of their sincere prayers. When we live by faith and die in the faith, we can be assured that a Just and Holy God will not forget His certified promises regarding His willingness to answer the prayers offered in the Name of Jesus.

The ". . . golden vials full of odours, which are the prayers of the saints," shall be poured out before the mediatorial throne of Jesus some glorious day. When that gladsome hour shall arrive on the wings of time, we shall see the triumph of the tears we have shed in the hours of agonizing prayer. We shall see the Father glorified in the Son.

We are living in a passing world filled with fears and doubts; but we can live in this transient world and not be filled with its fears and doubts regarding the answer to our prayers. The inspired Psalmist said,

> *"Trust in him at all times; ye people, pour out your heart before him: God is a refuge for us." — Psa. 62:8*

God's certified promises relating to prayer give us the inalienable right to say,

> *"Hear my cry, O God; attend unto my prayer. From the end of the earth will I cry unto thee, when my heart is overwhelmed: lead me to the rock that is higher than I." — Psa. 61:1, 2*

The Scriptures encourage us to pray incessantly and importunately knowing within ourselves that God will answer our petitions in His own time, and according to His own will. Let us offer up prayers with strong crying and tears unto Him that is able to save to the uttermost. Let us pray without ceasing until the hour comes for our immortal prayer to be poured out like sweet incense poured out of golden vials.

CHAPTER 14: CHRIST PLEADS HIS WILL

"Father, I will that they also, whom thou hast given me, be with me where I am . . ." — John 17:24

Jesus presented the precious legacy of His prayer when He offered His intercessory prayer preserved for us by John. The Lord let His disciples have the pleasure of knowing what His intercession for them in heaven as their High Priest was like. The disciples had heard the Saviour pray for them many times, but they had never heard Him pray as He did at this particular time. They must have been deeply impressed by the simplicity of His approach to the Father. They heard Him pray with the implicit confidence of the Beloved Son, Who is co-equal and eternal with the Father. They must have realized that Christ breathed into His intercessory prayer the efficacy and power of His endless life.

Jesus presented the priceless legacy of His prayer to the Father when He said, "Father, I will that they also, whom thou hast given me, be with me where I am; that they may behold my glory, which thou gavest me: for thou lovedst me before the foundation of the world." These gracious words of Jesus reveal His final will regarding the blessed estate of the redeemed. His inalienable right to plead His will before the Father is based on His finished work in the world. He said,

> *"I have glorified thee on the earth: I have finished the work which thou gavest me to do." — v. 4*

Jesus made it clear that His intercessory prayer is an integral part of His redemptive work on the cross. His finished work and His final will are one in the Divine plan of salvation.

It has pleased the Saviour to disclose the final fulfillment of all He has willed and devised for His purchased people. The pleasing prospect of being with Him where He is shall be fulfilled to the glory of the Father and to the everlasting admiration and joyful acclamation of His adoring saints.

It was difficult for the disciples to understand the Saviour's avowed purpose to go away. Their minds were sorely perplexed and their hearts troubled by the disturbing fact of His sufferings and death. They thought that He was leaving them alone to serve and suffer in a world hostile toward all they believed and preached. Perhaps they had almost reached the point of accepting final defeat when Jesus revived their faltering courage, saying,

> *"Let not your heart be troubled: ye believe in God, believe also in me. In my Father's house are many mansions: if it were not so, I would have told you. I go to prepare a place for you." — John 14:1, 2*

Let us emphasize His gracious words, ". . . a place for you." Our Lord revealed the purpose of His departure when He uttered these immortal words. He lifted the veil between time and eternity to establish the faith of His troubled people. He enabled His ransomed saints to see the heavenly home of the soul with the eyes of their hearts. He would have His people rest their faith on His comforting words, "In my Father's house are many mansions . . ."

There will be no homeless children in the family of God. All shall dwell in stately mansions throughout the endless day. This unfriendly world has no permanent abiding place for the children of God. They were born in this world, and many shall be buried in this world, but this passing world is not their home. They have no continuing city on the earth. God's people are citizens of the celestial City, the heavenly Jerusalem, which John saw coming down from heaven, prepared as a bride adorned for her husband.

Perhaps we are disposed to think of the eternal pleasure and ineffable joys to be obtained in the place prepared for His people. We try to visualize the beauty of the City whose Builder and Maker is God. We are inclined to wonder about the skill of the Infinite Artist who has blended the seven prismatic colors of white light to enhance the resplendent glory of the holy habitation of the redeemed.

While meditating on the blessed hope of heaven let us not overlook the fact that our expectations are based on the finished work of Christ. Jesus said to the Father, "I have finished the work which thou gavest me to do." He made no mention of the price paid in blood and tears to prepare the place where we could be with Him to all eternity. He prays like One returning home after having completed an assigned task.

His vicarious sufferings on the middle cross provided the necessary fitness of moral character for us to share eternal bliss with Him in the Father's house. His intercessory prayer assures us that we can be sanctified through the truth. It is His will to cleanse us by His blood and present us holy and unblameable and unreproved in His sight. (Colossians 1:22.)

We have every reason to believe that we can avail ourselves of the blessed benefits of His finished work, and come to the end of life's journey and receive a grand welcome into the City of God. His finished work and final will are the sure foundation on which we rest our hope to be with Him where He is, and to behold His glory.

Jesus possessed a peculiar joy in achieving His Father's purpose in redemption. He had a peculiar pleasure in providing a place in the Father's house for His trusting people. His joy in bringing many sons unto glory enabled Him to triumph over His physical sufferings and anguish of soul.

The merciless mockery of the multitude, the scorning sneers of the scribes, and the reproaches of the riotous rabble could not turn Him from His fixed purpose to finish His work according to the will of the Father. The stripes, spittle, blood, and bruises could not defeat Him. The insults and indignities heaped upon Him could not overwhelm His fervent love for His homeless saints. Being numbered with the transgressors, He was crucified on a lonely hill called Calvary. He suffered, the Just for the unjust, that He might bring us to God.

He was despised by foes, derided by fanatics, and deserted by friends, but He triumphed over sin and death, and returned to the right hand of the majesty on High, and ever lives to make intercession for His saints.

It would be utterly impossible to imagine the overwhelming despair and dreadful disappointment that would sweep over the souls of the redeemed if Christ's prayer should not be answered. The black raven of despair would croak the dirge of eternal death on the graves of the godly. The living sons of God would lift up their voices in unutterable lament and bewail the day they heard the hope of the Gospel.

We have no fears and doubts regarding the final triumph of Christ's intercessory prayer. He has presented His petition as a legacy to be shared by His trusting people. His last will and testament has been signed by His nail-scarred hand and sealed by the Holy Spirit. Every word uttered in His immortal intercession shall be answered in full.

The voice of His supplication has been heard in high heaven, and the language of His weeping has been interpreted before the mercy seat of pure gold. His tears shall triumph and His petition shall be granted.

It is almost unbelievable that our Lord can find pleasure in holy fellowship with His ransomed people to all eternity. His prayer shows us that it is His will to dwell with His people in the sacred bond of love throughout all ages, world without end.

The greatest pleasure to be enjoyed in heaven will be the unspeakable pleasure of being with the Saviour for evermore. The glory of His presence shall make glad the City of God.

We would find no pleasure in beholding the beauty of the Father's house of many mansions if Christ were not present to fill it with the light of His countenance. The brightness of His glory, and beauty of His Person shall enhance the happiness of the redeemed. The river of life, the fruitful trees, and the anthems of angels enhance the joys of the habitation of the holy people, but these blessed realities would fail to satisfy the citizens of the land of endless day unless the glorified Son were present to receive their eternal praise.

Let us continue to pray that our Lord will count us worthy to receive the legacy of His intercessory prayer presented to the Father. Let us not fail to obtain the spiritual fitness provided for us in His finished work. We must ever be mindful of the fact that without holiness no man shall see the Lord.

Let us take comfort in the Saviour's immortal prayer, "Father, I will that they also, whom thou hast given me, be with me where I am; that they may behold my glory, which thou gavest me: for thou lovedst me before the foundation of the world."

The Soul of Prayer

~ ※ ~

By *P. T. Forsyth*

The 1916 Edition

~ ※ ~

Dedication

To

MRS. WATERHOUSE

Lomberdale Hall, in the High Peak

There is, high among the hills, a garden with a walk—a terraced walk. The moors lie round it, and the heights face it; and below the village drowses; while far, far afield, the world agonizes in a solemn tragedy of righteousness (where you, too, have your sepulchres[1])—a tragedy not quite divorced from the war in heaven, nor all unworthy of the glorious cusp of sky that roofs the riot of the hills.

The walk begins with a conservatory of flowers and it ends in an old Gothic arch—rising, as it were, from beauty natural and frail to beauty spiritual and eternal. And it curves and twines between rocky plants, as if to suggest how arduous the passage from the natural to the spiritual is. And it has, half-way, a little hermitage on it, like a wayside chapel, of old carved and inscribed stones. And the music and the pictures! Close by, the mowers whir upon the lawn, and the thrush flutes in the birch hedge; beyond, in the gash of the valley, the stream purrs up through the steep woods; still farther, the limestone rocks rise fantastic, like castles in the air; and, over all, the lark still soars and sings in the sun (as he does even in Flanders), and makes melody in his heart to the Lord.

That terrace was made with a purpose and a welcome at will. And it is good to pace the Italian paving, to tread the fragrance from the alyssum in the seams, to brood upon the horizons of the far, long wolds[2], with their thread of road rising and vanishing into busy Craven, and all the time to think greatly of God and kindly of men—faithfully of the past, lovingly of the present, and hopefully of the future.

So in our soul let us make a cornice road for God to come when He will, and walk upon our high places. And a little lodge and shelter let us have on it, of sacred stones, a shrine of ancient writ and churchly memories. Let us make an eyrie there of large vision and humane, a retreat of rest and refitting for a dreadful world. May He show us, up there apart, transfigured things in a noble light. May He prepare us for the sorrows of the valley by a glorious peace, and for the action of life by a fellowship gracious, warm, and noble (as even earthly friendships may be). So may we face all the harsh realisms of Time in the reality, power, and kindness of the Eternal, whose Mercy is as His Majesty for ever.

Chapter I: The Inwardness of Prayer

It is a difficult and even formidable thing to write on prayer, and one fears to touch the Ark. Perhaps no one ought to undertake it unless he has spent more toil in the practice of prayer than on its principle. But perhaps also the effort to look into its principle may be graciously regarded by Him who ever liveth to make intercession as itself a prayer to know better how to pray. All progress in prayer is an answer to prayer—our own or another's. And all true prayer promotes its own progress and increases our power to pray.

---

[1] Original British spelling has been kept throughout.
[2] Open country.

The worst sin is prayerlessness. Overt sin, or crime, or the glaring inconsistencies which often surprise us in Christian people are the effect of this, or its punishment. We are left by God for lack of seeking Him. The history of the saints shows often that their lapses were the fruit and nemesis of slackness or neglect in prayer. Their life, at seasons, also tended to become inhuman by their spiritual solitude. They left men, and were left by men, because they did not in their contemplation find God; they found but the thought or the atmosphere of God. Only living prayer keeps loneliness humane. It is the great producer of sympathy. Trusting the God of Christ, and transacting with Him, we come into tune with men. Our egoism retires before the coming of God, and into the clearance there comes with our Father our brother. We realize man as he is in God and for God, his Lover. When God fills our heart He makes more room for man than the humanist heart can find. Prayer is an act, indeed *the* act, of fellowship. We cannot truly pray even for ourselves without passing beyond ourselves and our individual experience. If we should begin with these the nature of prayer carries us beyond them, both to God and to man. Even private prayer is common prayer—the more so, possibly, as it retires from being public prayer.

Not to want to pray, then, is the sin behind sin. And it ends in not being able to pray. That is its punishment—spiritual dumbness, or at least aphasia, and starvation. We do not take our spiritual food, and so we falter, dwindle, and die. "In the sweat of your brow ye shall eat your bread." That has been said to be true both of physical and spiritual labour. It is true both of the life of bread and of the bread of life.

Prayer brings with it, as food does, a new sense of power and health. We are driven to it by hunger, and, having eaten, we are refreshed and strengthened for the battle which even our physical life involves. For heart and *flesh* cry out for the living God. God's gift is free; it is, therefore, a gift to our freedom, i.e. renewal to our moral strength, to what makes men of us. Without this gift always renewed, our very freedom can enslave us. The life of every organism is but the constant victory of a higher energy, constantly fed, over lower and more elementary forces. Prayer is the assimilation of a holy God's moral strength.

We must work for this living. To feed the soul we must toil at prayer. And what a labour it is! "He prayed in an agony." We must pray even to tears if need be. Our cooperation with God is our receptivity; but it is an active, a laborious receptivity, an importunity that drains our strength away if it do not tap the sources of the Strength Eternal. We work, we slave, at receiving. To him that hath this laborious expectancy it shall be given. Prayer is the powerful appropriation of power, of divine power. It is therefore creative.

Prayer is not mere wishing. It is asking—with a will. Our will goes into it. It is energy. *Orare est laborare.* We turn to an active Giver; therefore we go into action. For we could not pray without knowing and meeting Him in kind. If God has a controversy with Israel, Israel must wrestle with God. Moreover, He is the Giver not only of the answer, but first of the prayer itself. His gift provokes ours. He beseeches us, which makes us beseech Him. And what we ask for chiefly is the power to ask more and to ask better. We pray for more prayer. The true "gift of prayer" is God's grace before it is our facility.

Thus prayer is, for us, paradoxically, both a gift and a conquest, a grace and a duty. But does that not mean, is it not a special case of the truth, that all duty is a gift, every call on us a blessing, and that the task we often find a burden is really a boon? When we look up from under it it is a load, but those who look down to it from God's side see it as a blessing. It is like great wings—they increase the weight but also the flight. If we have no duty to do God has shut Himself from us. To be denied duty is to be denied God. No cross no Christ. "When pain ends gain ends too."

We are so egoistically engrossed about God's giving of the answer that we forget His gift of the prayer itself. But it is not a question simply of willing to pray, but of accepting and using as God's will the gift and the power to pray. In every act of prayer we have already begun to do God's will, for which above all things we pray. The prayer within all prayer is "Thy will be done." And has that petition not a special significance here? "My prayer is Thy Will. Thou didst create it in me. It is Thine more than mine. Perfect Thine own will"—all that is the paraphrase, from this viewpoint, of "Hear my prayer." "The will to pray," we say, "is Thy will. Let that be done both in my petition and in Thy perfecting of it." The petition is half God's will. It is God's will inchoate. "Thy will" (in my prayer) "be done (in Thy answer). It is Thine both to will and to do. Thy will be done in heaven— in the answer, as it is done upon earth—in the asking."

Prayer has its great end when it lifts us to be more conscious and more sure of the gift than the need, of the grace than the sin. As petition rises out of need or sin, in our first prayer it comes first; but it may fall into a subordinate place when, at the end and height of our worship, we are filled with the fullness of God. "In that day ye shall ask Me nothing." Inward sorrow is fulfilled in the prayer of petition; inward joy in the prayer of thanksgiving. And this thought helps to deal with the question as to the hearing of prayer, and especially its answer. Or rather as to the place and kind of answer. We shall come one day to a heaven where we shall gratefully know that God's great refusals were sometimes the true answers to our truest prayer. Our soul is fulfilled if our petition is not.

When we begin to pray we may catch and surprise ourselves in a position like this. We feel to be facing God from a position of independence. If He start from His end we do from ours. We are His *vis-a-vis;* He is ours. He is an object so far as we are concerned; and we are the like to Him. Of course, He is an object of *worship.* We do not start on equal terms, march up to Him, as it were, and put our case. We do more than approach Him erect, with courteous self-respect shining through our poverty. We bow down to Him. We worship. But still it is a voluntary, an independent, submission and tribute, so to say. It is a reverence which we make and offer. We present something which is ours to give. If we ask Him to give we feel that we begin the giving in our worship. We are outside each other; and we call, and He graciously comes.

But this is not the Christian idea, it is only a crude stage of it (if the New Testament is to guide us). We are there taught that only those things are perfected in God which He begins, that we seek only because He found, we beseech Him because He first besought us (2 Cor. v. 20). If our prayer reach or move Him it is because He first reached and moved us to pray. The prayer that reached heaven began there, when Christ went forth. It began when God turned to beseech us in Christ—in the appealing Lamb slain before the foundation of the world. The Spirit went out with the power and function in it to return with our soul. Our prayer is the answer to God's. Herein is prayer, not that we prayed Him, but that He first prayed us, in giving His Son to be a propitiation for us. The heart of the Atonement is prayer—Christ's great self-offering to God in the Eternal Spirit. The whole rhythm of Christ's soul, so to say, was Godhead going out and returning on itself. And so God stirs and inspires all prayer which finds and moves Him. His love provokes our sacred forwardness. He does not compel us, but we cannot help it after that look, that tone, that turn of His. All say, "I am yours if you will"; and when we will it is prayer. Any final glory of human success or destiny rises from man being God's continual creation, and destined by Him for Him. So we pray because we were made for prayer, and God draws us out by breathing Himself in.

We feel this especially as prayer passes upwards into praise. When the mercy we besought comes home to us its movement is reversed in us, and it returns upon itself as thanksgiving. "Great blessings which are won with prayer are worn with thankfulness." Praise is the converted consecration of the egoism that may have moved our prayer. Prayer may spring from self-love, and be so far natural; for nature is all of the craving and taking kind. But praise is supernatural. It is of pure grace. And it is a sign that the prayer was more than natural at heart. Spare some leisure, therefore, from petition for thanksgiving. If the Spirit move conspicuously to praise, it shows that He also moved latently the prayer, and that within nature is that which is above it. "Prayer and thanks are like the double motion of the lungs; the air that is drawn in by prayer is breathed forth again by thanks."

Prayer is turning our will on God either in the way of resignation or of impetration. We yield to His Will or He to ours. Hence religion is above all things prayer, according as it is a religion of will and conscience, as it is an ethical religion. It is will and Will. To be religious is to pray. Bad prayer is false religion. Not to pray is to be irreligious. "The battle for religion is the battle for prayer; the theory of religion is the philosophy of prayer." In prayer we do not think out God; we draw Him out. Prayer is where our thought of God passes into action, and becomes more certain than thought. In all thought which is not mere dreaming or brooding there is an element of will; and in earnest (which is intelligent) prayer we give this element the upper hand. We do not simply spread our thought out before God, but we *offer* it to Him, turn it on Him, bring it to bear on Him, press it on Him. This is our great and first sacrifice, and it becomes pressure on God. We can offer God nothing so great and effective as our obedient acceptance of the mind and purpose and work of Christ. It is not easy. It is harder than any idealism. But then it is very mighty. And it is a power that grows by exercise. At first it groans, at last it glides. And it comes to this, that, as there are thoughts that seem to think themselves in us, so there are prayers that pray themselves in us. And, as those are the best thoughts, these are the best prayers. For it is the Christ at prayer who lives in us, and we are conduits of the Eternal Intercession.

Prayer is often represented as the great means of the Christian life. But it is no mere means, it is the great end of that life. It is, of course, not untrue to call it a means. It is so, especially at first. But at last it is truer to say that we live the Christian life in order to pray than that we pray in order to live the Christian life. It is at least as true. Our prayer prepares for our work and sacrifice, but all our work and sacrifice still more prepare for prayer. And we are, perhaps, oftener wrong in our work, or even our sacrifice, than we are in our prayer—and that for want of its guidance. But to reach this height, to make of prayer our great end, and to order life always in view of such a solemnity, in this sense to pray without ceasing and without pedantry—it is a slow matter. We cannot move fast to such a fine product of piety and feeling. It is a growth in grace. And the whole history of the world shows that nothing grows so slowly as grace, nothing costs as much as free grace; a fact which drives us to all kinds of apologies to explain what seems the absence of God from His world, and especially from His world of souls. If God, to our grief, seems to us far absent from history, how does He view the distance, the absence, of history from Him?

A chief object of all prayer is to bring us to God. But we may attain His presence and come closer to Him by the way we ask Him for other things, concrete things or things of the Kingdom, than by direct prayer for union with Him. The prayer for deliverance from personal trouble or national calamity may bring us nearer Him than mere devout aspiration to be lost in Him. The poor woman's prayer to find her lost sovereign may mean more than the prayer of many a cloister. Such distress is often meant by God as the initial means and exercise to His constant end of reunion with Him. His patience is so long and kind that He is willing to begin with us when we are no farther on than to use Him as a means of escape or relief. The holy Father can turn to His own account at last even the exploiting egoism of youth. And He gives us some answer, though the relief does not come, if He keeps us praying, and ever more instant and purified in prayer. Prayer is never rejected so long as we do not cease to pray. The chief failure of prayer is its cessation. Our importunity is a part of God's answer, both of His answer to us and ours to Him. He is sublimating our idea of prayer, and realizing the final purpose in all trouble of driving us farther in on Himself. A homely image has been used. The joiner, when he glues together two boards, keeps them tightly clamped till the cement sets, and the outward pressure is no more needed; then he unscrews. So with the calamities, depressions, and disappointments that crush us into close contact with God. The pressure on us is kept up till the soul's union with God is set. Instant relief would not establish the habit of prayer, though it might make us believe in it with a promptitude too shallow to last or to make it the principle of our soul's life at any depth. A faith which is based chiefly on impetration might become more of a faith in prayer than a faith in God. If we got all we asked for we should soon come to treat Him as a convenience, or the request as a magic. The reason of much bewilderment about prayer is that we are less occupied about faith in God than about faith in prayer. In a like way we are misled about the question of immortality because we become more occupied with the soul than with God, and with its endless duration more than its eternal life, asking if we shall be in eternity more than eternity in us.

In God's eyes the great object of prayer is the opening or restoring of free communion with Himself in a kingdom of Christ, a life communion which may even, amid our duty and service, become as unconscious as the beating of our heart. In this sense every true prayer brings its answer with it; and that not "reflexly" only, in our pacification of soul, but objectively in our obtaining a deeper and closer place in God and His purpose. If prayer is God's great gift, it is one inseparable from the giver; who, after all, is His own great gift, since revelation is His Self-donation. He is actively with us, therefore, as we pray, and we exert His will in praying. And, on the other hand, prayer makes us to realize how far from God we were, i.e. it makes us realize our worst trouble and repair it. The outer need kindles the sense of the inner, and we find that the complete answer to prayer is the Answerer, and the hungry soul comes to itself in the fullness of Christ.

Prayer is the highest use to which speech can be put. It is the highest meaning that can be put into words. Indeed, it breaks through language and escapes into action. We could never be told of what passed in Christ's mountain midnights. Words fail us in prayer oftener than anywhere else; and the Spirit must come in aid of our infirmity, set out our case to God, and give to us an unspoken freedom in prayer, the possession of our central soul, the reality of our inmost personality in organic contact with His. We are taken up from human speech to the region of the divine Word, where Word is deed. We are integrated into the divine consciousness, and into the dual soliloquy of Father and Son, which is the divine give and take that upholds the world. We discover how poor a use of words it is to work them into argument and pursue their dialectic consequences. There is a deeper movement of speech than that, and a more inward mystery, wherein the Word does not spread out to wisdom, nor broods in dream, but gathers to power and condenses to action. The Word becomes Flesh, Soul, Life, the active conquering kingdom of God.

Prayer, as it is spoken, follows the principle of the Incarnation with its twofold movement, down and up.[3] It is spirit not in expression only, but in deed and victory. It is speech become not only movement, but moral action and achievement; it is word become work; as the Word from being Spirit became flesh, as Christ from prophet became priest, and then Holy Spirit. It is the principle of the Incarnation, only with the descending movement reversed. "Ye are gods." God became man in His Son's outgoing that man might become divine; and prayer is in the train of the Son's return to the Father, a function of the Ascension and Exaltation, in which (if we may not say man becomes God) we are made partakers of the divine nature, not ontologically, but practically, experimentally. It is the true response, and tribute, and trophy to Christ's humiliation. Man rises to be a co-worker with God in the highest sense. For it is only action, it is not by dream or rapture, far less in essence, that we enter communion with an active being—above all with the eternal Act of God in Christ that upholds the world. As such communion prayer is no mere *rapport,* no mere contact. It is the central act of the soul, organic with Christ's; it is that which brings it into tune with the whole universe as God's act, and answers the beating of its central heart. It is a part and function of the creative, preservative, and consummatory energy of the world.

What is true religion? It is not the religion which contains most truth in the theological sense of the word. It is not the religion most truly thought out, nor that which most closely fits with thought. It is religion which comes to itself most powerfully in prayer. It is the religion in which the soul becomes very sure of God and itself in prayer. Prayer contains the very heart and height of truth, but especially in the Christian sense of truth—reality and action. In prayer the inmost truth of our personal being locks with the inmost reality of things, its energy finds a living Person acting as their unity and life, and we escape the illusions of sense, self, and the world. Prayer, indeed, is the great means for appropriating, out of the amalgam of illusion which means so much for our education, the pure gold of God as He wills, the Spirit as He works, and things as they are. It is the great school both of proficiency and of veracity of soul. (How few court and attain proficiency of soul!) It may often cast us down, for we are reduced by this contact to our true dimensions—but to our great peace.

Prayer, true prayer, does not allow us to deceive ourselves. It relaxes the tension of our self-inflation. It produces a clearness of spiritual vision. Searching with a judgment that begins at the house of God, it ceases not to explore with His light our own soul. If the Lord is our health He may need to act on many men, or many moods, as a lowering medicine. At His coming our self-confidence is shaken. Our robust confidence, even in grace, is destroyed. The pillars of our house tremble, as if they were ivy-covered in a searching wind. Our lusty faith is refined, by what may be a painful process, into a subtler and more penetrating kind; and its outward effect is for the time impaired, though in the end it is increased. The effect of the prayer which admits God into the recesses of the soul is to destroy that spiritual density, not to say stupidity, which made our religion cheery or vigorous because it knew no better, and which was the condition of getting many obvious things done, and producing palpable effect on the order of the day. There are fervent prayers which, by making people feel good, may do no more than foster the delusion that natural vigour or robust religion, when flushed enough, can do the work of the kingdom of God. There is a certain egoist self-confidence which is increased by the more

---

[3] See the last chapter of *Person and Place of Christ.*

elementary forms of religion, which upholds us in much of our contact with men, and which even secures us an influence with them. But the influence is one of impression rather than permeation, it overbears rather than converts, and it inflames rather than inspires. This is a force which true and close prayer is very apt to undermine, because it saps our self-deception and its Pharisaism. The confidence was due to a lack of spiritual insight which serious prayer plentifully repairs. So by prayer we acquire our true selves. If my prayer is not answered, I am. If my petition is not fulfilled, my person, my soul, is; as the artist comes to himself and his happiness in the exercise of the talent he was made for, in spite of the delay and difficulty of turning his work to money. If the genius is happy who gets scope, the soul is blessed that truly comes to itself in prayer.

Blessed, yet not always happy. For by prayer we are set tasks sometimes which (at first, at least) may add to life's burden. Our eyes being opened, we see problems to which before we were blind, and we hear calls that no more let us alone. And I have said that we are shown ourselves at times in a way to dishearten us, and take effective dogmatism out of us. We lose effect on those people who take others at their own emphatic valuation, who do not try the spirits, and who have acquired no skill to discern the Lord in the apostle. True searching prayer is incompatible with spiritual dullness or self-complacency. And, therefore, such stupidity is not a mere defect, but a vice. It grew upon us because we did not court the searching light, nor haunt the vicinity of the great white Throne. We are chargeable with it because of our neglect of what cures it. Faith is a quickening spirit, it has insight; and religious density betrays its absence, being often the victim of the sermon instead of the *alumnus* of the gospel. It is not at all the effect of ignorance. Many ignorant people escape it by the exercise of themselves unto godliness; and they not only show wonderful spiritual acumen, but they turn it upon themselves; with a result, often, of great but vigilant humility, such as is apt to die out of an aggressive religion more eager to bring in a kingdom coming than to trust a Kingdom come. They are self-sufficient in a godly sort, and can even carry others, in a way which reveals the action of a power in them beyond all natural and unschooled force. We can feel in them the discipline of the Spirit. We can read much habitual prayer between their lines. They have risen far above religion. They are in the Spirit, and live in a long Lord's day. We know that they are not trying to serve Christ with the mere lustiness of natural religion, nor expecting to do the Spirit's work with the force of native temperament turned pious. There are, even amongst the religious, people of a shrewd density or nimble dullness who judge heavenly things with an earthly mind. And, outside the religious, among those who are but interested in religion, there may be a certain gifted stupidity, a witty obtuseness; as among some writers who *sans gene* turn what they judge to be the spirit of the age upon the realities of Eternity, and believe that it dissolves them in spray. Whether we meet this type within the Church or without, we can mostly feel that it reveals the prayerless temper whatever the zeal or vivacity may be. Not to pray is not to discern—not to discern the things that really matter, and the powers that really rule. The mind may see acutely and clearly, but the personality perceives nothing subtle and mighty; and then it comforts and deludes itself by saying it is simple and not sophisticated; and it falls a victim to the Pharisaism of the plain man. The finer (and final) forces, being unfelt, are denied or decried. The eternal motives are misread, the spell of the Eternal disowned. The simplicity in due course becomes merely bald. And all because the natural powers are unschooled, unchastened, and unempowered by the energy of prayer; and yet they are turned, either, in one direction, to do Christian work, active but loveless, or, on the other, to discuss and renounce Christian truth. It is not always hard to tell among Christian men those whose thought is matured in prayer, whose theology there becomes a hymn, whose energy is disciplined there, whose work there becomes love poured out, as by many a Salvationist lass, and whose temper is there subdued to that illuminated humility in which a man truly finds his soul. "The secret of the Lord is with them that fear Him, and He will show them His covenant." The deeper we go into things the more do we enter a world where the mastery and the career is not to talent but to prayer.

In prayer we do not ask God to do things contrary to Nature. Rather here ascending Nature takes its true effect and arrives. For the God we invoke is the Lord and Destiny of the whole creation; and in our invocation of Him Nature ends on its own key-note. He created the world at the first with a final and constant reference to the new creation, whose native speech is prayer. The whole creation thus comes home and finds itself in our prayer; and when we ask from the God of the *whole* Creation we neither do nor expect an arbitrary thing. We petition a God in whom all things are fundamentally working together for good to such a congenial cry. So far from crossing Nature, we give it tongue. We lift it to its divinest purpose, function, and glory. Nature excels itself in our prayer. The Creation takes its true effect in personality, which at once resists it, crowns it, and understands it; and personality takes true effect in God—in prayer. If there be a divine teleology in Nature at all, prayer is the telos. The world was made to worship God, for God's glory. And this purpose is the world's providence, the principle of creation. It is an end present all along the line and course of natural evolution; for we deal in prayer most closely with One to whom is no after nor before. We realize the simultaneity of Eternity.

When we are straitened in prayer we are yet not victims of Nature, we are yet free in the grace of God—as His own freedom was straitened in Christ's incarnation, not to say His dereliction, to the finishing of His task. It is hard, it is often impossible, for us to tell whether our hour of constriction or our hour of expansion contributes more to the divine purpose and its career. Both go to make real prayer. They are the systole and diastole of the world's heart. True prayer is the supreme function of the personality which is the world's supreme product. It is personality with this function that God seeks above all to rear—it is neither particular moods of its experience, nor influential relations of it with the world. The praying personality has an eternal value for God as an end in itself. This is the divine fullness of life's time and course, the one achievement that survives with more power in death than in life. The intercession of Christ in heaven is the continuity and consummation of His supreme work on earth. To share it is the meaning of praying in the Spirit. And it has more effect on history than civilization has. This is a hard saying, but a Christian can say no otherwise without in so far giving up his Christianity.

"There is a budding morrow in midnight." And every juncture, every relation, and every pressure of life has in it a germ of possibility and promise for our growth in God and grace; which germ to rear is the work of constant and progressive prayer. (For as a soul has a history, prayer has its progress.) This germ we do not always see, nor can we tend it as if we did. It is often hidden up under the earthly relations, and may there be lost—our soul is lost. (It can be lost even through love.) But also it may from there be saved—and we escape from the fowler's net. Its growth is often visible only to the Saviour whom we keep near by prayer, whose search we invoke, and for whose action we make room in prayer. Our certainty of Him is girt round with much uncertainty, about His working, about the steps of His process. But in prayer we become more and more sure that He is sure, and knows all things, and hesitates or falters never, and commands all things to His end. All along Christ is being darkly formed within us as we pray; and our converse with God goes on rising to become an element of the intercourse of the Father and the Son, whom we overhear, as it were, at converse in us. Yet this does not insulate us from our kind; for other people are then no more alien to us, but near in a Lord who is to them what He is to us. Private prayer may thus become more really common prayer than public prayer is.

And so also with the universe itself as we rise in Christ to prayer. Joined with its Redeemer, we are integrated into its universality. We are made members of its vast whole. We are not detained and cramped in a sectional world. We are not planted in the presence of an outside, alien universe, nor in the midst of a distraught, unreconciled universe, which speaks like a crowd, in many fragments and many voices, and drags us from one relation with it to another, with a Lo, here is Christ, or there. But it is a universe wholly vocal to us, really a universe, and vocal as a whole, one congenial and friendly, as it comes to us in its Christ and ours. It was waiting for us—for such a manifestation of the Son of God as prayer is. This world is not now a desert haunted by demons. And it is more than a vestibule to another; it is its prelude in the drama of all things. We know it in another knowledge now than its own. Nature can never be understood by natural knowledge. We know it as science never can—as a whole, and as reality. We know it as we are known of God—altogether, and not in pieces. Having nothing, and praying for everything, we possess all things. The faith that energizes in Christian prayer sets us at the centre of that whole of which Nature is the overture part. The steps of thought and its processes of law fade away. They do not cease to act, but they retire from notice. We grasp the mobile organization of things deep at its constant and trusty heart. We receive the earnest of our salvation—Christ in us.

> There, where one centre reconciles all things,
> The world's profound heart beats.

We are planted there. And all the mediation of process becomes immediate in its eternal ground. As we are going there we feel already there. "They were willing to receive Him into the boat, and straightway the boat was at the land whither they were going." We grasp that eternal life to which all things work, which gives all the waxing organization its being and meaning—for a real organism only grows because it already is. That is the mark of a real life. And soul and person is the greatest organism of all. We apprehend our soul as it is apprehended of God and in God, the timeless God—with all its evolution, past or future, converted into a divine present. We are already all that we are to be. We possess our souls in the prayer which is real communion with God. We enter by faith upon that which to sight and history is but a far future reversion. When He comes to our prayer He brings with Him all that He purposes to make us. We are already the "brave creature" He means us to be. More than our desire is fulfilled—our soul is. In such hour or visitation we realize our soul or person at no one stage of it, but in its fullness, and in the context of its whole and final place in history, the world, and eternity. A phase which has no meaning in itself, yet carries, like the humble mother of a great genius, an eternal meaning in it. And we can seize that meaning in prayer; we can pierce to what we are at our true centre and true destiny, i.e. what we are to God's grace. Laws and injunctions such as "Love your neighbour," even "Love your enemy," then become life principles, and they are law pressures no more. The yoke is easy. Where all is forgiven to seventy times seven there is no friction and no grief any more. We taste love and joy. All the pressure of life then goes to form the crystals of faith. It is God making up His jewels.

When we are in God's presence by prayer we are *right,* our will is morally right, we are doing His will. However unsure we may be about other acts and efforts to serve Him we know we are right in this. If we ask truly but ask amiss, it is not a sin, and He will in due course set us right in that respect. We are sure that prayer is according to His will, and that we are just where we ought to be. And that is a great matter for the rightness of our thought, and of the aims and desires proposed by our thought. It means much both as to their form and their passion. If we realize that prayer is the acme of our right relation to God, if we are sure that we are never so right with Him in anything we do as in prayer, then prayer must have the greatest effect and value for our life, both in its purpose and its fashion, in its spirit and its tenor. What puts us right morally, right with a Holy God (as prayer does), must have a great shaping power on every part and every juncture of life. And, of course, especially upon the spirit and tenor of our prayer itself, upon the form and complexion of our petition.

The effect of our awful War[4] will be very different on the prayerful and the prayerless. It will be a sifting judgment. It will turn to prayer those who did not pray, and increase the prayer of those who did. But some, whose belief in God grew up only in fair weather and not at the Cross, it will make more sceptical and prayerless than ever, and it will present them with a world more confused and more destitute of a God than before; which can only lead to renewed outbreaks of the same kind as soon as the nations regain strength. The prayerless spirit saps a people's moral strength because it blunts their thought and conviction of the Holy. It must be so if prayer is such a moral blessing and such a shaping power, if it pass, by its nature, from the vague volume and passion of devotion to formed petition and effort. Prayerlessness is an injustice and a damage to our own soul, and therefore to its history, both in what we do and what we think. The root of all deadly heresy is prayerlessness. Prayer finds our clue in a world otherwise without form and void. And it draws a magic circle round us over which the evil spirits may not pass. "Prayer," says Vinet, "is like the air of certain ocean isles, which is so pure that there vermin cannot live. We should surround ourselves with this atmosphere, as the diver shuts himself into his bell ere he descends into the deep."

If there must be in the Church a communion of belief, there must be there also a communion of prayer. For the communion of prayer is the very first form the communion of belief takes. It is in this direction that Church unity lies. It lies behind prayer, in something to which prayer gives effect, in that which is the source and soul of prayer—in our relation with God in Christ, in our new creation. Prayer for Church unity will not bring that unity; but that which stirs, and founds, and wings prayer will. And prayer is its chief exercise. The true Church is just as wide as the community of Christian prayer, i.e. of due response to the gospel of our reconcilement and communion with God. And it is a thing almost dreadful that Christians who pray to the same God, Christ, and Saviour should refuse to unite in prayer because of institutional differences.

A prayer is also a promise. Every true prayer carries with it a vow. If it do not, it is not in earnest. It is not of a piece with life. Can we pray in earnest if we do not in the act commit ourselves to do our best to bring about the answer? Can we escape some kind of hypocrisy? This is especially so with intercession. What is the value of praying for the

---

[4] The First World War.

poor if all the rest of our time and interest is given only to becoming rich? Where is the honesty of praying for our country if in our most active hours we are chiefly occupied in making something out of it, if we are strange to all sacrifice for it? Prayer is one form of sacrifice, but if it is the only form it is vain oblation. If we pray for our child that he may have God's blessing, we are really promising that nothing shall be lacking on our part to be a divine blessing to him. And if we have no kind of religious relation to him (as plenty of Christian parents have none), our prayer is quite unreal, and its failure should not be a surprise. To pray for God's kingdom is also to engage ourselves to service and sacrifice for it. To begin our prayer with a petition for the hallowing of God's name and to have no real and prime place for holiness in our life or faith is not sincere. The prayer of the vindictive for forgiveness is mockery, like the prayer for daily bread from a wheat-cornerer. No such man could say the Lord's Prayer but to his judgment. What would happen to the Church if the Lord's Prayer became a test for membership as thoroughly as the Creeds have been? The Lord's Prayer is also a vow to the Lord. None but a Christian can pray it, or should. Great worship of God is also a great engagement of ourselves, a great committal of our action. To begin the day with prayer is but a formality unless it go on in prayer, unless for the rest of it we pray in deed what we began in word. One has said that while prayer is the day's best beginning it must not be like the handsome title-page of a worthless book.

"Thy will be done." Unless that were the spirit of all our prayer, how should we have courage to pray if we know ourselves at all, or if we have come to a time when we can have some retrospect on our prayers and their fate? Without this committal to the wisdom of God, prayer would be a very dangerous weapon in proportion as it was effective. No true God could promise us an answer to our every prayer. No Father of mankind could. The rain that saved my crop might ruin my neighbour's. It would paralyse prayer to be sure that it would prevail as it is offered, certainly and at once. We should be terrified at the power put into our foolish hands. Nothing would do more to cure us of a belief in our own wisdom than the granting of some of our eager prayers. And nothing could humiliate us more than to have God say when the fulfilment of our desire brought leanness to our souls. "Well, you would have it." It is what He has said to many. But He said more, "My grace is sufficient for thee."

Chapter II: The Naturalness of Prayer

We touch the last reality directly in prayer. And we do this not by thought's natural research, yet by a quest not less laborious. Prayer is the atmosphere of revelation, in the strict and central sense of that word. It is the climate in which God's manifestation bursts open into inspiration. All the mediation of Nature and of things sinks here to the rear, and we are left with God in Christ as His own Mediator and His own Revealer. He is directly with us and in us. We transcend these two thousand years as if they were but one day. By His Spirit and His Spirit's creative miracle God becomes Himself our new nature, which is yet our own, our destined Nature; for we were made with His image for our "doom of greatness." It is no mere case of education or evolution drawing out our best. Prayer has a creative action in its answer. It does more than present us with our true, deep, latent selves. It lays hold on God, and God is not simply our magnified self. Our other self is, in prayer, our Creator still creating. Our Maker it is that is our Husband. He is Another. We feel, the more we are united with Him in true prayer, the deep, close difference, the intimate otherness in true love. Otherwise prayer becomes mere dreaming; it is spiritual extemporizing and not converse. The division runs not simply between us and Nature, but it parts us within our spiritual self, where union is most close. It is a spiritual distinction, like the distinction of Father and Son in heaven. But Nature itself, our natural selves, are involved in it; because Nature for the Christian is implicated in Redemption. It "arrives." It is read in a new script. The soul's conflict is found in a prelude in it. This may disturb our pagan joy. It may quench the consolations of Nature. The ancient world could take refuge in Nature as we cannot. It could escape there from conscience in a way impossible to us, because for us body runs up into soul, and Nature has become organic with spirit, an arena and even (in human nature) an experience of God's will. It groans to come to itself in the sons of God. Redemption is cosmic. We do not evade God's judgment there; and we put questions about His equity there which did not trouble the Greek. If we take the wings of the morning and dwell in the uttermost parts of the earth, God still besets us behind and before. We still feel the collision of past and future, of conduct and conscience. If we try to escape from His presence there, we fail; the winds are His messengers, the fires His ministers, wars and convulsions instruments of His purpose. He is always confronting us, judging us, saving us in a spiritual world, which Nature does not stifle, but only makes it more universal and impressive than our personal strife. In Nature our *vis-a-vis* is still the same power we meet as God in our soul.

> *The voice that rolls the stars along*
> *Speaks all His promises.*

Our own natural instincts turn our scourges, but also our blessings, according as they mock God or serve Him. So Nature becomes our chaperone for Christ, our tutor whose duty is daily to deliver us at Christ's door. It opens out into a Christ whose place and action are not historic only, but also cosmic. The cosmic place of Christ in the later epistles is not apostolic fantasy, extravagant speculation, nor groundless theosophy. It is the ripeness of practical faith, faith which by action comes to itself and to its own.

Especially is this pointed where faith has its most pointed action as prayer. If cosmic Nature runs up into man, man rises up into prayer; which thus fulfils Nature, brings its inner truth to pass, and crowns its bias to spirit. Prayer is seen to be the opening secret of creation, its destiny, that to which it all travails. It is the burthen of evolution. The earnest expectation of the creation waits, and all its onward thrust works, for the manifestation of the sons of God. Nature comes to itself in prayer. Prayer realizes and brings to a head the truth of Nature, which groans being burdened with the passion of its deliverance, its relief in prayer. *"Magna ars est conversari cum Deo."* "The art of prayer is Nature gone to heaven." We become in prayer Nature's true artists (if we may so say), the vehicles of its finest and inmost passion. And we are also its true priests, the organs of its inner commerce with God, where the Spirit immanent in the world meets the Spirit transcendent in obedient worship. The sum of things for ever speaking is heard in heaven to pray without ceasing. It is speaking not only to us but in us to God. Soliloquy here is dialogue. In our prayer God returns from His projection in Nature to speak with Himself. When we speak to God it is really the God who lives in us speaking through us to Himself. His Spirit returns to Him who gave it; and returns not void, but bearing our souls with Him. The dialogue of grace is really the monologue of the divine nature in self-communing love. In prayer, therefore, we do true and final justice to the world. We give Nature to itself. We make it say what it was charged to say. We make it find in thought and word its own soul.

It comes to itself not in man but in the praying man, the man of Christian prayer. The Christian man at prayer is the secretary of Creation's praise. So prayer is the answer to Nature's quest, as God is the answer to prayer. It is the very nature of nature; which is thus miraculous or nothing at its core.

Here the friction vanishes, therefore, between prayer and natural law. Nature and all its plexus of law is not static, but dynamic. It is not interplay, but evolution. It has not only to move, but to arrive. Its great motive power is not a mere instinct, but a destiny. Its system is not a machine, but a procession. It is dramatic. It has a close. Its ruling power is not what it rises from, but what it moves to. Its impulse is its goal immanent. All its laws are overruled by the comprehensive law of its destination. It tends to prayer. The laws of Nature are not like iron. If they are fixed they are only fixed as the composition is fixed at H_2O of the river which is so fluid and moving that I can use it at any time to bear me to its sea. They are fixed only in so far as makes them reliable, and not fatal, to man's spirit. Their nature is constant, but their function is not stiff. What is fixed in the river is the constancy of its fluidity. "Still glides the stream, and shall for ever glide." The greatest law of Nature is thus its bias to God, its *nisus*[5] to return to His rest. This comes to light chiefly in man's gravitation to Him, when His prodigal comes home to Him. The forwardest creation comes to itself in our passion for God and in our finding of Him in prayer. In prayer, therefore, we do not ask God to do things contrary to Nature, though our request may seem contrary to sections of it which we take for the whole. We ask Him to fulfil Nature's own prayer.

The atmosphere of prayer seems at first to be the direct contrary of all that goes with such words as practical or scientific. But what do we mean by practical at last but that which contributes to the end for which the world and mankind were made? The whole of history, as the practical life of the race, is working out the growth, the emancipation of the soul, the enrichment and fortifying of the human spirit. It is doing on the large scale what every active life is doing on the small—it is growing soul. There is no reality at last except soul, except personality. This alone has eternal meaning, power, and value, since this alone develops or hampers the eternal reality, the will of God. The universe has its being and its truth for a personality, but for one at last which transcends individual limits. To begin with the natural plane, our egoism constructs there a little world with a definite teleology converging on self, one which would subdue everybody and everything to be tributary to our common sensible self. On a more spiritual (yet not on the divine) plane the race does the like with its colossal ego. It views and treats the universe as contributory to itself, to the corporate personality of the race. Nature is here for man, man perhaps for the superman. We are not here for the glory of God, but God is here for the aid and glory of man. But either way all things are there to work together for personality, and to run up into a free soul. Man's practical success is then what makes for the enhancement of this ego, small or great. But, on the Christian plane, man himself, as part of a creation, has a meaning and an end; but it is in God; he does not return on himself. God is his nisus and drift. God works in him; he is not just trying to get his own head out. But God is Love. All the higher science of Nature, therefore, is an exposition of its work in the service of souls and their love. It is the science of a Nature which is the *milieu* and the machinery that give the soul its bent to love, and turn it out its true self in love. All the practice and science of the world is there, therefore, to reveal and realize love and love's communion. It is all a

---

[5] Striving.

stage, a scenery, a plot, for a *dénounement* where beings mingle, and each is enriched by all and all by each. It all goes to the music of that love which binds all things together in the cosmic dance, and which makes each stage of each thing prophetic of its destined fullness only in a world so bound. So science itself is practical if prayer end and round all. It is the theory of a cosmic movement with prayer for its active end. And it is an ethical science at last, it is a theology, if the Christian end is the real end of the whole world. All knowledge serves love and love's communion. For Christian faith a universe is a universe of souls, an organism of persons, which is the expression of an Eternal Will of love. This love is the real presence which gives meaning, and movement, and permanence to a fleeting world of sense. And it is by prayer that we come into close and conscious union with this universe and power of love, this living reality of things. Prayer (however miraculous) is, therefore, the most natural thing in the world. It is the effectuation of all Nature, which comes home to roost there, and settles to its rest. It is the last word of all science, giving it contact with a reality which, as science alone, it cannot reach. And it is also the most practical thing in all man's action and history, as doing most to bring to pass the spiritual object for which all men and all things exist and strive.

Those who feel prayer stifled by the organization of law do not consider that law itself, if we take a long enough sweep, keeps passing us on to prayer. Law rises from Nature, through history, to heaven. It is integrated historically, i.e. by Christ's cross and the Church's history, with the organization of love. But that is the organization of Eternity in God, and it involves the interaction of all souls in a communion of ascending prayer. Prayer is the native movement of the spiritual life that receives its meaning and its soul only in Eternity, that works in the style and scale of Eternity, owns its principles, and speaks its speech. It is the will's congenial surrender to that Redemption and Reconciliation between loving wills which is God's Eternity acting in time. We beseech God because He first besought us.

So not to pray on principle means that thought has got the better of the will. The question is whether thought includes will or will thought; and thought wins if prayer is suppressed. Thought and not personality is then in command of the universe. If will is but a function of the idea, then prayer is but a symptom, it is not a power. It belongs to the phenomenology of the Infinite, it is not among its controls.

Prayer is doing God's will. It is letting Him pray in us. We look for answer because His fullness is completely equal to His own prayers. Father and Son are perfectly adequate to each other. That is the Holy Spirit and self-sufficiency of the Godhead.

If God's will is to be done on earth as it is in heaven, prayer begins with *adoration*. Of course, it is thanks and petition; but before we give even our prayer we must first receive. The Answerer provides the very prayer. What we do here rests on what God has done. What we offer is drawn from us by what He offers. Our self-oblation stands on His; and the spirit of prayer flows from the gift of the Holy Ghost, the great Intercessor. Hence praise and adoration of His work in itself comes before even our thanksgiving for blessings to us. At the height of prayer, if not at its beginning, we are preoccupied with the great and glorious thing God has done for His own holy name in Redemption, apart from its immediate and particular blessing to us. We are blind for the time to ourselves. We cover our faces with our wings and cry "Holy, holy, holy is the Lord God of hosts; the fullness of the earth is His glory." Our full hearts glorify. We magnify His name. His perfections take precedence of our occasions. We pray for victory in the present war, for instance, and for deliverance from all war, for the sake of God's kingdom—in a spirit of adoration for the deliverance there that is not destroyed, or foiled, even by a devilry like this. If the kingdom of God not only got over the murder of Christ, but made it its great lever, there is nothing that it cannot get over, and nothing it cannot turn to eternal blessing and to the glory of the holy name. But to the perspective of this faith, and to its vision of values so alien to human standards, we can rise only in prayer.

But it would be unreal prayer which was adoration only, with no reference to special boons or human needs. That would be as if God recognized no life but His own—which is very undivine egoism, and its collective form is the religion of mere nationalism. In true prayer we do two things. We go out of ourselves, being lost in wonder, love and praise; but also, and in the same act, we go in upon ourselves. We stir up *all that is within us* to bless and hallow God's name. We examine ourselves keenly in that patient light, and we find ourselves even when our sin finds us out. Our nothingness is not burned and branded into us as if we had above only the starry irony of heaven. Our heart comes again. Our will is braced and purified. We not only recall our needs, but we discover new ones, of a more and more intimate and spiritual kind. The more spiritual we grow, the more we rise out of the subconscious or the unconscious. We never realize ourselves as we do when we forget ourselves after this godly sort in prayer. Prayer is not falling back upon the abyss below the soul; even as the secret of the Incarnation is sought in vain in that non-moral zone. Prayer is not what might be called the increased drone or boom of an unspeakable Om. But we rise in it to more conscious and positive relation with God the Holy—the God not abysmal but revealed, in whose revelation the thoughts of many hearts are revealed also, and whose fullness makes need almost as fast as it satisfies it.

After adoration, therefore, prayer is *thanksgiving* and petition. When we thank God our experience "arrives". It finds what it came for. It fulfills the greatest end of experience. It comes to its true self, comes to its own, and has its perfect work. It breathes large, long, and free, *sublimi anhelitu*[6]. The soul runs its true normal course back to God its Creator, who has stamped the destiny of this return upon it, and leaves it no peace till it finds its goal in Him. The gift we thank for becomes sacramental because it conveys chiefly the Giver, and is lost in Him and in His praise. It is He that chiefly comes in His saints and His boons. In real revelation we rise far above a mere interpretation of life, a mere explanation of events; we touch their Doer, the Life indeed, and we can dispense with interpretations, having Him. An occurrence thus becomes a revelation. It gives us God, in a sacrament. And where there is real revelation there is thanksgiving, there is eucharist; for God Himself is in the gift, and strikes His own music from the soul. If we think most of the gift, prayer may subtly increase our egoism. We praise for a gift to us. We are tempted to treat God as an asset, and to exploit him. But true prayer, thinking most of the Giver, quells the egoism and dissolves it in praise. What we received came for another end than just to gratify us. It came to carry God to us, and to lift us to Him and to the consent of His glory. The blessing in it transcends the enjoyment of it, and the Spirit of the outgoing God returns to Him not void, but bringing our souls as sheaves with Him.

So also with the *petition* in our prayer. It also is purified by adoration, praise, and thanksgiving. We know better what to pray for as we ought. We do not only bring to God desires that rise apart from Him, and that we present by an act of our own; but our desires, our will, as they are inspired are also *formed* in God's presence, as requests. They get

---

[6] Sublime breath.

shape. In thanks we spread out before Him and offer Him our past and present, but in petition it is our future.

But has petition a true place in the highest and purest prayer? Is it not lost in adoration and gratitude? Does adoration move as inevitably to petition as petition rises to adoration? In reply we might ask whether the best gratitude and purest thanks are not for answered petitions. Is there not this double movement in all spiritual action which centres in the Incarnation, where man ascends as God comes down? Does not man enlarge in God as God particularizes upon men? But, putting that aside, is the subsidence of petition not due to a wrong idea of God; as if our only relation were dependence, as if, therefore, will-lessness before Him were the devout ideal—as if we but acknowledge Him and could not act on Him? Ritschl, for example, following Schleiermacher, says, "Love to God has no sphere of action outside love to our brother." If that were so, there would be no room for petition, but only for worship of God and service of man without intercession. The position is not unconnected with Ritschl's neglect of the Spirit and His intercession, or with his aversion to the Catholic type of piety. If suffering were the only occasion and promptuary of prayer, then resignation, and not petition, might be the true spirit of prayer. But our desires and wills do not rise out of our suffering only, nor out of our passivity and dependence, but also out of our freedom (viewed both as a power and a peril), and out of our duty and our place in life; and therefore our petition is as due to God and as proper as our life's calling. If we may not will nor love, no doubt petition, especially for others, is a mistake. Of course, also, our egoism, engrossed with our happiness influences our prayer too often and too much. But we can never overcome our self-will by will-lessness, nor our greed of happiness by apathy. Petitions that are less than pure can only be purified by petition. Prayer is the salvation of prayer. We pray for better prayer. We can rise above our egoism only as we have real dealing with the will of God in petitionary prayer which does change His detailed intentions toward us though not His great will of grace and Salvation.

The element of adoration has been missed from worship by many observers of our public prayer. And the defect goes with the individualism of the age just past. Adoration is a power the egoist and individualist loses. He loses also the power both of thanksgiving and of petition, and sinks, through silence before God, to His neglect. For our blessings are not egoistically meant, nor do they remain blessings if so taken. They contemplate more than ourselves, as indeed does our whole place and work in the gift of life. We must learn to thank God not only for the blessings of others, but for the power to convey to others gifts which make them happier than they make us—as the gifts of genius so often do. One Church should praise Him for the prosperity of other Churches, for that is to the good of the gospel. And, as for petition, how can a man or a Church pray for their own needs to the omission of others? God's fundamental relation to us is one that embraces and blesses all. We are saved in a common salvation. The atmosphere of prayer is communion. Common prayer is the inevitable fruit of a gospel like Christ's.

Public prayer, therefore, should be in the main liturgical, with room for free prayer. The more it really is common prayer, and the more our relation with men extend and deepen (as prayer with and for men does extend them), the more we need forms which proceed from the common and corporate conscience of the Church. Even Christ did. As He rose to the height of His great world-work on the cross His prayer fell back on the liturgy of His people—on the Psalms. It is very hard for the ordinary minister to come home to the spiritual variety of a large congregation without those great forms which arose out of the deep soul of the Church before it spread into sectional boughs or individual twigs.

Common prayer is not necessarily public. To recite the Litany on a sick-bed is common prayer. Christ felt the danger of common prayer as public prayer (Matt. vi. 5, 6). And this is specially so when the public prayer is "extempore." To keep that real calls for an amount of private prayer which perhaps is not for every one. "Extempore" prayers are apt to be private prayers in public, like the Pharisee's in the temple, with too much idiosyncrasy for public use; or else they lose the spontaneity of private prayer, and turn as formal as a liturgy can be, though in another (and perhaps deadlier) way. The prayers of the same man inevitably fall more or less into the same forms and phrases. But private prayer may be more common in its note than public prayer should be private in its tone. Our private prayer should be common in spirit. We are doing in the act what many are doing. In the retired place we include in sympathy and intercession a world of other men which we exclude in fact. The world of men disappears from around us but not from within. We are not indifferent to its weal or woe in our seclusion. In the act of praying for ourselves we pray for others, for no temptation befalls us but what is common to man; and in praying for others we pray with them. We pray for their prayers and the success of their prayers. It is an act of union. We can thus be united even with churches that refuse to pray or unite with us.

Moreover, it is common prayer, however solitary, that prevails most, as being most in tune with the great first goal of God's grace—the community. So this union in prayer gives to prayer an ethical note of great power and value. If we really pray with others, it must clear, and consolidate, and exalt our moral relations with them everywhere. Could we best the man with whom and for whom we really pray? There is a great democratic note in common prayer which is also true prayer. "Eloquence and ardour have not done so much for Christ's cause as the humble virtues, the united activity, and the patient prayers of thousands of faithful people whose names are quite unknown." And we are united thus not only to the living but to the long dead. "He who prays is nearer Christ than even the apostles were," certainly than the apostles before the Cross and Resurrection.

We have been warned by a man of genius that the bane of so much religion is that it clings to God with its weakness and not with its strength. This is very true of that supreme act of religion of which our critics know least—of the act of prayer. So many of us pray because we are driven by need rather than kindled by grace. Our prayer is a cry rather than a hymn. It is a quest rather than a tryst. It trembles more than it triumphs. It asks for strength rather than exerts it. How different was the prayer of Christ! All the divine power of the Eternal Son went to it. It was the supreme form taken by His Sonship in its experience and action. Nothing is more striking in Christ's life than His combination of selflessness and power. His consciousness of power was equal to anything, and egoism never entered Him. His prayer was accordingly. It was the exercise of His unique power rather than of His extreme need. It came from His uplifting and not His despair. It was less His duty than His joy. It was more full of God's gift of grace than of man's poverty of faith, of a holy love than of a seeking heart. In His prayer He poured out neither His wish nor His longing merely, but His will. And He knew He was heard always. He knew it with such power and certainty that He could distribute His value, bless with His overflow, and promise His disciples they would be heard in His name. It was by His prayer that He countered and foiled the godless power in the world, the kingdom of the devil. "Satan hath desired to have thee—but I have prayed for thee." His prayer means so much for the weak because it arose out of this strength and its exercise. It was chiefly in His prayer that He was the Messiah, and the Revealer and Wielder of the power and kingship of God. His power with God was so great that it made His disciples feel it could only be the power of God; He prayed in the Eternal Spirit whereby He offered Himself to God. And it was so great because it was spent on God alone. So true is it that the kingdom of God comes not with observation, that the greatest things Christ did for it were done in the night and not in the day; His prayers meant more than His miracles. And His great triumph was when there were none to see, as they all forsook Him and fled. He was mightiest in His action for men not when He was acting on men but on God. He felt the dangers of the publicity where His work lay, and He knew that they were only to be met in secrecy. He did most for His public in entire solitude; there He put forth all His power. His nights were not always the rest of weakness from the day before, but often the storing of strength for the day to come. Prayer (if we let Christ teach us of it) is mightiest in the mightiest. It is the ether round the throne of the Most High. Its power answers to the omnipotence of grace. And those who feel they owe everything to God's grace need have no difficulty about the range of prayer. They may pray for everything.

A word, as I close this chapter, to the sufferers. We pray for the removal of pain, pray passionately, and then with exhaustion, sick from hope deferred and prayer's failure. But there is a higher prayer than that. It is a greater thing to pray for pain's conversion than for its removal. It is more of grace to pray that God would make a sacrament of it. The sacrament of pain! That we partake not simply, nor perhaps chiefly, when we say, or try to say, with resignation, "Thy will be done." It is not always easy for the sufferer, if he remain clear-eyed to see that it is God's will. It may have been caused by an evil mind, or a light fool, or some stupid greed. But, now it is there, a certain treatment of it is God's will; and that is to capture and exploit it for Him. It is to make it serve the soul and glorify God. It is to consecrate its elements and make it sacramental. It is to convert it into prayer.

God has blessed pain even in causing us to pray for relief from it, or profit. Whatever drives us to Him, and even nearer Him, has a blessing in it. And, if we are to go higher still, it is to turn pain to praise, to thank Him in the fires, to review life and use some of the energy we spend in worrying upon recalling and tracing His goodness, patience, and mercy. If much open up to us in such a review we may be sure there is much more we do not know, and perhaps never may. God is the greatest of all who do good by stealth and do not crave for every benefit to be acknowledged. Or we may see how our pain becomes a blessing to others. And we turn the spirit of heaviness to the garment of praise. We may stop grousing and get our soul into its Sunday clothes. The sacrament of pain becomes then a true Eucharist and giving of thanks.

And if there were a higher stage than all it would be Adoration—when we do not think of favours or mercies to us or ours at all, but of the perfection and glory of the Lord. We feel to His Holy Name what the true artist feels towards an unspeakable beauty. As Wordsworth says:

> *I gazed and gazed,*
> *And did not wish her mine.*

There was a girl of 15, tall, sweet, distinguished beyond her years. And this is how Heine ran into English at the sight of her:

> No flower is half so lovely,
>   So dear, and fair, and kind.
> A boundless tide of tenderness
>   Flows over my heart and mind.
> And I pray. (There is no answer
>   To beauty unearthly but prayer.)
> God answer my prayer, and keep you
>   So dear, and fine, and fair.

Chapter III: The Moral Reactions of Prayer

All religion is founded on prayer, and in prayer it has its test and measure. To be religious is to pray, to be irreligious is to be incapable of prayer. The theory of religion is really the philosophy of prayer; and the best theology is compressed prayer. The true theology is warm, and it steams upward into prayer. Prayer is access to whatever we deem God, and if there is no such access there is no religion; for it is not religion to resign ourselves to be crushed by a brute power so that we can no more remonstrate than resist. It is in prayer that our real idea of God appears, and in prayer that our real relation to God shows itself. On the first levels of our religion we go to our God for help and boon in the junctures of our natural life; but, as we rise to supernatural religion, gifts become less to us than the Giver; they are not such as feed our egoism. We forget ourselves in a godly sort; and what we court and what we receive in our prayer is not simply a boon but communion—or if a boon, it is the boon which Christians call the Holy Spirit, and which means, above all else, communion with God. But lest communion subside into mere meditation it must concentrate in prayer. We must keep acquiring by such effort the grace so freely given. There is truly a subconscious communion, and a godliness that forgets God well, in the hourly life of taxing action and duty; but it must rise to seasons of colloquy, when our action is wholly with the Father, and the business even of His kingdom turns into heart converse, where the yoke is easy and the burden light. Duty is then absorbed in love—the deep, active union of souls outwardly distinct. Their connection is not external and (as we might say) inorganic; it is inward, organic, and reciprocal. There is not only action but interplay, not only need and gift but trust and love. The boon is the Giver Himself, and its answer is the self of the receiver. *Cor ad cor loquitur.*[7] All the asking and having goes on in a warm atmosphere, where soul passes into soul without fusion, person is lost in person without losing personality, and thought about prayer becomes thought in prayer. The greatest, deepest, truest thought of God is generated in prayer, where right thought has its essential condition in a right will. The state and act of true prayer contains the very substance and summit of Christian truth, which is always there in solution, and becomes increasingly explicit and conscious. To grow in grace is to become more understanding in prayer. We make for the core of Christian reality and the source of Christian power.

Our atonement with God is the pregnant be-all and end-all of Christian peace and life; and what is that atonement but the head and front of the Saviour's perpetual intercession, of the outpouring of His sin-laden soul unto death? Unto death! That is to say, it is its outpouring utterly. So that His entire self-emptying and His perfect and prevailing prayer

---

[7] Heart speaks to heart.

are one. In this intercession our best prayer, broken, soiled, and feeble as it is, is caught up and made prayer indeed and power with God. This intercession prays for our very prayer, and atones for the sin in it. This is praying in the Holy Ghost, which is not necessarily a matter either of intensity or elation. This is praying "for Christ's sake." If it be true that the whole Trinity is in the gospel of our salvation, it is also true that all theology lies hidden in the prayer which is our chief answer to the gospel. And the bane of so much theology, old and new, is that it has been denuded of prayer and prepared in a vacuum.

Prayer draws on our whole personality; and not only so, but on the whole God. And it draws on a God who really comes home nowhere else. God is here, not as a mere presence as He is in Nature, nor is He a mere pressure as He closes in upon us in the sobering of life. We do not face Him in mere meditation, nor do we cultivate Him as life's most valuable asset. But He is here as our Lover, our Seeker, our Visitant, our Interlocutor; He is our Saviour, our Truth, our Power, nay, our Spiritual World. In this supreme exercise of our personality He is at once our Respondent and our Spiritual Universe. Nothing but the experience of prayer can solve paradoxes like these. On every other level they are absurd. But here deep answers deep. God becomes the living truth of our most memorable and shaping experience, not its object only but its essence. He who speaks to us also hears in us, because He opens our inward ear (Rom. viii. 15; Gal. iv. 6). And yet He is Another, who so fully lives in us as to give us but the more fully to ourselves. So that our prayer is a soliloquy with God, a monologue *a deux.*

There is no such engine for the growth and command of the moral soul, single, or social, as prayer. Here, above all, he who will do shall know. It is the great organ of Christian knowledge and growth. It plants us at the very centre of our own personality, which gives the soul the true perspective of itself; it sets us also at the very centre of the world in God, which gives us the true hierarchy of things. Nothing, therefore, develops such "inwardness" and yet such self-knowledge and self-control. Private prayer, when it is made a serious business, when it is formed prayer, when we pray audibly in our chamber, or when we write our prayers, guided always by the day's record, the passion of piety, and above all the truths of Scripture, is worth more for our true and grave and individual spirituality than gatherings of greater unction may be. Bible searching and searching prayer go hand in hand. What we receive from God in the Book's message we return to Him with interest in prayer. Nothing puts us in living contact with God but prayer, however facile our mere religion may be. And therefore nothing does so much for our originality, so much to make us our own true selves, to stir up all that it is in us to be, and hallow all we are. In life it is not 'dogged that does it' in the last resort, and it is not hard work; it is faculty, insight, gift, talent, genius. And what genius does in the natural world prayer does in the spiritual. Nothing can give us so much power and vision. It opens a fountain perpetual and luminous at the centre of our personality, where we are sustained because we are created anew and not simply refreshed. For here the springs of *life* continually rise. And here also the eye discerns a new world because it has second sight. It sees two worlds at once. Hence, the paradoxes I spoke of. Here we learn to read the work of Christ which commands the world unseen. And we learn to read even the strategy of Providence in the affairs of the world. To pray to the Doer must help us to understand what is done. Prayer, as our greatest work, breeds in us the *flair* for the greatest work of God, the instinct of His kingdom and the sense of His track in Time.

Here, too, we acquire that spiritual veracity which we so constantly tend to lose; because we are in contact with the living and eternal reality. Our very love is preserved from dissimulation, which is a great danger when we love men and court their love. Prayer is a greater school and discipline of divine love than the service of man is. But not if it is cut off from it.

And no less also is it the school of repentance, which so easily can grow morbid. We are taught to be not only true to reality, but sincere with ourselves. We cannot touch God thus without having a light no less searching than saving shed upon our own hearts; and we are thus protected from Pharisaism in our judgment of either self or friend or foe—especially at present of our foe. No companion of God can war in His name against man without much self-searching and self-humiliation, however reserved. But here humility turns into moral strength.

Here we are also regathered in soul from the fancies that bewilder us and the distractions that dissolve us into the dust of the world. We are collected into peace and power and sound judgment, and we have a heart for any fate, because we rest in the Lord whose judgments are salvation. What gives us our true stay gives us our true self; and it protects us from the elations and despairs which alternate in ourselves by bringing home to us a Saviour who is more to us than we are to ourselves. We become patient with ourselves because we realize the patience of God. We get rid of illusions about ourselves and the world because our intimacy is with the real God, and we know that we truly are just what we are before Him. We thus have a great peace, because in prayer, as the crowning act of faith, we lay hold of the grace of God the Saviour. Prayer alone prevents our receiving God's grace in vain. Which means that it establishes the soul of a man or a people, creates the moral personality day by day, spreads outward the new heart through society, and goes to make a new ethos in mankind. We come out with a courage and a humanity we had not when we went in, even though our old earth remove, and our familiar hills are cast into the depth of the sea. The true Church is thus co-extensive with the community of true prayer.

It is another paradox that combines the vast power of prayer both on the lone soul and on the moral life, personal and social, with the soul's shyness and aloofness in prayer. Kant (whose genius in this respect reflected his race) has had an influence upon scientific thought and its efficiency far greater than upon religion, though he is well named the philosopher of Protestantism. He represents (again like his race) intellectual power and a certain stiff moral insight, but not spiritual atmosphere, delicacy, or flexibility, which is rather the Catholic tradition. Intellectualism always tends to more force than finish, and always starves or perverts ethic. And nowhere in Kant's work does this limitation find such expression as in his treatment of prayer, unless it be in his lack of any misgiving about treating it at all with his equipment or the equipment of his age. Even his successors know better now—just as we in England have learned to find in Milton powers and harmonies hidden from the too great sagacity of Dr. Johnson or his time. Kant, then, speaks of prayer thus. If we found a man (he says) given to talking to himself we should begin to suspect him of some tendency to mental aberration. Yet the personality of such a man is a very real thing. It is a thing we can be more sure of than we can of the personality of God, who, if He is more than a conclusion for intellectual thought, is not more than a postulate for moral. No doubt in time of crisis it is an instinct to pray which even cultivated people do not, and need not, lose. But if any such person were surprised even in the attitude of private prayer, to say nothing of its exercise, he would be ashamed. He would think he had been discovered doing something unworthy of his intelligence, and would feel about it as educated people do when found out to be yielding to a superstition about the number thirteen.

A thinker of more sympathy and delicacy would have spoken less bluntly. Practical experience would have taught him discrimination. He would have realized the difference between shame and shyness, between confusion at an unworthy thing and confusion at a thing too fine and sacred for exposure. And had his age allowed him to have more knowledge and taste in history, and especially the history of religion, he would have gone, not to the cowardice of the ordinary cultivated man, but to the power and thoroughness of the great saints or captains of the race—to Paul, to Thomas a Kempis, to Cromwell with his troops, or Gustavus Adolphus with his. I do but humbly allude to Gethsemane. But Kant belonged to a time which had not realized, as even our science does now, the final power of the subtler forces, and the overwhelming effect in the long run of the impalpable and elusive influences of life. Much might be written about the effect of prayer on the great history of the world.

Chapter IV: The Timeliness of Prayer

Let him pray now that never prayed before,
And him that prayed before but pray the more.

The nearer we are driven to the God of Christ, the more we are forced on paradox when we begin to speak. I have been led to allude to this more than once. The *magnalia Dei*[8] are not those great simplicities of life on which some orders of genius lay a touch so tender and sure; but they are the great reconciliations in which life's tragic collisions come to lie "quiet, happy and supprest." Such are the peaceful paradoxes (the paradox at last of grace and nature in the Cross) which make the world of prayer such a strange and difficult land to the lucid and rational interpreters of life. It is as miraculous as it is real that the holy and the guilty should live together in such habitual communion as the life of prayer. And it is another paradox that combines the vast power of prayer for the active soul, whether single or social, with the same soul's shyness and aloofness in prayer.

There is a tendency to lose the true balance and adjustment here. When all goes well we are apt to overdo the aloofness that goes with spiritual engagement, and so to sacrifice some of its power and blessing for the soul. Prayer which becomes too private may become too remote, and is apt to become weak. (Just as when it is too intimate it becomes really unworthy, and may become absurd even to spiritual men; it does so in the trivialities associated sometimes with the answer to prayer.) It is neither seemly nor healthy to be nothing but shy about the greatest powers in life. If we felt them as we should, and if we had their true vitality in us, we could not be so reserved about them. Some churches suffer much from extempore prayer, but perhaps those suffer more that exclude it. It at least gives a public consecration to prayer private and personal, which prayer, from the nature of it, must be extempore and "occasional." The bane of extempore prayer is that it is confused with prayer unprepared; and the greatest preparation for prayer is to pray. The leader of prayer should be a man of prayer—so long as prayer does not become for him a luxury which really unfits him for liturgy, and private devotion does not indispose him for public worship. Delicacy and propriety in prayer are too dearly bought if they are there at

---

[8] Mighty works of God (Acts 2:11).

the cost of its ruling power in life, private and public, and of its prevailing power with God.

It is one of the uses of our present dreadful adversity[9] that we are driven to bring the great two-handed engine of prayer frankly to the fore. There is probably a greater volume of personal prayer to-day than for generations we have had in this somewhat silent people, and there is less embarrassment in owning it. One hears tales of the humour in the trenches, but not so much of the prayer which appears, from accounts, to be at least equally and visibly there. And it is not the prayer of fear, either at home or abroad, but of seriousness, of a new moral exaltation, or at least deepening, a new sense of realities which are clouded by the sunshine of normal life. How can we but pray when we send, or our hearts go out to those who send, the dearest to a noble peril, or lose them in a noble death; or when we melt to those who are cast into unspeakable anxiety by the indirect effects of such a war upon mind or estate? We are helpless then unless we can pray. Or how can we but pray as we regain, under the very hand and pressure of God, the sense of judgment which was slipping from our easy and amiable creed? Above the aircraft we hear the wings of the judgment angel; their wind is on our faces; how should we not pray? We now discuss with each other our prayers as we have seldom done before; and we do it for our practical guidance, and not merely our theological satisfaction. We ask our neighbours' judgment if we may pray for victory when we can be so little sure as we are in the increased complexity of modern issues that all the right is on one side; or when our enemy is a great nation to which the Christianity and the culture of the world owe an unspeakable debt, whether for reformation or illumination. And if Christian faith and prayer is a supernatural, and therefore an international, thing, should it be exploited in the interest of national rivalries and tutelary gods?

Truly the course of events has made the answer to this question easier than at first. We are driven by events to believe that a great moral blindness has befallen Germany; that its God, ceasing to be Christian, has become but Semitic; that it has lost the sense of the great imponderables; that the idolatry of the State has barrack-bound the conscience of the Church and stilled that witness of the kingdom of God which beards kings and even beheads them. We are forced to think that the cause of righteousness has passed from its hands with the passing from them of humanity, with the submersion of the idea of God's kingdom in nationality or the cult of race, with the worship of force, mammon, fright, and ruthlessness, with the growth of national cynicism in moral things, and with the culture of a withering, self-searing hate which is the nemesis of mortal sin, and which even God cannot use as He can use anger, but must surely judge. This people has sinned against its own soul, and abjured the kingdom of God. That settles our prayer for victory. We must pray for the side more valuable for the kingdom of God—much as we have to confess.

It would more than repay much calamity if we were moved and enlarged to a surer sense, a greater use, and a franker confession of the power of prayer for life, character, and history. There is plenty of discussion of the present situation, historic, ethical, or political, and much of it is competent, and even deep. There is much speculation about the situation after the War, at home and abroad. But its greatest result may be the discredit of elegant, paltering, and feeble types of religion, the end of the irreligious wits and fribbles, and the rise of a new moral seriousness and a new spiritual realism. Many will be moved, in what seems the failure of civilization, to a new reliance on the Church, and especially

---

[9] The First World War.

on the more historic, ethical, and positive Churches, which have survived the paganism of culture and which ride the waves of storm. Yet even these impressions can evaporate unless they are fixed by action. And the action that fixes them in their own kind is prayer— prayer which is really action. A religion of prosperity grows dainty, petty, sentimental, and but pseudo-heroic. We unlearn our fathers' creed that religion is, above all things, an act, that worship is the greatest act of which man is capable, and that true worship culminates in the supreme labour, and even sorrow, of real prayer. This is man at his utmost; and it has for it near neighbours all the great things that men or nations do. But when a nation must go to righteous war it embarks on one of the very greatest acts of its life, especially if its very existence as a servant of God's kingdom hang on it. A state of war is really the vast and prolonged act of a corporate soul, with a number of minor acts organized into it. It is capable of being offered to a God whose kingdom is a public campaign moving through history, and coming by the faith, toil, peril, sacrifice, grief, and glory of nations, as well as of hearts and souls. It is not possible to separate moral acts so great and solemn as the act of prayer (especially common and corporate prayer) and the act of war; nor to think them severed in the movement, judgment, and purpose of the Eternal. And we are forced into paradox again. The deeper we go down into the valley of decision the higher we must rise (if we are to possess and command our souls) into the mount of prayer, and we must hold up the hands of those whose chief concern is to prevail with God. If we win we shall have a new sense of power amid all our loss and weakness; but what we shall need most of all is the power to use that power, and to protect us from our victory and its perilous sequels, whether of pride or poverty. And if we do not win we shall need it more. There will be much to sober us either way, more perhaps than ever before in our history.

But that is not all, and it is not enough. As Christian people we need something to sanctify that very sobering and to do for the new moral thoughtfulness itself what that does for the peace-bred levity of the natural man. For such a purpose there is no agent like prayer—serious, thinking, private prayer, or prayer in groups, in small, grave, congenial, understanding groups—prayer with the historic sense, church-nurtured and Bible-fed. Public prayer by all means, but, apart from liturgical form, the more open the occasions and the larger the company the more hard it may be to secure for such prayer the right circumstances or the right lead. Public facility is apt to outstrip the real intimacy and depth with God. While on the other hand, the prayer that freely rises and aptly flows in our audience of God may be paralyzed in an audience of men. So that public prayer does not always reflect the practice of private petition as the powerful factor it is in Christian life and history. It does not always suggest a door opened in heaven, the insight or fellowship of eternal yet historic powers in awful orbits. It does not always do justice to our best private prayer, to private prayer made a business and suffused with as much sacred mind as goes to the more secular side even of the Christian life. Should ministers enlist? it is asked. But to live in true and concrete prayer is to be a combatant in the War, as well as a statesman after it, if statesmen ought to see the whole range of forces at work. The saintly soldier still needs the soldier saint. Yet so much prayer has ceased to be a matter of thought, will, or conflict, and religion therefore has become so otiose, that it is not easy even for the Christian public to take such a saying as more than a phrase. This is but one expression of a general scepticism, both in the Church and out, about prayer, corporate or private, as power with God, and therefore as momentous in the affairs of life and history. But momentous and effectual it must be. Other things being equal, a voluntary and convinced army is worth more than a conscript one. So to know that we are morally right means worlds for our shaping of the things that face us and must be met; and we are never so morally right as in proficient prayer with the Holy One and the Just. It has, therefore, a vast effect on the course of things if we believe at all in their moral destiny. More is wrought by it than the too wise world wots; and all the more as it is the prayer of a great soul or a great Church. It is a power behind thrones, and it neutralizes, at the far end, the visible might of armies and their victories. It settles at last whether morality or machinery is to rule the world. If it lose battles, it wins in the long historic campaign. Whereas, if we have no such action with God, we lose delicacy of perception in the finer forces of affairs; we are out of touch and understanding with the final control in things, the power that is working to the top always; we become dense in regard to the subtle but supreme influences that take the generals and chancellors by surprise; and we are at the mercy of the sleepless action of the kingdom of evil on the world. It is a fatal thing to under estimate the enemy; and it is in Christian prayer, seriously and amply pursued, that the soul really learns to gauge evil's awful and superhuman power in affairs. I am speaking not only of the single soul, perhaps at the moment not chiefly, but of the soul and prayer of a society like the true Church or a sobered people. The real power of prayer in history is not a fusillade of praying units of whom Christ is the chief, but it is the corporate action of a Saviour-Intercessor and His community, a volume and energy of prayer organized in a Holy Spirit and in the Church the Spirit creates. The saints shall thus judge the world and control life. Neither for the individual nor for the Church is true prayer an enclave in life's larger and more actual course. It is not a sacred enclosure, a lodge in some vast wilderness. That is the weak side of pietism. But, however intimate, it is in the most organic and vital context of affairs, private and public, if all things work together, deeply and afar, for the deep and final kingdom of God. Its constant defeat of our egoism means the victory of our social unity and its weal. For the egoist neither prays nor loves. On the other hand, such prayer recalls us from a distraught altruism, teeming with oddities, and frayed down to atomism by the variety of calls upon it; because the prayer is the supreme energy of a loving will and believing soul engaged with the Love that binds the earth, the sun, and all the stars. So far is it from being the case that love to God has no sphere outside love to man that our love to man perishes unless it is fed by the love that spends itself on God in prayer, and is lifted thereby to a place and a sway not historic only, but cosmic.

Our communion with God in Christ rose, and it abides, in a crisis which shook not the earth only, but also heaven, in a tragedy and victory more vast, awful, and pregnant than the greatest war in history could be. Therefore the prayer which gives us an ever-deeper interest and surer insight into that eternal moral crisis of the Cross gives us also (though it might take generations) a footing that commands all the losses or victories of earth, and a power that rules both spirit and conscience in the clash and crash of worlds. As there is devoted thought which ploughs its way into the command of Nature, there is thought, still more devoted, that prays itself into that moral interior of the Cross, where the kingdom of God is founded once for all on the last principle and power of the universe, and set up, not indeed amid the wreck of civilization, but by its new birth and a baptism so as by fire. Prayer of the right kind, with heart and soul and strength and mind, unites any society in which it prevails with those last powers of moral and social regeneration that settle history and that reside in the creative grace of the Cross, which is God's true omnipotence in the world. "O God, who showest Thine almighty power most chiefly in having mercy and forgiving." Such speech as this may to some appear tall and rhetorical;

but it would have so seemed to no father of the church, ancient or modern, taking apostolic measure of the place and moment of Christ in society, history, or the universe.

If war is in any sense God's judgment on sin, and if sin was destroyed by the judgment in Christ and on Him, let us pray with a new depth and significance to-day, "O Lamb of God, that takest away the sin of the world, grant us Thy peace. Send us the peace that honours in act and deed that righteous and final judgment in Thy Cross of all historic things, and that makes therein for Thy Kingdom on earth as in heaven. Give peace in our time, O Lord, but, peace or war, Take the crown of this poor world."

Chapter V: The Ceaselessness of Prayer

Prayer as Christian freedom, and prayer as Christian life—these are two points I would now expand.

I. First, as to the moral freedom involved and achieved in prayer.

Prayer has been described as religion in action. But that as it stands is not a sufficient definition of the prayer which lives on the Cross. The same thing might be said about the choicest forms of Christian service to humanity. It is true enough, and it may carry us far; but only if we become somewhat clear about the nature of the religion at work. Prayer is certainly not the action of a religion mainly subjective. It is the effective work of a religion which hangs upon the living God, of a soul surer of God than of itself, and living not its own life, but the life of the Son of God. To say prayer is faith in action would be better; for the word "faith" carries a more objective reference than the word "religion." Faith is faith in another. In prayer we do not so much work as interwork. We are fellow workers with God in a reciprocity. And as God is the freest Being in existence, such co-operant prayer is the freest thing that man can do. It we were free in sinning, how much more free in the praying which undoes sin! If we were free to break God's will, how much more free to turn it or to accept it! Petitionary prayer is man's cooperation in kind with God amidst a world He freely made for freedom. The world was made by a freedom which not only left room for the kindred freedom of prayer, but which so ordered all things in its own interest that in their deepest depths they conspire to produce prayer. To pray in faith is to answer God's freedom in its own great note. It means we are taken up into the fundamental movement of the world. It is to realize that for which the whole world, the world as a whole, was made. It is an earnest of the world's consummation. We are doing what the whole world was created to do. We overleap in the spirit all between now and then, as in the return to Jesus we overleap the two thousand years that intervene. The object the Father's loving purpose had in appointing the whole providential order was intercourse with man's soul. That order of the world is, therefore, no rigid fixture, nor is it even a fated evolution. It is elastic, adjustable, flexible, with margins for freedom, for free modification in God and man; always keeping in view that final goal of communion, and growing into it by a spiritual interplay in which the whole of Nature is involved. The goal of the whole cosmic order is the "manifestation of the sons of God," the realization of complete sonship, its powers and its confidences.

Thus we rise to say that our prayer is the momentary function of the Eternal Son's communion and intercession with the Eternal Father. We are integrated in advance into the final Christ, for whom, and to whom, all creation moves. Our prayer is more than the acceptance by us of God's will; it is its assertion in us. The will of God is that men should pray everywhere. He wills to be entreated. Prayer is that will of God's making itself good. When we entreat we give effect to His dearest will. And in His will is our eternal liberty. In this will of His ours finds itself, and is at home. It ranges the liberties of the Father's house. But here prayer must draw from the Cross, which is the frontal act of our emancipation as well as the central revelation of God's own freedom in grace. The action of the Atonement and of its release of us is in the nature of prayer. It is the free return of the Holy upon the Holy in the Great Reconciliation.

II. Then, secondly, as to prayer being the expression of the perennial new life of faith in the Cross. The Christian life is prayer without ceasing.

When we are told to pray without ceasing, it seems to many tastes to-day to be somewhat extravagant language. And no doubt that is true. Why should we be concerned to deny it? Measured language and the elegant mean is not the note of the New Testament at least. Mhoen zyan, said the Greek—too much of nothing. But can we love or trust God too much? Christian faith is one that overcomes and commands the world in a passion rather than balances it. It triumphs in a conclusive bliss, it does not play off one part against another. The grace of Christ is not but graciousness of nature, and He does not rule His Church by social tact. The peace of God is not the calm of culture, it is not the charm of breeding. Every great forward movement in Christianity is associated with much that seems academically extravagant. Erasmus is always shocked with Luther. It is only an outlet of that essential extravagance which makes the paradox of the Cross, and keeps it as the irritant, no less than the life of the world—perhaps because it is the life of the world. There is nothing so abnormal, so unworldly, so supernatural, in human life as prayer, nothing that is more of an instinct, it is true, but also nothing that is less rational among all the things that keep above the level of the silly. The whole Christian life in so far as it is lived from the Cross and by the Cross is rationally an extravagance. For the Cross is the paradox of all things; and the action of the Spirit is the greatest miracle in the world; and yet it is the principle of the world. Paradox is but the expression of that dualism which is the moral foundation of a Christian world. I live who die daily. I live another's life.

To pray without ceasing is not, of course, to engage in prayer without break. That is an impossible literalism. True, "They rest not day and night, saying, Holy, holy, holy, Lord God Almighty, who wert, and art, and art to come." But it is mere poverty of soul to think of this as the iteration of a doxology. It is deep calling unto deep, eternity greeting eternity. The only answer to God's eternity is an eternal attitude of prayer.

Nor does the phrase mean that the Church shall use careful means that the stream and sound of prayer shall never cease to flow at some spots of the earth, as the altar lamp goes not out. It does not mean the continuous murmur of the mass following the sun round the world, incessant relays of adoring priests, and functions going on day and night.

But it means the constant bent and drift of the soul—as the Word which was from the beginning (John i. 1). All the current of its being set towards Him. It means being "in Christ," being in such a moving, returning Christ—reposing in this godward, and not merely godlike life. The note of prayer becomes the habit of the heart, the tone and tension of its new nature; in such a way that when we are released from the grasp of our occupations the soul rebounds to its true bent, quest, and even pressure upon God. It is the soul's habitual appetite and habitual food. A growing child of God is always hungry. Prayer is not identical with the occasional act of praying. Like the act of faith, it is a whole life thought of as action. It is the life of faith in its purity, in its vital action. Eating and speaking are necessary to life, but they are not living. And how hidden prayer may be—beneath even gaiety! If you look down on Portland Race you see but a shining sea; only the pilot knows the tremendous current that pervades the smiling calm.

So far is this "pray without ceasing" from being absurd because extravagant that every man's life is in some sense a continual state of prayer. For what is his life's prayer but its ruling passion? All energies, ambitions and passions are but expressions of a standing *nisus* in life, of a hunger, a draft, a practical demand upon the future, upon the unattained and the unseen. Every life is a draft upon the unseen. If you are not praying towards God you are towards something else. You pray as your face is set—towards Jerusalem or Babylon. The very egotism of craving life is prayer. The great difference is the object of it. To whom, for what, do we pray? The man whose passion is habitualy set upon pleasure, knowledge, wealth, honour, or power is in a state of prayer to these things or for them. He prays without ceasing. These are his real gods, on whom he waits day and night. He may from time to time go on his knees in church, and use words of Christian address and petition. He may even feel a momentary unction in so doing. But it is a flicker; the other devotion is his steady flame. His real God is the ruling passion and steady pursuit of his life taken as a whole. He certainly does not pray in the name of Christ. And what he worships in spirit and in truth is another God than he addresses at religious times. He prays to an unknown God for a selfish boon. Still, in a sense, he prays. The set and drift of his nature prays. It is the prayer of instinct, not of faith. It is prayer that needs total conversion. But he cannot stop praying either to God or to God's rival—to self, society, world, flesh, or even devil. Every life that is not totally inert is praying either to God or God's adversary.

What do we really mean, whom do we mean, when we say, "My God"? In what sense mine? May our God not be but an idol we exploit, and in due course our doom?

There is a fearful and wonderful passage in Kierkegaard's *Entweder-Oder* which, if we transfer it to this connection, stirs thoughts deeper than its own tragedy. The seduced, heart-broken, writes to the seducer.

"John! I do not say *my* John. That I now see you never were. I am heavily punished for ever letting such an idea be my joy. Yet—yet, mine you are—*my* seducer, *my* deceiver, *my* enemy, *my* murderer, the spring of my calamity, the grave of my joy, the abyss of my misery. I call you mine, and I am thine—thy curse for ever. Oh, do not think I will slay you and put a dagger into you. But flee where you will, I am yours, to the earth's end yours. Love a hundred others but I am yours. I am yours in your last hour, I am yours, yours, yours—your curse."

Beware lest the whole trend of the soul fix on a deity that turns a doom. There is a prayer which makes God our judgment as well as one which makes Him our joy.

Prayer is the nature of our hell as well as our heaven.

Our hell is ceaseless, passionate, fruitless, hopeless, gnawing prayer. It is the heart churning, churning grinding itself out in misery. It is life's passion and struggle surging back on itself like a barren, salt, corroding sea. It is the heart's blood rising like a fountain only to fall back on us in red rain. It is prayer which we cannot stop, addressed to nothing, and obtaining nothing. It calls into space and night. Or it is addressed to self, and it aggravates the wearing action of self on self. Our double being revolves on itself, like two millstones with nothing to grind.

And prayer is our heaven. It goes home to God, and attains there, and rests there. We are "in Christ," whose whole existence is prayer, who is wholly for us. He is there to extinguish our hell and make our heaven—far more to quench our wrath and our seething than God's.

To cultivate the ceaseless spirit of prayer, use more frequent acts of prayer. To learn to pray with freedom, force yourself to pray. The great liberty begins in necessity.

Do not say, "I cannot pray, I am not in the spirit." Pray till you are in the spirit. Think of analogies from lower levels. Sometimes when you need rest most you are too restless to lie down and take it. Then compel yourself to lie down, and to lie still. Often in ten minutes the compulsion fades into consent, and you sleep, and rise a new man.

Again, it is often hard enough to take up the task which in half an hour you enjoy. It is often against the grain to turn out of an evening to meet the friends you promised. But once you are in their midst you are in your element.

Sometimes, again, you say, "I will not go to church. I do not feel that way." That is where the habit of an ordered religious life comes in aid. Religion is the last region for chance desires. Do it as a duty, and it may open out as a blessing. Omit it, and you may miss the one thing that would have made an eternal difference. You stroll instead, and return with nothing but an appetite—when you might have come back with an inspiration. Compel yourself to meet your God as you would meet your promises, your obligations, your fellow men.

So if you are averse to pray, pray the more. Do not call it lip-service. That is not the lip-service God disowns. It is His Spirit acting in your self-coercive will, only not yet in your heart. What is unwelcome to God is lip-service which is untroubled at not being more. As appetite comes with eating, so prayer with praying. Our hearts learn the language of the lips.

Compel yourself often to shape on your lips the detailed needs of your soul. It is not needful to inform God, but to deepen you, to inform yourself before God, to enrich that intimacy with yourself which is so necessary to answer the intimacy of God. To common sense the fact that God knows all we need, and wills us all good, the fact of His infinite Fatherhood, is a reason for not praying. Why tell Him what He knows? Why ask what He is more than willing to give? But to Christian faith and to spiritual reason it is just the other way. Asking is polar cooperation. Jesus turned the fact to a use exactly the contrary of its deistic sense. He made the all-knowing Fatherhood the ground of true prayer. We do not ask as beggars but as children. Petition is not mere receptivity, nor is it mere pressure; it is filial reciprocity. Love loves to be told what it knows already. Every lover knows that. It wants to be asked for what it longs to give. And that is the principle of prayer to the all-knowing Love. As God knows all, you may reckon that your brief and humble prayer will be understood (Matt. vi. 8). It will be taken up into the intercession of the Spirit stripped of its dross, its inadequacy made good, and presented as prayer should be. That is praying in the Holy Ghost. Where should you carry your burden but to the Father, where Christ took the burden of all the world? We tell God, the heart searcher, our heavy thoughts to escape from brooding over them. "When my spirit was overwhelmed within me, Thou knewest my path." (Ps. cxlii. 3). So Paul says the Spirit intercedes for us and gives our broken prayer divine effect (Rom. viii. 26). To be sure of God's sympathy is to be inspired to prayer, where His mere knowledge would crush it. There is no father who would be satisfied that his son should take everything and ask for nothing. It would be thankless. To cease asking is to cease to be grateful. And what kills petition kills praise.

Go into your chamber, shut the door, and cultivate the habit of praying audibly. Write prayers and burn them. Formulate your soul. Pay no attention to literary form, only to spiritual reality. Read a passage of Scripture and then sit down and turn it into a prayer, written or spoken. Learn to be particular, specific, and detailed in your prayer so long as you are not trivial. General prayers, literary prayers, and stately phrases are, for private prayer, traps and sops to the soul. To formulate your soul is one valuable means to escape formalizing it. This is the best, the wholesome, kind of self-examination. Speaking with God discovers us safely to ourselves We "find" ourselves, come to ourselves, in the Spirit. Face your special weaknesses and sins before God. Force yourself to say to God exactly where you are wrong. When anything goes wrong, do not ask to have it set right, without asking in prayer what it was in you that made it go wrong. It is somewhat fruitless to ask for a general grace to help specific flaws, sins, trials, and griefs. Let prayer be concrete, actual, a direct product of life's real experiences. Pray as your actual self, not as some fancied saint. Let it be closely relevant to your real situation. Pray without ceasing in this sense. Pray without a break between your prayer and your life. Pray so that there is a real continuity between your prayer and your whole actual life. But I will bear round upon this point again immediately.

Meantime, let me say this. Do not allow your practice in prayer to be arrested by scientific or philosophic considerations as to *how* answer is possible. That is a valuable subject for discussion, but it is not entitled to control our practice. Faith is at least as essential to the soul as science, and it has a foundation more independent. And prayer is not only a necessity of faith, it is faith itself in action.

Criticism of prayer dissolves in the experience of it. When the soul is at close quarters with God it becomes enlarged enough to hold together in harmony things that oppose, and to have room for harmonious contraries. For instance: God, of course, is always working for His Will and Kingdom. But man is bound to pray for its coming, while it is coming all the time. Christ laid stress on prayer as a necessary means of bringing the Kingdom to pass. And it cannot come without our praying. Why? Because its coming is the prayerful frame of soul. So again with God's freedom. It is absolute. But it reckons on ours. Our prayer does not force His hand; it answers His freedom in kind. We are never so active and free as in prayer to an absolutely free God. We share His freedom when we are "in Christ."

If I must choose between Christ, who bids me pray for everything, and the savant, who tells me certain answers are physically and rationally impossible, must I not choose Christ? Because, while the savant knows much about nature and its action (and much more than Christ did), Christ knew everything about the God of nature and His reality. He knew more of what is possible to God than anybody has ever known about what is possible in nature. On such a subject as prayer, anyone is a greater authority who wholly knows the will of God than he who only knows God's methods, and knows them but in part. Prayer is not an act of knowledge but of faith. It is not a matter of calculation but of confidence—"that our faith should not stand in the wisdom of men, but in the power of God." Which means that in this region we are not to be regulated by science, but by God's self-revelation. Do not be so timid about praying wrongly if you pray humbly. If God is really the Father that Christ revealed, then the principle is—take everything to Him that exercises you. Apart from frivolity, such as praying to find the stud you lost, or the knife, or the umbrella, there is really no limitation in the New Testament on the contents of petition. Any regulation is as to the spirit of the prayer, the faith it springs from. In all distress which mars your peace, petition must be the form your faith takes—petition for rescue. Keep close to the New Testament Christ, and then ask for anything you desire in that contact. Ask for everything you can ask in Christ's name, i.e. everything desirable by a man who is in Christ's kingdom of God, by a man who lives for it at heart, everything in tune with the purpose and work of the kingdom in Christ. If you are in that kingdom, then pray freely for whatever you need or wish to keep you active and effective for it, from daily bread upwards and outwards. In all things make your requests known. It will not unhinge such faith if you do not obtain them. At least you have laid them on God's heart; and faith means confidences between you and not only favours. And there is not confidence if you keep back what is hot or heavy on your heart. If prayer is not a play of the religious fantasy, or a routine task, it must be the application of faith to a concrete actual and urgent situation. Only remember that prayer does not work by magic, and that stormy desire is not fervent, effectual prayer. You may be but exploiting a mighty power; whereas you must be in real contact with the real God. It is the man that most really has God that most really seeks God.

I said a little while ago that to pray without ceasing also meant to pray without a breach with your actual life and the whole situation in which you are. This is the point at which to dwell on that. If you may not come to God with the occasions of your private life and affairs, then there is some unreality in the relation between you and Him. If some private crisis absorbs you, some business or family anxiety of little moment to others but of much to you, and if you may not bring that to God in prayer, then one of two things. Either it is not you, in your actual reality, that came to God, but it is you in a pose—you in some role which you are trying with poor success to play before Him. You are trying to pray as another person than you are,—a better person, perhaps, as some great apostle, who should have on his worshipping mind nothing but the grand affairs of the Church and Kingdom, and not be worried by common cares. You are praying in court-dress. You are trying to pray as you imagine one should pray to God, i.e. as another person than you are, and in other circumstances. You are creating a self and a situation to place before God. Either that or you are not praying to a God who loves, helps, and delivers you in every pinch of life, but only to one who uses you as a pawn for the victory of His great kingdom. You are not praying to Christ's God. You are praying to a God who cares only for the great actors in His kingdom, for the heroic people who cherish nothing but the grand style, or for the calm people who do not deeply feel life's trials. The reality of prayer is bound up with the reality and intimacy of life.

And its great object is to get home as we are to God as He is, and to win response even when we get no compliance. The prayer of faith does not mean a prayer absolutely sure that it will receive what it asks. That is not faith. Faith is that attitude of soul and self to God which is the root and reservoir of prayer apart from all answer. It is what turns need into request. It is what moves your need to need God. It is what makes you sure your prayer is heard and stored, whether granted or not. "He putteth all my tears in His bottle." God has old prayers of yours long maturing by Him. What wine you will drink with Him in His kingdom! Faith is sure that God refuses with a smile; that He says No in the spirit of Yes, and He gives or refuses always in Christ, our Great Amen. And better prayers are stirred by the presence of the Deliverer than even by the need of deliverance.

It is not sufficiently remembered that before prayer can expect an answer it must be itself an answer. That is what is meant by prayer in the name of Christ. It is prayer which answers God's gift in Christ, with Whom are already given us all things. And that is why we must pray without ceasing, because in Christ God speaks without ceasing. Natural or instinctive prayer is one thing; supernatural prayer is another; it is the prayer not of instinct but of faith. It is our word answering God's. It is more the prayer of fullness even than of need, of strength than of weakness—though it be "a strength girt round with weakness." Prayer which arises from mere need is flung out to a power which is only remembered, or surmised, or unknown. It is flung into darkness and uncertainty. But in Christian prayer we ask for what we need because we are full of faith in God's power and word, because need becomes petition at the touch of His word. (I always feel that in the order of our public worship prayer should immediately follow the lesson, without the intrusion of an anthem. And for the reason I name—that Christian prayer is our word answering God's). We pray, therefore, in Christ's name, or for His sake, because we pray as answering the gift in Christ. Our prayer is the note the tremulous soul utters when its chords are smitten by Him. We then answer above all things God's prayer to us in His cross that we would be reconciled. God so beseeches us in Christ. So that, if we put it strongly, we may say that our prayer to God in Christ is our answer to God's prayer to us there. "The best thing in prayer is faith," says Luther.

And the spirit of prayer in Christ's name is the true child-spirit. A certain type of religion is fond of dwelling on faith as the spirit of divine childhood; and its affinities are all with the tender and touching element in childhood. But one does not always get from the prophets of such piety the impression of a life breathed in prayer. And the notion is not the New Testament sense of being children of God. That is a manlier, a maturer thing. It is being sons of God by faith, and by faith's energy of prayer. It is not the sense of being as helpless as a child that clings, not the sense of weakness, ignorance, gentleness, and all that side of things. But it is the spirit of a prayer which is a great act of faith, and therefore a power. Faith is not simply surrender, but *adoring* surrender, not a mere sense of dependence, but an act of intelligent committal, and the confession of a holiness which is able to save, keep, and bless for ever.

How is it that the experience of life is so often barren of spiritual culture for religious people? They become stoic and stalwart, but not humble; they have keen sight, but no insight. Yet it is not the stalwarts but the saints that judge the world, i.e. that take the true divine measure of the world and get to its subtle, silent, and final powers. Whole sections of our Protestantism have lost the virtue of humility or the understanding of it. It means for them no more than modesty or diffidence. It is the humility of weakness, not of power. To many useful, and even strong, people no experience seems to bring this subtle, spiritual intelligence, this finer discipline of the moral man. No rebukes, no rebuffs, no humiliations, no sorrows, seem to bring it to them. They have no spiritual history. Their spiritual biography not even an angel could write. There is no romance in their soul's story. At sixty they are, spiritually, much where they were at twenty-six. To calamity, to discipline of any kind, they are simply resilient. Their religion is simply elasticity. It is but lusty life. They rise up after the smart is over, or the darkness fades away, as self-confident as if they were but seasoned politicians beaten at one election, but sure of doing better at the next. They are to the end just irrepressible, or persevering, or dogged. And they are as juvenile in moral insight, as boyish in spiritual perception, as ever.

Is it not because they have never really had personal religion? That is, they have never really prayed with all their heart; only, at most, with all their fervour, certainly not with strength and mind. They have never "spread out" their whole soul and situation to a god who knows. They have never opened the petals of their soul in the warm sympathy of His knowledge. They have not become particular enough in their prayer, faithful with themselves, or relevant to their complete situation. They do not face themselves, only what happens to them. They pray with their heart and not with their conscience. They pity themselves, perhaps they spare themselves, they shrink from hurting themselves more than misfortune hurts them. They say, "If you knew all you could not help pitying me." They do not say, "God knows all, and how can He spare me?" For themselves, or for their fellows, it is the prayer of pity, not of repentance. We need the prayer of self-judgment more than the prayer of fine insight.

We are not humble in God's sight, partly because in our prayer there is a point at which we cease to pray, where we do not turn everything out into God's light. It is because there is a chamber or two in our souls where we do not enter in and take God with us. We hurry Him by that door as we take Him along the corridors of our life to see our tidy places or our public rooms. We ask from our prayers too exclusively comfort, strength, enjoyment, or tenderness and graciousness, and not often enough humiliation and its fine strength. We want beautiful prayers, touching prayers, simple prayers, thoughtful prayers; prayers with a quaver or a tear in them, or prayers with delicacy and dignity in them. But searching prayer, humbling prayer, which is the prayer of the conscience, and not merely of the heart or taste; prayer which is bent on reality, and to win the new joy goes through new misery if need be—are such prayers as welcome and common as they should be? Too much of our prayer is apt to leave us with the self-complacency of the sympathetically incorrigible, of the benevolent and irremediable, of the breezy octogenarian, all of whose yesterdays look backward with a cheery and exasperating smile.

It is an art—this great and creative prayer—this intimate conversation with God. *"Magna ars est conversari cum Deo,"* says Thomas a Kempis. It has to be learned. In social life we learn that conversation is not mere talk. There is an art in it, if we are not to have a table of gabblers. How much more is it so in the conversation of heaven! We must learn that art by practice, and by keeping the best society in that kind. Associate much with the great masters in this kind; especially with the Bible; and chiefly with Christ. Cultivate His Holy Spirit. He is the grand master of God's art and mystery in communing with man. And there is no other teacher, at last, of man's art of communion with God.

Chapter VI: The Vicariousness of Prayer

I

The work of the ministry labours under one heavy disadvantage when we regard it as a profession and compare it with other professions. In these, experience brings facility, a sense of mastery in the subject, self-satisfaction, self-confidence; but in our subject the more we pursue it, the more we enter into it, so much the more are we cast down with the overwhelming sense, not only of our insufficiency, but of our unworthiness. Of course, in the technique of our work we acquire a certain ease. We learn to speak more or less freely and aptly. We learn the knack of handling a text, of conducting church work, or dealing with men, and the like. If it were only texts or men we had to handle! But we have to handle the gospel. We have to lift up Christ—a Christ who is the death of natural self-confidence—a humiliating, even a crushing Christ; and we are not always alive to our uplifting and resurrection in Him. We have to handle a gospel that is a new rebuke to us every step we gain in intimacy with it. There is no real intimacy with the gospel which does not mean a new sense of God's holiness, and it may be long before we realize that the same holiness that condemns is that which saves. There is no new insight into the Cross which does not bring, whatever else come with it, a deeper sense of the solemn holiness of the love that meets us there. And there is no new sense of the holy God that does not arrest His name upon our unclean lips. If our very repentance is to be repented of, and we should be forgiven much in our very prayers, how shall we be proud, or even pleased, with what we may think a success in our preaching? So that we are not surprised that some preachers, after what the public calls a most brilliant and impressive discourse, retire (as the emperor retired to close his life in the cloister) to humble themselves before God, to ask forgiveness for the poor message, and to call themselves most unprofitable servants—yea, even when they knew themselves that they had "done well." The more we grasp our gospel the more it abashes us.

Moreover, as we learn more of the seriousness of the gospel for the human soul, we feel the more that every time we present it we are adding to the judgment of some as well as to the salvation of others. We are not like speakers who present a matter that men can freely take or leave, where they can agree or differ with us without moral result. No true preacher can be content that his flock should believe in him. That were egoism. They must believe with him. The deeper and surer our gospel is the more is our work a judgment on those to whom it is not a grace. This was what bore upon the Saviour's own soul, and darkened His very agony into eclipse. That He, who knew Himself to be the salvation of His own beloved people, should, by His very love, become their doom! And here we watch and suffer with Him, however sleepily. There is put into our charge our dear people's life or death. For to those to whom we are not life we are death, in proportion as we truly preach, not ourselves, but the real salvation of Christ.

How solemn our place is! It is a sacramental place. We have not simply to state our case, we have to *convey* our Christ, and to convey Him effectually as the soul's final fate. We are sacramental elements, broken often, in the Lord's hands, as He dispenses His grace through us. We do not, of course, believe that orders are an ecclesiastical sacrament, as Rome does. But we are forced to realize the idea underlying that dogma—the sacramental nature of our person, work, and vocation for the gospel. We are not saviours. There is only one Saviour. But we are His sacraments. We do not believe in an ecclesiastical priesthood; but we are made to feel how we stand between God and the people as none of our flock do. We bring Christ to them, and them to Christ, in sacrificial action in a way far more moral, inward, and taxing than official priesthood can be. As ministers we lead the sacerdotal function of the whole Church in the world—its holy confession and sacrifice for the world in Christ.

We ought, indeed, to feel the dignity of the ministry; we must present some protest against the mere fraternal conception which so easily sinks into an unspiritual familiarity. But still more than the dignity of the ministry do its elect feel its solemnity. How can it be otherwise? We have to dwell much with the everlasting burnings of God's love. We have to tend that consuming fire. We have to feed our life where all the tragedy of life is gathered to an infinite and victorious crisis in Christ. We are not the fire, but we live where it burns. The matter we handle in our theological thought we can only handle with some due protection for our face. It is one of the dangerous industries. It is continually acting on us, continually searching our inner selves that no part of us may be unforgiven, unfed, or unsanctified. We cannot hold it and examine it at arm's length. It enters into us. It evokes the perpetual comment of our souls, and puts us continually on self-judgment. Our critic, our judge, is at the door. Self-condemnation arrests denunciation. And the true apostle can never condemn but in the spirit of self-condemnation.

But, after all, our doom is our blessing. Our Judge is on our side. For if humiliation be wrung from us, still more is faith, hope, and prayer. Everything that rebukes our self-satisfaction does still more to draw out our faith. When we are too tired or doubtful to ask we can praise and adore. When we are weary of confessing our sin we can forget ourselves in a godly sort and confess our Saviour. We can say the creed when we cannot raise the song. He also hath given us the reconciliation. The more judgment we see in the holy cross the more we see it is judgment unto salvation. The more we are humbled the more we "roll our souls upon Christ." And we recover our self-possession only by giving our soul again and again to Christ to keep. We win a confidence in self-despair. Prayer is given us as wings wherewith to mount, but also to shield our face when they have carried us before the great white throne. It is in prayer that the holiness comes home as love, and the love is established as holiness. At every step our thought is transformed to prayer, and our prayer opens new ranges of thought. His great revelation is His holiness, always outgoing in atoning love. The Christian revelation is not "God is love" so much as "love is God." That is, it is not God's love, but the infinite power of God's love, its finality, omnipotence, and absoluteness. It is not passionate and helpless love, but it has power to subdue *everything* that rises against it. And that is the holiness of love—the eternal thing in it. We receive the last reconciliation. Then the very wrath of God becomes a glory. The red in the sky is the new dawn. Our self-accusation becomes a new mode of praise. Our loaded hearts spring light again. Our heavy conscience turns to grave moral power. A new love is born for our kind. A new and tender patience steals upon us. We see new ways of helping, serving, and saving. We issue into a new world. We are one with the Christ not only on His cross, but in His resurrection. Think of the resurrection power and calm, of that solemn final peace, that infinite satisfaction in the eternal thing eternally achieved, which filled His soul when He had emerged from death, when man's worst had been done, and God's best had been won, for ever and for all. We have our times of entrance into that Christ. As we were one with Him in the likeness of His death, so we are in the likeness of His resurrection. And the same Eternal Spirit which puts the preacher's soul much upon the cross also raises it continually from the dead. We overcome our mistakes, negligences, sins; nay, we rise above the sin of the whole world, which will not let our souls be as good as they are. We overcome the world, and take courage, and are of new cheer. We are in the Spirit. And then we can preach, pray, teach, heal. And even the unclean lips then put a new thrill into our sympathy and a new tremor into our praise.

If it be not so, how shall our dangerous work not demoralize us, and we perish from our too much contact with holy things.

The minister's holiest prayer is hardly lawful to utter. Few of his public would comprehend it. Some would dismiss it with their most opprobrious word. They would call it theological. When he calls to God in his incomprehensible extremity they would translate it into an appeal to Elijah (Matt. xxvii. 47). For to them theology is largely mythology.

We are called at the present day to a reconstruction of the old theology, a restatement of the old gospel. We have to reappropriate and remint the truth of our experienced Christianity. But what a hardship it is that this call should search us at a time when the experimental power of our Christianity has abated, and the evangelical experience is so low and so confused as it often is! It must be the minister's work to recover and deepen this experience for the churches, in the interest of faith, and of the truth in which faith renders account of itself. Theological inadequacy, and especially antagonism to theology, means at root religious defect. For the reformation of belief we must have a restoration of faith. And a chief engine for such recovery of faith is for us what it was for Luther and his like—prayer. And it is not mindless prayer, but that prayer which is the wrestling of the conscience and not merely the cry of the heart, the prayer for reconciliation and redemption and not merely for guidance and comfort, the prayer of faith and not merely of love.

I saw in a friend's house a photograph from (I think) Durer—just two tense hands, palms together, and lifted in prayer. It was most eloquent, most subduing. I wish I could stamp the picture on the page here and fit it to Milton's line:

> *The great two-handed engine at our door.*[10]

II

Public prayer is, on the whole, the most difficult part of the work of the minister. To help the difficulty I have always claimed that pulpit notes of prayer may be used. "The Lord's Prayer" itself is of this nature. It is not a prayer, but a scheme of prayer, heads of prayer, or buoys in the channel. But even with the use of all helps there are perils enough. There are prayers that, in the effort to become real, are much too familiar in their fashion of speech. A young man began his prayer, in my own hearing, with the words, "O God, we have come to have a chat with Thee." It was gruesome. Think of it as a sample of modern piety for the young! No prayers, certainly no public prayers, should be "chats with God." Again, other prayers are sentimental prayers. George Dawson's volume has this fault. The prayers of the Church should not be exposures of the affectional man. The public prayer of the Church, as the company of grace, is the saved soul returning to God that gave it; it is the sinner coming to the Saviour, or the ransomed of the Lord returning to Zion; it is the sanctified with the sanctifier; it is not primarily the child talking to the Father—though that note may prevail in more private prayers. We are more than stray sheep reclaimed. We are those whose defiant iniquity has lain upon Christ for us all.

But the root of the difficulty of public prayer lies farther back than in the matter of style. It lies in the difficulty of private prayer, in its spiritual poverty, its inertia, its anemia. What culture can deal with the rooted difficulty that resides there, out of sight, in the inner man of the heart, for lack of the courage of faith, for sheer spiritual fecklessness? Yet the preparation for prayer is to pray. The prayer of the Church is learned in the chamber. The culture needed is the practice of prayer. It is only prayer that teaches to pray. The minister ought never to speak before men in God's name without himself first speaking to God in man's name, and making intercession as for himself so for his people.

Intercession! We are properly vigilant that the minister do not sever himself from his people in any sacerdotal way. But for all that, is the minister's personal and private prayer on exactly the same footing as a layman's? It is a question that leads to the distinction between intercessory and vicarious prayer. The personal religion of the minister is vicarious even when it is not intercessory. Great indeed is the spiritual value of private intercession. The *intercessory* private prayer of the minister is the best corrective of the *critical* spirit or the grumbling spirit which so easily besets and withers us to-day. That reconciliation, that pacification of heart, which comes by prayer opens in us a fountain of

---

[10] Lycidas.

private intercession, especially for our antagonists. Only, of course, it must be private. But the minister is also praying to his people's good even when he is not interceding on their behalf, or leading them in prayer. What he is for his Church he is with his whole personality. And so his private and personal prayers are vicarious for his people even when he does not know it. No Christian man lives for himself, nor believes for himself. And if the private Christian in his private prayers does not pray, any more than he lives, unto himself alone, much more is this true for the minister. His private prayers make a great difference to his people. They may not know what makes his spell and blessing; even he may not. But it is his most private prayers; which, thus, are vicarious even where not intercessory.

What he is for his Church, I have said, he is with his whole personality. And nothing gives us personality like true prayer. Nothing makes a man so original. We cannot be true Christians without being original. Living faith destroys the commonplaceness, the monotony of life. Are not all men original in death? *"Je mourrai seul."*[11] Much more are they original and their true selves in Christ's death, and in their part and lot in that. For true originality we must be one, and closely one, with God. To be creative we must learn with the Creator. The most effectual man in history was he who said, "I live; yet not I, but Christ liveth in me." What a reflection on our faith that so much piety should be humdrum, and deadly dull! Private prayer, when it is real action, is the greatest forge of personality. It places a man in direct and effective contact with God the Creator, the source of originality, and especially with God the Redeemer as the source of the new creation. For the minister personality is everything—not geniality, as it is the day's fashion to say, but personality; and prayer is the spring of personality. This impressive personality, due to prayer, you may often have in "the peasant saint." And in some cases its absence is as palpable. Hence comes vulgarity in prayer, essential vulgarity underlying much possible fineness of phrase or manner. Vulgarity in prayer lies not so much in its offenses to good taste in style as in its indications of the absence of spiritual *habit* and reality. If the theology of rhetoric destroys the theology of reality in the sermon, how much more in prayer!

Prayer is for the religious life what original research is for science—by it we get direct contact with reality. The soul is brought into union with its own vaster nature—God. Therefore, also, we must use the Bible as an original; for indeed, the Bible is the most copious spring of prayer, and of power, and of range. If we learn to pray from the Bible, and avoid a mere *cento* of its phrases, we shall cultivate in our prayer the large humane note of a universal gospel. Let us nurse our prayer on our *study* of our Bible; and let us, therefore, not be too afraid of *theological* prayer. True Christian prayer must have theology in it; no less than true theology must have prayer in it and must be capable of being prayed. "Your theology is too difficult," said Charles V to the Reformers; "it cannot be understood without much prayer." Yes, that is our arduous puritan way. Prayer and theology must interpenetrate to keep each other great, and wide, and mighty. The failure of the habit of prayer is at the root of much of our light distaste for theology. There is a conspiracy of influences round us whose effect is to belittle our great work. Earnest ministers suffer more from the smallness of their people than from their sins, and far more than from their unkindness. Our public may kill by its triviality a soul which could easily resist the assaults of opposition or wickedness. And our newspaper will greatly aid their work. Now, to resist this it is not enough to have recourse to prayer and to cultivate

---

11 I'll die alone.

devotion. Unfortunately, there are signs in the religious world to show that prayer and piety alone do not save men from pettiness of interest, thinness of soul, spiritual volatility, the note of insincerity, or foolishness of judgment, or even vindictiveness. The remedy is not prayer alone, but prayer on the scale of the whole gospel and at the depth of searching faith. It is considered prayer—prayer which rises above the childish petitions that disfigure much of our public pietism, prayer which issues from the central affairs of the kingdom of God. It is prayer with the profound Bible as its book of devotion, and a true theology of faith for half of its power. It is the prayer of a mind that moves in Bible passion, and ranges with Bible scope, even when it eschews Bible speech and "the language of Canaan."

And yet, with all its range, it is prayer with *concentration*. It has not only thought but will in it. The great reason why so many will not decide for Christ is that Christ requires from the world concentration; not seclusion and not renunciation merely, but concentration. And we ministers have our special form of that need. I am speaking not of our share in the common troubles of life, but of those specially that arise from the ministerial office and care. No minister can live up to his work on the casual or interjectional kind of prayer that might be sufficient for many of his flock. He must think, of course, in his prayers—in his private prayers—and he must pray his faith's thought. But, still more, in his praying he must act. Prayer is not a frame of mind, but a great energy. He must rise to conceive his work as an active function of the work of Christ; and he must link his faith, therefore, with the intercession which covers the whole energy of Christ in His kingdom. In this, as in many ways, he must remember, to his great relief and comfort, that it is not he who is the real pastor of his church, but Christ, and that he is but Christ's curate. The final responsibility is not his, but Christ's, who bears the responsibility of all the sins and frets, both of the world and, especially, of the Church.

The concentration, moreover, should correspond to the positivity of the gospel and the Bible. Prayer should rise more out of God's Word and concern for His kingdom than even out of our personal needs, trials, or desires. That is implied in prayer in Christ's name or for Christ's sake, prayer from His place in the midst of the Kingdom. *Our* Prayer-book, the Bible, does not prescribe prayer, but it does more—it inspires it. And prayer in Christ's name is prayer inspired by His first interest—the gospel. Do not use Christ simply to countersign your egoist petition by a closing formula, but to create, inspire, and glorify it. Prayer in Christ's name is prayer for Christ's object—for His Kingdom, and His promise of the Holy Ghost.

If we really pray for that and yet do not feel we receive it, probably enough we have it; and we are looking for some special form of it not ours, or not ours yet. We may be mistaking the fruits of the Spirit for His presence. Fruits come late. They are different from signs. Buds are signs, and so are other things hard to see. It is the Spirit that keeps us praying for the Spirit, as it is grace that keeps us in grace. Remember the patience of the missionaries who waited in the Spirit fifteen years for their first convert. If God gave His Son *unasked*, how much more will He give His Holy Spirit to them that *ask* it! But let us not prescribe the form in which He comes.

The true close of prayer is when the utterance expires in its own spiritual fullness. That is the true Amen. Such times there are. We feel we are at last laid open to God. We feel as though we "did see heaven opened, and the holy angels, and the great God

Himself."[12] The prayer ends itself; *we* do not end it. It mounts to its heaven and renders its spirit up to God, saying, "It is finished." It has its perfect consummation and bliss, its spiritually natural close and fruition, whether it has answer or not.

Chapter VII: The Insistency of Prayer

In all I have said I have implied that prayer should be strenuously *importunate*.[13] Observe, not petitionary merely, nor concentrated, nor active alone, but importunate. For prayer is not only meditation or communion. Nor ought it to be merely submissive in tone, as the "quietist" ideal is. We need not begin with "Thy will be done" if we but end with it. Remember the stress that Christ laid on importunity. Strenuous prayer will help us to recover the masculine type of religion—and then our opponents will at least respect us.

I would speak a little more fully on this matter of importunity. It is very closely bound up with the reality both of prayer and of religion. Prayer is not really a power till it is importunate. And it cannot be importunate unless it is felt to have a real effect on the Will of God. I may slip in here my conviction that far less of the disbelief in prayer is due to a scientific view of nature's uniformity than to the slipshod kind of prayer that men hear from us in public worship; it is often but journalese sent heavenwards, or phrase-making to carry on. And I would further say that by importunity something else is meant than passionate dictation and stormy pertinacity—imposing our egoist will on God, and treating Him as a mysterious but manageable power that we may coerce and exploit.

The deepening of the spiritual life is a subject that frequently occupies the attention of religious conferences and of the soul bent on self-improvement. But it is not certain that the great saints would always recognize the ideal of some who are addicted to the use of the phrase. The "deepening of the spiritual life" they would find associated with three unhappy things.

1. They would recoil from a use of Scripture prevalent in those circles, which is atomistic individualist, subjective, and fantastic.

2. And what they would feel most foreign to their own objective and penetrating minds might be the air of introspection and self-measurement too often associated with the spiritual thus "deepened"—a spiritual egoism.

3. And they would miss the note of judgment and Redemption.

We should distinguish at the outset *the deepening of spiritual life* from the *quickening of spiritual sensibility*. Christ on the cross was surely deepened in spiritual experience, but was not the essence of that dereliction, and the concomitant of that deepening, the dulling of spiritual sensibility?

There are many plain obstacles to the deepening of spiritual life, amid which I desire to name here only one; it is prayer conceived merely, or chiefly, as *submission*, resignation, quietism. We say too soon, "Thy will be done"; and too ready acceptance of a situation as His will often means feebleness or sloth. It may be His will that we surmount His will. It may be His higher will that we resist His lower. Prayer is an act of will much more than of sentiment, and its triumph is more than acquiescence. Let us submit when we *must*, but let us keep the submission in reserve rather than in action, as a ground tone rather than the stole effort. Prayer with us has largely ceased to be *wrestling*. But is that

---

[12] Handel's words, on completing the Messiah.
[13] Persistent.

not the dominant scriptural idea? It is not the sole idea, but is it not the dominant? And is not our subdued note often but superinduced and unreal?

I venture to enlarge on this last head, by way of meeting some who hesitate to speak of the power of prayer to alter God's will. I offer two points:

I. Prayer may really change the will of God, or, if not His will, His intention.

II. It may, like other human energies of godly sort, take the form of resisting the will of God. Resisting His will may be doing His will.

I. As to the first point. If this is not believed the earnestness goes out of prayer. It becomes either a ritual, or a soliloquy only overheard by God; just as thought with the will out of it degenerates into dreaming or brooding, where we are more passive than active. Prayer is not merely the meeting of two moods or two affections, the laying of the head on a divine bosom in trust and surrender. That may have its place in religion, but it is not the nerve and soul of prayer. Nor is it religious reverie. Prayer is an encounter of *wills*— till one will or the other give way. It is not a spiritual exercise merely, but in its maturity it is a cause acting on the course of God's world.[14] It is, indeed, by God's grace that prayer is a real cause, but such it is. And of course there must be in us a faith corresponding to the grace. Of course also there is always, behind all, the readiness to accept God's will without a murmur when it is perfectly evident and final. "My grace is sufficient for thee." Yes, but there is also the repeated effort to alter its form according to our sanctified needs and desires. You will notice that in Paul's case the power to accept the sufficiency of God's grace only came in the course of an importunate prayer aiming to turn God's hand. Paul ended, rather than began, with "Thy will be done." The peace of God is an end and not a beginning.

"Thy will be done" was no utterance of mere resignation; thought it has mostly come to mean this in a Christianity which tends to canonize the weak instead of strengthening them. As prayer it was a piece of active cooperation with God's will. It was a positive part of it. It is one thing to submit to a stronger will, it is another to be one with it. We submit because we cannot resist it; but when we are one with it we cannot succumb. It is not *a* power, but *our* power. But the natural will is not one with God's; and so we come to use these words in a mere negative way, meaning that we cease to resist. Our will does not accept God's, it just stops work. We give in and lie down. But is that the sense of the words in the Lord's Prayer? Do they mean that we have no objection to God's will being done? or that we do not withstand any more? or even that we accept it gladly? Do they not mean something far more positive—that we actively will God's will and aid it, that it is the whole content of our own, that we put into it all the will that there can be in prayer, which is at last the great will power of the race? It is our heart's passion that God's will be done and His kingdom come. And can His kingdom come otherwise than as it is a passion with us? Can His will be done? God's will was not Christ's consent merely, nor His pleasure, but His meat and drink, the source of His energy and the substance of His work.

Observe, nothing can alter God's grace, His will in that sense, His large will and final purpose—our racial blessing, our salvation, our redemption in Jesus Christ. But for that will He is an infinite opportunist. His ways are very flexible. His *intentions* are amenable

---

[14] This position is excluded by Schleiermacher's view of religion as absolute dependence, because that leaves room for no action of man on God. And it is one of the grave defects of so great a saint as Robertson.

to us if His *will* is changeless. The steps of His process are variable according to our freedom and His.

We are living, let us say, in a careless way; and God proposes a certain treatment of us according to our carelessness. But in the exercise of our spiritual freedom we are by some means brought to pray. We cease to be careless. We pray God to visit us as those who hear. Then He does another thing. He acts differently, with a change caused by our freedom and our change. The treatment for deafness is altered. God adopts another treatment—perhaps for weakness. We have by prayer changed His action, and, so far, His will (at any rate His intention) concerning us. As we pray, the discipline for the prayerless is altered to that for the prayerful. We attain the thing God did not mean to give us unless He had been affected by our prayer. We change the conduct, if not the will, of God to us, the *Verhalten*[15] if not the *Verhaltniss*[16].

Again, we pray and pray, and no answer comes. The boon does not arrive. Why? Perhaps we are not spiritually ready for it. It would not be a real blessing. But the persistence, the importunity of faith, is having a great effect on our spiritual nature. It ripens. A time comes when we are ready for answer. We then present ourselves to God in a spiritual condition which reasonably causes Him to yield. The new spiritual state is not the answer to our prayer, but it is its effect; and it is the condition which makes the answer possible. It makes the prayer effectual. The gift can be a blessing now. So God resists us no more. Importunity prevails, not as mere importunity (for God is not bored into answer), but as the importunity of God's own elect, i.e. as obedience, as a force of the Kingdom, as increased spiritual power, as real moral action, bringing corresponding strength and fitness to receive. I have often found that what I sought most I did not get at the right time, not till it was too late, not till I had learned to do without it, till I had renounced it in principle (though not in desire). Perhaps it had lost some of its zest by the time it came, but it meant more as a gift and a trust. That was God's right time—when I could have it as though I had it not. If it came, it came not to gratify me, but to glorify Him and be a means of serving Him.

One recalls here that most pregnant saying of Schopenhauer: "All is illusion—the hope or the thing hoped." If it is not true for all it is true for very many. Either the hope is never fulfilled or else its fulfilment disappoints. God gives the hoped for thing, but sends leanness into the soul. The mother prays to have a son—and he breaks her heart, and were better dead. Hope may lie to us, or the thing hoped may dash us. But though He slay me I will trust. God does not fail. Amid the wreck of my little world He is firm, and I in Him. I justify God in the ruins; in His good time I shall arrive. More even than my hopes may go wrong. I may go wrong. But my Redeemer liveth; and, great though God is as my Fulfiller, He is greater as my Redeemer. He is great as my hope, but He is greater as my power. What is the failure of my hope from Him compared with the failure of His hope in me? If He continue to believe in me I may well believe in Him.

God's object with us is not to give just so many things and withhold so many; it is to place us in the tissue of His kingdom. His best answer to us is to raise us to the power of answering Him. The reason why He does not answer our prayer is because we do not answer Him and His prayer. And His prayer was, as though Christ did beseech us, "Be ye reconciled." He would lift us to confident business with Him, to commerce of loving wills.

---

15 Behavior.
16 Circumstances.

The painter wrestles with the sitter till he gives him back himself, and there is a speaking likeness. So man with God, till God surrender His secret. He gives or refuses things, therefore, with a view to that communion alone, and on the whole. It is that spiritual personal end, and not an iron necessity, that rules His course. Is there not a constant spiritual interaction between God and man as free spiritual beings? *How* that can be is one of the great philosophic problems. But the fact that it is is of the essence of faith. It is the unity of our universe. Many systems try to explain *how* human freedom and human action are consistent with God's omnipotence and omniscience. None succeed. *How* secondary causes like man are compatible with God as the Universal and Ultimate Cause is not rationally plain. But there is no practical doubt that they are compatible. And so it is with the action of man on God in prayer. We may perhaps, for the present, put it thus, that we cannot change the will of God, which is grace, and which even Christ never changed but only revealed or effected; but we can change the intention of God, which is a manner of treatment, in the interest of grace, according to the situation of the hour.

If we are guided by the Bible we have much ground for this view of prayer. *Does not Christ set more value upon importunity than on submission?* "Knock, and it shall be opened." I would refer also not only to the parable of the unjust judge, but to the incident of the Syrophoenician woman, where her wit, faith, and importunity together did actually change our Lord's intention and break His custom. Then there is Paul beseeching the Lord thrice for a boon; and urging us to be instant, insistent, continual in prayer. We have Jacob wrestling. We have Abraham pleading, yea, haggling, with God for Sodom. We have Moses interceding for Israel and asking God to blot his name out of the book of life, if that were needful to save Israel. We have Job facing God, withstanding Him, almost bearding Him, and extracting revelation. And we have Christ's own struggle with the Father in Gethsemane.

It is a wrestle on the greatest scale—all manhood taxed as in some great war, or some great negotiation of State. And the effect is exhaustion often. No, the result of true, prayer is not always peace.

II. As to the second point. This wrestle is in a certain sense a resisting of God. You cannot have wrestling otherwise; but you may have Christian fatalism. It is not mere wrestling with ourselves, our ignorance, our self-will. That is not prayer, but self-torment. Prayer is wrestling with God. And it is better to fall thus into the hands of God than of man—even than your own. It is a resistance that God loves. It is quite foreign to a godless, self-willed defiant resistance. In love there is a kind of resistance that enhances it. The resistance of love is a quite different thing from the resistance of hostility. The yielding to one you love is very different from capitulating to an enemy:

> *Two constant lovers, being joined in one,*
> *Yielding unto each other yield to none —*

i.e. to no foreign force, no force foreign to the love which makes them one.

So when God yields to prayer in the name of Christ, to the prayer of faith and love, He yields to Himself who inspired it, as He sware by Himself since none was greater. Christian prayer is the Spirit praying in us. It is prayer in the solidarity of the Kingdom. It is a continuation of Christ's prayer, which in Gethsemane was a wrestle, an αγωνια[17] with the Father. But if so, it is God pleading with God, God dealing with God—as the true

---

[17] Anguish.

atonement must be. And when God yields it is not to an outside influence He yields, but to Himself.

Let me make it still more plain. When we resist the will of God we may be resisting what God wills to be temporary and to be resisted, what He wills to be intermediary and transcended. We resist because God wills we should. We are not limiting God's will, any more than our moral freedom limits it. That freedom is the image of His, and, in a sense, part of His. We should defraud Him and His freedom if we did not exercise ours. So the prayer which resists His dealing may be part of His will and its fulfilment.

Does God not will the existence of things for us to resist, to grapple with? Do we ourselves not appoint problems and make difficulties for those we teach, for the very purpose of their overcoming them? We set questions to children of which we know the answer quite well. The real answer to our will and purpose is not the solution but the grappling, the wrestling. And we may properly give a reward not for the correct answer, but for the hard and honest effort. That work is the prayer; and it has its reward apart from the solution.

That is a principle of education with us. So it may be with God. But I mean a good deal more by this than what is called the reflex action of prayer. It that were all it would introduce an unreality into prayer. We should be praying for exercise, not for action. It would be prayer with a theological form, which yet expects no more than a psychological effect. It would be a prayer which is not sure that God is really more interested in us than we are in Him. But I mean that God's education has a lower stage for us and a higher. He has a lower will and a higher, a prior and a posterior. And the purpose of the lower will is that it be resisted and struggled through to the higher. By God's will (let us say) you are born in a home where your father's earnings are a few shillings a week, like many an English labourer. Is it God's will that you acquiesce in that and never strive out of it? It is God's will that you are there. Is it God's will that you should not resist being there? Nay, it may be His will that you should wisely resist it, and surmount His lower, His initial, will, which is there for the purpose. That is to say, it is His will that you resist, antagonize, His will. And so it is with the state of childhood altogether.

Again: Is disease God's will? We all believe it often is—even if man is to blame for it. It may be, by God's will, the penalty on human ignorance, negligence, or sin. But let us suppose there were only a few cases where disease is God's will. It was so in the lower creatures, before man lived, blundered, or sinned. Take only one such case. Is it God's will that we should lie down and let the disease have its way? Why, a whole profession exists to say no. Medicine exists as an antagonism to disease, even when you can say that disease is God's will and His punishment of sin. A doctor will tell you that resignation is one of his foes. He begins to grow hopeless if the patient is so resigned from the outset as to make no effort, if there be no will to live. Resistance to this ordinance of God's is the doctor's business and the doctor's ally. And why? Because God ordained disease for the purpose of being resisted; He ordained the resistance, that from the conflict man might come out the stronger, and more full of resource and dominion over nature.

Again, take death. It is God's will. It is in the very structure of man, in the divine economy. It is not the result of sin; it was there before sin. Is it to be accepted without demur? Are doctors impious who resist it? Are we sinning when we shrink from it? Does not the life of most people consist in the effort to escape it, in the struggle for a living? So also when we pray and wrestle for another's life, for our dear one's life. "Sir, come down ere my child die." The man was impatient. How familiar we are with his kind! "Do, please, leave your religious talk, which I don't understand; get doing something; cure my child." But was that an impious prayer? It was ignorant, practical, British, but not quite faithless. And it was answered, as many a similar prayer has been. But, then, if death be God's will, to resist it is to resist God's will. Well, it is His will that we should. Christ, who always did God's will, resisted His own death, slipped away from it often, till the hour came; and even *then* He prayed with all his might against it when it seemed inevitable. "If it be possible, release Me." He was ready to accept it, but only in the last resort, only if there was no other way, only after every other means had been exhausted. To the end He cherished the fading hope that there might be some other way. He went to death voluntarily, freely, but—shall we say reluctantly?—resisting the most blessed act of God's will that ever was performed in heaven or on earth; resisting, yet sure to acquiesce when that was God's clear will.

The whole nature, indeed, is the will of God, and the whole of grace is striving with nature. It is our nature to have certain passions. That is God's will. But it is our calling of God to resist them as much as to gratify them. They are there as God's will to be resisted as much as indulged. The redemption from the natural man includes the resistance to it, and the release of the soul from what God Himself appointed as its lower stages—never as its dwelling place, and never its tomb. So far prayer is on the lines of evolution.

Obedience is the chief end. But obedience is not mere submission, mere resignation. It is not always acquiescence, even in prayer. We obey God as much when we urge our suit, and make a real petition of it, as when we accept His decision; as much when we try to change His will as when we bow to it. The kingdom of heaven suffereth violence. There is a very fine passage in Dante, Parad. xx. 94 (Longfellow):

> *Regnum coelorum suffereth violence*
> > *From fervent love, and from that living hope*
> > *That overcometh the divine volition.*
> *Not in the way that man o'ercometh man;*
> > *We conquer it because it will be conquered,*
> > *And, conquered, conquers by benignity.*

It is His will—His will of grace—that prayer should prevail with Him and *extract* blessings. And how we love the grace that so concedes them! The answer to prayer is not the complaisance of a playful power lightly yielding to the playful egoism of His favorites. "Our antagonist is our helper." To struggle with Him is one way of doing His will. To resist is one way of saying, "Thy will be done." It was God's will that Christ should deprecate the death God required. It pleased God as much as His submission to death. But could it have been pleasing to Him that Christ should pray so, if no prayer could ever possibly change God's will? Could Christ have prayed so in that belief? Would faith ever inspire us to pray if the God of our faith must be unmoved by prayer? The prayer that goes to an inflexible God, however good He is, is prayer that rises more from human need than from God's own revelation, or from Christian faith (where Christian prayer should rise). It is His will, then, that we should pray against what seems His will, and what, for the lower stage of our growth, is His will. And all this without any unreality whatever.

Let us beware of a pietist fatalism which thins the spiritual life, saps the vigour of character, makes humility mere acquiescence, and piety only feminine, by banishing the will from prayer as much as thought has been banished from it. "The curse of so much religion" (I have quoted Meredith) "is that men cling to God with their weakness rather than with their strength."

The popularity of much acquiescence is not because it is holier, but because it is easier. And an easy gospel is the consumption that attacks Christianity. It is the phthisis to faith.

Once come to think that we best say "Thy will be done" when we acquiesce, when we resign, and not also when we struggle and wrestle, and in time all effort will seem less pious than submission. And so we fall into the ecclesiastical type of religion, drawn from an age whose first virtue was submission to outward superiors. We shall come to canonize decorum and subduedness in life and worship (as the Episcopal Church with its monarchical ideas of religion has done). We shall think more of order than of effort, more of law than of life, more of fashion than of faith, of good form than of great power. But was subduedness *the* mark of the New Testament men? Our religion may gain some beauty in this way, but it loses vigour. It may gain style, but it loses power. It is good form, but mere aesthetic piety. It may consecrate manners, but it impoverishes the mind. It may regulate prayer by the precepts of intelligence instead of the needs and faith of the soul. It may feed certain pensive emotions, but it may emasculate will, secularize energy, and empty character. And so we decline to a state of things in which we have no shocking sins—yes, and no splendid souls; when all souls are dully correct, as like as shillings, but as thin, and as cheap.

All our forms and views of religion have their test in prayer. Lose the importunity of prayer, reduce it to soliloquy, or even to colloquy, with God, lose the real conflict of will and will, lose the habit of wrestling and the hope of prevailing with God, make it mere walking with God in friendly talk; and, precious as that is, yet you tend to lose the reality of prayer at last. In principle you make it mere conversation instead of the soul's great action. You lose the food of character, the renewal of will. You may have beautiful prayers—but as ineffectual as beauty so often is, and as fleeting. And so in the end you lose the reality of religion. Redemption turns down into mere revelation, faith to assent, and devotion to a phase of culture. For you lose the power of the Cross and so of the soul.

Resist God, in the sense of rejecting God, and you will not be able to resist any evil. But resist God in the sense of closing with God, cling to Him with your strength, not your weakness only, with your active and not only your passive faith, and He will give you strength. Cast yourself into His arms not to be caressed but to wrestle with Him. He loves that holy war. He may be too many for you, and lift you from your feet. But it will be to lift you from earth, and set you in the heavenly places which are theirs who fight the good fight and lay hold of God as their eternal life.

Other Books on Prayer

And there are also many other things which Jesus did, the which, if they should be written every one, I suppose that even the world itself could not contain the books that should be written. Amen. — John 21:25

Sermon Recordings by T. M. Anderson at https://place.asburyseminary.edu

The Complete Works of E.M. Bounds on Prayer (ISBN 9781640322431)

How I Know God Answers Prayer by Rosalind Goforth

Quiet Talks on Prayer by S. D. Gordon

Treatise on Prayer by John Knox

Spirit of Prayer by William Law

Prevailing Prayer by D. L. Moody

With Christ in the School of Prayer by Andrew Murray

The Life of Prayer by A. B. Simpson

www.ingramcontent.com/pod-product-compliance
Lightning Source LLC
LaVergne TN
LVHW021121080426
835509LV00011B/1366